Joan

CHILDREN — THE NEW LAW

THE CHILDREN ACT 1989

CHILDREN —
THE NEW LAW
THE CHILDREN ACT 1989

Andrew Bainham LLB, LLM, Solicitor

Senior Lecturer in Law
University of East Anglia

FAMILY LAW
1990

Published by
Family Law, a publishing
imprint of Jordan & Sons Ltd
21 St Thomas Street
Bristol BS1 6JS

© Jordan & Sons Limited 1991

Reprinted April 1990
Reprinted March 1991
Reprinted November 1991
Reprinted April 1992
Reprinted April 1993

British Library Cataloguing in Publication Data

Bainham, Andrew
  Children : the new law, the Children Act 1989
  1. England. Children. Law
  I. Title
  344.202′87

ISBN 0 85308 115 8

Printed and bound in Great Britain by Bookcraft (Bath)

FOREWORD

The Children Act 1989 has claims to be the most important piece of legislation affecting the family enacted in the twentieth century. The Act is a massive technical achievement, in which the Law Commission, draftsmen, officials, and ministers involved can legitimately take pride. The Act is also, in a rather different way, a striking example of the acceptable face of the law-making process – for it is based on extensive consultation, and the Government has, throughout, shown itself ready to listen to the concerns and worries to which change in so sensitive an area must inevitably give rise.

The Act is complex, and those professionally affected by it – whether lawyer, social worker, doctor, or police officer – need a sure guide to its provisions. But what is needed is far more than a detailed guide to the minutiae of the Act's provisions. The Act involves fundamental changes in legislative policy affecting the rôle of the courts and local authorities; and it also marks a significant shift in the relationship between the family and the State.

Andrew Bainham's book is, of course, a reliable guide to the detailed provisions of the law. But it also does something which is far more important: it focuses attention on those broader issues, which are essential to an understanding of the new law.

We now have two years or more to prepare for the implementation of the new law. That time will be well spent in pondering on the changes at all levels which are going to be needed in professional practice relating to the family. I am confident that Andrew Bainham's book will meet a real need in helping those affected to identify what has to be done.

STEPHEN CRETNEY
November 1989

PREFACE

The Children Bill has finally become the Children Act almost a year since its introduction in the House of Lords. Those familiar with the law affecting children will probably agree with the Lord Chancellor's assessment that the Act effects 'the most comprehensive and far-reaching reform of child law in living memory'. Certainly, this is an area of law which will never be the same again. My aim in writing this book is to make these wide-ranging reforms more intelligible to those who confront them, whether as practitioners, students of family law and child law, or simply because they have an interest in children and their position in the legal system. I hope that the book will be used at this time by those wishing to acquaint themselves with the changes before they occur, but also in the coming years leading up to and following implementation of the legislation. For this reason, I have made liberal use of the present tense in an attempt to describe and analyse the legal position on the assumption that the Act is in force. In fact, implementation is not expected before Autumn 1991 and could be after this.

My primary purpose has been to highlight and explore the new law which the Act introduces. As far as possible, I have endeavoured to follow the structure of the Act in order to facilitate cross-reference from the commentary to the text itself. Thus, after the introductory chapter most of the remaining chapters correspond with individual parts of the Act. An exception is Chapter 7 which covers all those parts which constitute a substantial re-enactment of existing law. This chapter is, therefore, more descriptive and less analytical than the rest. In line with the general scheme, the discussion of jurisdictional and procedural matters (which might have appeared early in the book) has been left to the final chapter.

As well as bringing about many and varied changes to the law and practice affecting children, the Act raises some fascinating philosophical and theoretical issues. Among the more important are the move towards fusion of public and private law (both at the substantive and procedural level), the conceptualisation of a voluntary partnership between parents and the State and the redefinition of parenthood to emphasise the 'responsibilities' rather than 'rights' of parents. I have tried, where possible, to offer some tentative views on these more theoretical questions. A controversial feature of the Act is the comparatively large amount of detail which has been left to regulations and rules of court. Inevitably, this has meant that the discussion of certain matters, especially procedural rules, is somewhat speculative.

For the sake of consistency, I have generally used male pronouns throughout when referring to children, parents and others having the care of children. I recognise that the use of female pronouns would have been equally appropriate. The equality of mother and father is perhaps encapsulated best in the gender-neutral term 'parent' and by the primary status of 'parenthood' which the Act asserts.

In writing this book, I have received the help and encouragement of several people to whom I am indebted. As well as agreeing to write the foreword, Stephen Cretney read parts of the manuscript and saved me from a number of errors. Any which remain are my sole responsibility. I would like to thank him for his help and, more generally, for his valued support and interest in my work. Christine Christopher typed most of the manuscript with characteristic cheerfulness. Sue Sargant took over the typing at a crucial and difficult stage and saw this through to completion. Both of them gave me invaluable secretarial support in the face of time constraints and their normal commitments at the University of East Anglia. My thanks also go to the staff at Jordans.

Most of all, I must thank my wife Wendy for allowing me to immerse myself again in theoretical questions about the welfare of children while she bore the brunt of the all too practical considerations of the welfare of our own children. I dedicate this book to Wendy, Sami and especially Rhys, born on 2 May 1989. It seems that my children are keeping pace with my books. I had better think twice before I write another!

ANDREW BAINHAM
November 1989

CONTENTS

TABLE OF CASES

TABLE OF STATUTES

TABLE OF STATUTORY INSTRUMENTS

CHAPTER ONE

The Background and Purposes
of the Act

1. Introduction

1.1 The Children Act 1989 is undoubtedly one of the most radical and far-reaching reforms of the private and public law affecting children. In private law, orders for custody and access are completely abolished and are replaced by new forms of order to be known respectively as 'residence' and 'contact' orders. The concept of parental 'rights' disappears and the legal status of parenthood is re-defined in terms of 'responsibility'. A clear distinction is drawn between parenthood and guardianship with parents ceasing to be the legal guardians of their children. In the unmarried family there are major reforms designed to improve the legal standing of fathers. The legal standing of relatives and other non-parents having an interest in particular children is also significantly advanced. The custodianship procedure, which took ten years to implement, is swept away at a stroke and is in effect subsumed by a much more flexible regime providing non-parents with access to the courts for the purpose of seeking the new range of orders introduced by the Act.

1.2 The changes to public law are no less dramatic. The Act creates a more marked division between voluntary and compulsory arrangements for the public care of children. 'Voluntary Care' as it has been known will no longer exist. Where children are looked after or accommodated by a local authority, they will no longer technically be in the 'care' of that authority for legal purposes. If the authority wishes to obtain the legal powers associated with parenthood it will henceforth be obliged to obtain these by court order. It will no longer be possible to secure a compulsory transfer of parental responsibility by administrative resolution. The basis for compulsory intervention is completely re-cast by the introduction of a single composite ground for care and supervision orders. This takes the place of the previous range of freestanding conditions under the Children and Young Persons Act 1969, the grounds for resolutions assuming parental rights under the Child Care Act 1980 and the different basis for committal to care in those family proceedings in which this was possible. The Act provides greater opportunities for judicial challenge to decisions of local authorities regarding contact between children in care and other individuals. It also establishes a new code for the emergency protection of children thought to be at risk of abuse or neglect.

1.3 Wardship currently exists alongside the statutory children's jurisdictions. It has been used by individuals as an alternative to other family proceedings and, in recent years, increasingly by local authorities wishing to circumvent the technicalities of care proceedings. The future of wardship and its relationship to the reformed statutory scheme is one of the most controversial and uncertain aspects of the Act. The Act imposes severe restrictions on the circumstances in which authorities may resort to wardship but is otherwise silent as to the place of wardship under the new law.

1.4 The Act brings about important procedural and jurisdictional changes. It creates a concurrent jurisdiction over family proceedings in the High Court, county court and magistrates' court. These arrangements are intended to be flexible and they incorporate provision for the transfer of cases between these levels of court where this is thought appropriate. The initial allocation of cases between the three courts is at present rather uncertain and will be left to rules of court. Many other detailed aspects of the legislation will also be left to secondary legislation.

1.5 The Act received the Royal Assent on 16 November 1989. Apart from a few provisions which deal with immediately pressing matters (ss 89, 96 (3) to (7) and para 36 of Sch 12), the Act will come into force 'on such date as may be appointed by order made by the Lord Chancellor or the Secretary of State' (108(2)). There is the usual formula that 'different dates may be appointed for different provisions of this Act and in relation to different cases' (s.108(3)). The Lord Chancellor has, however, indicated in Parliament that every effort will be made to implement the Act in its entirety although this will not be before Autumn 1991 at the earliest. There is concern to avoid the progressive implementation which has dogged previous legislation affecting children, notably the Children Act 1975.

2.   The Origins and Foundations of the Legislation

1.6 The Act broadly derives from two major reviews. The private law affecting children (custody and guardianship in particular) was subjected to extensive examination by the Law Commission in its *Review of Child Law* which it instigated in 1984. Working papers were published on *Guardianship* (No.91(1985)), *Custody* (No.96 (1986)), *Care, Supervision and Interim Orders in Custody Proceedings* (No.100 (1987)) and *Wards of Court* (No.101 (1987)). The Commission consulted widely with interested bodies and individuals and this process culminated in its *Report on Guardianship and Custody* (No.172 (1988)). This Report substantially forms the basis of Parts I and II and has an influence on other parts of the Act. It should be said that, with the exception of s.100 which imposes restrictions on the use of wardship by local authorities, most of what the Law Commission had to say about wardship in its working paper on that subject was not incorporated in its final report and is not embodied in the legislation. The Commission's provisional suggestions of options for reform of the inherent wardship jurisdiction met with a mixed reception and resulted in the decision to postpone making any substantial recommendations in this respect until after the reform of the statutory jurisdictions brought about by the Act.

1.7 Meanwhile, also in 1984, an equally comprehensive review of the public law relating to children was undertaken by an Interdepartmental Working Party set up on the recommendation of the House of Commons Social Services Committee. It published its *Review of Child Care Law* (hereafter 'the Review') in 1985 which contained over two hundred recommendations for reform in this sphere. Most (but not all) of these were accepted by the Government in January 1987 in a White Paper entitled *The Law on Child Care and Family Services* (Cmnd 62) (hereafter 'the White Paper'). These two documents together are the principal source of Parts III, IV and V of the Act.

1.8 Parts VI (Community Homes), VII (Voluntary Homes and Voluntary Organisations), VIII (Registered Children's Homes), IX (Private Arrangements for Fostering Children) and XI (the Secretary of State's Supervisory Functions and Responsibilities) are substantial re-enactments, with minor modifications, of previous legislation governing these matters. They are included in the Act since the intention is to bring together, as far as possible, in a single code all the public and private law affecting children. Part XII deals with Miscellaneous and General Matters. The most significant provisions here are s 92 prescribing the courts with jurisdiction in proceedings under the Act and s 100 restricting the use of wardship in local authority cases. Part X deals with the regulation of child-minding and day care for young children and substantially modifies the existing legislation on this.

1.9 Before leaving the general scheme of the Act it should be noted that many important items of detail are tucked away in its fifteen schedules. This extensive use of schedules was criticised during the passage of the Bill as was the liberal usage of enabling powers resulting in many important matters being left to regulations or rules of court. Whatever view is taken of the legitimacy of this approach to the legislative process, the important point is that serious students of the legislation, and those concerned with its operation in practice, cannot afford to ignore the schedules. In particular, Sch 2 (which contains most of the detailed duties of local authorities towards children being looked after by them) and Sch 3 (which lays down the new scheme for supervision orders) are deserving of special mention.

1.10 It would not be right to conclude this account of the background to the Act without mentioning a number of other important influences on the process of reform. Foremost among these is, perhaps, the *Report of the Inquiry into Child Abuse in Cleveland 1987* conducted by Lord Justice Butler-Sloss (1988 Cm 41 (hereafter 'the Butler-Sloss Report')). This exposed the apparent over-zealous treatment by protection agencies in Cleveland of cases of alleged child sexual abuse in that region. In particular, it highlighted the absence of adequate legal safeguards for parents where their children were summarily removed from them under emergency procedures. Part V of the Act which, inter alia, abolishes the place of safety order and introduces a new 'emergency protection order' should, at least in part, overcome some of the difficulties which were experienced in Cleveland. These changes to emergency procedures were already accepted by the Government before the Cleveland crisis erupted but there can be little doubt that the speed with which it moved to secure the passage of the Act is in part attributable to the public clamour arising from the Cleveland affair. That said, the Act is far from a categorical endorsement of the Butler-Sloss recommendations. Following publication of the Butler-Sloss report the Lord Chancellor issued a consultation paper and the Government took the results of this process into account in finally determining the content of the Bill. The proposal of Butler-Sloss that an 'Office of Child Protection' be established has not been taken up. Moreover, Butler-Sloss was in favour of maintaining the role of wardship in child care cases and favoured a relaxation of the judicially-imposed restrictions preventing parents and other interested individuals from using it where a child is in care (See *A v Liverpool City Council* [1982] AC 363 and *Re W (A minor) (Wardship:Jurisdiction)* [1985] AC 791). In fact, the Act takes us in the opposite direction. It does nothing to liberate parents and others from these restraints on using wardship and, instead, extends the restrictions to prevent local authorities from resorting to the jurisdiction in specified circumstances. While the new measures achieve a certain symmetry in the respective positions of parents and local authorities their effect is to put in doubt the future of a jurisdiction which many regard as a valuable backdrop to the statutory procedures.

Other reports of public inquiries into the deaths of individual children at the hands of those responsible for looking after them have formed part of the background to the legislation and have had their influence on parts of it. These include *A Child in Trust: Report of the Panel of Inquiry Investigating the Circumstances Surrounding the death of Jasmine Beckford* (London Borough of Brent (1985)); *A Child in Mind: Protection of Children in a Responsible Society, Report of the Commission of Inquiry into the Circumstances surrounding the death of Kimberley Carlile* (London Borough of Greenwich (1987)) and *Whose Child? The Report of the Public Inquiry into the death of Tyra Henry* (London Borough of Lambeth (1987)).

1.11 A further influence on the legislation was undoubtedly the decision of the House of Lords in *Gillick v West Norfolk and Wisbech Area Health Authority* [1986] 1 AC 112. This recognised the older child's capacity for decision-making in the medical context where he possesses sufficient maturity and understanding. It was also held that the child's decision was capable of superseding any parental right or power over upbringing. According to Lord Scarman the parental right 'yields to the child's right to make his own decisions when he reaches a sufficient understanding and intelligence to be capable of making up his mind on the matter requiring decision'.

The judgments have given rise to considerable speculation about the legal competence of children for taking a range of decisions affecting their lives. The Act recognises, in several places, the importance of ascertaining and taking into account the wishes of children to an extent commensurate with their age and understanding. The issue which has provoked some disagreement, and which formed the basis of a number of proposed amendments in Parliament, is whether the preferences of a mature child should not only be taken into account but should be *determinative* of the matter in question. If accepted, this interpretation of *Gillick* would in effect have removed the courts' discretion to decide what are the best interests of children and would have obliged them to uphold the autonomy of children to the exclusion of all else. Not surprisingly, this interpretation was not accepted by the Government and is not generally supported by the Act. We shall, nonetheless, have to return to the crucially important question of the weight to be attached to children's wishes when examining a number of the Act's provisions.

1.12 A final influence on the legislative process has been the United Kingdom's obligations as a signatory to the European Convention on Human Rights and Fundamental Freedoms. Increasingly, there has been pressure from Europe for reform of English law to give effect to the fundamental rights of parents and children especially in relation to family life which is protected by Article 8. In several recent decisions the higher courts in England have made reference to the Convention (see, for example, *Re K D (A Minor)(Ward:Termination of Access)* [1988] 1 All ER 577). Undoubtedly, many of the reforms relating to care procedures, (and in particular those giving parents and others the right to challenge contact decisions by local authorities) have been inspired, if not positively mandated, by the state's obligations under the Convention. Indeed, in 1988 the Government was able to head off a challenge under the Convention by an unmarried father (regarding his lack of standing vis à vis his child in care) only on the basis of the reforms to be effected by the Act (*K v United Kingdom*, Application No 11468/85. Friendly settlement achieved in April 1988).

While discussing the European dimension, it is interesting to note that the new legislation does not embrace any new or revolutionary concept of children's rights. The Act makes many references to the 'best interests' or 'welfare' of children but nowhere is there to be found any mention of their 'rights'. This may, of course, simply be a matter of choice of terminology especially since the Act abolishes the notion of 'rights' for parents. But doubtless it will only be a matter of time before the substance of the legislation is tested in the European Court for its conformity with the Convention.

3. The Aims and Purposes of the Act

1.13 The Act seeks to bring together the private and public law relating to the care, protection and upbringing of children and the provision of services to them and their families. The primary objective is to incorporate, with some exceptions, all the relevant statute law into a single code which is simpler, more accessible and comprehensible than the amorphous mass of complex statutory provisions which reflected the piecemeal development of child law over a considerable number of years. A glance at the Repeal Schedule to the Act (Sch 15) reveals the extent of the reforms. Eight post-war statutes are repealed in full. They are the Nurseries and Child-Minders Regulation Act 1948, the Guardianship of Minors Act 1971, the Guardianship Act 1973, the Children Act 1975, the Child Care Act 1980, the Foster Children Act 1980, the Children's Homes Act 1982 and the Children and Young Persons (Amendment) Act 1986. Others, including the Children and Young Persons Act 1969 and the Domestic Proceedings and Magistrates' Court Act 1978, have been so substantially amended that their operation is now limited to criminal provisions or provisions affecting only adults. It is remarkable that, at least in terms of volume, so much has been replaced by so little.

1.14 It must be stressed that the partial fusion of private and public law which the Act brings about is something which it is imperative to grasp at the outset. The cardinal principles enshrined in Part I will (at least in theory) apply with equal force in private disputes affecting children and public proceedings for care or supervision. A good example is the innovative 'non-intervention' principle in s.1(5) to the effect that courts should not make orders with respect to children unless satisfied that to do so would be better for the child than refraining from making any order at all. This principle applies as much to the question whether a care order should be made as it does to the question whether a residence or other order should be made on divorce. Moreover, this marriage of private and public law does not consist solely of the sharing of some common principles. A second major objective of the legislation is 'to provide a consistent set of legal remedies which will be available in all courts and in all proceedings' (Brenda Hoggett, *The Children Bill: The Aim* [1989] 19 Fam. Law 217). Thus, the orders available in private family proceedings or broadly equivalent orders will also be available in public care proceedings and vice versa. A good example is the new 'residence order' which the Act introduces. No doubt this will be sought primarily in private proceedings, especially divorce, but there is nothing to prevent an individual seeking such an order where the child is in the care of a local authority. If granted its effect, under s 91(1), will be to discharge the care order. Conversely, the effect of granting a care order is to discharge automatically any existing residence order. There is, therefore, intended to be a flexibility and interchangeability about the new scheme which is quite uncharacteristic of the old law. There are, however, some limits to the common availability of remedies. Where the child is in care (i.e. by virtue of a care order) no 's 8 orders' other than a residence order may be made. This is designed to prevent unwarranted interference by the courts with the discharge of the authority's statutory obligations to children being looked after by it. Where, however, the child is not in care, but is merely being looked after by the authority under a voluntary arrangement, these other orders may be sought. A 'contact order' might, for example, be requested by an individual interested in preserving his or her relationship with the child.

This interrelationship between private and public law and procedures may come as a surprise to those who have been accustomed to the more rigid demarcation of family and care proceedings which existed before the Act. It is something which needs to be kept in mind when considering the constituent parts of the Act.

1.15 Some of the guiding principles which permeate the legislation should also be appreciated. Among these are the paramountcy of the welfare of children, the primary responsibility of parents for the care of their children and the durability and continuity of this responsibility, the voluntary partnership between parents and the state and the need to avoid the harm which can be caused to children by delays or the protracted litigation of disputes concerning them.

4. The Relevance of the Old Law

1.16 An issue which must be broached at this stage is the relevance of the many authorities on the old law as precedents or aids to interpretation of the new law. Since the Act replaces the former statutory scheme with a completely new statutory regime for child law it is tempting to offer the view that all previously decided cases, for example those on custody, access or care orders, have been jettisoned. It is probably technically correct to say that they cannot be regarded as binding. This is because the new orders are not synonymous with the old. Custody orders are not the same as residence orders in their legal effect although they may be regarded as having a broad equivalence. Decisions on what should influence the courts in granting or withholding the former cannot simply be transplanted as authorities on the circumstances in which the latter should be granted or withheld. The same may be true of access and contact orders.

Having said that, it would seem likely that the body of principles which has emerged over the years will be used as a guide to the interpretation of the Act. Leading authorities are likely to be regarded as highly persuasive unless they clearly conflict with the principles embodied in the Act. Some principles established under the old law have an immutable quality which will surely transcend the changes brought about by the Act. The well-established rule that siblings should be kept together wherever possible (accepted in both custody and adoption) is perhaps an example of the kind of principle which ought to survive. (See, for example, *C v C* [1988] 18

Fam.Law 338, *Adams v Adams* [1984] FLR 768 and *Re C (A minor) (Adoption: Conditions)* [1988] 1 All ER 705).

1.17 Where it appears that a decision is inconsistent with the express provisions or the basic objectives of the Act, it must be taken to have been impliedly overruled by it. A good illustration of this would appear to be the comparatively recent decision of the Court of Appeal in *Riley v Riley* [1986] 2 FLR 429. Here the Court appeared to set its face against joint custodial arrangements which contemplate the physical sharing of a child's care in two separate homes. This decision cannot stand either with the underlying philosophy of the legislation or with the express language of s 11(4).

5. The Structure of the Book

1.18 This analysis of the legislation attempts to follow the structure of the Act as nearly as possible. Chapters 2 to 6 broadly correspond with Parts I to V of the Act. Chapter 7 covers Parts VI to XI which are, as noted above, substantially re-enactments of existing law and therefore deserving of less detailed treatment in a book which is attempting to analyse what is new. The final chapter is devoted to a discussion of jurisdictional and procedural matters and the important question of the place of wardship in the new scheme. Much of the detail here has been consigned to rules of court. Where possible an indication of what is likely to be included in the rules is given. The wardship question is considered at some length because of its crucial significance in the operation of the system. The general availability of a non-statutory jurisdiction such as wardship in which a broad welfare criterion applies in the determination of disputes could, as the Law Commission noted in its working paper, make a nonsense of the statutory code.

CHAPTER TWO

General Principles

1. The Welfare of the Child

(a) The welfare principle

2.1 Section 1(1) re-enacts, with one modification, the cardinal principle in child law that in proceedings concerned with the upbringing of a child, or the administration of a child's property or the application of any income arising from it, the child's welfare shall be the court's paramount consideration.

The welfare principle originated in the Guardianship of Infants Act 1925 and was later incorporated in s 1 of the Guardianship of Minors Act 1971. Those familiar with the old law will notice immediately that the statutory formula has changed in that welfare is no longer expressed to be 'first and paramount' but simply 'paramount'. This is not intended to bring about any change of substance in the relative importance to be attached to the child's welfare in litigated disputes. Rather the omitted words were considered otiose given the settled interpretation of the principle by Lord MacDermott in *J v C* [1970] AC 668. In that case he said that the principle meant:

'... more than that the child's welfare is to be treated as the top item in a list of items relevant to the matters in question.'
In his view it connoted:
'a process whereby, when all the relevant facts, relationships, claims and wishes of parents, risks, choices and other circumstances are taken into account and weighed, the course to be followed will be that which is most in the interests of the child's welfare as that term has now to be understood. That is the first consideration because it is of first importance and the paramount consideration because it rules upon or determines the course to be followed.'

The effect of this interpretation is to make welfare the *sole* consideration since it is the court's sole concern to arrive at a determination of what is in the child's best interests and to make orders which reflect this. Other factors are relevant only in so far as they can assist the court in ascertaining the best solution for the child. It follows that to describe welfare as the 'first' consideration adds nothing. If it is the sole consideration it must, by definition, be first in importance. It was also thought that the original form of words had caused some confusion in practice as certain courts had attempted to balance the child's interests against other considerations, notably the claims of a so-called 'unimpeachable parent'.

Under the new provision it is clear that these other considerations are relevant only as an integral part of the court's investigation of the child's position. The original draft Bill annexed to the Law Commission's report had attempted to put this beyond doubt by writing into the Statute that the child's welfare should be the court's 'only concern'. The term 'paramount' was ultimately preferred since there was anxiety that the court should not feel obliged to refuse to hear evidence which did not bear directly on what was best for the child. It was thought desirable to preserve a wider approach in which the court would be required to examine *all* the circumstances before concluding what was best for a child. This would mean, for example, that it would be quite proper for the court to admit and consider evidence relating to the personal and economic circumstances of the various adults involved in the proceedings. Indeed it is difficult to visualise how a court could discharge its functions properly without doing so. The point is that it will often be impossible to segregate or compartmentalise the interests of children and adults.

2.2 It is important to be clear about the circumstances in which the welfare principle will operate. It should be said immediately that it only applies in the course of litigation, although it has sometimes been suggested that the discharge of responsibilities by parents is governed by it. It does not, for example, apply to the statutory obligations of local authorities towards children being looked after by them. While they are under a general duty to 'safeguard and promote the welfare' of such children they are not obliged to regard it as 'paramount' (See Part III and the discussion in Chapter 4).

The application of the principle in court proceedings is pervasive but not universal. The reference to 'the court' in s 1(1) applies to all courts having jurisdiction under the Act and therefore extends to the High Court, county court and magistrates' court (s 92(7)). The general principles in Part I apply (with limited exceptions) to *all* proceedings under the Act. Accordingly, the welfare principle, prima facie, applies as much in proceedings for care or supervision under Part IV as it does in the various private proceedings arising under Part II. But this is a deceptively simplistic analysis since there are important differences in the way in which the principle operates in these two very different types of action.

In private disputes concerning the upbringing of a child it operates in the unrestrained or undiluted manner explained by Lord MacDermott. This has not been true, and is still not the case, in relation to care proceedings. We shall see that care (and supervision) orders may only be made where the reformulated ground in s 31(2) is satisfied. They may *not* be made simply because the court thinks that the welfare of the child requires it. But assuming that the new ground is made out, the welfare principle will *only at this stage* come into play. In other words, the court will make the order only if satisfied that it is in the best interests of the child to do so. The more limited application of the welfare principle in care proceedings reflects the need to set limits to the power of the state to intervene in the family, by defining more specifically the circumstances in which this is permissible. It was for this reason that the Review rejected a broad welfare criterion as the basis for care orders (Review, para 15.10).

2.3 In certain types of proceedings which may affect children the welfare principle does not apply. This is true of many legal disputes which are predominantly concerned with issues between the adult members of a family. In these proceedings the welfare of children can range in its relevance from being the 'first' consideration to being wholly irrelevant. Some examples may serve to elucidate the position.

In adoption proceedings the child's welfare is the 'first' consideration both for adoption agencies and for courts deciding whether to grant adoption orders (Adoption Act 1976, s 6). This is also true in proceedings relating to the adjustment of property and financial matters on divorce (Matrimonial Causes Act 1973, s 25(1)). What this means is that in these proceedings the child's welfare is the most important single factor but is not the sole factor. Other considerations are also relevant, especially the interests of the adult parties. It is conceivable that these other factors may, singly or collectively, outweigh the interests of the child. In proceedings to exclude an adult partner from the family home the welfare of any children of the union is a relevant factor (Matrimonial Homes Act 1983 s 1(3)) but is not expressed to be either 'first' or 'paramount'. Thus, while it must be weighed alongside other factors, including the conduct of the adult parties and their respective housing needs, it must not be elevated above these other considerations in importance. (See particularly the House of Lords' decision in *Richards v Richards* [1984] AC 174.) In divorce proceedings the child's welfare is not relevant *at all* on the question of whether the decree itself should be granted as opposed to the specific question of the care and upbringing of the child.

These nuances are more than mere subtleties. The weighting of the child's welfare in different proceedings is in reality the mechanism whereby Parliament stipulates the relative importance to be attached to the often conflicting interests of children and adults. It is vital that this should be understood.

2.4 The Law Commission suggested a second modification to the welfare principle which has not been embodied in the Act. This was that 'the interests of the child whose future happens to be at issue in the proceedings before the court should not in principle prevail over those of other children likely to be affected by the decision'. It went on to recommend that under the reformulated principle 'the welfare of any child likely to be affected by the decision should be the court's only concern' (Report No. 172, paras 13 to 14). The obvious example which springs to mind is the welfare of any children in a divorcing spouse's reconstituted family. The interests of these children will not now fall within the ambit of the welfare principle. But this is far from saying that they are irrelevant. It may well be that the court will take the view that the interests of the child directly before the court are inextricably bound up with the overall family situations of the parties. In these circumstances the interests of the children in a second family must surely be a relevant circumstance in ascertaining what is required to give effect to the best interests of the child directly involved in the proceedings as a 'child of the family' (defined in s 105(1)).

(b)   The statutory checklist

2.5   The Act breaks new ground in enjoining the court to have regard to a checklist of factors in arriving at its determination of the child's best interests. The inclusion of such a list is recognition that the welfare principle, despite the high ideals which it represents, is an essentially indeterminate concept. It is one thing to say that the court should act to protect the best interests of children and quite another to establish definitively where these lie. Section 1(3) is an attempt to structure judicial discretion by requiring the court *in every case* to have regard to the matters set out there. Other checklists already exist in other proceedings such as those relating to property and financial matters on divorce (Matrimonial Causes Act 1973, s 25(2)) and proceedings with respect to occupation of the matrimonial home (Matrimonial Homes Act 1983, s 1(3)). The hope is that the inclusion of the new requirements will inject greater consistency and clarity into the law. It is thought that adult parties will be assisted in their efforts to understand the basis of court orders affecting children and that out-of-court agreements will be facilitated.

2.6   The checklist is mandatory in those proceedings in which it applies. These are proceedings where :
- (a)   the court is considering whether to make, vary or discharge a s 8 order, and the making, variation or discharge of the order is opposed by any party to the proceedings; or
- (b)   the court is considering whether to make, vary or discharge an order under Part IV (s 1(4)).

In short, the checklist must be operated in all *contested* private proceedings under Part II and all proceedings under Part IV *whether contested or uncontested*. The reason for the exemption of uncontested private proceedings was that there might otherwise be a danger of unnecessary court involvement in these cases. It is a central tenet of the new scheme that courts should be involved in family arrangements only where the child's welfare positively requires this. Nonetheless, the exemption does provide an interesting contrast with the position in property and financial proceedings on divorce. In that context, the statutory checklist applies whether or not the application is contested. This is not thought to have caused any particular difficulty or to have imposed an undue burden on the courts.

It should be noted that the checklist does not apply to the emergency procedures under Part V. There is obvious force in the argument that a requirement to apply the checklist might inhibit the immediate action required to protect a child in danger. It will however have to be applied in any subsequent proceedings for an interim or final care order.

2.7 Section 1(3) sets out the particular matters which the court is required to consider. They are:

(a) the ascertainable wishes and feelings of the child concerned (considered in the light of his age and understanding);
(b) his physical, emotional and educational needs;
(c) the likely effect on him of any change in his circumstances;
(d) his age, sex, background and any characteristic of his which the court considers relevant;
(e) any harm which he has suffered or is at risk of suffering;
(f) how capable each of his parents, and any other person in relation to whom the court considers the question to be relevant, is of meeting his needs;
(g) the range of powers available to the court under the Act in the proceedings in question.

Unlike other statutory lists this one does not in terms contain a 'sweeping-up' provision directing the court to have regard to 'all the circumstances of the case' or some similar form of words. The relevance of other circumstances must be implied from the direction to have regard *in particular* to the enumerated factors. Where the court wishes to have information about matters not included in the list the proper course will presumably be for it to make a specific request that they be dealt with in any welfare report prepared in connection with the proceedings.

2.8 The legislation more typically provides no guidance on the relative weight to be attached to individual factors. Prima facie, equal weight should be given to each of them but there would appear to be nothing to prevent the court deciding to regard some matters as more important than others in individual cases. Indeed, this is probably part and parcel of the court's general quest to ascertain the child's best interests. The checklist is, after all, only an aid to this process.

2.9 Two factors in the list are worth looking at more closely. The final factor is the only one which does not relate directly to children's needs. Its special purpose is 'to try to ensure that the court chooses the order which is most appropriate in the interests of the child's welfare in the particular case, rather than the one which happens to have been sought' (Hoggett, *The Children Bill: The Aim* [1989] 19 Fam.Law 217 at p. 220).

The other factor is the first in the list. In common with a number of other provisions in the Act, this gives statutory recognition to the claims of older children to have an independent say on issues affecting them. Section

1(3)(*a*) is in line with the test propounded in the *Gillick* case in making reference to the age and understanding of the child. Suppose, however, that the child in question *is* of sufficient maturity and understanding to be capable of arriving at an independent decision. Does this mean that his views should *determine* the matter? If so, this would have the effect of making the child's *wishes*, and not his welfare, the paramount consideration. To paraphrase Lord MacDermott, they would rule upon the course to be followed.

During the passage of the Bill several amendments were tabled (which might collectively be termed the 'Gillick amendments') which would have produced this effect in relation to a range of decisions to be taken under the Act. It was pointed out in Parliament that legislation in the States of Ohio and Georgia, and in Australia and West Germany does require the courts to give effect to the preferences of older children in specified circumstances. This principle has not been accepted here and the general position taken throughout the Act is that the court must take proper account of children's wishes but is never obliged to follow them. In this way a compromise has been struck which has been graphically described by Brenda Hoggett as 'an attempt to achieve a balance between those who believe that the child, as he grows older, is entitled to determine his fate and those who believe not only that he is not so entitled, but that it is an abuse of his childhood even to attempt to ascertain his wishes' (supra, at p. 220). Put another way, the Act is attempting to provide a legal framework in which the child's alternative claims to independence and protection may receive proper consideration. The protective element in this thinking was evident in the debates in Parliament. There was a very real fear that children's views might on occasions be unreliable or induced by parental pressure. It was also felt by some that they should not have to bear the burden of having to choose between one parent or the other.

Having said that the Act is trying to achieve the right balance, it has unquestionably shifted this towards a greater degree of involvement in decision-making for children. It is perhaps at least psychologically significant that children's views appear at the top of the statutory checklist. This is a marked change from the position taken in the Law Commission's draft checklist set out in its working paper on *Custody* (No. 96, para 6.38) where this factor appeared *last* in a list of thirteen. As a matter of law there is no authority for saying that children's wishes are to be accorded any greater priority or weight than the other specified factors. Yet it is difficult to escape the feeling that in practice they are going to be seen as increasingly important. Certainly their strategic place at the head of the checklist provides no excuse for omission by oversight. Finally, it should be said that even before the Act it had been judicially recognised that it could be futile for the court to attempt to override the settled wishes of an older child (See, for example, *M v M (Minor: Custody Appeal)* [1987] 1 WLR 404.)

(c) The non-intervention principle

2.10 Section 1(5) enshrines one of the most innovative and influential principles in the Act. It provides:

> 'Where a court is considering whether or not to make one or more orders under this Act with respect to a child, it shall not make the order or any of the orders unless it considers that doing so would be better for the child than making no order at all.'

This provision reflects a basic philosophy underlying the legislation that the primary responsibility for children should rest with parents and that this should not be unnecessarily disturbed by court intervention. Parental responsibility is conceived to have a continuing or enduring quality. Parents do not cease to be parents because they are divorced. Neither do they cease to be parents where their child is being looked after compulsorily or voluntarily by a local authority despite the fact that, in either instance, an individual parent's continuing ability to play an active role in the upbringing of his child may be unrealistic.

2.11 The Law Commission expressed concern that in divorce proceedings orders for custody and access were too readily seen as 'part of the package'. It noted the likelihood that in recent years there had been an increase in relatively amicable divorces in which the parents were able to make responsible arrangements for the child without the need for a court order. It thought that where a child already had a good relationship with both parents the law should seek to disturb this as little as possible. Otherwise it felt that there might be a danger that court orders could have the undesirable effect of polarising parents' roles and perhaps alienating the child from one of them. Equally, it thought that the principle should apply to care and supervision orders since 'local authority services for families should be provided on a voluntary basis and compulsory intervention confined to cases where compulsion itself is necessary' (Report No.172, para 3.2 et seq.).

The effect of s 1(5) is that in *all* family proceedings the court must specifically direct its attention to the comparative effects of making an order and of not doing so, as far as these can be predicted. An order of any kind should only be made where it is perceived to be the most effective way of safeguarding or protecting the child's welfare. As part of this process, the court may decide that an order other than that specifically sought is desirable. It has power to make this order instead (s 1(3)(g), supra, para 2.7).

2.12 The most important situation in which the non-intervention principle will operate in practice is on divorce. Section 41 of the Matrimonial Causes Act 1973 has been radically amended to absolve the court from its duty to make the so-called 'declaration of satisfaction' before making a decree absolute (Sch 12, para 31). The old section required the court to form a judgment as to the arrangements made by divorcing parents for the children of the family. The Law Commission thought that this could lead to the making of orders for custody and access simply as a matter of routine even in uncontested cases where the parties were in total agreement about what should happen to the children (Report No. 172, para 3.5 et seq). The Act now gives effect to the recommendation that parents should continue to be required to provide the court with details of the proposed arrangements for the child but that the court's duty should be limited to considering whether it should exercise any of its powers under the Act in the light of the disclosed arrangements. It may, for example, order a welfare report where there is some reason to suppose that the parties' proposals are in some way unsatisfactory. Clearly it may have to consider making residence or contact orders in disputed cases. Where the court considers that it may wish to exercise its power but needs further time for consideration, it may in exceptional cases order that the decree should not be made absolute until it directs this.

2.13   The essential effect of the amendment to s 41 is that there is no longer any universal requirement of judicial approval for private agreements relating to children on divorce. The objective is, again, to reinforce the responsibility of parents by placing public confidence in their good sense. The reform of s 41 is welcome since it was generally accepted that the procedure did not work well in practice. The central point, which was made many times, was that there was very little a court could usefully do where the parties themselves were agreed on the future care and upbringing of their children. While this is undoubtedly true, s 41 was an important symbolic affirmation of the principle that there is a *public* interest in the well-being of the children of divorce. It is a matter of regret that the recasting of the court's function on divorce should have been relegated to a schedule of 'minor amendments' where it may languish unnoticed. It is in no sense a minor amendment and should preferably have appeared in the main body of the Act.

(d)   Avoidance of delay

2.14   Section 1(2) provides that in any proceedings in which any question relating to the upbringing of a child arises the court should have regard to the general principle that any delay in determining the question is likely to prejudice the welfare of the child. This is more appropriately considered when we examine the new powers of the court to order a timetable in family proceedings (infra, para 3.52 et seq).

2.   Parental Responsibility for Children

(a)   The allocation of parental responsibility

2.15   Where a child's mother and father were married to each other at the time of his birth they each have parental responsibility for him (s 2(1)). This essentially confirms the former rule in s 1(1) of the Guardianship Act 1973 which provided that a mother should have the same 'rights and authority' as the law allowed to a father. The change in terminology reflects the view of the Law Commission (and that of the majority of the House of Lords in *Gillick*) that the parental position vis à vis a child is more accurately described as 'responsibility'. We shall come to the meaning of the new legal concept of 'parental responsibility' in due course. For the moment it is sufficient to observe that married parents have equality before the law in all matters relating to the upbringing of their child.

2.16 The Act asserts parenthood to be the primary legal status. It abolishes the common law notion of parental guardianship whereby the married father (but not the married mother) was regarded as the natural guardian of the child. When the mother acquired equal parental rights and authority under the 1973 Act, the legislation did nothing about the superior, or at least additional, status of the father as guardian. This anachronistic rule is now abolished, thereby completing the process of achieving legal equality for married parents (s 2(4)). At the same time it produces a more clear-cut distinction between parents and non-parental guardians. Guardianship is now, with one exception, a status confined to non-parents appointed to assume parental responsibility on the death of a parent. The exception relates to the unmarried father who is without parental responsibility during the lifetime of the mother. He may be appointed guardian by the mother and acquire this responsibility by virtue of that status on her death.

2.17 Section 2(2) reaffirms the legal position governing the automatic acquisition of parental responsibility outside marriage. It vests it exclusively in the mother (as was previously the case under s 85(7) of the Children Act 1975 and s 1(7) of the Guardianship Act 1973). The father does not have parental responsibility and, if he wants it, must acquire it by one of the formal legal procedures provided by the Act.

The unmarried father's automatic legal position is best described as a 'parent without parental responsibility'. The term 'parent' under the Act applies to *all* parents including unmarried fathers but the Act distinguishes between those fathers with or without parental responsibility. This represents something of a change since previously the unmarried father fell outside the statutory definition of 'parent' for the purposes of most legal issues such as care or adoption. He is now to be regarded as a 'parent' in accordance with s 1 of the Family Law Reform Act 1987 (s 2(3)). This enacted the general principle that references in all future legislation:

> 'to any relationship between two persons shall, unless the contrary intention appears, be construed without regard to whether or not the father and mother of either of them, or the father and mother of any person through whom the relationship is deduced, have or had been married to each other at any time.'

The broad effect of this complex provision is that the unmarried father will always qualify as a parent unless a contrary intention appears in a statute. But this is only part of the picture since this legal status of parenthood will be no great advantage where the parental responsibility which normally attaches to it is expressly withheld. This is the father's automatic legal position and it is also the case that certain provisions of the Act, notably those governing the right to remove a child being looked after by a local authority under Part III, only apply to someone who has this parental responsibility whether a parent or not. The unmarried father is, thus, prohibited from removing the child not because he lacks parental status but because he does not have parental responsibility for the child except where he has previously acquired this formally (s 20(8)).

(b)   Shared parental responsibility and the right of independent action

2.18   The Act confirms that more than one person can have parental responsibility for the same child at the same time (s 2(5)). This is, of course, self-evident in the case of married parents. There are other instances in which responsibility may be shared between a parent and non-parent, such as a guardian or step-parent, or between a parent and a local authority where the child is in care. Because parental responsibility can be shared, a person who has it does not cease to have it solely because some other person also acquires parental responsibility in relation to the child (s 2(6)). This important rule encapsulates the ethos of continuing parental responsibility to which reference has already been made and which is a salient feature of the legislation. A parent does not, for example, lose parental responsibility because a third party such as a foster parent, grandparent or step-parent succeeds in acquiring it by means of a residence order (see Chapter 3). This will be likely to arise on many occasions following divorce when the mother remarries and the step-father obtains a joint residence order in favour of himself and the mother. The divorced natural father will still retain his parental responsibility in these circumstances. Most remarkably, perhaps, a parent will not lose responsibility where a local authority acquires it under a care order though it has been necessary for the Act to impose some restrictions on the *exercise* of this responsibility by the parent (see Chapter 5).

The effect of s 2(6) is that parental responsibility is not lost *solely* because it is also acquired by someone else. It will, however, be lost where an adoption order is made since, in this case, it is expressly provided by statute that parental responsibility should be wholly transferred to the adoptive parents (Adoption Act 1976, s 12(3)(*a*)).

2.19   Where parental responsibility is shared, each person in whom it is vested may act independently in meeting that responsibility except where statute expressly requires the consent of more than one person in a matter affecting the child (s 2(7)).

This right to take unilateral action was recognised in the case of married parents by s 1(1) of the Guardianship Act 1973 which stated that their rights and authority were 'exercisable by either without the other'. This was thought to be qualified by s 85(3) of the Children Act 1975 which appeared to prohibit the independent exercise of parental powers where someone else possessing parental rights signified his disapproval of the proposed course of action before it took place. The generally accepted interpretation of these provisions was that a person with parental rights (in the former terminology) had no right to be consulted before another person with parental rights took action in relation to the child. But it was equally accepted that each holder of parental rights did have a veto power provided that he was forewarned of the impending action.

2.20 The Act introduces a major change by abolishing this power of veto. The effect of the new provisions is that each parent (or other person with parental responsibility) may act alone whether or not anyone else with parental responsibility objects. This is subject to two qualifications. The first is that independent action may not be taken where statute requires each person with parental responsibility to act. The obvious example is adoption where each parent's consent must either be obtained or dispensed with before an order can be made (s 16(1) of the Adoption Act 1976). The other limitation is that no-one may exercise parental responsibility in a way which is incompatible with a court order relating to the child (s 2(8)). In the light of this statutory endorsement of independent action it hardly needs saying that the Act has not created any rights of consultation before action is taken.

The Act draws no distinction between every day trivial matters and major decisions, perhaps in the educational or medical sphere. Where those sharing responsibility disagree strongly on issues like this the statutory scheme places the onus on the person objecting to a course of action to seek a court order preventing it. This will be either a 'prohibited steps order' or, perhaps, a 'specific issue order' if judicial regulation of an area of upbringing is required rather than prohibition of some specific action (s 8(1) discussed in Chapter 3).

2.21 It is conceivable that this scheme may give rise to some difficulties in practice. It appears to rely on the assumption that an objecting parent will have time to take the appropriate legal steps to block action in relation to the child. But without a right of consultation that parent may not discover the proposed action until it is too late. In this situation the parental responsibility of the objector appears more illusory than real. The problem may be accentuated where parents are separated or divorced. The failure of the Act to incorporate rights of consultation may well impede one of the central objectives of the reforms which is to achieve a norm of parental co-operation following divorce.

(c) Delegation of parental responsibility

2.22 The Act distinguishes between the surrender or transfer of parental responsibility and its temporary delegation. It provides that a person with parental responsibility 'may not surrender or transfer any part of that responsibility to another but may arrange for some or all of it to be met by one or more persons acting on his behalf' (s 2(9)).

The embargo on relinquishing parental responsibility altogether has its roots in the common law (*Vansittart v Vansittart* (1858) 2 De G & J 249). It eventually found expression in s 85(2) of the Children Act 1975. The rule is grounded in public policy that parents should not be able to abdicate from their legal responsibility by private agreement but only with a court order allowing them to do so. On the other hand, there has never been any objection to a temporary delegation of responsibility where a parent arranges for his child to be looked after for a short time by someone else, for example, a relative, friend or baby-sitter. The legitimacy of this practice is now expressly recognised whether the arrangement is made with a person already possessing parental responsibility or someone who does not have this (s 2(10)). There is one qualification to this power of temporary delegation. A parent may not escape from his basic legal duty to ensure that the child is properly looked after. In other words he may incur liability under the criminal law or civil law if the child suffers harm as a result of a parent's failure to satisfy himself that the arrangements for temporary care of the child are adequate (s 2(11)).

2.23 This statutory confirmation of the right to delegate responsibility is designed, inter alia, to clarify (particularly for the benefit of third parties) the legal standing of temporary carers. The Law Commission suggested that it would be helpful if, for example, a school could feel confident in accepting the decision of someone nominated as a temporary 'guardian' by parents in their absence (Report No. 172, para 2.13). What, then, is the precise legal status of the temporary carer? The position before the Act was that anyone with 'actual custody' of a child (as defined by s 87 of the Children Act 1975) had the same duties as those imposed on a person with 'legal custody'. These were not defined but were basically those arising under the criminal law and the law of tort. In particular, there could be legal liability for ill-treatment or neglect of the child. It was almost certainly also the case that these duties implied certain concomitant legal powers. How, for example, could a duty to protect an infant from physical harm be discharged without a legal power to control the physical movements of that child?

The position was sufficiently uncertain that the Act now seeks to clarify the powers of temporary carers by providing them with a legal basis to 'do what is reasonable in all the circumstances of the case for the purpose of safeguarding or promoting the child's welfare' (s 3(5)). What is reasonable will be a question of fact but the Law Commission offered the view, with specific reference to medical treatment, that consent to major elective surgery would not be authorised whereas it would be reasonable for a carer to agree to whatever was medically advised in the case of an accident to the child (Report No. 172, para 2.16). It should be apparent that a temporary delegation of parental responsibility does not confer on the carers the more fundamental legal incidents of parenthood. Thus, they may not appoint guardians or consent to adoption. Finally, it is important to bear in mind that these arrangements are not legally binding on parents and may be revoked by them at will. This is similar in nature to the position where a child is being voluntarily looked after by a local authority. Here again parents may remove the child without notice (see Chapter 4). The policy in each case is not to deter parents from seeking voluntary help with their children.

3. The Meaning of Parental Responsibility

2.24 Somewhat illogically, the definition of the fundamental concept of parental responsibility appears after the provisions dealing with its allocation between parents. The Act states that it amounts to 'all the rights, duties, powers, responsibilities and authority which by law a parent of a child has in relation to the child and his property.' (s 3(1)). This is reminiscent of the former definition of parental 'rights' in s 85(1) of the Children Act 1975 and is about as useful. It really tells us nothing about the nature or extent of parent powers and duties which have to be deduced from an examination of the general law. The primary purpose of the Act is however to simplify the ambiguous and confusing terminology which has characterised previous attempts to describe the parent's position in law. Thus all previous references in legislation to 'rights, duties, responsibilities and authority' are replaced by the unitary concept of 'responsibility'. At the same time this represents a distinct shift of emphasis away from proprietorial notions of 'rights' and towards the idea that any powers which parents have derive from duty or responsibility.

2.25 This revision of language does not effect any significant substantive change. Parents have always had legal powers to take action to control their children's upbringing and, of course, they still have them. In exercising them they have a wide, but not unlimited, discretion. This is the essence of the legal relationship between parents and children. Neither the concept of 'rights' nor the concept of 'responsibility' conveys this relation particularly accurately. Whatever its jurisprudential inadequacies may be (and this is not the place to explore these) the new concept of parental responsibility has won the day and will now serve to determine who has the legal authority to act in relation to a child in such matters as education, medical care, where the child is to live, what name he is to have and all other aspects of upbringing and welfare. The temptation to produce a definitive list of the spheres of parental responsibility was rejected as impracticable.

2.26 At common law there were thought to be some distinctions between the respective legal powers of parents and guardians. In particular it was doubtful whether parents possessed the authority to administer or deal with the child's property. This power was undoubtedly vested in guardians of the child's estate. A primary objective of the legislation is to assimilate as far as possible the legal powers of parents and guardians. Accordingly, it is expressly provided that parental responsibility shall include the rights, powers and duties which a guardian of the child's estate would have had in relation to a child and his property (s 3(2)). These include the right of the guardian to receive or recover in his own name, for the benefit of the child, property of whatever description and wherever situated which the child is entitled to receive or recover (s 3(3)). In practice this is likely to be most useful in confirming a parent's right to receive a legacy on his child's behalf.

2.27 As we have seen, parental responsibility is largely concerned with the power to regulate matters of upbringing. Certain other legal incidents are characteristics of being a parent rather than of possessing parental responsibility. Thus, even parents who do not possess this have the duty to maintain the child. They also have succession rights which are a feature of being related to the deceased in a particular way. These incidents, therefore, attach to the unmarried father without parental responsibility but do not pass to a non-parent who obtains this under a residence order. The Act confirms this position which existed under the old law (s 3(4)).

4.   Acquisition of Parental Responsibility by the Unmarried Father

2.28 We saw that the unmarried father acquires no parental responsibility simply by virtue of his paternity. The issue of automatic parental 'rights' for unmarried fathers received an exhaustive airing during the Law Commission's work on illegitimacy which culminated in the Family Law Reform Act 1987. The arguments against giving automatic rights prevailed and this position is maintained by the Act. The father must, therefore, take formal legal steps to obtain parental responsibility if he wishes to have it. There are two mechanisms in the Act for this purpose. He may either apply to the court for a 'parental responsibility order' or enter into a 'parental responsibility agreement' with the mother (s 4(1)).

2.29 The court application originated in s 4 of the Family Law Reform Act 1987 where the order was known as a 'parental rights order'. The change in the 1989 Act is a purely semantic one in line with the other revised terminology discussed above. The view was expressed by certain commentators on the 1987 Act that the s 4 order would be unlikely to be granted where it was opposed by the mother. It was initially seen primarily as a device for sharing parental responsibility between cohabiting unmarried parents. This view must now be re-assessed in the light of the fact that in 1987 there existed no mechanism for the formal sharing of parental responsibility by unmarried parents without recourse to the courts. Since the Act now introduces such a mechanism it may well be that the judicial procedure will be used only where the mother and father cannot agree to share responsibility. The court will have to apply the welfare principle in deciding whether it should override the mother's wishes and make the order.

2.30 The 'parental responsibility agreement' is another of the Act's innovations. The idea that unmarried parents might voluntarily agree to share parental responsibility was resisted at the time of the illegitimacy reforms primarily because of fears that this might lead to what was seen as a further erosion of the institution of marriage. Eventually the Law Commission came around to the view that these agreements would be desirable. Judicial proceedings were considered to be 'unduly elaborate, expensive and unnecessary unless the child's mother objects to the order' (Report No. 172, para 2.18). Hence the Act follows the recommendation for the introduction of agreements which will have the same legal effect as s 4 orders.

In view of the importance and seriousness of these legal effects it is provided that no agreement will be effective unless it is made in the prescribed form and has been recorded in the prescribed manner. The precise form of the agreement and the manner in which it is to be recorded is to be left to regulations made by the Lord Chancellor (s 4(2)). The Commission envisaged a simple paper procedure in the county court with a small standard fee. It is expected that the regulations will institute such a procedure.

Where the mother does not wish to share responsibility with the father during her lifetime, she will still have the option of appointing him a guardian to take over responsibility for the child on her death.

2.31 Both the court order and the agreement may only be terminated by the court on the application of any person who has parental responsibility for the child or, with the leave of the court, the child himself (s 4(3)). Leave may only be granted where the court is satisfied that the child has sufficient understanding to make the proposed application (s 4(4)). This is another statutory formulation of the *Gillick* test.

There is one restriction on the court's power to order termination. It is prohibited during any time in which a residence order in favour of the father remains in force (s 12(4)). The reasoning is that where the father is looking after the child under a residence order it is a necessary concomitant of this that he should have formal legal responsibility for the child.

5. Guardians

(a) General

2.32 Sections 5 and 6 constitute a new statutory code governing the appointment and removal of guardians and the legal effects of guardianship. They replace, with important modifications, the relevant provisions of the Guardianship of Minors Act 1971. There are two major changes. First, the formal requirements for the private appointment of guardians are relaxed in an attempt to encourage and facilitate more appointments. Secondly, a new rule is introduced (subject to one exception) that where there is a surviving parent a guardian's appointment should take effect only on the death of that parent.

(b) The appointment of guardians

2.33 The Act maintains the basic position that guardians may be appointed either by the court or by private appointment. Section 5(1) governs court appointments. It empowers the court to appoint an individual applicant guardian where:

(a) the child has no parent with parental responsibility for him; or

(b) a residence order has been made with respect to the child in favour of a parent or guardian who has died while the order was in force.

Such an appointment may be made on application or of the court's own motion in family proceedings (s 5(2)).

The court's power to appoint a guardian must be considered alongside the more wide-ranging and flexible powers which it has under s 8. It may make orders to resolve all questions relating to upbringing (contact, prohibited steps and special issue orders) and to provide that the child may live with someone other than a parent or guardian (residence orders). A person in whose favour a residence order is made will acquire virtually all the responsibilities of a parent. In the light of these other powers the policy of the Act is that the court should appoint a guardian only where it is necessary to provide a complete substitute for a deceased parent. Where a parent is still alive, but a complete substitute-parent is considered to be in the best interests of the child, the appropriate procedure is adoption rather than guardianship.

2.34 Section 5(1)(*a*) covers the situation where both parents are dead and did not themselves appoint a guardian. It also encompasses the circumstances which may arise on the death of an unmarried mother. In the latter situation, although the father may be alive, he will not be a 'parent with parental responsibility' unless he took steps to acquire it during the life of the mother. He may, of course, acquire it on the death of the mother if she privately appointed him guardian. Where none of these mechanisms was used the Court may appoint a guardian and one option would clearly be to appoint the father himself.

Section 5(1)(*b*) allows a court appointment to be made where a residence order was in force in relation to a parent or guardian who then died. This broadly corresponds with the policy on private appointments where, as we shall see, these may take immediate effect where the deceased parent had physical care of the child under a residence order. Most obviously, this provision covers the situation of the death of a divorced parent. It was not thought desirable that a surviving parent, without a residence order in his favour, should automatically be entitled to resume the care of the child by virtue of his continuing parental responsibility. Without the appointment of a guardian he would probably be entitled to do so since a person with parental responsibility may take any action in relation to the child which is not incompatible with a court order. While a residence order is in force, it would be incompatible with this to remove the child from the residential parent. But on the death of that parent the residence order terminates and it would be a proper exercise of parental responsibility to resume the physical care of the child in these circumstances. Where the residential parent wishes to prevent this scenario arising on her death the answer will be to appoint a guardian to share parental responsibility with the surviving parent. Failing this, s 5(1)(*b*) allows the court to appoint a guardian. Where there is actual or potential disagreement between the guardian and surviving parent the court may need to back-up the appointment with one or more s 8 orders, especially perhaps a residence order in the guardian's favour.

2.35 Guardians may be privately appointed by parents with parental responsibility and by guardians themselves (s 5(3) and (4)). An unmarried father, without parental responsibility, may not appoint a guardian. There is no restriction or control on the character of persons who may be appointed. The Law Commission did canvass the possibility of extending to guardians the controls applying to the supervision and disqualification of foster parents but this was ultimately rejected as unworkable and, on balance, undesirable (Report No.172, para 2.32). The statutory confirmation of a guardian's own right to appoint a guardian to take his place in the event of his death is part of the general policy of the Act in favour of assimilating the legal position of parents and guardians by giving full parental responsibility to the latter.

2.36 The Act breaks new ground by allowing private appointments to be effective if made in writing, dated and signed. Where the appointment is made by will it will be effective, although not signed by the testator, provided it is signed at his direction in accordance with the requirements of s 9 of the Wills Act 1837. In other cases, the appointment will be effective if it is made in writing and signed at the direction of the person making the appointment in his presence and in the presence of two witnesses who each attest the signature (s 5(5)). This is a substantial relaxation of the formal requirements which previously recognised only appointments made by deed or will. The simpler method should encourage more appointments. It is particularly designed to overcome the widespread reluctance to make wills which is prevalent in the case of younger adults. Most of them would prefer not to contemplate death at all if they can avoid doing so. Nevertheless, it is precisely this group who are most likely to have younger children who might become orphaned. It should be emphasised that this less formal method of appointment in writing does not prevent an appointment by the more traditional means of a deed or will. Indeed it is likely that most appointments will continue to be made by will.

2.37 Two final points on appointments may be noted. The first is that the Act confirms that private appointments may continue to be made jointly by two or more persons (s 5(10)). The clearest example is the mutual choice by two parents of an individual to act as guardian should they die together suddenly. The second point is that the methods of appointment discussed above are exhaustive (s 5(13)). There is no other means of appointing a guardian than that provided by s 5.

(c) The legal effects of guardianship

2.38 It is provided that an appointed guardian has parental responsibility for the child concerned (s 5(6)). He thus acquires a legal status which is closely akin to parenthood. In particular, he has all the decision-making powers over upbringing inherent in the concept of parental responsibility and, importantly, the right to undertake the physical care of the child except where this is withheld from him by virtue of a residence order in favour of someone else. It is intended that guardians should become parents to the child in the fullest sense since they are in effect complete replacements for deceased parents. It was also considered that the somewhat obscure distinction between guardianship of the person and guardianship of the estate, which existed at common law, should be abolished. This is achieved by the application of the single concept of parental responsibility to guardians and by restricting the circumstances under which the inherent jurisdiction of the High Court may be exercised to appoint a guardian of the estate to circumstances (and subject to conditions) prescribed by rules of court (s 5(11) and (12)). Guardians are therefore, to all intents and purposes, placed in the same legal position as parents, at least so far as the care and upbringing of the child are concerned.

2.39 We now come to what is undoubtedly the most controversial change to the law of guardianship wrought by the Act. The issue is the legal position of an appointed guardian where there is a surviving parent. The new rules are contained in s 5(7) to (9) which must be read together. Prior to the Act every guardian's appointment took effect immediately on the death of the appointing parent. The guardian would then act jointly with a surviving parent subject to the court's power to intervene to resolve disputes between them.

The broad effect of the new rules is that the appointment will not take place until the death of the second or surviving parent *unless* the deceased parent had a residence order which was operative at the date of his death. This general rule may be divided into several sub-rules. In each case we are concerned with the position immediately before the death of the deceased and the legal effect which his death will have. The position is as follows:

(i)   Where the child had no parent with parental responsibility (i.e. apart from the deceased himself) the appointment takes effect immediately (s 5(7));

(ii)   Where the child *did* have another parent with parental responsibility but the deceased had a residence order in his favour, again the appointment takes effect immediately (s 5(7));

As noted above, the legal position is identical where the court makes an appointment in these circumstances;

(iii) Where the child *did* have another parent with parental responsibility and the deceased did *not* have a residence order in his favour at the time of death, the appointment will take place only 'when the child no longer has a parent who has parental responsibility for him' (s 5(8)). In simple language this means on the death of the surviving parent;

(iv)   Where the surviving parent *also* had a residence order in his favour, in addition to that in favour of the deceased (i.e. a 'joint' residence order), the appointment will again take effect only on the death of the survivor (s 5(9)). This sub-rule is designed to cater for the situation where the child has been living partly in the household of one parent and partly with the other parent under what might be termed a 'time-sharing arrangement'. In these circumstances the court is also precluded from appointing a guardian following the death of one parent (s 5(9)).

2.40   The objective of this framework is 'to balance the claims of the surviving parent and the wishes of the deceased in the way which will be best for the child' (Report No. 172, para 2.27). The new rules are readily understandable where the child was living with *both* parents in a united family before the death of one of them. In that context the new law protects the surviving parent from interference by an outsider. If the survivor wishes informally to seek the help of the appointed guardian this may be done without jeopardising his parental status. If the appointed guardian wishes to challenge this position the Act now shifts the onus on to him to obtain a s 8 order.

The position may be less satisfactory where the parents were separated or divorced. The Act takes the position that a residential parent ought to be able to exclude the non-residential parent from the physical care of the child in the event of his death. The survivor will, of course, have joint parental responsibility with the guardian but will have the onus of bringing the child's position before the court in the event of a disagreement between them. This is not very easy to reconcile with the ethos of continuing parental responsibility following divorce. It casts the non-residential parent in the role of an outsider who is liable to interfere with the child rather than that of a concerned parent who is anxious to step in to the breach left by the deceased. Again it is questionable how realistic it is to talk of parental responsibility where the individuals concerned do not also have the physical care of the child.

(d) The revocation, disclaimer and termination of guardianship

2.41 The appointment of a guardian may be revoked in the following circumstances:

(i)   where it is expressly revoked by a written and dated instrument signed by the person who made the appointment (s 6(2)). These written requirements are the same as for the original appointment;

(ii)   where the written document is destroyed with the intention of revoking the appointment either by the person making the appointment or by someone else at his direction and in his presence (s 6(3));

(iii) where a later appointment has been made by written instrument, will or codicil by the same person in respect of the same child unless it is clear, expressly or impliedly, that the purpose of the later appointment is to appoint an additional guardian (s 6(1));

(iv)   where the appointment was made in a will or codicil which is subsequently revoked either deliberately or by operation of law, for example, by marriage (s 6(4)).

2.42 An appointed guardian may disclaim his appointment within a reasonable time of his first knowing that the appointment has taken effect (s 6(5)). The disclaimer must be in writing and signed. Curiously, the Act does not expressly require the document to be dated but this must be implied since the disclaimer must be within a reasonable time of the appointment. It will, thus, be necessary to know when the purported disclaimer took place. The disclaimer will be ineffective unless it is recorded in accordance with any regulations made by the Lord Chancellor (s 6(6)). This requirement is for the purpose of resolving any doubts which may arise concerning the person with parental responsibility for a child in the event of a parent's death. As a matter of good practice, any parent or guardian wishing to appoint a guardian should (and in most cases almost certainly will) secure the prior consent of the intended guardian before making the appointment. This will obviously reduce the risk of a subsequent disclaimer.

2.43 The court may terminate the appointment of a guardian at any time in the same circumstances in which it may make the original appointment (supra, para 2.33) (s 6(7)). It has an unfettered discretion and a general power to do so. The power was previously vested solely in the High Court but is now extended by the Act to the county court and magistrates' court which also have a concurrent jurisdiction to appoint guardians. Removal of a guardian is most likely to occur where the court considers him to be an undesirable individual who is unfit to have parental responsibility or where the guardian is at loggerheads with a surviving parent with whom he is sharing responsibility. Where the court exercises the power of removal it may have to consider ordering the appointment of a new guardian in order to prevent a hiatus in legal responsibility for the child.

6. Welfare Reports

(a) Circumstances in which a report may be ordered

2.44 The court is given a complete discretion to decide what welfare reports (if any) to order when considering any question with respect to a child under the Act (s 7(1)). It may request a report from either a probation officer or a local authority. Where an authority is requested to produce a report it must arrange for one of its own officers or some other appropriate person to prepare it. The power of the court to order a report is extended to *all* proceedings under the Act. Previously there were some proceedings in which this could not be done. Moreover, the separate criteria for ordering reports which applied in different proceedings are abolished in favour of the general power to do so wherever the court feels that a report would assist on any question relevant to the welfare of a child.

Where the court requests a report from a probation officer or officer of a local authority's social services department these persons are under a statutory duty to comply with the request (s 7(5)). The court is not precluded from requesting a report from some other independent source such as the officer of a voluntary organisation which has been directly concerned with the child. But there is no corresponding duty on the organisation or its officer to accede to the court's request.

2.45 It was suggested in Parliament that the court should be *obliged* to order a report in every case. This position had previously been rejected by the Law Commission which was mindful of the resource implications which this would entail and the need to target the limited time of welfare officers on the cases (usually contested) in which a report would be most valuable. It also pointed out that welfare reports could be a source of delay and that the court might have to balance this against the potential advantages to be gained from a report (Report No.172, para 6.15). Obviously, in practice, there is a greater likelihood that the court will wish to order a report in a contested case but it would be unwise to assume that the court will never wish to order one in an uncontested case. It should also be remembered that in deciding whether to order a report the court will be guided by the general principle in s 1(5) and will not order one unless it is satisfied that this is better for the child than not doing so.

(b) Content and presentation of the report

2.46 Regulations may specify matters which must be dealt with in welfare reports unless the court orders otherwise (s 7(2)). This follows the recommendation of the Law Commission which was concerned with two particular types of cases (Report No. 172, paras 6.19 to 6.20).

The first was where a non-parent might apply (probably with leave) for a residence order under s 8 where that person would under the former law have been qualified to apply for a custodianship order under s 33 of the Children Act 1975. It will be recalled that the entire custodianship regime has been abolished by the Act. In the vast majority of custodianship proceedings it was a formal requirement that a detailed report be obtained from the relevant local authority (Children Act 1975, s 40). Regulations prescribed the matters which the report should cover. It is envisaged that new regulations made under the 1989 Act may prescribe that similar matters be covered where this type of case is the subject of any application for an order under the Act.

The second type of case is where a court is considering making a care or supervision order in private family proceedings. The Commission thought that the protection offered to the child ought to be as close as possible to that in ordinary care proceedings. Accordingly, it is envisaged that rules of court may provide in these cases for an independent welfare report to be obtained from a welfare officer or a member of the panel of guardians ad litem.

2.47   A welfare report requested under the Act may be made in writing, or orally, as the court requires (s 7(3)). Normally it will be in writing but it was considered that the provision for oral reports under the rules governing magistrates' courts could usefully be expanded to all courts having jurisdiction under the Act. A written report may, therefore, be supplemented by an oral report at the hearing. It is expected that the rules of court will require disclosure of written reports to the parties and provide for the right to put questions at the hearing to the officer responsible for the report.

(c)   The relevance of the welfare report

2.48   The court is entitled to have regard to any statement in the report and any evidence given in respect of the matters covered by it notwithstanding the normal rules of evidence (s 7(4)). The relaxation of the technical rules of evidence in relation to welfare reports was again expressly governed by rules of court in the magistrates' court and also seems to have been accepted practice in the higher courts (see, particularly *Re H (A Minor), Re K (Minors) (Child Abuse: Evidence)* [1989] 2 FLR 313 in which the Court of Appeal reviewed the rules of evidence applicable in children cases and generally, Chapter 8, infra). The main purpose of the provision is to put it beyond doubt that hearsay evidence in welfare reports may be taken into account in proceedings under the Act. The reasoning is that welfare reports are provided for the benefit of the court and that anything which can assist it in its task of ascertaining the child's best interests should be admissible. Proceedings relating to children are not to be seen as a contest between adults and in practice it is uncommon for a party to take a point on the technical rules of evidence.

Concern was voiced in Parliament that where hearsay is relied upon the source of it should be disclosed to the parties. It is not envisaged that the rules of court will require this but it will be open to the court to discount any statement which is not properly supported. As the Lord Chancellor has said a court is 'well able to separate the wheat from the chaff in a welfare officer's report without going into too much detail and description of what is wheat on the one hand and chaff on the other' (*House of Lords, Official Report*, December 19, 1988, col 1215).

2.49 The Act is silent on the question of the weight which ought to be attached to welfare reports. A number of decisions have emphasised the court's obligation to give reasons when departing from the recommendations in a report. (See, for example, *Stephenson v Stephenson* [1985] FLR 1140 and *Cadman v Cadman* (1982) 3 FLR 275). These decisions should hold good under the reformed legislation but it might have been better if this issue had been expressly confronted by the Act.

CHAPTER THREE

Orders Relating to Children in Family Proceedings

1. Introduction

3.1 Part II of the Act radically reforms the nature of the orders which can be made in respect of children and the basis upon which they can be granted in public and private proceedings. The orders prescribed in this Part will arise predominantly in private family proceedings while those relating to care and supervision in Part IV will arise primarily in public proceedings. Yet both of these types of proceedings are 'family proceedings' for the purposes of the legislation and the general principle is that all orders should be available in all proceedings. Thus, it will be possible for 'private' or 's 8 orders' to be granted in proceedings in which a local authority is seeking the care or supervision of a child. Likewise, it will be possible for 'public' orders relating to care and supervision to be made in the course of private family proceedings such as divorce. The orders are, therefore, intended to be interchangeable and as far as possible to have equivalent effects. The 'private' residence order will, for example, be similar, (though not identical) in its legal effect to the 'public' care order. Both vest 'parental responsibility' in the person in whose favour they are made. The overall objective is to create a consistent and unified scheme in place of the confusing morass of almost incomprehensible orders and procedural niceties which existed before the Act. At the same time the much-simplified orders are intended to be wide enough to deal with every practical issue which could arise in relation to the care or upbringing of children. They are to be widely available so that they may be made in all proceedings in all courts. In this way it is to be hoped that some duplication of proceedings which was necessary under the old law in order to achieve complementary purposes will be avoided.

3.2 The defects of the old law were substantial. First, the orders which were available differed according to the proceedings in which they were sought. The divorce courts, for example, applied their own concept of 'custody' which had a different meaning to that of 'legal custody' which applied in proceedings under the Domestic Proceedings and Magistrates' Courts Act 1978, the Guardianship of Minors Act 1971 and the Children Act 1975. In particular, courts exercising jurisdiction under these Acts had no power to make orders for *joint* legal custody whereas joint custody orders were becoming an increasingly common phenomenon in the divorce courts.

Secondly, there was considerable doubt about the precise legal effects of those orders. According to one view, neither order removed the non-custodial parent's right to have a say in matters of upbringing. (*Dipper v Dipper* [1981] Fam. 31). A different view was commonly held by practitioners according to research conducted on behalf of the Law Commission (see J.A. Priest and J.C. Whybrow, *Custody Law and Practice in Divorce and Domestic Courts* (1986), Supplement to Law Commission Working Paper No. 96). This was that the person with sole custody (usually the mother) had the *exclusive* right to take decisions on upbringing. Put colloquially, the effect of the order was thought to place her 'in the driving seat'. This ambiguity concerning the effects of custody orders led to a sharp division of opinion on the merits and demerits of making orders for joint custody and to serious regional discrepancies in the granting of these orders.

Thirdly, there were major inconsistencies in the orders which might be made in favour of 'non-parents'. These depended, at least in part, on whether the applicant was a step-parent, relative, foster parent or some other third party. Even within these categories there were unjustifiable distinctions. Step-parenthood derived from remarriage following divorce was, for example, treated more favourably than step-parenthood arising from marriage to a widowed or previously unmarried parent. Furthermore, the different rules on locus standi in various family proceedings were unnecessarily restrictive in their effect on non-parents.

3.3   The beauty of the new scheme is that it simplifies the orders available and at the same time goes a long way towards assimilating the position of parents and non-parents before the courts. Two caveats must, however, be entered at this stage. The first is that a parent will generally retain his parental responsibility *whether or not* he has a residence order in his favour. This is not so in the case of non-parents who only obtain parental responsibility *by virtue* of a residence order. The second is that, although the Act does much to improve the access of non-parents to the courts, the circumstances in which they may seek orders are still considerably more restricted than those which apply to parents.

3.4   The structure of Part II is as follows:

Section 8 introduces and defines four new types of order and contains the expansive definition of 'family proceedings' in which these orders may be made. Section 10 deals with the powers of the court to make the various orders. It provides that certain classes of individuals may apply for orders as of right while others are required to obtain the leave of the court. Section 9 imposes some specific restrictions on the making of s 8 orders. Sections 11 to 13 flesh out the scheme and deal with various specific matters relating to s 8 orders including the effect of cohabitation, change of the child's name and removal of the child from the jurisdiction. Sections 12, 14 and parts of s 11 are directly concerned with residence orders. They should be read with the definition of residence orders in s 8 since it is impossible to appreciate the nature of these orders in isolation from their relationship to the distribution of parental responsibility.

Section 15 and Sch 1 constitute a self-contained code for financial relief and, to a limited extent, property orders for children. They are a substantial re-enactment, with only minor modifications, of existing legislation governing these matters. Consequently, proportionately less space is devoted here to this aspect.

Finally, s 16 introduces 'family assistance orders' which are related to, but distinct from, supervision orders. The purpose is to provide for a less coercive kind of order where a family requires short-term help.

2.   General Principles Relating to Section 8 Orders

(a)   Types of order under s 8

3.5   Section 8 introduces four new types of order viz 'a contact order', a 'prohibited steps order', 'a residence order' and 'a specific issue order'. We must look at each of these in turn beginning with the residence order which is by far the most significant.

(i)   The residence order

3.6   The Act states with deceptive simplicity that a residence order 'means an order settling the arrangements to be made as to the person with whom a child is to live' (s 8(1)). This definition is as noteworthy for what it does not say as it is for what it does say. It does not tell us in terms what effect the order has on the allocation of parental responsibility and we have to turn to s 12(2) to elucidate this. This explains that, in the case of anyone who is not a parent or guardian of the child, that person 'shall have parental responsibility for the child, while the residence order remains in force.'

Non-parents who have a residence order are therefore automatically vested with parental responsibility as a concomitant of the order. The purpose of this is self-evident. If someone is to have the physical care of a child he must also have the power to determine matters of upbringing which goes with parental responsibility. Unless the Act had made express provision to this effect parental responsibility would not have been assured. This is because a residence order is precisely what it says it is i.e. an order regulating where a child is to live. It does not per se confer or take away any parental responsibility.

3.7   Let us apply this analysis to the position of parents (or guardians). They are people who do have parental responsibility quite apart from any residence order. Where a residence order is made, its effect is simply to regulate where the child is to live. Apart from this one matter all other aspects of parental responsibility remain undisturbed. In the context of divorce, this means in essence that *both* parents retain the parental responsibility which they had during the marriage. The only change is that the 'non-residential' parent (assuming that a sole residence order is made) will not have the right (or responsibility if this is preferred) to look after the child. This would appear to be broadly in line with the *Dipper* philosophy noted above. Where a residence order is in favour of a non-parent, the parent will again retain joint parental responsibility with that person (s 2(6)).

3.8   The idea which needs to be grasped is that the concepts of residence and parental responsibility are distinct. In a functioning family they are both features of the parent-child relationship but they may become detached from one another, at least as far as one parent is concerned, on divorce or where long-term substitute care is arranged for the child.

The position of the unmarried father is perhaps the best illustration of this separation of the notions of residence and responsibility. Where he successfully obtains a residence order this will not per se be enough to give him the parental responsibility which (we shall assume) he does not already have. Accordingly, it will be necessary for him to secure a separate order giving him the parental responsibility which he needs in order to have a legal basis for looking after the child. Thus, it is provided that the court *must* make a 'parental responsibility order' in his favour when it grants him a residence order (s 12(1)). Moreover, in order to ensure the continuity of parental responsibility where the child is living with the father, the court is prevented from terminating the order for parental responsibility while the residence order remains in force (s 12(4)).

3.9   The idea that the parent without the residence order continues to have parental responsibility despite it is fundamental to the philosophy of the Act. Parents do not cease to be parents where they are no longer primarily responsible for looking after their child. This is a subtle notion for a lawyer to understand, let alone a layman. It probably does not represent the perception of custody orders currently held by the person in the street. Those responsible for advising in practice will bear the heavy burden of getting this across to their clients.

What, then, does this continuing parental responsibility mean in practical terms? At least in theory, it means that the non-residential parent has the right to be involved in, and express opinions on, all questions relating to the child's upbringing. Third parties such as schools, hospitals or clergymen should therefore continue to regard the non-residential parent as a parent and deal with him on an equal footing with the residential parent. He is entitled to exercise his parental responsibility at all times when the child is with him since responsibility 'runs with the child'. Technically, he is also entitled to exercise responsibility where the child is *not* physically with him although, realistically this may be practically impossible. The exercise of responsibility in either case is subject only to the limitation that it must not be executed in a way which is incompatible with a court order (s 2(8)).

It is for this reason that he is not entitled to remove the child from the physical care of the residential parent. This would be incompatible with the residence order.

3.10 All of this must be carefully explained if parents are to understand properly their continuing obligations. The question which a parent is most like to raise is this: 'How can it be said that I have parental responsibility if I am not entitled to object to something which my ex-spouse is doing in relation to my child and I am not even entitled to be told about it before it occurs?' There is no answer to this except the unsatisfactory one that the objecting parent may take the issue to the court if he is quick enough. In truth, upbringing will be determined and executed for the most part by the residential parent and it requires some intellectual effort to regard the parental responsibility of the non-residential parent as anything more than symbolic . Where the new scheme *can* be expected to score some success is in the reshaping of societal attitudes, particularly those of individual divorcing couples. The Act establishes a norm that ex-spouses remain parents and *ought* to retain a commitment to their child. This should not simply be off-loaded on to the other parent and/or the state.

3.11 Yet in one sense the Act gives the non-residential parent a remarkable power. When the child is actually with him he will himself be able to take any manner of decision which is not expressly prohibited by court order. He may act independently, without consultation with the residential parent, and in serious matters as well as every day trivial affairs. There would, for instance, apparently be nothing to prevent him from authorising major elective surgery for the child despite his being aware of the residential parent's opposition to this. This is the price which may occasionally have to be paid for the principle of independent parental action which has been considered sacrosanct. In practice, vigilance may need to be shown in order to prevent this kind of problem arising. Where it is known in advance that there is likely to be a serious bone of contention between divorcing parents the correct course of action will be to seek either a prohibited steps order or a specific issue order at the time of the divorce.

3.12 Although, prima facie, parental responsibility carries with it the power to determine all matters of upbringing the Act recognises that it should not embrace the power to take certain fundamental actions which are a characteristic feature of the relationship between a natural parent or guardian and his child. Thus a residence order in favour of a non-parent, despite conferring parental responsibility will not give the right:

  (a) to consent or refuse to consent to an application to free the child for adoption under s 18 of the Adoption Act 1976;
  (b) to agree or refuse to agree to an adoption order itself, or an order under s 55 of the 1976 Act; or
  (c) to appoint a guardian (s 12(3)).

These fundamentals were sometimes referred to as 'the residual rights of the natural guardian' under the old law although this expression was strictly only accurate in relation to the father. Under the new law it is not necessary for these 'rights' to be preserved for the non-residential parent since he will retain them anyway by virtue of remaining a parent and keeping parental responsibility (in the fullest sense in which a parent automatically has this by operation of law). What the Act confirms is that a non-parent cannot acquire these fundamental incidents of status by way of residence and parental responsibility orders.

3.13 Closely allied to the above are the issues of changing the child's name and taking the child out of the country. The former was often described as falling within the residual rights of the natural guardian so as to preclude independent or unilateral action by a mother. The automatic position in law was, therefore, that one parent was not authorised to change the child's name without the consent of the other or an order of the court. Where a change had *in fact* been effected the court would apply the welfare principle to determine whether a reversion to the original name should be ordered. It could ratify the change where it believed this to be in the child's best interests (for the approach taken under the old law see particularly *W v A (Child: Surname)* [1981] Fam. 14 in which previous case law is considered). Divorcing parents were given notice of the prohibition on unilateral changes of name by rules of court (r 92(8) of the Matrimonial Causes Rules 1977). The same rules also provided that a divorce court making an order for custody, care or control should incorporate a prohibition on removing the child from *England and Wales* without the leave of the court (r 94(2)). Both of these restrictions were designed to emphasise the importance of the continuing link between the child and the non-custodial parent and the damage which might be caused to this by the contemplated moves.

3.14 The Act re-enacts these prohibitions but relaxes the second by confining it to removals from the *United Kingdom* (s 13(1)). Where a residence order is in force no person may cause the child to be known by a new surname or remove him from the UK without either the written consent of every person with parental responsibility or the leave of the court. The court may grant general leave or leave for specified purposes (s 13(3)). More significantly, perhaps, the residential parent is entitled to remove the child for any period of less than one calendar month (s 13(2)). This will obviously cover the case of most holidays abroad and its purpose is to relieve the residential parent from the obligation to secure the consent of the other parent or the court for a comparatively short trip. It should be remembered, however, that such a trip could be arranged without the knowledge of the non-residential parent. Again, the point must surely be made that this may leave the non-residential parent wondering how much responsibility for the child he really has. Where there is genuine concern that the residential parent may be about to use a short-term expedient as a cloak for abduction it will be open to the other parent to seek a prohibited steps order. But this may be unrealistically optimistic. Potential abductors are not in the habit of giving notice of their intentions. In the final analysis, the Act is taking a calculated risk. It is an attempt to balance the inconvenience which would be caused to the majority of responsible parents against the dangers created by a much smaller number of irresponsible ones. As the Solicitor-General put it in Committee, it is important to assess the potential operation of the Act's provisions on 'perfectly normal and reasonable behaviour as well as on unreasonable behaviour' (*Hansard,* May 16 1989, col 72).

3.15 Finally, before leaving the subject of residence orders, we must consider s 11(4). Despite being tucked away in a section containing a rag-bag of miscellaneous provisions, this is a massively important subsection. It states:

> 'Where a residence order is made in favour of two or more persons who do not themselves all live together, the order may specify the periods during which the child is to live in the different households concerned.'

The effect of this is to empower the court to make *joint* residence orders and to sanction the practice of 'time-sharing' which is prevalent in certain jurisdictions in the United States. The idea has not been one which has caught on in England and the Court of Appeal clearly disapproved of this type of order in *Riley v Riley* [1986] 2 FLR 429. In that case the court criticised, as a matter of principle, an order which had provided for joint physical care and control despite the apparent success of the order for a period of almost five years. The Court reasoned that a child needed a settled home and that the original order which had provided for the child to live alternate weeks with each of her parents had been wrong.

3.16 *Riley* cannot stand with s 11(4) and must be considered to have been overruled by it. This does not mean that orders like this will immediately flood in under the new law or that this would necessarily be desirable. But, as the Law Commission acknowledged, there will be *some* instances in which such arrangements are practicable and desirable and it is intended that residence orders should be sufficiently flexible to accommodate this type of arrangement. More commonly, a degree of time-sharing occurs where a child spends school term-time in the care of one parent and holidays with the other. The Commission felt that in circumstances like this a residence order covering both parents was more realistic than a sole residence order accompanied by a contact order (Report No.172, para 4.12).

3.17 The Commission was not in favour of a statutory *presumption* for time-sharing, or any other form of joint custodial arrangement, as a means of expressly encouraging the active participation by both parents in the care of a child following divorce. The courts have, thus, been left with a complete discretion to decide when orders contemplating a degree of shared residence are workable and desirable. An important responsibility will again rest on those advising in practice to explore the possibilities for maximum involvement of both parents in upbringing following divorce. The incidence of this type of order will in due course reveal something about how serious parents and the courts are about the much-vaunted principle of continuing parental responsibility. A willingness to share the physical care of a child, to provide directly for his many needs and to put up with some material inconvenience is, in the final analysis, a more realistic acceptance of parental responsibility than some nebulous notion of ongoing parenthood from a distance. It is fair to say, of course, that the principle in s 1(5) will mean that in some cases the absence of an order reflects a high level of parental cooperation over care and upbringing.

3.18 We must now consider briefly the difference between a joint residence order under the new law and a joint custody order under the old law. The form of joint custody which has been employed by the English divorce courts differs markedly from the concept of joint custody in certain other jurisdictions. It is most appropriately described as joint *legal* custody as opposed to joint physical custody. Its effect was thought to leave daily care and control of the child in one parent while sharing between the parents the power and responsibilities for major decisions on upbringing (for cases in which the order was used see *Jussa v Jussa* [1972] 2 All ER 600; *Cafell v Cafell* [1984] FLR 169 and *Hurst v Hurst* [1984] FLR 867). What was uncertain under this regime was whether the parent without care and control had a right to be consulted about these major issues. The better view was, perhaps, that such a right of consultation did exist since the very nature of the order was to ensure that the 'absent parent' retained an equally active role in influencing the way in which the child was to be brought up.

If this is right, the Act brings about a major change since, as we have seen, each parent (whether residential or not) has a wholly independent right to take action in relation to the child without consulting the other parent and the previous right of veto which parents enjoyed has also been removed. What the Act has in effect done is to create a norm of *joint independent parenting*. It certainly does not establish a standard of *parental cooperation* and there is no principle of voluntary partnership between estranged parents which in any way approximates to the principle of voluntary partnership between parents and the state enshrined in Part III of the Act.

3.19 A residence order made in the magistrates' court may be enforced, on proof of proper service, under s 63(3) of the Magistrates' Courts Act 1980 as if it were an order requiring the person in breach to produce the child to the person with the residence order (s 14(1) and (2)). This enables the justices to impose a fine of up to £50 per day (subject to a maximum of £2,000) while the breach continues. Alternatively, the person in default may be committed to custody for a period of up to 2 months or until the default has been remedied. A residence order made in the higher courts may be enforced in the ordinary way in contempt proceedings.

(ii) The contact order

3.20   A contact order means:

> 'an order requiring the person with whom a child lives, or is to live, to allow the child to visit or stay with the person named in the order, or for that person and the child otherwise to have contact with each other' (s 8(1)).

The order replaces the access order and introduces a subtle change of emphasis. The old form of access order was 'parent-centred' in that it provided for the parent to have access to the child. The new contact order is 'child-centred' in form, concentrating on allowing the *child* to visit or stay with a named individual, usually a parent. This is more in keeping with the view expressed judicially that access is properly to be regarded as a right of the child rather than a right of the parent (per Wrangham J in *M v M (Child: Access)* [1973] 2 All ER 81).

3.21   It is interesting to compare contact orders under s 8 with the new 'contact code' under s 34 which applies where a child is in the care of a local authority. This is considered in depth in Chapter 5 but for the moment it is sufficient to note that it provides, inter alia, for a presumption of reasonable contact between a child and his parent, guardian or other person with a residence order immediately before the child was taken into care. No such statutory presumption expressly applies where the child is not in care. The court's discretion over contact is completely unfettered. It is likely that the courts will follow previous decisions on access to the effect that a parent should not be deprived of contact with a child unless there is a risk of some harm to the child (see, for example, *S v S and P* [1962] 2 All ER 1). Nonetheless, it is perhaps regrettable that the legislation does not enshrine the presumption of reasonable contact wherever a child is physically apart from a parent.

3.22   It will be apparent from what was said earlier about joint residence orders that contact orders will only be appropriate where the plan is that the child will spend significantly more time in one household than in another. The general objective is that s 8 orders should be flexible and accordingly the form of contact ordered may differ greatly from case to case. It may range from 'staying' contact at one end of the spectrum to contact by letters or telephone at the other. It is expected that the usual order will be for reasonable contact leaving it to the parties to work out their own arrangements. The court may define contact in cases of difficulty, may impose conditions or make directions as to how the order is to be put into effect (s 11(7)). This may be appropriate where the various adults concerned cannot agree on a major issue of upbringing. If the court does not intervene here, the parent exercising contact with the child may also exercise parental responsibility while the child is with him in a manner liable to cause friction.

Finally, it must be remembered that the court, following the general principle in s 1(5), may feel that it is not in the best interests of the child for it to make *any* order for contact where the parties have been able to work out acceptable arrangements between themselves.

(iii)   The prohibited steps order

3.23   This order is defined as:

> 'an order that no step which could be taken by a parent in meeting his parental responsibility for a child, and which is of a kind specified in the order, shall be taken by any person without the consent of the court' (s 8(1)).

3.24   Both this and the 'specific issue order' are primarily concerned with what might be called 'single issues'. The traditional procedure for resolving disputes over particular matters affecting children has been wardship . We noted that the future of wardship is uncertain following the implementation of the current statutory reforms but for the moment at least it will continue to exist alongside the statutory jurisdictions. What is clear is that one of the express objectives of the reforms is to cut down the circumstances under which it will be necessary to resort to wardship by incorporating its more useful features into the statutory code itself (Report No.172, para 4.20). The availability of these two types of orders should cut down the need to have recourse to wardship.

Certain automatic restrictions come into play where a child is made a ward of court. These include a prohibition on marriage and on removal of the child from the jurisdiction. More significantly, wardship freezes the status quo and prevents any 'important step' being taken with respect to the child without the court's consent. The court is technically seised of the 'custody' of the child and therefore (at least theoretically) is 'parent' to the child with an active continuing role. In practice the court is unlikely to become actively involved until someone objecting to a course of action makes an application to the court to prevent it. The Law Commission thought that the 'important step' prohibition in wardship was too vague and that a court wishing to impose restrictions on the exercise of parental responsibility by individuals should spell out more precisely the prohibited spheres of activity. The new prohibited steps order is designed for just this purpose.

3.25   An obvious issue at this point is the relationship between the new orders and the wardship procedure. This general question is considered in Chapter 8 but we must at least mention here s 9(5)(*b*). The effect of this is to prevent the court from making a prohibited steps or specific issue order 'in any way which is denied to the High Court by s 100(2) in the exercise of its inherent jurisdiction with respect to children'. Section 100(2) relates to the restrictions on access to wardship which the Act imposes on local authorities. The basic position is that an authority may not use wardship without leave which will only be granted where the result which the authority is trying to achieve could not be achieved under the statutory scheme. The restriction in s 9(5)(*b*) is to ensure that the authority does not circumvent these restrictions by applying for s 8 orders.

3.26 Section 9(5)(*a*) further restricts the use of prohibited steps and specific issue orders by preventing the court from making them 'with a view to achieving a result which could be achieved by making a residence or contact order'. The point here is that, under the statutory code, residence and contact orders are conceived to be the primary orders and the other two orders are in the nature of 'back-up' orders. The Commission's view was that they ought not therefore be used as a substitute for a primary order.

(*iv*)   *The specific issue order*

3.27   This is defined as:

> 'an order giving directions for the purpose of determining a specific question which has arisen, or which may arise, in connection with any aspect of parental responsibility for a child' (s 8(1)).

The order is closely allied to the prohibited steps order. The main difference would appear to be that a specific issue order can do more than merely prohibit a course of action. It can *regulate* a sphere of upbringing by (if necessary) detailed directions from the court. A little-used procedure existed under s 1(3) of the Guardianship Act 1973 for similar purposes. This could, however, only be invoked by parents. The more usual procedure was wardship which was also the only option for non-parents. The specific issue order should in future be used as an alternative to wardship. It is important to note, however, that the Act's restrictions on wardship do not apply to private individuals. Judicially created restrictions apply to them where the child is in care. Where, however, the child is not in care wardship will continue as an alternative option for individuals wishing to obtain a ruling on single issues affecting a child. In fact it may be a preferred option since, unlike an application for a s 8 order, there is never any requirement of leave. We shall return to these matters in Chapter 8.

The restrictions on prohibited steps orders discussed above apply equally to specific issue orders.

3.   Power of the Court to make Section 8 Orders

(a)   Proceedings in which orders may be made

3.28   The court may make a s 8 order in 'any family proceedings in which a question arises with respect to the welfare of any child' (s 10(1)). 'Section 8 order' is defined to include the four orders discussed above and 'any order varying or discharging such an order' (s 8(2)). The important question is therefore: What are 'family proceedings' for these purposes? The proceedings falling within this expression are very wide-ranging. They are:

(i)   Proceedings under the inherent jurisdiction of the High Court in relation to children; and

(ii)   Proceedings under:

(a) Parts I, II and IV of the 1989 Act;
(b) The Matrimonial Causes Act 1973;
(c) The Domestic Violence and Matrimonial Proceedings Act 1976;
(d) The Adoption Act 1976;
(e) The Domestic Proceedings and Magistrates' Courts Act 1978;
(f) Sections 1 and 9 of the Matrimonial Homes Act 1983; and
(g) Part III of the Matrimonial and Family Proceedings Act 1984 (s 8(3) and (4)).

It is expressly provided that the definition does not include proceedings on an application for leave under s 100(3) by local authorities. Also absent from the definition are proceedings under Part V of the Act relating to emergency protection orders. Part V constitutes a special code governing the emergency protection of children and it would be inappropriate for s 8 orders to be made generally available in those circumstances.

3.29 It can be seen that the proceedings in which s 8 orders may be made are many and varied. But broadly they fall into two categories. First, there are proceedings under the Act itself. These might be categorised as the 'children jurisdictions' since they are specifically concerned with the care and upbringing of children. Secondly, there are the proceedings under the other listed enactments which are, with the exception of those under the Adoption Act 1976, essentially 'adult jurisdictions'. They are predominantly concerned with disputes between adult family members, for example divorce, financial provision and property adjustment, domestic violence and occupation of the matrimonial home. They are, equally, all proceedings in which the interests of children may be relevant and, in some cases, in which orders specifically relating to children may be made.

The Law Commission considered collecting in a single statute all the courts' powers to deal with children whether in relation to the care and upbringing or financial provision for them. But, on balance, it felt that it was 'convenient for the statutes dealing primarily with the affairs of adults to contain all those of the provisions relating to children which cannot readily be separated from those relating to adults.' It also observed the different weighting of the child's welfare in these adult jurisdictions (see Chapter 2). Where, on the other hand, the courts' powers related exclusively to children the Commission thought that it was convenient that they should be collected in one statute. This has now been effected by Parts I, II and IV of the Act (see Report No.172, para 1.8).

3.30 The Act at the same time achieves much greater uniformity between the adult and children's jurisdictions in that the orders available in relation to children in each case are now uniformly s 8 orders and orders under Part IV of the Act. This approach confers some notable powers on the courts in certain types of proceedings which they did not possess before the Act. This is true of proceedings under the Domestic Violence and Matrimonial Proceedings Act 1976 or the Matrimonial Homes Act 1983 for non-molestation or exclusion orders. The Commission felt that it was highly artificial that the court was empowered in these proceedings to exclude a spouse from the matrimonial home, at least in part on the strength of its assessment of the needs of the children, but could not at the same time order that the children should live with the parent remaining in the home or regulate the contact which they should have with the other parent. These powers are now available since the proceedings fall within the wide ambit of family proceedings.

3.31 Adoption is a special case which remains largely outside the present reforms and continues to be governed by its own statutory code in the Adoption Act 1976. But adoption proceedings are, as we have seen, within the definition of family proceedings so that s 8 orders are available as an alternative to an adoption order.

3.32 The relationship between adoption orders and residence orders will be an important one. Those having knowledge of the old law will recall that the courts were directed by statute to have regard to the lesser alternatives of custodianship or divorce court custody in the case of adoption applications made by relatives and step-parents (Children Act 1975, s 37(1) and (2) and ss 14(3) and 15(4) of the Adoption Act 1976 respectively). These provisions followed the recommendations of the Houghton/Stockdale Report on the Adoption of Children (1972, Cmnd 5107). The essence of the statutory directives was that, in this type of case, the drastic effects of adoption might not be desirable and might, in particular, distort family relationships, for example by turning a grandparent into a parent or a parent into a sibling. In the case of step-parent adoptions, there were fears that adoption might be used as a device for cutting off one side of the family from any connection with the child. The original purpose of the statutory provisions was therefore to encourage the courts to think in terms of alternative orders which would not have these undesirable effects. Decided cases produced differing interpretations of the statutory provisions but, eventually, the view emerged judicially that their effect was simply to require the court to decide which order would be best for the child. (See, for example *Re D (Minors)(Adoption by Step-parent)* (1981) 2 FLR 102 and *Re S (A Minor)(Adoption or Custodianship)* [1987] Fam. 98.)

3.33 This is in effect the position taken by the Act. By bringing adoption proceedings within the meaning of family proceedings the court is empowered to make s 8 orders wherever it feels that these would be better for children than adoption orders. But it should not be overlooked that the former statutory directives (whatever they meant) have been removed by the Act. Any encouragement for the courts to think in a particular way has been abandoned. This is consistent with the non-interventionist stance taken under other parts of the Act. The theory seems to be that the courts can be trusted to exercise extremely flexible powers and discretions, on a case by case basis, in the best interests of children.

(b) Applications for section 8 orders

3.34 Section 10 contains the details on who is entitled to apply for s 8 orders. The broad scheme is that certain individuals are *entitled* to apply while others require *leave*. In both cases, s 8 orders may be made in one of three ways i.e.:

  (i)   on applications in the course of family proceedings;
  (ii)   on the court's own motion in the course of family proceedings or
  (iii)   on a freestanding application (i.e. an application for the specific purpose of obtaining a s 8 order) in the absence of any other proceedings (s 10(1) and (2)).

It is envisaged that, wherever possible, in order to avoid duplication the orders will be made in the course of existing family proceedings. (Report No. 172, para 4.33).

(i) Persons entitled to apply without leave

3.35 Those entitled to apply as of right for *any* s 8 order are parents (which expression includes the unmarried father), guardians and persons in whose favour a residence order has been made with respect to a child (s 10(4)). The inclusion of guardians is another illustration of the Act's objective to extend full parental status to them. Those with residence orders in their favour will usually only require access to the courts for the purpose of seeking prohibited steps or special issue orders or the variation or discharge of the residence orders themselves. The general point which applies to all three categories is that their connection with the child is so patently close that it would be inappropriate to present them with the hurdle of applying for leave in order to obtain a hearing before the court.

3.36 In addition to the above categories, certain other persons may apply for a *residence or contact order* without leave. They are:

  (a)   any party to a marriage (whether or not subsisting) in relation to whom the child is a child of the family;
  (b)   any person with whom the child has lived for a period of at least three years;
  (c)   any person who:

      (i)   in any case where a residence order is in force with respect to the child, has the consent of each of the persons in whose favour the order was made;
      (ii)   in any case where the child is in the care of a local authority, has the consent of that authority; or
      (iii)   in any other case, has the consent of each of those (if any) who have parental responsibility for the child (s 10(5)).

3.37   The unifying factor connecting these disparate groups is that it would be presumed that leave would be granted as a matter of course. Any requirement of leave would therefore be likely to prove an unnecessary formality. On the other hand prohibited steps and specific issue orders are sufficiently unusual that the preliminary filter of leave is appropriate to sift out unmeritorious applications.

3.38   Group (a) embraces primarily step-parents who are in the process of divorce. It is highly likely that they will have 'treated' any children of their spouses as members of their family. As the law stood before the Act these people would have had a right to apply for custody or access in the matrimonial proceedings. The Law Commission thought it wrong that they should be denied the opportunity of applying to the courts *during the subsistence of the marriage* where this was an option open to them on divorce. Thus, they may now apply for residence or contact orders either during or after the termination of the marriage. This has the additional benefit of removing the discrimination which previously existed between the different categories of step-parents. All now have ready access to the court however they came to be step-parents. 'Child of the family' for these purposes is defined by s 105(1) in terms which are identical to those used in s 88(1) of the Domestic Proceedings and Magistrates' Courts Act 1978. This definition was preferred over that in s 52(1) of the Matrimonial Causes Act 1973 since the latter definition excluded children who were at some time, but no longer, boarded out with the parties to the marriage by a local authority or voluntary organisation. The definition under the Act excludes only those who are *currently* in this position. Subject to this, a child of the family is:

'(a)   a child of both parties or
(b)   any other child ... who has been treated by both of those parties as a child of their family.'

Since this definition is a re-enactment of existing law it is likely that the case law on the former provision will be accepted as an authoritative interpretation of the new provision. (See *D v D (Child of the Family)* (1981) 2 FLR 93, *M v M (Child of the Family)* (1981) 2 FLR 39, *A v A (Family: Unborn Child)* [1974] Fam 6 and *W v W (Child of the Family)* [1984] FLR 796.)

3.39   Groups (b) and (c) essentially include those who would have been qualified to bring an application for custodianship under s 33 of the Children Act 1975. They will now need to apply for a residence order to provide security against removal of the child from their care. In the case of group (b) it is provided that the period of three years' residence need not be continuous but must not have begun more than five years before, or ended more than three months before, the making of the application (s 10(10)). The different sub-categories in group (c) are united by the common feature that in each case the applicant will have the consent of the person whose legal position would be affected by the application — essentially the person or institution having parental responsibility for the child. Again, a leave requirement would be a perfunctory exercise in this type of case. People in this category benefit under the new law in that the former requirement of one year's residence for a custodianship application does not apply to applications for s 8 orders made with the relevant consents.

3.40 Those entitled to apply without leave may be extended by rules of court (s 10(7)). Grandparents were singled out under the old law for various purposes, in particular for seeking access orders in proceedings instituted by parents. It may be that rules of court will in due course bring them within the categories of those entitled to apply as of right. In any event, many grandparents may well fall within one or more of the existing categories. Failing this, it is extremely unlikely that they (or other interested relatives) would experience difficulty in obtaining leave where their application is motivated by a genuine concern for the child.

3.41 A person who would not otherwise be entitled without leave to apply for variation or discharge of a s 8 order is entitled to do so where the order was made on his application or where he was named in a contact order.

(ii) Persons entitled to apply with leave

3.42 The statutory scheme is intended to be sufficiently flexible to enable *anyone* with a genuine interest in the child's welfare to get before the court. At present wardship performs the function of affording access to the courts to interested individuals who have no locus standi in the various statutory proceedings affecting children. In order to obviate the necessity of recourse to wardship, the general principle under the Act is that anyone not entitled to apply as of right may do so with leave. The point should be made that for some people the new approach is more restrictive than the old since anyone was entitled to apply in wardship proceedings *without* leave except where the application was vexatious. On the other hand, it is not expected that anyone with a demonstrable interest in a child will find the requirement of leave unduly onerous. It exists merely as a 'filter to protect the child and his family against unwarranted interference in their comfort and security, while ensuring that the child's interests are properly respected.' (Report No. 172, para 4.41).

3.43 The Act enumerates the factors which the court must take into account in deciding whether to grant leave. They are:

(a) the nature of the proposed application for the section 8 order;
(b) the applicant's connection with the child;
(c) any risk there might be of that proposed application disrupting the child's life to such an extent that he would be harmed by it; and
(d) where the child is being looked after by a local authority:

  (i)   the authority's plans for the child's future; and
  (ii)   the wishes and feelings of the child's parents (s 10(9)).

Perhaps one surprising omission from the list is the wishes and feelings of the child. The reasoning, presumably, is that we are concerned here only with a preliminary application and not with the final determination of the child's welfare. Before reaching its *final* decision the court must have proper regard to the child's wishes (s 1(3)). Against this it might be said that, if leave is refused, the child concerned may have missed the opportunity of presenting his views to the court.

3.44 One solution for the child might be to bring an application for a s 8 order himself. The Act draws a distinction between children who have attained sixteen and those under that age. So far as the former group is concerned, the court is prevented from making any s 8 order, other than one discharging or varying an existing order, unless it is satisfied that the circumstances of the case are exceptional (s 9(7)). Moreover, no s 8 order may have effect for a period which will end after the child has attained sixteen, again unless the circumstances are exceptional (s 9(6)). These provisions in effect recognise the autonomy of 'children', perhaps more appropriately referred to as young people. It is assumed that those in this age group are able to make up their own minds about the persons with whom they wish to live or have contact. It was in fact well-established before the Act that the courts would not generally seek to override the wishes of young people of this age on the basis that any order made might lack efficacy. (See, for example *Krishnan v Sutton LBC* [1969] 3 All ER 1367 but cf *Re SW (A Minor)(Wardship: Jurisdiction)* [1986] 1 FLR 24.) Exceptional circumstances might exist where, for example the child is mentally handicapped and the court feels that its protection is required. Indeed, Lord Templeman in *Re B (A Minor)* [1987] 2 WLR 1213 took the view that the court's prior approval would *always* be required for a sterilisation operation which, in that case, concerned a girl of seventeen. Under the new law someone would, it seems, be obliged to apply for a specific issue order in this sort of case.

3.45 Where the child is under sixteen the Act allows him to apply *with leave*. The normal factors prescribed by s 10(9) on other applications for leave do *not* apply to applications by a child. Instead, the court may only grant leave where it is satisfied that the child has sufficient understanding to make the proposed application (s 10(8)).

This apparent exercise in paternalism appears to have one flaw. The child may be applying for leave because no other interested adult has been willing to intervene on his behalf. If the court refuses leave on the basis that the child lacks the necessary understanding to make the application, the result may be that it abdicates altogether from taking a decision on his welfare. This is a general problem inherent in the *Gillick* principles which the Act adopts. Assessments based on maturity or understanding rule out of court the very children who may be most in need of protection because they are immature, mentally retarded or otherwise vulnerable. Where leave is refused it may, however, still be possible for the child to make himself a ward of court. Moreover, it should be remembered that the child will automatically be a party in care and supervision proceedings where his views will almost always be conveyed by his guardian ad litem. It is, nevertheless, arguable that it would have been better if the Act had placed children themselves in a category of those entitled to apply without leave.

4.   Restrictions on the Court's Power to make Section 8 Orders

3.46   Section 9 imposes a number of specific restrictions on the granting of s 8 orders. We have already discussed the limitations in s 9(5) on making prohibited steps and special issue orders and those in s 9(6) and (7) on making any s 8 orders where a child has attained sixteen. Section 9 contains three other restrictions all of which are to some extent concerned with the relationship between s 8 orders and the statutory powers and responsibilities of local authorities under Parts III and IV.

(a)   Restrictions where the child is in care

3.47   The court is prevented from making any s 8 order, *other than a residence order*, in respect of a child who is in the care of a local authority (s 9(1)).

The first thing to note about this is that the restriction only applies where the child is 'in care' in the technical sense, i.e. where the child has been committed to the authority's care by an order under s 31. It does *not* apply where the child is merely being looked after by an authority under a voluntary arrangement covered by Part III of the Act. Neither will it apply where a supervision order is made under Part IV. In these instances the full panoply of orders is available to the court. Suppose, for example that an unmarried mother arranges for the local authority to look after her child. The father would here be able to apply to the court as of right for any s 8 order if he felt that his potential contribution was being overlooked by the authority.

The other feature to note about this provision is that residence orders *are* available where a child is in care. We have to jump to s 91(1) to discover that where a residence order is made with respect to a child in care its effect is to discharge the care order. Conversely, a care order will have the effect of discharging any existing residence order (s 91(2). Staying with the example of the unmarried father, the availability of residence orders where the child is in care overcomes, from his point of view, the adverse effects of certain decisions under the old law. These were to the effect that the courts should not exercise their jurisdiction to make custody or access orders under ss 9 and 14 of the Guardianship of Minors Act 1971 where the child was in care. They arrived at this position by applying an analogy with the judicial restraints on the use of wardship where a child was in care (see, particularly, the House of Lords' decision *M v H* [1988] 3 All ER 5). The father may now seek a residence order and, if he succeeds, this will have the effect of removing the child from care and (by virtue of the accompanying parental responsibility order) giving him legal responsibility for the child. If he wishes to challenge a decision of the authority relating to his *contact* with the child, this will have to be by invoking the special code governing contact decisions where a child is in care (s 34).

3.48 It will be seen from the above example that the subsidiary s 8 orders relating to prohibited steps and specific issues will not be available at all where a child is in care. The Act gives effect to the non-interventionist stance taken by the courts to the use of wardship where a child is in care. We consider this in depth in Chapter 8. It should be emphasised however that these restrictions had been judicially extended to situations where a child was in *voluntary care* as opposed to compulsory care (see particularly *W v Nottinghamshire County Council* [1986] 1 FLR 565). Whether or not wardship is available, it will be possible under the Act to seek *any* s 8 order where the child is being accommodated by an authority without a care order. Ironically, this represents something of a reversion to the position taken over twenty years ago by Lord Denning MR in *Re S (An Infant)* [1965] 1 WLR 483 where he emphasised the transitory nature of the authority's position where a care order had not been made and the need to make the court's protection available in these circumstances.

3.49 The basic philosophy behind the Act is, as we shall see, that a clear line must be drawn between voluntary and compulsory arrangements involving local authorities. Where the authority has formally acquired parental responsibility for the child (as it does under a care order by virtue of s 33(3)), the theory is that it should be allowed to exercise this without undue external interference. It is for this reason that s 8 orders are generally unavailable apart from residence orders. The purpose of a residence order is not to challenge the exercise of the authority's powers in relation to a child in its care. It is rather to remove that child from care altogether. An application for a residence order, rather than one for discharge of the care order (which would have basically the same effect) will prove particularly useful where the child's parents were divorced or separated. This is because the order will not only discharge the care order but will determine with which parent the child is to live.

(b) Restrictions on applications by local authorities

3.50 No application may be made by a local authority for a residence or contact order and no court is empowered to make such an order in favour of a local authority (s 9(2)).

This restriction must be read with s 100 which sets limits to the use of wardship by local authorities as a means of securing control over a child. There is nothing to prevent an authority seeking leave to apply for a prohibited steps or specific issue order. The basic thinking behind these provisions is that since Parliament has bothered to define with particularity the circumstances under which state intervention in the family is to be allowed (s 31), the local authority should not have a 'soft option' available to it, whether this is in wardship or by means of a residence or contact order. If the authority is concerned enough about a child to feel that it must intervene, it must do so under the statutory scheme, specifically set up for this purpose. It must either persuade the person looking after the child to let it accommodate the child under Part III or it must obtain an emergency protection order, care or supervision order under Parts IV and V.

Some may express regret that a lesser form of order is not available to the authority to cover situations where the authority is concerned about a child but does not wish to go so far as to seek one of the orders under Parts IV or V. Nevertheless, the scheme of the Act is that the authority will either have to take decisive action or refrain from intervening. Again, the purpose is to accentuate the divide between voluntary and compulsory arrangements.

(c) Restrictions on local authority foster parents

3.51   Section 9(3) places restrictions on applications for leave by public foster parents and, as a result of a Commons' amendment, certain former public foster parents (*Hansard*, 11 May, 1989, col 62). A person who is, or was at any time during the last six months, a local authority foster parent may not apply for leave unless:

(a)   he has the consent of the authority;

(b)   he is a relative of the child; or

(c)   the child has lived with him for at least three years preceding the application. The three years does not have to be continuous but must have begun not more than five years before making the application (s 9(4)).

The purpose of the amendment was to cover the situation where a child is removed from a public foster parent just before an application is made. It was thought that the policy reasons against allowing public foster parents to make applications as of right for leave applied just as much to this situation. Different considerations were however thought to apply to those local authority foster parents who were also relatives. Here the 'special family ties' were thought to make it more appropriate for a court rather than a local authority to take a decision on the child's future.

3.52   It should be emphasised that we are concerned here only with *public* foster parents, i.e. those with whom a child has been boarded out by a local authority. There are no such restrictions on *private* foster parents i.e. those with whom a child has been placed privately, usually by parents. Private foster parents simply have to satisfy the ordinary requirements for leave. Most significantly, perhaps, they will be able to apply for a s 8 order *immediately* provided they have the consent of the individual with parental responsibility. This is not an option open to public foster parents unless they can also secure the consent of the authority.

3.53 The Act, then, takes an especially restrictive attitude to the position of public foster parents. It does so in order to meet the concern that the confidence of parents in the voluntary child care system be maintained. It is a central objective of the reforms to encourage society in general, and individual parents in particular, to think more positively about voluntary public assistance in the case of family difficulty (see Chapter 4). Confidence would, it was feared, be undermined if parents thought that they were liable to face early applications by foster parents the effect of which could be to water down their parental responsibility. If a residence order were made they would be obliged to share responsibility with the foster parents and, more importantly, would be prevented from resuming the care of the child. This might operate as a severe disincentive to voluntary arrangements with local authorities. Moreover, it was considered important that parents should not feel exposed to a *greater* risk of losing their children by entering public arrangements than they would face by making private arrangements. There was also concern that the authorities themselves should not be unduly hindered in their efforts to make plans for children, whether for rehabilitation or long-term substitute care, by premature applications from short-term foster parents (Report No. 172, para 4.43). The Act, therefore, effects a compromise between meeting these anxieties and providing for the legitimate claims of some foster parents seeking legal security in looking after children.

5. Specific Matters Relating to Section 8 Orders

(a) Delay and the timetable in family proceedings

3.54 Section 11 together with s 1(2) introduce a striking procedural change relating to orders for children. They assert (supra, para 2.14) the general principle that delay in legal proceedings is prejudicial to the welfare of children, require the court to specify a timetable within which the steps required to dispose of an action must be taken and give the court power to make directions to this end. The Law Commission received evidence of serious concern, especially among the judiciary, about delays in children cases (for an example of judicial disapproval of delay see Ewbank J in *Stockport MBC v B and Stockport MBC v L* [1986] 2 FLR 80). The Commission took the view that protracted litigation was damaging to children because of the uncertainty which it created in their lives and because of the prejudice which it would cause to the party who was not living with the child. A lengthy delay would make it that much more difficult for him to convince the court that the status quo should be disturbed.

3.55 The central feature of the new regime is that *the court*, rather than the adult parties, will be required to take the initiative in ensuring the expeditious progress of children cases. This is to be achieved in the following ways:

(i)   In any proceedings in which any question with respect to the upbringing of a child, arises the court must have regard to the general principle that any delay in determining the question is likely to prejudice the welfare of the child concerned (s 1(2)). The Commission was in favour of a presumption that delay would be prejudicial unless the contrary was shown. This is probably the effect of the above provision which makes reference to 'likely' prejudice from delay. There may, thus, be circumstances in which *some* delay may be justifiable. The example suggested by the Commission was where the benefit to the child of a full welfare report might offset the detriment of having to wait for it (Report No. 172, para 4.57).

(ii)   The court is then required in any proceedings relating to s 8 orders (a) to draw up a timetable with a view to determining the question without delay and (b) give such directions as it considers appropriate for the purpose of ensuring, so far as is reasonably practicable, that the timetable is adhered to (s 11(1)).

The court's duty is to be discharged in the light of any rules of court which may:

(a)   specify periods within which specified steps must be taken; and

(b)   make other provision for the purpose of ensuring, so far as is reasonably practicable, that the questions before the court are determined without delay (s 11(2)).

(b) Directions, conditions and other supplementary provisions

3.56 If the new scheme has a hallmark it is its flexibility. The objective is that the court's powers should be as flexible as possible to deal with all questions raised as to the welfare of the children before it. Two provisions in s 11 give effect to this purpose.

3.57 First, where a court has power to make a s 8 order, it may do so at any time during the course of the proceedings even though it is not in a position to dispose finally of those proceedings (s 11(3)).

The Law Commission disapproved of the rigidity of the distinction drawn in certain proceedings between 'interim' and 'final' orders and of the time limits on making the former orders. The Act abolishes both the distinction and the time limits. The purpose of the above provision is simply to confirm that the court may continue to make orders at any time during the course of proceedings before it. These changes are intended to remove some of the technicality which previously existed in certain proceedings to give effect to the flexibility principle.

3.58 Secondly, the court has power to incorporate directions, conditions and other provisions in s 8 orders (s 11(7)). The wording of the Act could hardly be wider. Again the purpose is to give the court a complete discretion to back up its orders by attaching terms to them which are tailored to the circumstances of individual cases. Accordingly, a s 8 order may:

(a) contain directions about how it is to be carried into effect;

(b) impose conditions which must be complied with by any person:

    (i)   in whose favour the order is made; or

    (ii)   who is a parent; or

    (iii)   who is a non-parent with parental responsibility; or

    (iv)   with whom the child is living;

(c) be made to have effect for a specified period, or contain provisions which are to have effect for a specified period;

(d) make such incidental, supplemental or consequential provisions as the court thinks fit (s 11(7)).

Given the width of these powers it is difficult to visualise circumstances in which a court would find its hands tied in trying to follow a course of action which it considers to be in the best interests of the child before it. This is an important consideration in its own right but it is also important in achieving the aim of cutting down reliance on wardship. A prime reason why this has been used in some cases has been as a means of getting around limitations on the powers of courts under various statutes. (For an excellent example of this use of wardship, where the court lacked statutory power to take the desired action, see *Re H (A Minor)(Wardship: Jurisdiction)* [1978] Fam 65.) This phenomenon should become increasingly rare under the reformed legislation.

(c) The effect of cohabitation

3.59 Where a residence order is made in favour of one or two parents who each have parental responsibility for the child, the order will cease to have effect if the parents live together for a continuous period of more than six months (s 11(5)).

A similar provision existed before the Act with respect to custody orders. The rationale is that it is unrealistic to keep the order alive where the child is in fact living with both parents. It is also reasoned that it would be unfair, should they separate again after a long period of cohabitation for one of them to be placed in an automatically stronger position than the other (Report No. 172, para 4.13). For the order to lapse, both parents must have parental responsibility. The rule does not apply where this is vested solely in one of them. Neither does it apply to step-parents.

3.60 A similar rule applies to contact orders. A contact order which requires the residential parent to allow the child to visit, or otherwise have contact with, his other parent will cease to have effect if the parents live together for a continuous period of more than six months (s 11(6)).

6. Financial Relief for Children

3.61 Section 15 and Sch 1 constitute a new statutory code governing financial relief and property adjustment for children. Schedule 1 consists of the re-enactment (with minor modifications) of previous legislation under which these types of order could be made.

It will be recalled that the Law Commission took the view that only those statutes which deal *exclusively* with orders for children could be brought within the Act. It is, therefore, those statutes which governed, inter alia, orders for financial relief for children (but not adults) which are incorporated in Sch 1, viz the relevant parts of the Guardianship of Minors Act 1971, the Guardianship Act 1973, the Children Act 1975 and the Family Law Reform Act 1987.

3.62 It is not possible in a work of this size to deal in any detail with the many provisions in Sch 1. The following are some of the salient points which can usefully be made:

(i)   Applications for financial provision or property adjustment for children qualify as 'family proceedings' for the purposes of the Act so that the court is empowered to make s 8 orders without the necessity of a separate application.

(ii)   Conversely, where the court makes a s 8 order it is also empowered to make financial and property orders of its own motion.

(iii) The full range of orders is available to the court on the application of a parent, guardian or person with the benefit of a residence order (para 1(1)).

(iv)   The orders which the court may make against a parent include secured and unsecured periodical payments, lump sums, settlement orders and transfer of property orders (para 1(2)).

(v)   The factors which the court is to take into account are reproduced from s 25 of the Matrimonial Causes Act 1973. These include, inter alia 'the manner in which the child was being, or was expected to be, educated or trained'. (para 4(1)(*f*)). This did not apply in certain proceedings under the old law.

(vi)   The orders are also available against step-parents to whom the child concerned is a child of the family.

(vii) The court has power to vary or discharge the various orders on the same basis as that which applied under the previous legislation. The court's enforcement powers are also re-enacted (paras 6, 7 and 12).

(viii) The powers of a magistrates' court under s 60 of the Magistrates' Courts Act 1980 to revoke, revive or vary an order for periodical payments do not apply to any order under Sch 1 (s 15(2)).

7. Family Assistance Orders

3.63 Section 16 introduces a new type of order known as the 'family assistance order' (FAO). The Law Commission thought that there was a case for distinguishing between the different circumstances in which traditional supervision orders might be made. In future it was envisaged that there would be two distinct types of order. The first would be in favour of local authorities and would be based on harm or likely harm to the child. It could impose requirements on the parents as well as the child. The main concern here would be child protection. The second would be made in favour of a welfare or probation officer and would have the quite different aim of providing short-term help to parents following separation or divorce, to smooth the transition period for them and to encourage cooperation between them. The Act brings out this distinction by providing for two differently named orders to be available in family proceedings. The first type of order continues to be known as a 'supervision order'. We shall consider this along with the other provisions of Part IV in Chapter 5. The second type of order has been re-named the 'family assistance order'.

3.64 The court has power to make an FAO whenever family proceedings take place and the court has power to make an order under Part II of the Act (s 16(1)). It is not necessary that the court should actually make such an order. The FAO will require either a probation officer to be made available or a local authority to make an officer of the authority available to advise, assist and (where appropriate) befriend any person named in the order. Those who may be named are any parent or guardian, any person with whom the child is living or in whose favour a contact order has been made and the child himself (s 16(2)).

3.65 There are two restrictions on the making of FAOs (s 16(3)). The first is that the court must be satisfied that the circumstances of the case are exceptional. This is in line with the previous requirements for care and supervision orders in family proceedings. It is questionable how far this is a desirable limitation. If members of the family appear to require short-term help and are willing to consent to this, it is arguable that this hurdle should not exist. Perhaps in practice this requirement will prove to be a formality where there appears to be a genuine need for assistance.

The second limitation is that the order may only be made with the consent of every person to be named in it other than the child. The reasoning is that the whole concept of the order is to offer *voluntary* assistance and promote cooperation and that any form of compulsion would be out of place. The absence of a requirement to obtain the consent of the child himself is readily understandable in the case of young children but is surely questionable with respect to mature adolescents bearing in mind the other '*Gillick* provisions' in the Act.

3.66 The order may place obligations on the persons named in it to keep in touch with the welfare officer. It may also direct any of them to take specified steps with a view to enabling the officer concerned to be kept informed of the address of any person named in the order and to be allowed to visit any such person (s 16(4)).

This is primarily directed to the situation where a parent or other adult is being uncooperative with the officer about access to the child named in the order. The obligation is, however, limited to keeping in touch and allowing visits. The wider range of requirements which may be imposed under a supervision order (see Chapter 5) cannot be incorporated into an FAO, thus emphasising the essentially non-coercive nature of the latter.

The order will last for a maximum period of six months and a shorter period may be specified in the order, thus emphasising its short-term nature (s 16(5)). The period will run from the date when the order is made.

3.67   Where an FAO is in force at the same time as a s 8 order, the welfare officer concerned may refer to the court the question whether the s 8 order should be varied or discharged (s 16(6)). The Act gives him no power to seek a care order since no ground for this will have been established when the FAO was originally made. It was suggested by the Law Commission that where an officer expresses concern about the child this may be the kind of case in which the court ought to refer the child's situation to the local authority for investigation. (See Chapter 6.)

3.68   The essential aim of the FAO is then to provide a more limited order where a full supervision order is not justified. Before the Act, this limited form of assistance could only be given under a supervision order whether or not this order was strictly required. In order to bring out the aim and purpose of the order, the Commission has suggested that, as a matter of good practice, the court should make plain at the outset why the order is needed and what it is hoped will be achieved by it (Report No.172, para 5.20).

CHAPTER FOUR

Local Authority Support for Children and Families

1. Introduction

4.1 Parts III and IV of the Act replace the existing legislation on voluntary and compulsory care procedures and local authority support for families. Services to families and voluntary care were governed by the Child Care Act 1980 and compulsory care by the Children and Young Persons Act 1969. The Act repeals the 1980 Act in its entirety and the relevant parts of the 1969 Act. The 1980 Act regulated the treatment of children in care and the duties of the local authority towards them. This part of the 1980 Act applied to all children in care whether they had arrived there voluntarily, by virtue of a care order under the 1969 Act or by order of a court in family proceedings.

A wholly separate statutory regime applied to particular groups of children including the mentally handicapped and physically disabled. The provision of services to these children was governed by health and welfare legislation, the principal statutes being the National Health Service Act 1977, the National Assistance Act 1948 and the Chronically Sick and Disabled Persons Act 1970.

The Review and White Paper accepted that it would be in the interests of all the children concerned that there should be a unification of child care law and the relevant parts of the health and welfare legislation so that, in particular, the legal protections afforded by child care law might be extended to handicapped and disabled children. Thus, Part III of the Act represents a single code setting out the law on the provision of voluntary services by local authorities to children and families. The same services are now to be available to all children on the same basis, regardless of why they need them.

4.2 In contrast to this unification principle, Parts III and IV create a sharp division between voluntary services and compulsory care. A major criticism of the old law was that the distinction between *voluntary* and *compulsory* care had become blurred. Voluntary receptions into care had too often resulted in the local authority subsequently acquiring compulsory control of the child by administrative resolution under s 3 of the 1980 Act. This was thought to have resulted in a negative image of voluntary care and to have operated as a disincentive to the use of local authority services by families in difficulty. The thrust of the reforms effected by the Act is therefore to present voluntary services in a more positive way and to emphasise their supportive character. In theory this has always been the objective of the legislation but in practice too many voluntary arrangements have drifted into compulsion. The Act attempts to emphasise voluntary services and in various ways gives effect to the 'voluntary partnership' principle which was at the forefront of the Review and White Paper. Parents and the state (as represented by the local authority) are considered to be in voluntary partnership with one another in making arrangements to safeguard the welfare of children.

4.3 Those provisions in previous legislation which were inconsistent with this partnership principle are abolished. The Act does away with the 's 3 resolution' which enabled authorities to acquire compulsory powers to retain a child in their care against parental wishes. The procedure was purely administrative, albeit subject to later challenge in the juvenile court, and was widely considered to offend against the rules of natural justice. Also abolished is the twenty-eight day notice requirement for removal of a child who had been in voluntary care for over six months (s 13 1980 Act). The responsibilities of local authorities to children being looked after by them are spelled out more precisely than before and it is now clear that parents retain their parental responsibility where these arrangements are made. Responsibility does not pass to the authority except in so far as it is expressly delegated by parents. The general statutory duty under s 1 of the 1980 Act is recast and the specific duty to diminish the need to receive a child into voluntary care is removed. This was felt to be inconsistent with the character of voluntary services which ought to be encouraged rather than discouraged.

4.4 It cannot be emphasised too strongly that a child who is being accommodated by a local authority under Part III i.e. without a care order, is not 'in care' in the legal sense. It is quite wrong to refer to such a child in this way although, clearly, he will for many purposes be treated similarly to a child who was received into 'voluntary care' under s 2 of the 1980 Act. Only those children who are being looked after by virtue of a care order based on the criteria in s 31 are now 'in care'. The distinction is no mere technicality – it is vital and must be understood before the detail of Parts III and IV can be meaningfully examined. In some ways (perhaps many) the legal position of both groups of children is similar especially regarding their treatment by the authority. Similar duties apply, for example, in relation to such matters as placement, accommodation, education or religion. But, in other ways, there are major legal differences which reflect the wholly different basis (i.e. voluntary or compulsory) on which they are being accommodated by the authority.

4.5 This chapter and Part III are concerned with *voluntary* arrangements between parents and local authorities. *Compulsory* procedures are considered in Chapter 5 and fall within Part IV of the Act. The reader should however recall what was said above to the effect that the statutory duties of authorities towards children being looked after by them apply *equally* to all children regardless of whether they arrived in local authority accommodation under voluntary or compulsory arrangements.

4.6 The structure of Part III is as follows. Section 17 is concerned with the provision of services by local authorities to children and families. Section 18 deals with the emotive issue of day-care provision for the under-fives and certain other children. Section 19 provides for the periodic review of provision for day care services by local authorities. Section 20 replaces the procedure for voluntary reception into care and makes provision for the accommodation of children by local authorities. Section 21 deals with the provision of accommodation for children in police protection, on remand or in certain other similar circumstances. Section 22 specifies the general duties of authorities towards children being looked after by them and s 23 deals with the different ways in which they may be accommodated. These sections must be read with Part II of Sch 2 which contains further detailed duties of authorities. Section 24 establishes a new obligation for authorities to give advice and/or assistance to certain children. This reflects the concern which has been expressed in relation to older children leaving care. Section 25 governs the use of secure accommodation. Much of the detail here is left to regulations to be made under the Act. Section 26 provides for periodic reviews of the position of individual children being looked after by authorities. It also requires procedures to be set up by all authorities to receive representations regarding these children from the children themselves and from others. In reality 'representations' is a euphemism for 'complaints'. Section 27 provides for cooperation between authorities and s 28 for consultation with local education authorities. Section 29 and Part III of Sch 2 deal with financial contributions to the cost of family services and maintenance of children being looked after by authorities. Section 30 is concerned with a few miscellaneous matters.

Reference has been made above to Sch 2. This contains a great deal of detail which is impossible to analyse in depth in an introductory work of this nature. Much of this detail is nonetheless of practical importance, especially to local authority personnel. The comparatively small amount of space devoted to it here should not therefore be taken as an indication of its lack of importance.

2. Provision of Services for Children and Families

(a) The general duty

4.7 Section 17(1) replaces s 1 of the 1980 Act and lays down the general duty of local authorities to provide support services for children and families. It states:

'It shall be the general duty of every local authority . . .

(a)   to safeguard and promote the welfare of children within their area who are in need; and

(b)   so far as is consistent with that duty, to promote the upbringing of such children by their families,

by providing a range and level of services appropriate to those children's needs.'

4.8 The duty to provide services is therefore confined to those children who are 'in need'. The wording might give rise to the unfortunate impression that we are only concerned here with children from impoverished backgrounds. The use of the present tense might also suggest that the duty only arises where a child is already in a needy situation. It is clear that such interpretations are too restrictive of the authority's obligations which are concerned as much (if not more) with prevention as they are with cure. The preventive duty was spelled out more directly in the old section but this had pejorative connotations which led to the reformulation of the duty. The preventive duty still exists under the Act but it must be extracted from the definition of a child in need. The Act provides that a child shall be taken to be in need if:

(a) he is unlikely to achieve or maintain, or to have the opportunity of achieving or maintaining, a reasonable standard of health or development without the provision for him of services by a local authority under Part III;

(b) his health or development is likely to be significantly impaired, or further impaired, without the provision for him of such services; or

(c) he is disabled (s 17(10)).

4.9 It is evident from the wording of this provision that the authority must concern itself not only with those children who are already suffering from a low standard of health or development but also with those who would be likely to find themselves in this position unless the authority takes preventive action.

The Act provides a fuller definition of 'development', which includes 'physical, intellectual, emotional, social or behavioural development', and 'health' which means 'physical or mental health.' (s 17(11)). It also provides a detailed definition of 'disabled' children. 'Disabled' for these purposes means a child who is 'blind, deaf or dumb or suffers from mental disorder of any kind or is substantially and permanently handicapped by illness, injury or congenital deformity or such other disability as may be prescribed . . . (s 17(11)).' The original wording of the Bill contained a prospective element and incorporated within the definition those children who were 'likely' to be handicapped in any of the above ways. This was dropped as a result of a Commons' amendment (see *Hansard*, 16 May 1989, col 98). The purpose of the amendment was to align the definition of disabled children in the Act with the definition in the National Assistance Act 1948. Services for disabled *adults* will continue to be provided under the 1948 Act and it was felt that a common definition should apply to ensure consistency of provision between disabled adults and disabled children. In any event a child likely to become disabled would fall within the definition of a child in need since that definition embraces a prospective element.

Concern was expressed in Parliament that expressions such as 'blind, deaf or dumb' are unduly stigmatic and that it would have been better for the Act to have adopted a functional definition. It seems that the form of words was chosen in an effort to ensure that all those categories of children who are expected to fall within the scope of the authority's general duty are specifically included in the legislation. It also seems that the definition is wide enough to include those suffering from a *partial*, as opposed to total, disability. This, at least, was the view of the Secretary of State expressed in Committee (see *Hansard*, 16 May 1989, col 101).

4.10   Section 17 has in mind not simply services provided directly to children (although these are obviously included) but also services to members of their family. It is a major objective of the legislation to keep children in their families in the community wherever possible and this is written into the Act which requires authorities to promote the upbringing of children *by their families*. With this in mind any service provided by authorities may be for the family of a particular child in need or for any member of his family as long as it is provided with a view to safeguarding or promoting the child's welfare (s 17(3)). For this purpose 'family' (which is capable of being defined in many different ways) is given an expansive definition to include 'any person who has parental responsibility for the child and any other person with whom he has been living' (s 17(10)). The inclusion of the latter will enable authorities to give assistance to the person who is shouldering the daily burden of looking after the child whatever may be the technical legal position on parental responsibility for that child.

4.11   The services provided under this section may include giving assistance in kind or, in exceptional circumstances, in cash (s 17(6)). This repeats the formula in s 1 of the 1980 Act. It is well known that there has been a correlation between homelessness or adverse living conditions and voluntary receptions into care. This power allows an authority to make cash payments (commonly known as 's 1 money' under the old law) in an effort to improve home conditions for a family sufficiently to obviate the need to accommodate a child itself. It might, for example provide grants for furniture or household utilities to render the home habitable. As a matter of pure economics (to say nothing of the benefit to the child of continuing to live in his family) it might make sense for the authority to spend a comparatively small amount of money on family assistance rather than to incur the much higher cost of accommodating the child should the family situation ultimately prove to be intolerable. But it is not the function of the authority to provide income maintenance but rather social work support. Thus cash payments must not be used to usurp the role of the social security system however inadequate this may be in meeting the needs of a family. It is for this reason that

the payments may only be made in exceptional circumstances and not
routinely.

4.12 In certain circumstances an authority may seek to recoup the cost
of the services which it has provided to families under s 17. The assistance
which the authority gives may be either unconditional or subject to conditions
as to the repayment of the assistance or its value (in whole or in part)(s 17(7)).
This is qualified in that the authority must have regard to the means of
the child and each of his parents before giving any assistance or imposing
any condition (s 17(8)). This is taken a stage further by conferring an automatic
exemption from liability to repay in the case of an individual at any time
when he is in receipt of income support or family credit under the Social
Security Act 1986 (s 17(9)). It must be the case that a high proportion of
those likely to receive assistance in cash will already be wholly dependent
on means-tested state benefits.

4.13 Local authorities are required to facilitate the provision by others
of services which they have power to provide themselves under this Part
of the Act (s 17(5)(*a*)). Thus, they are empowered to make arrangements
for any person to act on their behalf in the provision of any service (s 17(5)(*b*).
In particular this authorises co-operation between authorities and voluntary
organisations and recognises the partnership between the public and private
sectors.

(b)   Specific powers and duties

4.14   Section 17 gives authorities a broad 'umbrella' power to provide services
to promote the care and upbringing of children (White Paper, para 18). The
more specific powers and duties which they have in discharging their
responsibilities under this section are contained in Part I of Sch 2. These
include:

(i)   a duty to take reasonable steps to identify the extent to which
there are children in need in their area (para 1(1));

(ii)   an obligation to publish information about the services which
they and others provide under this part of the Act and to
take such steps as are reasonably practicable to ensure that
this information is received by those who might benefit from
the services (para 1(2));

(iii) a duty to open and maintain a register of disabled children
within their area (para 2);

(iv)   a power to assess the needs of a child in need for present
purposes at the same time as assessing his needs for the purposes
of other relevant legislation (para 3);

(v)   a duty to take reasonable steps to prevent the ill-treatment
or neglect of children by the provision of services (para 4(1));

(vi)   a power to assist someone (possibly by the provision of cash)
with removal expenses and the costs of obtaining alternative

accommodation where that person is living with a child and the child is suffering, or is likely to suffer, ill-treatment at the hands of the person in question (para 5);

(vii)   a duty to minimise the effects of disability suffered by disabled children (para 6);

(viii)   a duty to take reasonable steps designed to reduce the need to bring proceedings for care or supervision orders, criminal proceedings, family proceedings which could result in them being placed in an authority's care or wardship proceedings, to encourage children not to commit criminal offences and to avoid the need to use secure accommodation (para 7);

(ix)   a duty to make provision for specified services to children in need who are living with their families (para 8);

(x)   a duty to provide 'family centres' at which a child, his parents and others may, inter alia, receive advice, guidance and counselling or take part in various activities of an occupational, social, cultural or recreational nature (para 9);

(xi)   a duty, where a child in need is living apart from his family, to take reasonable steps to enable him to live with them or to promote contact with them if, in the authority's opinion, it is necessary to do so to safeguard or promote his welfare (para 10).

4.15 Paragraph 7 (see (viii) above) should be mentioned. We saw that the Act removes the preventive duty which previously existed to diminish the need to receive children into *voluntary* care. The consideration which lay behind this change was the desire to present voluntary services as a positive option. This consideration does not apply to *compulsory* care proceedings and the other proceedings mentioned in para 7 which contemplate the removal of a child against parental wishes or some other non-consensual action being taken in relation to a child. Clearly, it is appropriate in relation to these relatively coercive measures that a preventive duty should be set out in the Act. There can be no dispute that it would be better if these steps could be avoided.

(c)   Day care for pre-school children and supervision of school children

4.16 Section 18 deals with the powers and duties of local authorities to provide for day care and other facilities primarily with respect to children under five but, to some extent, for children over school age outside school. The issue is an emotive one and resulted in one entire session in Committee being devoted to it (*Hansard*, 16 May 1989 (afternoon)). Contrary to the pattern in many European countries, there is no national plan in the UK relating to such facilities which are left to the discretion of individual authorities. Consequently, there is considerable regional variation in the amount and standard of services provided. There was considerable pressure in Parliament to impose stronger mandatory duties on authorities to provide services and to extend these to *all* children and not simply to those in need. These moves were resisted by the Government and the Act preserves the essentially permissive basis for the provision of services.

The Act distinguishes between children 'in need' as defined in s 17 and those falling outside this definition. It imposes a *duty* on every local authority to provide such day care for those in the former category, who are under five and not yet attending school, 'as is appropriate' (s 18(1)). It gives authorities a power to do so for those children in the latter category (s 18(2)). The mandatory language of s 18(1)) is deceptive since it is clear that authorities have a wide discretion in determining what day care provision they will make for children in need. They are obliged to provide only that which is appropriate. The original language of the Bill obliged authorities to make such provision 'as they consider appropriate'. Despite the slight modification in the wording, what is appropriate will still be a matter for individual authorities. This applies, a fortiori, to children not 'in need' where the language of s 18(2) is couched in permissive terms. It is certain that these provisions will perpetuate the regional differences referred to above. The argument that *all* children and *all* families could benefit from the universal availability of day-care facilities (and are thus in need of them in this less technical sense) has not been accepted.

4.17 Authorities are empowered to provide back-up support to those directly involved in providing day care facilities for children (s 18(3)). They may provide facilities for those who are caring for children in day care or who at any time accompany such children while they are in day care. 'Facilities' should include training, advice, guidance and counselling. Presumably it would also extend to the use of local authority premises for such activities as play-groups and perhaps, to the provision of transport. 'Day care' means any form of care or supervised activity provided for children during the day (whether or not it is provided on a regular basis) (s 18(4)). The obvious example of supervised activity for the under-fives would again seem to be play-groups. Day-care would include care in day nurseries and by child-minders. 'Supervised activity' is defined as 'an activity supervised by a responsible person' (s 18(7)).

4.18 Section 18(5) places authorities under similar duties to those in s 18(1) and (2) in relation to older children who are attending school. The original bill merely gave authorities a *power* to provide services for such children but, as a result of a Commons' amendment (*Hansard*, 16 May 1989, col 133) there is now a *duty* to provide for children 'in need' and a power to provide for others. Provision must be made for such care or supervised activities as is 'appropriate' outside school hours or during school holidays. It is unnecessary to repeat what was said above about the discretion which this gives to individual authorities.

The point of this provision is that many households in which *both* parents work have great difficulty in arranging child care between the hours of

4.00p.m. and 6.00p.m. when the school day has finished. Obviously, school holidays can give rise to similar problems. The White Paper (para 78) made reference to the considerable growth in recent years in private schemes for looking after children outside school hours while their parents were at work and in residential holidays for children. The Act confirms that authorities must ensure that *some* provision of this nature is made for children in need and that they may at their discretion support these facilities for other children.

4.19 Section 19 was added to the Bill in response to the widespread concern about the lack of coordination in day care provision for children. It places local authorities under a new duty to review periodically the whole spectrum of day care services in its area whether provided by local authorities or the private or voluntary sector.

4.20 The authority is required to undertake the initial review within one year of the commencement of s 19 and thereafter every three years (s 19(5). It must review the provision for day care which it makes itself, the availability of child-minders in its area with respect to children under eight and the provision for day care provided by persons required to register under s 71(1)(*b*) (which would include those involved with playgroups and day nurseries) (s 19(1)). The local authority must conduct the review in conjunction with the local education authority (s 19(2)). This is to emphasise the inextricable link between care and education and the need to facilitate coordination between the two bodies responsible for them. The review must also take account of provision for the under-eights which is exempt from the registration requirement (s 19(4)). There is a duty to consult and have regard to representations made by health authorities, health boards and other interested persons (s 19(7)). The latter group will include local voluntary groups, parents, employers and others. The authorities must then publish the result of the review as soon as is reasonably practicable and must include information about any proposals they may have with respect to the matters reviewed (s 19(6)).

The new duty falls well short of establishing a national plan or ensuring the availability of day care facilities for all children but may be seen as a move in the right direction.

3. Provision of Accommodation for Children

4.21 Section 20 is the legal foundation for what before the Act was known as 'Voluntary Care'. It establishes the basis upon which children may be looked after voluntarily (i.e. without the opposition of a parent or other person with parental responsibility) by a local authority. In order to appreciate the significance of the legal changes which it introduces it is necessary to compare it with ss 2 and 3 of the 1980 Act which it replaces. In particular, it should be noted that the previous power of authorities to acquire 'parental rights' by resolution is conspicuous by its absence.

(a)   Circumstances in which a child may be accommodated

4.22   Section 20(1) provides:

> 'Every local authority shall provide accommodation for any child in need within their area who appears to them to require accommodation as a result of:
>
> (a) there being no person who has parental responsibility for him;
> (b) his being lost or having been abandoned; or
> (c) the person who has been caring for him being prevented (whether or not permanently, and for whatever reason) from providing him with suitable accommodation or care.'

This is a substantial re-enactment, with some modifications to the wording, of s 2(1) of the 1980 Act. Essentially the authority is required to accommodate orphaned and abandoned children (where there is no individual exercising parental responsibility for them) and children whose parents or other carers are prevented by temporary or long-term illness or disability or any other reason from properly looking after them. The old s 2 contained a sweeping-up provision that, in all these cases, the intervention of the authority had to be necessary in the interests of the child's welfare. This has been omitted from the new provision but the clear implication of the several conditions in s 20(1) is that the authority's duty will only arise where its intervention is necessary in the interests of the child concerned.

(b)   Parental and other objections

4.23   The provision of accommodation for children in need is in the nature of a voluntary service which forms part of the range of services offered by local authorities to parents and children. In the case of orphaned or abandoned children it will obviously not be possible to obtain a positive consent from someone with parental responsibility for the child. In cases where such a person is available, and objects to the authority looking after the child, it will be necessary for the authority to resort to the compulsory measures in Parts IV and V where it is sufficiently concerned about the child.

4.24   The Act precludes the provision of accommodation where any person who has parental responsibility for the child objects (s 20(7)). This objection may prevent a voluntary arrangement coming into being at all or may be a superseding objection to the continuation of such an arrangement. A person with parental responsibility might, for example, be quite happy for a child to be looked after for respite purposes during some temporary difficulty but might subsequently wish to resume caring for the child. Following a Commons' amendment (*Hansard*, 18 May 1989, col 155) this right of objection by a person with parental responsibility is now qualified. It must be shown that the objector is himself willing and able to provide or arrange for alternative accommodation for the child. There was concern that an estranged father might wish to block a voluntary arrangement by a mother and the authority without having the intention of ensuring the proper accommodation of the child. Clearly similar considerations apply where the father is seeking to make an arrangement with an authority and an estranged mother is seeking to block it without accepting responsibility for the care of the child herself.

Subject to this, any person with parental responsibility 'may at any time remove the child from accommodation provided by or on behalf of the local authority' (s 20(8)). These objections by a person with parental responsibility do not apply where a residence order is in force and the person or persons in whose favour it is made agree to the child being looked after by the authority. This is also the case where a person with care of the child by virtue of an order under the High Court's inherent jurisdiction (usually wardship) agrees to the arrangement (s 20(9)). Where there is more than one such person, both must agree (s 20(10)).

4.25 These provisions give rise to two areas of difficulty.

The first is that some 'parents' and some people with 'parental responsibility' are, in certain circumstances, deprived of the right to object to voluntary arrangements made between an authority and another person with parental responsibility for the child. The unmarried father is a 'parent' within the terms of the Act but he is not (at least initially) a parent with parental responsibility. He will, therefore, have no power to prevent a child being looked after by an authority at the request of the mother, neither will he have any power to remove the child from local authority accommodation. The rationale appears to be that in the majority of cases children born out of wedlock will be looked after by their mothers from which it is apparently assumed that they alone should be placed in the position of making and terminating arrangements with Social Services. But difficulties can and do occur in practice where it is the *father* who is looking after the child and the mother who is unable or unwilling to exercise responsibility. In this type of case the Act gives the authority in effect a power to remove the child from the father's care *compulsorily* in the sense that *he* has no right of objection. He is, of course, able to seek residence or contact orders under s 8 but this is hardly as effective as the right to resist the child's removal in the first place. It may prove exceedingly difficult for him to persuade a court to upset the status quo where substitute care has been provided for the child before he has been able to get his application before the court. These difficulties did occasionally arise before the Act and have not been remedied by it (see *Re L (A Minor)* (1984) *The Times*, 21 June). While only a minority of fathers are likely to be affected the result may be quite devastating on those who are.

4.26 A second type of case is where a person with parental responsibility is deprived of his prima facie right of objection because someone else 'trumps' this with a residence order. The obvious example is that of the divorced 'non-residential' parent. He will have no right of objection where the parent with the residence order makes an arrangement with the authority. This is extraordinarily unsatisfactory. We saw in Chapter 3 that the purpose of a residence order is simply to regulate where a child is to live but otherwise to leave intact the full parental responsibility of both parents. Yet here it appears that this responsibility does not extend to the right to object to the child being accommodated by a public authority. The point must be made again that the principle of continuing parental responsibility may not add up to much in practical terms.

4.27 A second area of difficulty arising from these provisions concerns the anxiety that the interests of the authority in the well-being of a child being looked after by it may not be adequately protected. Section 2(3) of the 1980 Act provided that an authority was not authorised to keep a child in its care where any parent or guardian desired to take this over. But this apparent duty to hand over the child on demand was qualified by two other provisions. Section 2(2) required the authority to keep the child in its care so long as the welfare of the child appeared to the authority to require it. More significantly, s 13 provided that where a child had been in the care of the authority for at least six months a parent had to give the authority twenty-eight days' notice of his intention to resume the care of the child. Failure to do so constituted a criminal offence. The cumulative effect of these provisions was that the authority was not obliged to hand over a child immediately on request where it was concerned that this might jeopardise the child's welfare. Where the notice period applied its effect was to give the authority a 'breathing space' during which it could decide what further legal action (if any) it should take to secure a legal basis for retaining the care of the child (see *London Borough of Lewisham v Lewisham Juvenile Court Justices* [1980] AC 273).

The notice requirement has now been abolished by the 1989 Act. It was thought to be inconsistent with the new concept of the voluntary partnership between parents and local authorities (White Paper, para 22). It would seem that under the new law a parent (or other person with parental responsibility) will be acting quite lawfully in removing without notice a child who is being looked after by an authority (perhaps by foster parents) however long the arrangement may have been in existence. This has given rise to the concern that the authority may find itself powerless to prevent a removal where it considers that there is genuine doubt about the fitness of the parent or other individual to resume the physical care of the child. More often, perhaps, there may simply be concern that the child's present home should not be disturbed before the child has been properly prepared for the transition in caring arrangements. It appears that the authority may now be obliged to resort to the emergency procedures in Part V if it wishes to forestall an immediate removal (White Paper, para 23 and see Chapter 6).

4.28 There are two rather unsatisfactory features of this position. The first is that if there is a vacuum between the parental demand and the emergency action, the legal basis for the authority retaining the child (even for this short period) is unclear. It is suggested, however, that it probably does have authority to do so by virtue either of its general duty in s 22(3) to safeguard and promote the child's welfare or the power in s 3(5) to do what is reasonable in all the circumstances of the case for this purpose.

The other unsatisfactory aspect of these provisions is that an authority may need to have recourse to emergency procedures where it simply wishes to prepare the child for the return to his parents or where it just wishes to satisfy itself that the home circumstances are satisfactory before the child leaves his present accommodation. The authority does seem to have little choice here. If it cannot persuade the parent to wait for a short period it will either have to hand over the child more or less straight away or resort to coercive measures. A Lords' amendment which would have provided for twenty-four hours' notice by a parent and which, it is suggested, would have been a reasonable compromise was not accepted (*House of Lords, Official Report*, 20 December 1988, col 1335).

In the end, any period of notice was thought to detract unacceptably from the voluntary partnership principle.

(c) The child's point of view

4.29 Section 20(6) and (11) govern the relevance of the child's own views in determining whether he should be admitted to local authority accommodation. Again the Act draws a clear line between those over sixteen and those under that age. In the case of the former, parental or other objections will not prevent the young person concerned from being accommodated by the authority where he himself agrees to the arrangement (s 20(11)). This in effect accepts the complete autonomy of this age group to make their own decisions on where they should live. In most cases where a person of this age requests help from social services it is likely that there will have been a serious disruption of family relations. The young person concerned may have left home but may not have been able to become self-supporting or have found adequate housing. Unemployment and changes to Social Security law in s 4 of the Social Security Act 1988 did nothing to increase the chances of young people of this age making the transition to independence although the recent relaxation in Social Security regulations ought to ameliorate the situation. The essence of the new rules is that sixteen and seventeen-year-olds forced to live independently will be entitled to the higher rate of income support applicable to eighteen to twenty-four-year-olds.

4.30 The Act stops short of giving children under sixteen the right to decide this matter themselves. Instead it adopts the now familiar formula for ascertaining and taking their wishes into account to an extent commensurate with their age and understanding (s 20(6)).

Where a parent wishes a child of this age to be accommodated by an authority but the child objects it seems that the authority will have to balance their respective views in deciding whether or not the accommodation should be provided. The whole question of when a child reaches a sufficient age to decide when he should leave home is~unclear. The *Gillick* case might suggest that those who have reached the required level of maturity and understanding (whatever their age) should have the legal right to take this decision. Yet the Act establishes, at least in the present context, that this is not so. It is clearly the case that a child under sixteen may not be accommodated without compulsory measures against parental wishes. The more difficult situation will be where the parent wishes this and the child objects. Here s 20(6) attempts to strike a balance between the paternalistic view that children of this age should not have the entire burden of taking decisions like this upon themselves and recognition of their right to have some input into the discussions between their parents and the authority. It is nonetheless perhaps ironic, as pointed out by Lord Meston during the passage of the Bill (*House of Lords, Official Report*, 20 December, 1988, col 1338) that the authority should be obliged to provide accommodation against parental wishes for comparatively resourceful sixteen-year-olds but not duty-bound to offer shelter to arguably more vulnerable younger children. Obviously where they have done so as a result of suspected abuse or neglect the authority should consider applying for a care order.

4.31 It is quite likely that the conditions in s 20(1) giving rise to the authority's duty to accommodate children will not apply to those over sixteen. Accordingly, the Act makes separate provision for every authority to be under a duty to provide accommodation 'for any child in need within their area who has reached the age of sixteen and whose welfare the authority consider is likely to be seriously prejudiced if they do not provide him with accommodation' (s 20(3)). In most of these cases the teenager concerned will have a very unsatisfactory relationship with his parents. It does not follow that they would be unable to provide him with suitable accommodation. The Act thus confirms that the authority may provide him with accommodation even though a person with parental responsibility is able to do so if it considers that to do so would safeguard or promote the child's welfare (s 20(4)). The accommodation provided for a person who has attained sixteen, but is under twenty, may be in a community home which takes children who have reached the age of sixteen (s 20(5)). The purpose of this latter provision is to make it plain that a community home should not have to cater exclusively for sixteen-year-olds but can be used for them and other young people up to the age of twenty.

(d) Cooperation between authorities

4.32 Where a local authority provides accommodation for a child who is ordinarily resident in the area of another authority, that other authority may take over the provision of accommodation for the child within three months (or such longer period as may be prescribed) of receiving written notification of the child's situation (s 20(2)).

It should be noted that the authority has a discretion to decide whether or not to take over the care of the child. It is not obliged to do so. Any question arising as to the ordinary residence of a child is to be determined by agreement between the authorities concerned or, in default of agreement, by the Secretary of State (s 30(2)).

4. Provision of Accommodation for Children in Police Protection or Detention or on Remand

4.33 Local authorities are placed under a statutory duty to receive and accommodate children who are removed or kept away from home under the emergency procedures in Part V, in police protection and in other similar specified circumstances (s 21). These provisions are more appropriately discussed later when we consider emergency protection of children (see Chapter 6).

5. Duties of Local Authorities in Relation to Children looked after by them

(a) The general duty

4.34 The duties which local authorities have regarding children looked after by them apply equally to *all* such children whether they are formally 'in care' under a care order or being voluntarily provided with accommodation (s 22(1)). 'Accommodation' for these purposes is defined as that which is for a continuous period of more than twenty-four hours (s 22(2)). The general duty of authorities towards children being looked after by them was contained in Section 18(1) of the 1980 Act. This has now been recast and to appreciate fully the distinctions between the old and new duties it is necessary to take s 22(3) to (5) and compare these provisions with the former provision.

4.35 Section 22(3) states:

'It shall be the duty of a local authority looking after any child—

(a) to safeguard and promote his welfare; and
(b) to make such use of services available for children cared for by their own parents as appears to the authority reasonable in his case.'

Anyone having knowledge of the old law will notice immediately that, although the duty to safeguard and promote the welfare of the child is maintained, the child's welfare is no longer expressed to be the 'first consideration' for the authority. The obvious question must be whether this makes any difference. We saw in Chapter 2 that the welfare of the child is accorded varying degrees of significance depending on the legal context. The use of the 'first consideration' formula was thought to have the effect of prioritising the child's interests over other interests by making them the most important single factor, but not to render them the sole consideration as where they are expressed to be 'paramount'. The dropping of this wording must at least give rise to the suspicion that the Act has watered down the former statutory duty. Suppose, for example, the issue facing the authority is whether it should close a children's home. There were a number of reported instances under the old law of successful challenges by way of judicial review to home closures where it was shown that the authority had failed to give first consideration to the welfare of the individual children affected (see *Liddle v Sunderland BC* (1983) 13 Fam. Law 250; *R v Solihull MBC ex p C* [1984] FLR 363 and *R v Avon CC, ex p K* [1986] 1 FLR 443). There must now be some doubt whether challenges like this could succeed under the new law.

The essential problem is knowing what weight the authority is obliged to attach to the interests of children being looked after by it alongside other factors, particularly administrative convenience. The Act provides no definitive guidance on this. What is clear is that we are not concerned in this context with litigation in which an individual child's interests are the sole issue. The interests of *other* children in the same home would, for example, be clearly relevant. The authority may have to balance the interests of different children being accommodated by it and may also in some instances have regard to the wider public interest.

4.36   The authority's general duty is qualified in that it may act inconsistently with this where it thinks this is necessary 'for the purpose of protecting members of the public from serious injury' (s 22(6)). The Secretary of State may direct the authority to act in this way where he considers it necessary for the same reason (s 22(7)) and the authority is required to comply with such a direction (s 22(8)).

These provisions restate existing law with one modification. The Review took the position that it ought to be made clear that the child's welfare should only be overridden where 'serious harm' to members of the public could otherwise result. Previously the criterion was simply the perceived need for protection of the public.

(b)   Specific duties

(i)   The duty of consultation

4.37   We again confront the problem of weighting when we consider the relevance of the views expressed by the child, his parents and other interested adults regarding matters affecting a child being looked after by an authority. The Act makes much wider provision for consultation than ever existed previously. It provides:

> 'Before making any decision with respect to a child whom they are looking after, or proposing to look after, a local authority shall, so far as is reasonably practicable, ascertain the wishes and feelings of —
> (a) the child;

(b) his parents;

(c) any person who is not a parent of his but who has parental responsibility for him; and

(d) any other person whose wishes and feelings the authority consider to be relevant,

regarding the matter to be decided.' (s 22(4)).

4.38 The old provision simply directed the authority to ascertain the wishes of the *child* so far as was practicable. The addition of the various persons mentioned above is in keeping with the general aims of the legislation to allow parents and others directly concerned with the child to participate in the child's upbringing in partnership with the authority. It should be noted that consultation is mandatory. The only excuse for failing to consult will be where this is not reasonably practicable. This could be so where, for example, a parent cannot be contacted.

4.39 The Act goes on to deal with the authority's duty after it has ascertained the wishes of all relevant persons. The authority is required in making any decision to give due consideration:

(a) having regard to his age and understanding, to such wishes and feelings of the child as it has been able to ascertain;

(b) to such wishes and feelings of any person mentioned above as it has been able to ascertain; and

(c) to the child's religious persuasion, racial origin and cultural and linguistic background.

The question must be what is meant by 'due consideration'. In theory it should mean that the local authority personnel concerned are obliged to apply their minds to the representations which have been made as part of the consultation process. Failure to do so at all should be a ground for judicial review of any subsequent decision. But in practice it is more likely that the aggrieved individual will make a complaint under the procedure to be established under s 26. The difficulty with the consultation provisions is that it is likely to be a comparatively simple matter for the authority to listen to what is said and then dismiss it out of hand. There is certainly no indication in the Act that an authority is ever obliged to follow the wishes of a child, a parent or anyone else. Neither is there any indication of the relative importance of the respective views of the child, the parents, persons with parental responsibility or others. This appears to be left entirely to the authority's discretion except that, in the case of the child, his age and understanding will always effect the importance which may be attached to what he has said.

The appearance of the child's wishes as the first in the list may again be psychologically or symbolically significant but cannot be taken to elevate the standing of the child's views alongside the wishes of the various adults involved. Indeed to attach greater importance to children's views than to the views of their parents might operate as a disincentive to the use of voluntary arrangements by parents which would frustrate the main purpose of this aspect of the legislation.

4.40 The duty to take into account the child's religious persuasion, racial origin, and cultural and linguistic background is new and was specifically recommended in the Review (para 9.7). In previous legislation there have been various references to the child's religion and it is still a cardinal principle, even where a child is in care and the authority has acquired parental responsibility, that it should not change the child's religion (see Chapter 5). The Act now extends this position by requiring the authority to take the child's religion into account in taking any decision and by adding the child's racial origin and cultural and linguistic background as mandatory considerations. These factors are likely to be particularly relevant to the question of placement and, prima facie, suggest that efforts should be directed to placing the child with a family of similar race, culture and linguistic background. This is, of course, subject to the overriding consideration of the child's welfare which may in some cases dictate a different course of action, as where no foster parents from similar backgrounds are available or where those that are available are undesirable. The relevance of race and cultural and linguistic background in the context of *compulsory* state intervention is an extraordinarily difficult issue and we shall return to it later (see Chapter 5).

(ii)   The provision of accommodation

4.41 A local authority is obliged to provide a child in its care with accommodation (s 23(1)). The Act specifies the alternative ways in which a child (whether in care or being looked after under a voluntary arrangement) may be accommodated by the authority (s 23(2)). These are by:
  (a) placing the child with a family, a relative of his or any other suitable person (on terms as to payment determined by the authority), subject to qualifications in s 23(5) (discussed below);
  (b) maintaining him in a community home;
  (c) maintaining him in a voluntary home;
  (d) maintaining him in a registered children's home;
  (e) maintaining him in a home provided by the Secretary of State which is equipped with special facilities for children who need them;
  (f) making such other arrangements as:
     (i)   seem appropriate to the authority; and
     (ii)   comply with any regulations made by the Secretary of State.
  The legal regulation of these different types of accommodation is the subject of Chapter 7.

4.42 The above forms of accommodation are exhaustive but the purpose of category (f) is to allow the authority to provide accommodation which is not specified elsewhere in the list such as half-way houses and hostels. Again, the idea is to preserve a degree of flexibility. There is no statutory directive that an authority should prefer one form of accommodation over another. In particular, there is no presumption in favour of accommodating the child with relatives rather than with unrelated foster parents. Where an authority does decide to accommodate the child with an individual, that individual will generally be regarded as 'a local authority foster parent' for the purposes of the Act (s 23(3) and (4)) We saw earlier that this status has implications for eligibility to apply for residence orders under s 8 (see Chapter 3).

4.43 Regulations may be made concerning local authority foster placements. Schedule 2 specifies the matters which the regulations may cover (para 12). They include the health and education of the child concerned; the records to be kept by the authority; restrictions on the persons with whom a child may be placed; requirements that a foster parent is of the same religion as the child or is prepared to undertake to bring the child up in the child's religious persuasion; the supervision and inspection of premises; removal of the child from unsatisfactory living conditions and the discharge of an authority's duties by voluntary organisations.

4.44 Schedule 2 also lists some of the matters which may be covered in regulations made under s 23(2)(f) (para 13). These include the records to be kept by local authorities and the supervision by authorities of any arrangements made by them. Perhaps the most significant matter is that of notification. The regulations may provide for the persons to be notified of any proposed arrangements, the opportunities which such persons are to have to make representations and the persons to be notified of any proposed changes to the arrangements. It will be recalled that it is only the person with parental responsibility and, where there is a residence order, the person in whose favour it is made who will be dealing directly with an authority about voluntary arrangements. Other persons may well have a sufficient connection with the child that they should be notified of proposed arrangements and, ideally, have some input into these. The obvious examples are again the unmarried father without parental responsibility, the divorced non-residential parent and the extended family, especially grandparents. It is expected that these are the sort of categories which the regulations will cover.

4.45 The Act restricts the circumstances under which a child *in care* may be allowed to live with a parent or other person with parental responsibility (s 23(5)). It goes without saying that this only applies where the child is formally in care under a care order. The authority may only allow such an arrangement in accordance with regulations made under the Act. The purpose behind this is to ensure adequate safeguards before a child in care is allowed 'home on trial'. Public anxiety over this issue was aroused by the Jasmine Beckford inquiry. Following this the Children and Young Persons (Amendment) Act 1986 empowered the Secretary of State to make regulations to govern such matters as notification, consultation, medical and other supervision in such cases. It is anticipated that the new regulations will cover similar matters (Sch 2, para 14). The wording of the Act was criticised as too negative since it was said that it was inconsistent with the authority's duty to rehabilitate the child with his family. Accordingly, following a Commons' amendment, the Act now provides that (subject to any regulations made by the Secretary of State) any local authority looking after a child must make arrangements for him to live with a parent, person with parental responsibility, relative, friend or other person connected with him unless it would not be reasonably practicable or consistent with his welfare (s 23(6)). This amounts to a qualified rehabilitative duty. This is clearly an area in which the law has to strive to arrive at a sensitive balance between the rehabilitative and protective functions of local authorities.

4.46 Section 23(7) and (8) cater for some specific matters regarding the accommodation of children. First, the authority is required, so far as is reasonably practicable and consistent with his welfare, to secure that the accommodation provided for a child is near his home (s 23(7)(*a*)). There is a similar duty, subject to the same qualification, to secure that where an authority is looking after siblings they are accommodated together (s 23(7)(*b*)). The latter requirement reflects the general principle that it is desirable to keep brothers and sisters together where their original family has ceased to function. This was originally accepted in the context of custody disputes and has more recently been accepted as applicable to adoption (see the cases cited in Chapter 1).

4.47 The Act makes specific provision for the disabled child being looked after by the authority. It requires the authority, so far as is reasonably practicable, to secure that the accommodation is not unsuitable to his particular needs (s 23(8)). The Secretary of State has power to provide homes with particular facilities for children who need them (s 82(5)).

(iii)   The duty to maintain

4.48 The authority has a duty to maintain a child being looked after by it (s 23(1)(*b*)). The question of financial contributions from other persons to the child's maintenance or cost of services provided for him is considered below.

(iv)   The duty to promote and maintain contact between the child and his family

4.49 Paragraph 15 of Sch 2 is one of the more important provisions not to appear in the body of the Act. It governs the vital issue of the child's contact with his family. It should be considered along with s 34 which constitutes the new statutory code regulating disputes over contact where a child is *in care*. The present provisions relate to *all* children being looked after by an authority. Although a decision over contact may not be challenged under s 34 where a child is not in care there is no impediment to an application for a contact order under s 8 where a child is being looked after under a voluntary arrangement.

Leaving the question of challenges aside, the Act requires local authorities to endeavour to promote contact, so far as is reasonably practicable and consistent with his welfare, between the child and: (a) his parents; (b) any person with parental responsibility; and (c) any relative, friend or other person connected with him. The basic objective, as it was before the Act, is the reunification of the family. Paragraph 15 of Sch 2 must be read with s 23(6) (supra, para 4.45). These two provisions together with the general duty in s 17(1) to promote the upbringing of children *by their families* replace the former rehabilitative duty in s 2(3) of the 1980 Act. There are some who feel that the duty to rehabilitate the child with his family should have been spelled out more clearly in the Act. Instead it has to be deduced from the above provisions and from the central theme of the legislation which is one of support for the upbringing of children within their families and the use of substitute care for no longer than this is strictly necessary.

In order to facilitate the process of rehabilitation the Act imposes mutual obligations on the authority and parents or others with parental responsibility to keep in touch with one another. The authority must take reasonably practicable steps to keep these people informed of the child's whereabouts and they must keep the authority informed of their respective addresses (para 15(2)). There are also provisions for co-operation between authorities where a child moves from accommodation provided by one into accommodation provided by another (para 15(3) and (4)).

(v) Other powers and duties

4.50 The remaining paragraphs of Part II of Sch 2 deal with other aspects of the treatment of children being looked after by a local authority. The following are some of the more significant.

The authority has power in certain circumstances to make payments in respect of travelling expenses incurred in connection with visits to or by children. The payments may be made on grounds of financial hardship and where the circumstances warrant it (para 16). The authority is required to appoint an independent visitor where communication with or visits from parents or others with parental responsibility have been very infrequent and the appointment is in the best interests of the child (para 17). The authority may undertake any obligation by way of guarantee under any deed of apprenticeship or articles of clerkship on behalf of a child being looked after by it or qualifying for advice or assistance (para 18).

The authority may arrange for, or assist in arranging for a child to live outside England and Wales. Where the child is in care the approval of the court is required. The consent of the child is required before the court will give its approval unless it is satisfied that he lacks sufficient understanding to give or withhold consent. The consent of every parent or person with parental responsibility is also required. By analogy with adoption, the court may dispense with this where the relevant person cannot be found, is incapable of consenting or is withholding his consent unreasonably. The courts must also be satisfied that living abroad would be in the child's best interests and that suitable arrangements have been, or will be, made for his reception and welfare in the country in which he will live (para 19). In practice these issues are most likely to arise where a foster parent wishes to emigrate or where a suitable relative living abroad wishes to take over the care of the child.

Where a child looked after by an authority dies, the authority is required to notify the Secretary of State and, so far as is reasonably practicable, the parents and other persons with parental responsibility. Provision is also made for the authority to arrange the child's funeral and in certain circumstances to make payments to assist with travelling and other expenses in connection with attendance at the funeral (para 20).

6.   Advice and Assistance for Certain Children

4.51   Section 24 introduces substantial changes to the duties of local authorities with respect to young people leaving their care or ceasing to be looked after by them. These young people often find themselves in an unusually vulnerable position when seeking to make the transition to an independent life in the community. Those who are fortunate enough to have the benefit of a stable family life are not normally cut off from parental concern at an arbitrary age such as eighteen. They may expect to continue to be supported and advised by their parents after they have left the family home. On the other hand, young people leaving institutional care may well have no family on which to rely. They may find it difficult to obtain satisfactory living accommodation and, at worst, may be faced with homelessness. The high level of youth unemployment and changes to social security law to which we previously alluded have exacerbated these problems. Despite the rhetoric in the legislation about the need to take proper account of the wishes of children, as a practical matter the quest for independence is likely to be a difficult one for disadvantaged young people leaving local authority accommodation or foster care on attaining majority. The Act strengthens the duties of authorities to assist these young people.

4.52   The statutory obligations of authorities under the 1980 Act towards young people leaving care were confused and uncertain. The Act aims to rationalise and improve on existing provisions by expanding the circumstances under which authorities are obliged to offer help to young people who are being or have been looked after by them.

4.53   Section 24(1) adopts the logical position that the authority should begin to prepare a child for independent living while he is still being looked after by it. The authority must 'advise, assist and befriend him with a view to promoting his welfare when he ceases to be looked after by them.' This is the first time that there has been a general duty such as this. Previously duties only arose where a child was already in the process of leaving care.

4.54 The authority's duties towards children who have ceased to be looked after by it are also strengthened by extending the age of those qualifying for help from eighteen to twenty-one. Those qualifying for 'advice and assistance' under s 24 are persons within the area of the authority who are under twenty-one and who were, while sixteen or seventeen
  (a) looked after by a local authority;
  (b) accommodated by or on behalf of a voluntary organisation;
  (c) accommodated in a registered children's home;
  (d) accommodated:

  (i)   by any health authority or local education authority or
  (ii)   in any residential care home, nursing home or mental nursing home,

for a consecutive period of at least three months; or
  (e) privately fostered,
but are no longer so looked after, accommodated or fostered (s 24(2)).

The authority must in certain circumstances advise and befriend a qualifying person where it knows of his presence in its area and he has asked for help of a kind which the authority is empowered to give under s 24(s 24(4)). The duty only arises where the person concerned was looked after by the authority or a voluntary organisation. Where he was accommodated in one of the other ways the authority *may* help him. In either case the conditions for assistance are that he appears to be in need of advice and being befriended and, where he was not looked after by the authority, that the person by whom he was looked after does not have the facilities for advising or befriending him (s 24(5)). The latter condition is to ensure that the authority's duty will arise only where the voluntary organisation or other body who had primary responsibility for looking after the child, is unable to advise or befriend him themselves.

4.55 In exercising its duty or power to advise or befriend the authority has power at the same time to provide 'assistance' which may be in kind or, in exceptional circumstances, in cash (s 24(6) and (7)). It is expressly provided that assistance may be by way of a contribution to expenses incurred by virtue of living near the place where he is or will be employed or seeking employment or receiving education or training (s 24(8)). Again, in this context, cash payments must not, it would seem, be used as a substitute form of income support since this is the function of the social security system. It is, however, expressly provided that s 17(7) to (9) apply equally to assistance given under this section (s 24(10)). Accordingly, young people who are dependent on income support or family credit will be exempt from liability to repay any cash assistance.

4.56 Section 24(11) and (12) deal with cooperation and notification of a child's whereabouts between different authorities and voluntary organisations.

An authority which has been advising and befriending a child must inform any other authority in whose area the child proposes to live or is living of the position (s 24(11)). Where a child ceases to be accommodated by one of the bodies mentioned above on reaching the age of sixteen, the voluntary organisation, etc must inform the authority in whose area the child proposes to live (s 24(12)). These children will be qualifying persons for the purpose of the statutory powers and obligations of the authority under this section.

7.   Secure Accommodation

4.57   Apart from decisions relating to contact, decisions to place a child in secure accommodation are the only ones relating to the treatment of children looked after by local authorities which are directly subject to judicial control. The Criminal Justice Act 1982 inserted s 21A into the 1980 Act which, together with the Secure Accommodation Regulations, regulated the circumstances in which this type of accommodation could be used. They also governed the procedures for challenging the use of this accommodation in the juvenile court. Under these provisions no child could be locked up for more than seventy-two hours in any twenty-eight day period without the court's authority. The court might then authorise its use for up to three months and thereafter for periods of six months at a time. The position of wards of court in care caused some initial confusion but it was finally determined by regulations that only authorisation of the wardship court was required in those circumstances.

4.58   Section 25 essentially re-enacts these provisions with the details again being left to regulations. It provides that a child being looked after by an authority may not be placed or kept in accommodation provided for the purpose of restricting liberty (secure accommodation) unless it appears:
- (a)   that:
    - (i)   he has a history of absconding and is likely to abscond from any other description of accommodation; and
    - (ii)   if he absconds, he is likely to suffer significant harm; or
- (b)   that if he is kept in any other description of accommodation he is likely to injure himself or other persons. 'Harm' for the purposes of the Act means 'ill-treatment or the impairment of health or development' (ss 105(1) and 31(9)).

The essence of the above conditions is that the child should only be locked up for *protective* reasons and not as a mode of punishment. The concern is that children who are often the most abused should not be further punished by incarceration but should be helped in a positive way.

4.59   The Act empowers the Secretary of State to make regulations which specify a maximum period (currently seventy-two hours) beyond which a child may not be kept in secure accommodation without court authorisation and a maximum period for such authorisation. The regulations may empower the court to authorise extensions and provide that applications should be made only by local authorities (s 25(2)). The court for these purposes will be the magistrates' court, the county court or the High Court (as the case may be) and not the juvenile court as before.

More controversially, the Act gives the Secretary of State power to exempt or include categories of children, to modify these categories and to make other provisions for the purpose of determining whether a child of a description specified in the regulations may be placed or kept in secure accommodation (s 25(7)). These provisions apply equally to children in care and those being looked after under a voluntary arrangement subject to one important qualification. In the latter instance the parental right to remove the child from the authority (s 20(8)) takes precedence over any authorisation of the use of secure accommodation (s 25(9)). Where parents regard the authority's actions as inappropriate they may simply resume the child's care.

4.60 The court's primary function is to determine whether the relevant criteria for keeping a child in secure accommodation are satisfied in the case before it (s 25(3)). If it finds that they are, it must give its authorisation and specify the maximum period during which the child may be kept in the accommodation (s 25(4)). When adjourning an application, the court may make an interim order permitting the child to be kept in secure accommodation during the adjournment (s 25(5)). We consider the question of appeals in relation to these and other proceedings later (see Chapter 8). The court is prevented from exercising its powers where a child is not legally represented unless the child has failed the means test for legal aid or has been offered it and refused it (s 25(6)). Finally, the court may give directions in relation to any child which it has authorised to be detained in secure accommodation (s 25(8)).

4.61 One aspect of judicial control which remains rather uncertain under the reforms relates to wards of court. The authorisation of the use of secure accommodation by a judge in wardship was criticised in Parliament for being outside the statutory scheme and insufficiently controlled. The wardship court was said to be in a position where it could take the lead in locking-up children in contrast to the more passive role of the juvenile court. It could also authorise indefinite deprivations of liberty and was not subject to the time limits which the regulations imposed on juvenile courts. The child, as a ward, was not necessarily party to the proceedings and a local authority could not release a child even where the statutory conditions ceased to apply unless it first obtained the permission of the High Court. Taken together, these criticisms were alleged to amount to a breach of the child's rights under the European Convention on Human Rights (see Baroness David, *House of Lords, Official Report*, 17 January 1989, col 156).

The Act may now have changed all this by virtue of the general restrictions which it places on the use of wardship by local authorities under s 100(2). The effect of these is that the inherent wardship jurisdiction may not be used, inter alia, to put a child into care or to direct that a child be accommodated by or on behalf of a local authority. This presumably applies to directions that the child be placed in secure accommodation. If this is right, the problem of the open-ended powers of the wardship court will disappear and the statutory procedures will always govern the use of secure accommodation.

8. Reviews and Representations

(a) General

4.62 Section 26 provides for periodic reviews of the position of children being looked after by local authorities and for procedures to be established by authorities to receive and take into account representations from individuals concerning the treatment of such children. The objective of both mechanisms is to encourage long-term planning for children to prevent a situation in which they are allowed to drift and to subject authorities to a measure of accountability. The Review did not favour an extension of the court's powers to enable them to exert control over local authority decision-making. The basic distinction which it favoured was between 'major issues', such as the transfer of parental rights and duties, and the management of the child's case. The former were thought suitable for determination by the courts while the latter was considered to be the exclusive preserve of local authorities (Review, paras 2.20 et seq). The difficulty, acknowledged in the Review, is to decide which decisions taken by the authority ought to fall into which category. The Review was primarily influenced by the need to allow authorities, who have the daily care of the child, to 'take a grip on' the case and make firm and early decisions without the temptation to pass responsibility to another body (Review, para 2.24). It was thought that there were limits to what the courts could usefully contribute and that their particular strength lay in dispute resolution. But the practical questions of how the child should be brought up were considered to be appropriately left in the hands of the authorities who were responsible for putting them into effect. Accordingly, the Review took the position that a speedier and more informal complaints procedure was a better option than extension of the court's jurisdiction. It recommended that the existing system of reviews should be improved and strengthened and provision for complaints procedures should be expanded by requiring *all* local authorities to establish their own internal procedures which should contain an independent element.

4.63 Before turning to the provisions in the Act giving effect to these proposals, it should be noted that certain decisions do remain in the hands of the courts. This is now universally the case where an authority wishes to obtain a transfer of parental responsibility for the child. It is also the case with respect to the discharge of a child from care. Also, we have already seen that there is judicial control over decisions relating to contact and secure accommodation. Beyond this, the jurisdiction of the courts is the more limited one of judicial review which can only be successfully invoked where there has been some impropriety or irregularity in the exercise of an authority's discretion or some failure to comply with the correct statutory procedures (for an example of the use of judicial review before the Act see *R v Bedfordshire CC, ex p C; R v Hertfordshire CC, ex p B* [1987] 1 FLR 239).

(b) Reviews

4.64 The Act gives the Secretary of State power to make regulations requiring the case of each child who is being looked after by a local authority to be reviewed in accordance with those regulations (s 26(1)). Such a power existed under s 20(2) of the 1980 Act but this had not been exercised. Local authorities were obliged under s 27(4) of the 1969 Act to conduct a review in relation to every child in their care once every six months but there was no directive on the manner in which this was to be conducted or the matters which ought to be covered. The Act seeks to remedy this by specifying what reviews should include.

4.65 Section 26(2) states that the regulations may in particular make provision for the following matters:
(a) the manner in which each case is to be reviewed;
(b) the considerations to which the authority must have regard in conducting each review;
(c) the time when each case is to be first reviewed and the frequency of subsequent reviews. (It is expected that the regulations will prescribe the same six month interval for reviews (White Paper, para 30). It is likely that the initial review will have to be conducted within four weeks of the authority taking over the accommodation of the child (Review, para 9.8).);
(d) to require that, before conducting any review, the authority should seek the views of the child, his parents, any person with parental responsibility and any other person whose views the authority consider to be relevant. In each case these views should in particular be sought in relation to any particular matter which is under consideration as part of the review. (It should be noted here that the statutory requirement is simply one of consultation. The Act gives no-one any right to attend or participate in any meetings held as part of the review. Indeed, there is no statutory requirement that a meeting as such should take place. Concern was expressed about this in Parliament where it was pointed out that without such a provision the reviews could be discharged in a perfunctory manner. It was also suggested that, in the absence of rights of attendance and participation, there might be a risk that children and parents would have no confidence in decisions taken behind closed doors. The Lord Chancellor has indicated that these and other concerns will be taken into account in formulating the regulations.);

(e)   to require that the authority should consider, in the case of a child in care whether an application should be made to discharge the care order. (This re-enacts the duty in s 27(4) of the 1969 Act.);

(f)   to require that the authority should consider, in the case of a child in accommodation provided by the authority, whether the accommodation accords with the requirements of this part of the Act;

(g)   to require the authority to inform the child, as far as reasonably practicable, of any steps he may take under the Act;

(h)   to require the authority to make arrangements, including arrangements with other bodies providing relevant services, in order to implement any decision which the authority proposes to make in the course, or as a result, of the review;

(i)   to require the authority to notify details of the result of the review, and of any decision taken in consequence of it, to specified individuals. (Those concerned are basically those who were required to be consulted under (d) above.); and

(j)   to require that the authority monitor the arrangements which have been made with a view to ensuring that they comply with the regulations.

(c)   Representations

4.66   Every local authority is required to establish a procedure for considering any representations (including any complaint) made to them by a child being looked after by them, a parent, a person with parental responsibility or a local authority foster parent, or such other person as the authority considers has a sufficient interest in the child's welfare to warrant his representations being considered by it, about the discharge of any of the authority's functions under this part of the Act (s 26(3)).

Although the emphasis of the Act is on 'representations' we are in reality talking here principally about an avenue of redress for complaints. These may relate to the discharge of any function under the Act. The procedure may thus be invoked to challenge major decisions such as a change of placement or a serious medical issue or to complain about comparatively trivial annoyances.

The categories of those entitled to make representations are, perhaps, too restrictive. It appears, for example, that concerned members of the extended family are not included unless they have acquired parental responsibility for the child although their representations may be heard at the discretion of the authority. The sort of problem faced by an uncle, aunt and grandparents in *Re W (A Minor) (Wardship: Jurisdiction)* [1985] AC 791 does not seem to have been remedied. The basic complaint in that case was that the potential contribution of the relatives was not sufficiently taken into account by Social Services. If relatives like this are not to have an automatic right to utilise a complaints procedure the danger is that they will have to resort to something more drastic in order to have their views considered, i.e. bring an application for a s 8 order.

The justification for refusing to include a wider category of other interested persons given by the Lord Chancellor was that the procedure could not be open to everyone, and had to be reasonably selective, if it was to work. This is not a particularly convincing argument. It is surely right that those who can demonstrate a genuine interest in the child (whatever their personal connections with that child) should be entitled to express their views and should not have to rely on the goodwill of the authority. Moreover, there is good reason for feeling that people such as grandparents have much that they could offer a child. It is unfortunate that they may be forced to go to litigation in order to register their disapproval of an authority's treatment of a child.

4.67 The Review (para 9.12) recommended that the procedure should have an independent element built into it. The Act provides that it must ensure that at least one person who is not a member or officer of the authority takes part in the consideration of the representations and any discussions held about the action (if any) to be taken (s 26(4)).

Beyond this the Act does not prescribe the form of the procedure to be followed. The regulations to be made under this section are intended to set out *minimum* standards for procedures rather than dictate their format. The setting up of a procedure is therefore mandatory but each authority may decide how best to provide for it. It remains to be seen whether these procedures will prove to be an effective substitute for judicial control and how far they will meet the demands of natural justice. Concern has focussed on the fear that an essentially internal procedure may not be sufficiently independent of the authority despite the requirement of an independent element.

Authorities are required to give the procedure adequate publicity (s 26(8)). This should be seen alongside the more general duty of authorities to publish information on the services which they provide and to take reasonable steps to bring this information to those who might benefit from the services (Sch 2, para 1(2)).

4.68 Once it has considered a representation the authority is required to:

'(a) have due regard to the findings of those considering the representation; and
(b) take such steps as are reasonably practicable to notify (in writing)
    (i) the person making the representation;
    (ii) the child (if the authority considers that he has sufficient understanding); and
    (iii) such other persons (if any) as appear to the authority to be likely to be affected,
    of the authority's decision in the matter and their reasons for taking that decision and of any action which they have taken, or propose to take' (s 26(7)).

It is not clear from this whether the child, parent or other complainant
has any redress where a complaint is upheld. The section appears to lack
teeth in that it imposes no duty on the authority to redress a grievance
or, indeed, even to apply its mind to the question of redress. The only
course of action where the authority fails to act would seem to be a challenge
by way of judicial review on the basis that it has failed to perform its statutory
duty to 'have due regard' to the findings under the procedure.

9.   Cooperation between Authorities

4.69   We have seen that a number of provisions have dealt with aspects
of cooperation between different authorities. Section 27 is a general provision
designed to foster this. It gives a local authority power to request help from
other specified authorities where it appears that they may be able to assist
in the exercise of the authority's functions under the Act. The request should
specify the action which, it is thought, could assist. The other relevant
authorities and persons for these purposes are any other local authority,
any local education authority, any local housing authority, any health authority
and any person authorised by the Secretary of State for these purposes
(s 27(3)).

Section 27(1) is in permissive terms. There is no obligation on local
authorities to seek outside assistance. But where assistance is sought, the
authority whose help is requested must comply with the request 'if it is
compatible with their own statutory or other duties and obligations and
does not unduly prejudice the discharge of any of their functions' (s 27(2)).
Every local authority must also assist any local education authority with
the provision of services to any child in its area who has special educational
needs (s 27(4)).

4.70   Where a local authority complies with a request for assistance in relation
to a child or other person who is not ordinarily resident within its area,
it may recover expenses reasonably incurred in that connection from the
authority in whose area the child is ordinarily resident (s 29(9)). A similar
principle applies where accommodation is provided for a child under s 20(1)
who was when the authority began to look after him ordinarily resident
within the area of another local authority (s 29(7)). In each case, the question
of where the child is ordinarily resident is to be determined by agreement
between the authorities concerned or, in default of agreement, by the Secretary
of State (s 30(2)). Where, for example, a child is in need because of adverse
housing conditions or homelessness social services might approach the local
housing authority to see what (if anything) could be done to assist the family
and thereby obviate the need for the child to be looked after by the authority
under s 20. Where the vulnerability of the child is derived from the ill-
health of his parents again it may be desirable for social services to liaise
with the relevant health authority.

4.71 Section 28 is designed to ensure that there is full consultation between social services and the local education authority where a child looked after by the local authority is placed in a residential school or home with education provided on the premises. Consultation with the local education authority must, so far as is reasonably practicable, take place before such a placement is made (s 28(1)). The local authority must also inform the local education authority after such a placement is made (s 28(2)) and when the child ceases to be accommodated in the establishment (s 28(3)). This type of placement is particularly likely to be used in the case of handicapped children and those with special educational needs. The objective of these provisions is to ensure proper collaboration between the statutory agencies concerned about both the child's welfare and specifically his educational needs.

10. Contributions to the Cost of Local Authority Services

4.72 The Act allows local authorities to recoup the cost of providing services under s 17 or 18, other than advice, guidance or counselling, from specified individuals. They may make such charge for the service as they consider reasonable (s 29(1)).

Those who are liable to be charged are:
(a) where the service is provided for a child under sixteen, each of his parents;
(b) where it is provided for a child who has reached the age of sixteen, the child himself; and
(c) where it is provided for a member of the child's family, that member (s 29(4)).

Where such a charge is made it may be enforced as a civil debt (s 29(5)). In considering whether to make a charge the authority must have regard to the means of the recipient of the service. Where it is satisfied that these are insufficient for it to be reasonably practicable for him to pay the charge, it must not require him to pay more than he can reasonably be expected to pay (s 29(2)). Again, no-one is liable to pay anything while in receipt of income support or family credit (s 29(3)).

4.73 Contributions towards the maintenance of children being looked after by local authorities are governed by a detailed code constituted by s 29(6) and Part III of Sch 2. This is a re-enactment, with modifications, of Part V of the 1980 Act. The principal change is in para 21(2) of Sch 2. This provides that an authority may only recover contributions where it considers it reasonable to do so. The effect of this is to give the authority more discretion than it previously had to decide *not* to impose a charge. The charges are controversial and there is a substantial body of opinion in favour of their total abolition. Their unpopularity stems from the severe hardship which they can cause to individual families and the comparatively poor returns to local authorities. Inability to pay has meant that in many areas arrears are endemic. There has also been considerable inconsistency in the policies adopted by local authorities.

Despite this the Act leaves the existing system substantially intact except that it introduces a subtle change of emphasis. The pre-Act position was that an authority was *obliged* to require contributions (except where a family was exempted by virtue of their reliance on social security benefits) unless it considered it unreasonable to do so. Now there is no such presumption in favour of contributions. It is hoped that this will do something to prevent parents being discouraged from arranging for their children to be looked after by authorities for fear of the financial burden of doing so or from removing them for the same reason.

4.74 Other principal features of the scheme in Sch 2 are as follows:

(i)   A person is not liable to contribute towards maintenance in respect of any period while the child is allowed by the authority to live with a parent (para 21(5));

(ii)   There is no liability to contribute in certain instances where the child is being looked after on a short-term basis viz. where the child is the subject of an interim care order or accommodated under s 21 (para 21(7));

(iii)   The authority must initially seek to reach agreement with a contributor by serving a 'contribution notice' on him specifying the weekly sum which it thinks he ought to contribute(para 22);

(iv)   Where the authority and the contributor fail to reach agreement within one month of service of the notice or the contributor (having agreed) later withdraws his agreement, the authority may apply to the court for a 'contribution order'. The court may then make an order which must not specify a weekly sum greater than that in the original contribution notice. The court must have regard to the contributor's means in deciding the amount of the order. The order may subsequently be varied or revoked on the application of the contributor or the authority (para 23);

(v)   A contribution order made by a magistrates' court is enforceable as a magistrates' court maintenance order within the meaning of the Magistrates' Courts Act 1980 (para 24(1));

(vi)   One authority may recover contributions on behalf of another authority from a contributor in its area (para 24(2) et seq);

(vii)   The Secretary of State may make regulations as to the considerations to be taken into account by an authority in deciding whether it is reasonable to recover contributions and, if so, what the arrangements for payment should be. The regulations may also govern the procedures the authority must follow in reaching agreement with contributors or another authority (para 25).

11. The Authority's Powers in Relation to a Child looked after by it

4.75 This discussion of voluntary arrangements between families and local authorities should not conclude without a comment on the nature of the authority's legal powers under this type of arrangement. We have so far largely been concerned with the *duties* of authorities. Clearly authorities must possess concomitant *powers* in order to carry out these duties. But parental responsibility does not pass under voluntary arrangements. Thus, the authority has only those decision-making powers over upbringing which parents (or others with parental responsibility) delegate to it expressly or impliedly for the purpose of looking after the child (White Paper, para 27). We noted earlier that parental responsibility may not be voluntarily relinquished but may be temporarily delegated (see Chapter 2). It follows that the extent of an authority's powers must depend on the nature of the agreement reached with those having parental responsibility. These agreements should preferably be in writing and should cover matters such as the child's placement, medical care and schooling.

The essence of these arrangements is that the authority and the parents (or others) should at all times consult and work together in voluntary partnership for the benefit of the child. This idea of close cooperation and consultation on all important issues affecting the child does not apply, as we have seen, in the private sphere where parents separate. Why it is practically possible to make a cooperative arrangement work in the public sphere but not in the private sphere is a question which may at some time need to be addressed.

CHAPTER FIVE

Care and Supervision

1. Introduction

5.1 Part IV of the Act governs compulsory measures for public intervention in the family. Under the old law a child might enter the compulsory care of a local authority by virtue of one of a number of different statutory procedures. We have already mentioned the s 3 resolution procedure which was a mechanism for retaining compulsorily the care of a child who had entered care initially under a voluntary arrangement. Where the authority wished to take over the care of a child, whose parents were unwilling to come to a voluntary arrangement, it was generally required to commence care proceedings under the 1969 Act with a view to obtaining a care order from the juvenile court. Alternatively, the authority might prefer to commence wardship proceedings and seek a care and control order in its favour. This proved to be an increasingly popular option where the authority was genuinely anxious about a child but was doubtful about whether it might be able to satisfy the statutory grounds for a care order. Apart from wardship, courts having jurisdiction in certain family proceedings might also commit a child to care in the course of those proceedings. Divorce proceedings were the obvious example (see *R v G (Surrey County Council Intervening)* [1984] Fam. 100) but orders could also be made in other proceedings such as those relating to guardianship or adoption.

5.2 The basis upon which these various compulsory measures might be taken differed significantly. In the case of both s 3 resolutions and 1969 Act orders there were freestanding conditions which had to be satisfied. These conditions were quite distinct. The resolution grounds concentrated on the condition or behaviour of *parents*. The grounds for a care order were more *child-centred* in that they concentrated on the child's unsatisfactory situation whether this arose from abuse or neglect, exposure to moral danger, delinquency or being beyond parental control, etc. The basis for committing a child to care in family proceedings was, again, distinct. Here a court might make an order where there were 'exceptional circumstances making it impracticable or undesirable' for the child to be under the care of a parent or other individual (See, for example, s 43(1) of the Matrimonial Causes Act 1973).

5.3 One of the Act's primary aims is to remove the inconsistency and incoherence of these grounds and to unify the basis upon which parental responsibility may be compulsorily vested in the local authority (albeit shared with parents or others). It should be remembered that 'family proceedings' is now a generic term which describes all proceedings under the Act as well as other proceedings in which orders may be made relating to children and which have, more traditionally, been known as family proceedings. In *any* proceedings in which a compulsory care order is now sought by an authority the new statutory ground will have to be established. It was the case before the Act (see *Havering London Borough Council v S* [1986] 1 FLR 489), and it is manifestly the case under it, that an authority wishing to gain or retain compulsory control of a child must have a secure legal basis for doing so. The ground in s 31 is now the sole criterion which will apply in all proceedings in which care or supervision is sought.

5.4 Two matters must be emphasised. The first is that the effect of s 100(2) is to remove from local authorities the alternative option of commencing wardship proceedings with a view to obtaining care and control on an extra-statutory basis. There is no reason why a care order should not be sought in wardship proceedings but it may only be granted if the conditions in s 31 are proved to exist. Care orders will be made by 'the court', which expression includes the magistrates' court, the county court and the High Court. It has been indicated that most (if not all) care proceedings will be initiated and will take place in the magistrates' court but this will now be the new 'family proceedings court' rather than the juvenile court. Considerable concern has been expressed that this will deprive the authority, and others concerned, of the expertise of the High Court in complex cases. This function has until now been performed by wardship. The Act does, however, embrace a system for transferring cases between levels of court which it is hoped will accommodate at least some of this concern.

The second matter is that this requirement of a court order applies just as much where an authority is *already* looking after a child (for however long) as it does where the child is still at home. Where an authority is sufficiently concerned about a child being looked after by it under Part III that it desires to keep that child under its protection, it can now do so only by going to court and proving the ground in s 31. In either case it will now be easier for the authority to obtain an order in certain circumstances. The Act has removed one of the most serious inhibitions on compulsory action in that it will now be possible to secure an order on the strength of a *risk* of harm to a child who has not as yet been harmed. This was not possible under any of the statutory procedures discussed above and was a major reason why wardship was invoked by authorities.

5.5 The structure of Part IV is as follows. Section 31 establishes the new ground for care and supervision orders. Section 32 should be read with s 11 and s 1(2). It gives the court new powers to combat the problem of protracted litigation. Sections 11 and 32, taken together, are a good example of the way in which the Act is trying to bring together the public and private law affecting children by the application of common principles and common remedies. Section 33 specifies the effects of a care order. One of the worst deficiencies of the old law was that no one was quite certain of the precise legal effects of the various types of care orders on the distribution of parental powers and duties. Section 33 seeks to clarify these and, of course, it will be obvious by now that any inconsistencies which previously existed between the legal effects of the various routes into care have been removed at a stroke. There is only one basis for compulsory care. There can be no inconsistency. By far the most important legal effect is that, subject to express qualifications, the authority formally acquires parental responsibility for the child. This is merely a change of nomenclature since under the old law 'parental powers and duties' passed to the authority under a care order (1980 Act, s 10(2)). It is this feature which distinguishes the legal position of these children from other children being accommodated by the authority since, as we have seen, most of the Act's provisions governing the treatment of children by local authorities apply equally to both groups.

Section 34 constitutes the new statutory code regulating contact between parents and others with children in care. It has some features in common with s 12A to G of the 1980 Act which previously governed this issue. There are however some significant innovations, not least the enactment of a presumption of reasonable contact between the child and certain qualifying adults. Section 34 applies only to children in care and not to those merely being looked after by authorities. It should be compared with the provisions of para 15 of Sch 2 (see Chapter 4). The principal point of distinction is that s 34 provides for judicial control over contact decisions. It is assumed that this is not required in relation to voluntary arrangements because the authority, at least in theory, has no power to cut off contact between the child and his family. Section 35 deals with supervision orders and, in particular, the duties of the supervisor where a supervision order is made. Section 36 introduces the new 'education supervision order' which is designed to deal with the specific problem of truancy. Truancy used to be one of the freestanding conditions for a care order under the 1969 Act. The Review and White Paper did not consider it an appropriate use of care proceedings where truancy represented the *sole* reason for seeking to place the child in care. Where in future this is the single cause for concern the new form of order may be sought by a local education authority. It is only where absenteeism from school represents part of a wider family problem that care proceedings will be appropriate. The detailed rules governing supervision orders and education supervision orders are contained in Sch 3.

The remainder of Part IV is concerned with the powers of the court to direct local authorities to investigate a child's circumstances (s 37), to make interim orders (s 38), to discharge or vary care and supervision orders (s 39), to make orders pending appeals in cases involving care and supervision orders (s 40), and to appoint a guardian ad litem for the child (s 41).

2.   The Legal Basis for Care and Supervision Orders

5.6   Section 31 empowers the court to place a child in the care of a designated local authority, or under the supervision of that authority or a probation officer, on the application of any local authority or authorised person (s 31(1)). 'Authorised person' is defined to include the National Society for the Prevention of Cruelty to Children (NSPCC) and any of its officers and any person authorised by order of the Secretary of State to bring proceedings and any officer of a body so authorised (s 31(9)). The NSPCC was the only authorised person or body under the old law and it is named specifically in the Act in recognition of the valuable work of the Society over a large number of years. The old law did also permit the police to commence proceedings where the commission of a criminal offence by the child formed the basis of the application. The 'offence condition' has now been abolished and is, like all the other conditions, subsumed under the new statutory ground. The right of the police to commence proceedings has been abolished along with it. There is no indication at present that any body other than the NSPCC is likely to be authorised to commence proceedings. In the vast majority of cases proceedings will be brought by local authorities who, after all, have the direct responsibility for implementing the orders.

Where the NSPCC (or other 'authorised person') proposes to make an application it is required, where reasonably practicable and before it makes its application, to consult the local authority which appears to it to be the authority in whose area the child is ordinarily resident (s 31(6)). This is clearly intended to avoid duplication in the actions of the Society and the authority where both are concerned and involved with the welfare of the child. To reinforce this the court is precluded from entertaining an application by the Society if, at the time when it is made, the child concerned is the subject of an earlier unconcluded application for a care or supervision order, is already subject to such an order (s 31(7)). Again the purpose is to prevent the Society from cutting across the authority's responsibilities where it is already involved with the protection of the child. There is, of course, nothing to prevent close co-operation between the authority and the Society where the latter has information or evidence which may be of assistance. Indeed it is envisaged that this will often be the case and that co-operation is to be encouraged.

The 'designated authority' in a care order must be the one within whose area the child is ordinarily resident or, where the child does not reside in the area of a local authority, the authority within whose area any circumstances arose in consequence of which the order is being made (s 31(8)).

5.7   The court may not make a care or supervision order in relation to a child who has reached the age of seventeen or a married child who has attained sixteen (s 31(3)). This re-enacts the position under the 1969 Act. It should be recalled that a young person in this age group may *himself* approach the authority with a view to being provided with accommodation (see Chapter 4). The point is that the authority cannot take compulsory action. Before the Act the only course open to an authority wishing to secure compulsory control of a seventeen-year-old was to invoke the inherent jurisdiction of the High Court in wardship. Such an application succeeded in the remarkable case of *Re SW(A Minor) (Wardship: Jurisdiction)* [1986] 1 FLR 24 where an order was made in respect of a seventeen-year-old girl who was found to be beyond the control of her parents. This option has now been removed by s 100(2). Realistically the extent to which older teenagers can be controlled by courts or local authorities is a matter of considerable doubt. The Act recognises this and at the same time upholds the strong libertarian objections which cases like *Re S W* arouse.

5.8 An application under s 31 may be made on its own or in any other family proceedings (s 31(4)). The obvious situation in which care or supervision orders will be made is where the local authority commences proceedings specifically for this purpose. These proceedings, which under the old law were always referred to as 'care proceedings', now fall within the general definition of 'family proceedings' but will no doubt continue to be known by the former description where it is necessary to distinguish them from private family proceedings. Alternatively, an order may be made during the course of these other 'family proceedings'. This broadly corresponds with the power which previously existed to make these orders in divorce, adoption and certain other proceedings. There are, however, two significant modifications. The first is that these orders may now be made in *any* other family proceedings. The former position was that they could only be made in some family proceedings. The new power is potentially very wide bearing in mind the expansive definition of family proceedings (see Chapter 3). The second major change is that where these orders are sought in the course of family proceedings they may only be made if the ground in s 31 is satisfied. The Act, thus, harmonises the basis upon which orders may be made where proceedings are brought with the express purpose of seeking them with the position where they are sought during the course of existing proceedings.

5.9 We now come to the all-important s 31(2) which establishes the new ground for care and supervision orders. It provides:

> 'A court may only make a care order or supervision order if it is satisfied:
> (a) that the child concerned is suffering, or is likely to suffer, significant harm; and
> (b) that the harm, or likelihood of harm, is attributable to:
>   (i) the care given to the child, or likely to be given to him if the order were not made, not being what it would be reasonable to expect a parent to give to him; or
>   (ii) the child's being beyond parental control.'

This single composite ground replaces all the previous independent conditions to which reference has been made. The Review and White Paper had proposed the inclusion of a third element in the new ground to the effect that the order proposed would have to be 'the most effective means available to the court of safeguarding the child's welfare' (White Paper, para 59). It caused surprise in some quarters that this welfare criterion was apparently omitted from the Bill. In fact it was not. The point is that the general principles in Part I apply throughout the Act. The first of these is of course the 'welfare principle' in s 1(1). Section 1(5) also operates to preclude the court from making any order unless it considers it better for the child than not doing so. The cumulative effect of applying these provisions to orders under s 31 is broadly similar to that which was envisaged in the White Paper. As a matter of draftsmanship it might have been better, for the avoidance of doubt, if the welfare element had been specifically written into s 31.

5.10   At this point, any student or practitioner familiar with the old law may be puzzled. It used to be axiomatic that the welfare principle (then embodied in s 1 of the Guardianship of Minors Act 1971) did *not* apply in care proceedings (see particularly the explanation of Dunn J in *Re D(A Minor) (Justices' Decision Review)* [1977] Fam. 158 where he contrasts the position in care and wardship proceedings). It was a point which every teacher of family law drilled into every student of that subject. Moreover, the Review and White Paper specifically rejected a broad welfare criterion as the basis for care orders since it was feared that this would lead to widely varying and subjective interpretations and would not protect the family against unwarranted state intervention. How then can it possibly be that the principles in s 1 apply to care orders under s 31?

The answer is that they only come into the court's calculation *after the minimum conditions of s 31 are satisfied*. In other words, the court cannot make a care or supervision order just because it is convinced that the welfare of the child demands this. The statutory threshold must be crossed as an initial hurdle. Having cleared this, however, it is not inevitable that the court will feel that a care or supervision order is the best course to take. Parents may be willing to cooperate voluntarily with the authority. Perhaps they will agree to the child being looked after by it. In these circumstances the principles in s 1 will come into play and the court may decide that it would be better to make no order at all.

To recap, the precise relevance of the child's welfare in court proceedings is a matter of utmost importance. It is a highly sophisticated issue and to state baldly that the welfare principle in s 1 applies to Care and Supervision orders is unduly simplistic if not positively misleading. The relationship between s 1 and s 31 is a crucial aspect of the legislation and must be clearly understood.

5.11   The constituent elements of s 31(2) are charged with ambiguities and are bound to give rise to litigation. The attitude taken by the courts is likely to play a large part in determining whether the decision to curtail wardship is a success or a failure. If the ground is interpreted restrictively authorities may find themselves unable to act to protect children who might in the past have been made wards of court for this purpose. On the other hand a liberal interpretation will mean that authorities are more likely to be convinced that the reformed legislation really has rendered wardship redundant. We must now attempt a preliminary exploration of some of the more difficult issues inherent in the new ground.

5.12 Perhaps the most significant change is that it will now be possible for authorities to seek orders on the strength of *apprehended* harm to the child before any identifiable harm has yet been suffered. It was naturally the case that a prediction of what was likely to happen to a child in the future was an important element in the court's decision about whether to make a care or supervision order. But it had been decided that orders could not be made *solely* because of a perceived risk of future harm to the child (*Essex County Council v TLR and KBR (Minors)* (1978) 8 Fam. Law 15). The single most difficult scenario was the situation of the new-born baby who, while yet under hospital care, could only with difficulty be said to fall within the condition in s 1(2)(*a*) of the 1969 Act. Almost by definition, it could not be said that his health or development was *at that time* being avoidably impaired or neglected. Nonetheless, social services might be acutely worried about the child's well being if allowed to leave hospital with parents having a known propensity for abuse or neglect. The House of Lords did manage to stretch the language of the 1969 Act to cover the case of an infant born with drug-withdrawal symptoms derived from an addicted mother (*D (A Minor) v Berkshire County Council* [1987] 1 All ER 20). It did so by an imaginative and liberal interpretation which brought within the Act consideration of the past, present and future development of the child. This continuum was held to be wide enough to embrace maternal neglect of the unborn child by abuse of the mother's own body while pregnant.

This straining of the statutory provisions will no longer be necessary. Should the facts of the *Berkshire* case recur, it will now be possible for the court to make an order based entirely on the risk of harm to the child. In assessing this risk it would be open to the court to have regard to the mother's behaviour during pregnancy. But the days are gone when the court will be *obliged* to have primary regard to past and present conduct.

5.13 One situation in which the court found its hands tied remains unaltered by the Act. This is where the authority is concerned for the welfare of an unborn child. It is not open to the authority to take a 'pre-emptive strike' by obtaining a care order to regulate the mother's conduct in the closing stages of pregnancy. This is because the foetus falls outside the definition of 'child' for the purposes of the Act which means 'a person under the age of eighteen' (s 105(1)). Personhood is only recognised by the law (for example, the criminal law) where the child has an existence independent of that of the mother. It has also been decided by the Court of Appeal that a foetus cannot be made a ward or court (*Re F (In Utero)* [1988] 2 FLR 307).

In any event, even if it could, the authority would now be debarred from wardship by s 100(2). In these circumstances all it can do (if voluntary assistance is spurned) is wait for the child to be born, hoping that the birth is trouble-free, and then take immediate action predicated on the risk of harm to the now-living child.

5.14   The concept of 'harm' is the cornerstone of the new ground. It covers most of what was included in the several conditions under the 1969 Act. 'Harm' is defined as 'ill treatment or the impairment of health or development' (s 31(9)). The Act goes on to define each of these concepts. 'Development' includes 'physical, intellectual, emotional, social or behavioural development.' 'Health' includes 'physical or mental health'. 'Ill-treatment' embraces 'sexual abuse and forms of ill-treatment which are not physical'. The forms of harm encompassed are therefore extremely wide. In short, the concept of harm is sufficiently widely-drawn that it should cover all known forms of abuse or neglect.

5.15   The critical issue is really one of degree rather than kind. How much harm does a child have to suffer before an order can be made? The level required by the Act is 'significant' harm and it is clear that this is a relative notion. Section 31(10) provides:

> 'Where the question of whether harm suffered by a child is significant turns on the child's health or development, his health or development shall be compared with that which could reasonably be expected of a similar child.'

The difficulty in measuring the degree of detriment to a child is one which arises again when trying to assess the standard of care required of parents and we shall return to it in a moment. Suffice it to say at this point that it is not every minor deficiency in the child's health or development which will justify the making of a care order. The deficit or detriment must fall below that which can reasonably be expected for the particular child (see the Review, para 15.14).

5.16   The reference to a 'similar child' is designed to admit the child's subjective characteristics or handicaps as relevant factors in the court's assessment. The short point is that the special care required for some children, for example disabled children, is not required for children who do not have an equivalent disability. There was much debate during the passage of the Bill about the terminology used to express the relative needs of children and, in particular, whether the culture or background of children should be relevant to the court's task. This is better considered when we examine the standard of parental care, in which context the expression 'similar child' has been dropped. In assessing what harm is significant it does seem that Parliament was thinking primarily of the personal *attributes* of particular children rather than their family circumstances.

Before leaving the issue of 'harm' a word should be said about the assessment of 'likely' harm. Again, a relative test has to be applied. It is not every risk of harm which will justify an order. It is only those risks which are unacceptable. In deciding whether this is so, it is envisaged that the court will need to balance the chance of the harm occurring against the magnitude of that harm if it does occur (White Paper, para 60).

5.17　The second element in the new ground is a causative one. It must be shown that the harm or likelihood of harm to the child is attributable to an unacceptable standard of upbringing (s 31(2)(*b*)(i)) *or* to the child being beyond parental control (s 31(2)(*b*)(ii)). We must look at each of these alternatives in turn.

(i)　Parental upbringing

5.18　The first alternative is concerned with the standard of upbringing. Whatever degree of harm the child is suffering or likely to suffer, no order may be made unless this situation has been brought about by the standard of care 'not being what it would be reasonable to expect a parent to give him'. This phrase is the result of an amendment to meet objections to the original wording in the Bill which, as indicated above, made reference to a 'similar child'. It is clear that the original intention behind the inclusion of that phrase was to enable the particular attributes of the child (in the sense of physical, mental or emotional characteristics) to be taken into account in order to facilitate a comparison between the situation of the particular child before the court and other children with like characteristics. Again, the underlying objective was to strike a balance between the conflicting pressures of ensuring that state interference with family life should only occur in carefully defined circumstances and allowing this intervention where it was demonstrated that significant or likely harm could be traced to a perceptible deficiency in parental care (see Lord Mackay LC, *House of Lords, Official Report*, 19 January 1989, col 355). There was, nonetheless, a groundswell of opinion which felt that the original provision was ambiguous in that it did not make it clear whether cultural considerations and the social background of the child should be taken into account. There was also a division of opinion on whether this would be desirable.

5.19　On one view the state should demand the same minimum standard of care for children from impoverished backgrounds as it does for those from well-to-do backgrounds. It should also demand the same standards from the ethnic minorities as it does from parents forming part of the indigenous population. The opposing view is that some account should be taken of cultural pluralism and social inequality. The argument is that it is not reasonable to measure the standard of care by reference to some abstract ideal without also making some allowance for the different traditions of various communities and the greater difficulties faced by families suffering economic hardship.

It seems that the 'attributes' approach has won the day. The test in s 31(2)(b)(i) requires the court to have regard to the standard of care which it would be reasonable to expect a parent to give to the *child before it*, bearing in mind the child's particular needs according to *his* personal attributes. The court's focus of attention is to be on the needs of the child in question. The statutory formula is intended to avoid the problems inherent in making comparisons with hypothetical children and of listing specific attributes which might not be exhaustive (see Lord Mackay LC, *House of Lords, Official Report*, 16 March 1989, col 392). Despite this emphasis on the subjective characteristics of the child concerned it appears that the test of the parental standard of care is an *objective* one. The court must ask itself what it would have been *reasonable* to expect this parent to give this child and consider whether the parent in fact measured up to this standard.

5.20   It may yet be too early to discount altogether the cultural background or family circumstances of the child. This is because in deciding ultimately whether or not to make an order the court must apply the principles in s 1. In so doing it is bound to have regard to the checklist of factors in s 1(3). Section 1(3)(d) incorporates a reference to the 'background' of the child. It may, therefore, be that social and cultural considerations applying to the family's circumstances are to be disregarded in considering whether the minimum threshold conditions are satisfied but must be thrown into the balance when considering what is the best course of action to take.

It is interesting to speculate on what might be the outcome of a case like *Alhaji Mohammed v Knott* [1969] 1 QB 1 under the new law. That was a case which concerned the 'moral danger' condition under the 1969 Act. The Divisional Court took the view that a 13-year-old Nigerian girl could not be in moral danger where she was engaging in sexual relations with her husband to whom she was validly married under Nigerian law. It was accepted by the court that a girl of the same age, brought up in the English way of life, could have been in moral danger in these circumstances but that it was not permissible to apply the same standards to a Nigerian girl by ignoring her way of life and that of her husband. Would such a girl now be suffering significant harm under s 31 and would a parent be acting reasonably in allowing her to go through a ceremony of marriage at her age? If her ethnic background is to be ignored the answer must surely be that this is an unacceptable way of life for a 13-year-old. Indeed, marriage and sexual relations with a girl of this age (leaving aside the domicile factor) are prohibited by English law. At the second stage, however, the court would need to consider carefully whether the right course of action would be to make an order plucking the girl from her 'matrimonial' home and placing her in care.

(ii)   Parental control

5.21   The second alternative element in the new ground applies where the harm or likelihood of harm to the child is attributable to his being beyond parental control. By itself, the state of being beyond parental control was one of the freestanding conditions under the 1969 Act. In this previous incarnation it might accurately have been described as a 'status offence' and open to the libertarian objection that it sanctioned compulsory or coercive action against the child for non-criminal misbehaviour. This objection has at least been watered-down by the Act since it is no longer possible for a child to be taken into care on this basis unless the parental lack of control is accompanied by evidence of harm or likely harm to the child as a result. Nonetheless there is bound to exist a degree of tension between the principle that the state is empowered to 'control' children for their own benefit and the *Gillick* principles, recognised in other provisions in the Act. These would suggest that children depending on their age and maturity are entitled to behave contrary to parental wishes provided that they stay within the law.

5.22 The final stage in the court's adjudication process is to apply s 1 and consider whether an order is the most effective means of promoting the child's welfare. The importance of this stage is to direct the court's attention to all the available options which include a care order, supervision order or no order at all. It may decide not to make an order if compulsory measures are considered unnecessary. In order to enable the court to make an informed choice it will be essential for the authority to give it some idea of its general plans for the child. It is expected that the amount of detail in the projected plan will vary from case to case depending on how far it is possible for the authority to foresee what will be in the child's future interests (White Paper, para 60).

3. Avoidance of Delay and the Statutory Timetable

5.23 Section 32, together with s 1(2), obliges the court when hearing an application for an order under Part IV, viz. a care, supervision or contract order under s 34 to have regard to the general principle that any delay in disposing of the application is likely to prejudice the welfare of the child concerned. Again, the court must draw up a timetable with a view to disposing of the application without delay. There is provision for rules of court to impose more specific requirements to this end. The provisions of s 32 are identical to those in s 11 which govern s 8 orders and there is nothing to be gained by repeating what was said in Chapter 3 about the background to these provisions.

An attempt was made in Parliament to introduce an amendment which would have given the court a power to adjourn care proceedings specifically to direct attempts at a phased rehabilitation of parent and child. The juvenile court's inability to give such a direction was one of the defects of the 1969 Act which led for a short time to the successful use of wardship to achieve this purpose (see *Re J (A Minor)* [1984] 1 WLR 81). This attempt was resisted because adjournments cause delays and it was thought that this would be inconsistent with the policy of legislation to reduce these.

4. Care Orders

(a) Legal effects of a care order

5.24 Section 33 spells out the legal effects of a care order. We saw that these were uncertain under the old law. What was clear was that under the 1969 Act the juvenile court had no power to give directions to the authority regarding the plan for the child when in care. Where the child was committed to care in wardship or divorce proceedings it was equally clear that these courts *did* have the power to direct the authority. They might, for example, direct a programme of phased rehabilitation where this was not a course proposed by any of the parties (see *Re E (SA)(A Minor)(Wardship)* [1984] 1 All ER 289). They might direct a particular placement or order that a particular social worker be allocated to the child's case. The Act abolishes this power of the court to give directions. The purpose is to channel responsibility for the child to the authority and let it take a grip on the case by making firm and early decisions without the temptation of passing responsibility to another body (Review, para 2.24).

5.25 The crucial provision is s 33(3) which provides:

> 'While a care order is in force with respect to a child, the local authority designated by the order shall:
> (a) have parental responsibility for the child; and
> (b) have the power (subject to the following provisions of this section) to determine the extent to which a parent or guardian of the child may meet his parental responsibility for him.'

Since the authority has parental responsibility by virtue of the care order it has the right to retain the child's care and the power to determine all matters of upbringing except those which are specifically withheld from its control by s 33 (see below). Unlike its position where it is merely looking after a child, it does not have to rely on parental delegation of these powers. But this is only one side of the coin. The other is that parents remain parents even where a care order is made. They retain their parental responsibility and do not lose it simply because the authority also acquires it (s 2(5) and (6) and see Chapter 2). The effect is therefore that parental responsibility is *shared* between the authority and the parents (or a non-parent with parental responsibility prior to the order).

5.26 What does this sharing entail from a practical point of view? The position has now changed as a result of a Commons' amendment which arose from anxiety that parents might exercise their responsibility in a way which could undermine the authority's plans for the child. We shall come to this shortly. Prima facie, the effect of joint parental responsibility is that parents retain their voice in matters of upbringing and may also exercise parental responsibility when the child is allowed to be with them. This is not unlike the position of a non-residential parent on divorce. There is, however, a significant difference. The non-residential parent has no right of consultation on matters of upbringing. This is not so where a child is in care. It must be remembered that the duties of local authorities to children being looked after by them apply as much to those in care as to those accommodated under voluntary arrangements. Accordingly, the authority must consult with the same people, including parents, as it is obliged to consult under voluntary arrangements. It must also give due consideration to their views (see Chapter 4).

5.27 If parents have shared parental responsibility with the authority what is there to stop them physically removing the child from care? The answer is to be found by reading s 33(1) with s 2(8). The former provision states that one effect of a care order is to require the authority to receive the child into its care and to keep him in its care while the order remains in force. The corresponding provision in the 1980 Act specifically required the authority to keep the child in its care 'notwithstanding any claim by his parent or guardian' (s 10(1)). These words have been omitted from the new legislation but it is clear that no change in this effect of a care order was intended. Although parents retain their parental responsibility they may not act in any way which would be incompatible with an order under the Act (s 2(8)). Removal of the child would be incompatible with the care order given the duty of the authority to accommodate the child and retain his care during the subsistence of the order.

5.28 What if the authority allows the child 'home on trial'? While the child is physically under the authority's control, whether in institutional or foster care, the parental decision-making capacity which goes hand in hand with parental responsibility will amount in practical terms to little more than a right of consultation. But where the child is allowed home, prima facie, parents may discharge or exercise parental responsibility to the full. We noted that this normally includes the power of independent action (see Chapter 2). There was anxiety in Parliament that a parent could choose to exercise responsibility in a way which would be contrary to the wishes of the authority. He would be entitled to do so despite the authority's objections. The Bill was accordingly amended to make it clear that, although parental responsibility is shared in care cases the local authority must be in the driving seat 'to enable it to carry out its statutory duties'. The authority is given the power to control the *exercise* of parental responsibility by parents in a way which might undermine its own decision, for example relating to placement or education. It may, thus, determine the extent to which a parent may meet his parental responsibility for the child (s 33(3)(*b*)).

At the same time it is envisaged that this power will be exercised very sparingly and only where there is likely to be a clear conflict between the authority and a parent. Thus, the authority may only exercise this power where it is satisfied that it is necessary to do so in order to safeguard or promote the child's welfare (s 33(4)). Moreover, even where the power is exercised, it will not prevent a parent or guardian who has physical care of a child in care from doing what is reasonable in all the circumstances for the purpose of safeguarding or promoting his welfare (s 33(5)).

5.29   Where a care order has been made following an application by an authorised person (currently only the NSPCC), but the authority designated by the order was not notified of the application, the child may be kept in the care of the authorised person until received into the care of the authority (s 33(2)). This is obviously to prevent a hiatus in parental responsibility for the child. The situation should not occur very often in view of the duty of consultation with the authority which the Act places on the authorised person (s 31(6)).

5.30   The parental responsibility which an authority acquires under a care order is not quite as extensive in a number of respects as that which vests in parents. There are certain matters relating to a child which are considered sufficiently fundamental that they should not be under the control of the authority but should continue to be decided by parents or by order of the court. Three of these matters apply equally to other non-parents who have acquired parental responsibility by court order. They are the right to consent or refuse to consent to an application to free the child for adoption, to an adoption order itself and the right to appoint a guardian. The Act makes it clear that the authority does not acquire these rights under a care order (s 33(6)(*b*)) (cf the position of non-parents discussed in Chapter 3).

5.31   Additionally, the authority must not 'cause the child to be brought up in any religious persuasion other than that in which he would have been brought up if the order had not been made' (s 33(6)(*a*)). This re-enacts s 10(3) of the 1980 Act. The effect is to prevent the authority from changing the child's religion of its own motion. It is not necessarily precluded from doing so, it would seem, where *the child himself* requests the change and the authority considers it to be in his best interests. In arriving at such a decision the authority would be obliged to ascertain the wishes and feelings of the child and those of his parents or other person with parental responsibility and give due consideration to them.

5.32   There are restrictions on changing the child's name and removing him from the U.K. which correspond with those which apply where a residence order is made (s 33(7) and see Chapter 3). Neither of these steps may be taken by any person in relation to a child 'in care' without either the written consent of every person who has parental responsibility for the child or the leave of the court. Again the restriction on taking the child out of the country does not apply where this is for a period of less than one month (s 33(8)(*a*)). More significantly, perhaps, it does not apply to arrangements made by the authority for the child to live outside England and Wales under para 19 of Sch 2 (discussed in Chapter 4).

(b) Parental contact with children in care

5.33 Undoubtedly the single most important legal issue regarding a child in care is whether he should have contact, and if so how much, with his parents and other individuals. It is generally acknowledged that the child's eventual rehabilitation with his family is largely dependent on the quality and frequency of contact especially in the early stages of care. It was a major bone of contention that until 1983 parents and others interested in a child in care had no legal means of challenging access decisions by local authorities. In that year, largely as a result of European pressure as well as pressure at home, Parliament amended the 1980 Act to create a procedure for disputing access decisions in the juvenile court (see s 12A to G of the 1980 Act, introduced by s 6 and Sch 1 to the Health and Social Services and Social Security Adjudications Act 1983). The essential features were that an authority intending to refuse or terminate access was obliged to serve a formal notice on a parent, guardian or custodian of the child. This decision could then be challenged in the juvenile court by the person affected within six months. On the application the court had power to grant an order for access and could define this where necessary. The child's welfare was expressed to be the 'first and paramount' consideration. Either the parent (or other qualifying applicant) or the local authority could apply at a later stage to vary or discharge the order. An order might be suspended for seven days in an emergency where a magistrate was satisfied that the continuance of access would put the child's welfare seriously at risk. The Act also provided for a code of practice which laid down the principles of good practice for local authorities in promoting and maintaining access and in taking decisions about refusing or terminating it.

5.34 Section 34 takes the place of these provisions and constitutes the new code governing contact decisions. A number of points need to be emphasised at the outset. The first is that s 34 only applies to children in care. It does not apply to those being voluntarily accommodated. In the latter situation any challenge to the authority would have to be made by seeking a s 8 order, probably a contact order. The second point is that the authority is, irrespective of s 34, under a general duty to promote contact between all children being looked after by it and their families (Sch 2, para 15, discussed in Chapter 4). Section 34 is concerned primarily with providing a judicial procedure for resolving disputes about whether the authority is properly discharging its duties to promote and allow contact. The third point is that although the new section is seeking to achieve similar aims to the 1980 Act there are some very significant changes to the previous scheme. This is one area in which authorities are going to be subject to greater judicial scrutiny than has ever been the case before. There is some concern that the opening up of contact decisions to the courts may inhibit the authority in making positive plans for the child and may increase the pressure of court work.

5.35   Section 34(1) introduces the first major innovation by enacting a presumption of reasonable contact. It requires the authority to allow the child 'reasonable contact' with his parents, any guardian or person in whose favour a residence order was in force immediately before the care order was made or person who had the care of the child under an order made in the exercise of the High Court's inherent jurisdiction (usually in wardship proceedings). The change of terminology from 'access' to 'contact' mirrors the change in s 8. The duty to allow contact is qualified by s 34(6) which empowers the authority to refuse contact which would otherwise be required where:

> '(a)   they are satisfied that it is necessary to do so in order to safeguard or promote the child's welfare; and
> (b)   the refusal:
>   (i)   is decided upon as a matter or urgency; and
>   (ii) does not last for more than seven days.'

This is essentially the same basis upon which a magistrate might suspend an access order under the old law.

The broad effect of these provisions is, therefore, to create a presumption of reasonable contact which approximates to the presumption of reasonable access which, although not articulated by statute, has operated for many years in private disputes between parents (see the Review, para 21.1, and Chapter 3 generally). The presumption will only be displaced where the authority is satisfied that contact should be withheld as a matter of urgency in order to protect the child.

5.36   The limited categories of these entitled to the presumption of contact should be noted. They include the unmarried father since s 34(1) applies to all 'parents' and not just those with parental responsibility. On the other hand they do not extend to grandparents, siblings, uncles or aunts or other members of the extended family. Before leaping to criticise this omission it should be said that the general duty of the authority to promote and maintain contact between the child and his family should extend to these wider relatives since they should fall within the meaning of 'any other person connected with him' in para 15(1)(*c*) of Sch 2. Further, such persons may with *leave* apply to the court for a contact order where they are not happy with existing arrangements (discussed below).

It must be said, however, that these rights are not as concrete as those generated by s 34(1). That provision has the effect of placing the authority under a specific duty towards equally specific qualifying individuals. If the authority wishes to depart from this, the onus is on it to go to court and get the court's authorisation for doing so. This is quite different from the more vague obligation under Schedule 2. Furthermore, the onus to bring disputes concerning contact before the court is clearly on the relatives rather than on the authority.

5.37 Where the authority wishes to refuse contact between the child and one of the persons mentioned in s 34(1) it must obtain the court's authorisation. On an application for this purpose, or when the court initially makes the care order, the court may authorise refusal of contact with any person (s 34(4) and (5)). As we have seen, the authority may refuse contact in an emergency for up to seven days (s 34(6)) but thereafter it must obtain the court's authorisation if it wishes to continue to prohibit contact.

It should be said that this scheme represents a very distinct shift of emphasis from the pre-Act position. Under the previous law the authority was obliged to give notice of intended refusals or terminations of access but there was nothing to prevent it from imposing them in the first instance. The onus was on the aggrieved parent to bring proceedings before the juvenile court. The 1989 Act, in contrast, imposes *automatic* restraints and places the onus squarely on the authority to justify its proposed restrictions on contract to the court.

5.38 Where a parent or someone else having a connection with a child in care is dissatisfied with the amount of contact which he is being allowed by the authority, an application may be made to the court for an order defining contact (s 34(3)). Those qualified to make an application without leave are:

(a) anyone entitled to reasonable contact under s 34(1);
(b) the authority; and
(c) the child (s 34(2) and (3)).

The purpose of allowing the authority itself to make an application would appear to be to enable it to resolve disputes over contact without having to wait for a parent or other individual to commence proceedings. It may be advantageous to the authority to ascertain the precise extent of its legal obligations where parents or others are interfering with its attempts to make positive plans for a child. The court may make such order as it considers appropriate regarding contact between the child and any named person.

5.39 Applications under the 1980 Act could only be made where the authority refused or terminated access. It was not possible to apply on the basis that the amount of access allowed was inadequate. The authority might curtail drastically the amount of access allowed and it was expressly provided that it was not to be taken to have terminated access where it proposed to substitute new arrangements for existing arrangements (s 12B(4) of the 1980 Act). This was a serious defect which diluted considerably the principle of judicial control. Authorities were not subject to any control in making major restrictions on access usually with a view to phasing it out altogether and paving the way from long-term substitute care or adoption. It was this kind of action which led to abortive challenges in wardship. The leading case of *A v Liverpool City Council* [1982] AC 363 was just such a case. Here the mother's access had been reduced to one hourly supervised visit per month at a day nursery. The Act opens up authorities' decisions to much greater examination. It will now always be open to a qualified applicant to test the reasonableness of the amount of contact allowed by asking the court to review this and define it. The court may then specify the time, place and frequency of contact.

5.40 So far we have been considering those entitled to apply for contact without leave. The Act also allows applications to be brought by *any person* who obtains the leave of the court (s 34(3)(*b*)). This is very widely drawn and obviously extends to relatives but also to anyone else who can convince the court that he has a genuine interest in the child. The all-important question in practice is going to be the attitude taken by the courts to the leave requirement. Well intentioned relatives should not find it a difficult hurdle to surmount since its purpose is simply to act as a filter to prevent unmeritorious applications. It is arguable that relatives should have had an automatic right to apply but the requirement of leave was thought to be necessary to prevent applications becoming a 'free for all'. An important and influential policy consideration was the perceived need to allow the authority to get on with the job of planning the child's future and putting its plans into effect without being constantly harassed by applications from outsiders with different views of what is best for the child. These concerns are also behind s 91(17) which prohibits a further application under s 34 within six months of the refusal of a previous application without the leave of the court. This applies equally to applications for orders varying or discharging the original order. It does not apply to applications by the authority itself presumably on the basis that if the authority is seeking the court's assistance this should always be made available.

5.41 The Act gives the court flexible powers when defining or authorising the refusal of contact to impose such conditions as it thinks appropriate (s 34(7)). It may also vary or discharge any s 34 order on the application of the authority, the child or the person named in the order (s 34(9)). It may make a contact order either at the same time as the care order itself or later (s 34(10)). The provision for a contact order to be made contemporaneously with placing the child in care should be considered alongside s 34(11). This requires the court, before making any care order, to:

   (a) consider the arrangements which the authority has made, or proposes to make, for affording any person contact with a child; and
   (b) invite the parties to comment on those arrangements.

The intention here is to encourage parents and others to reach an initial agreement with the authority about contact arrangements. If this proves possible the court may not be called upon to make an order under s 34. There may also be a greater chance that a subsequent application will not arise since areas of potential disagreement may have been effectively removed. In any event the authority will need to present its plans for the child to the court before it decides to make a care order. Arrangements for contact with members of the family and other interested individuals ought to be an important element in these plans. The emphasis, as always, is on the voluntary partnership between parents and the authority where it is possible to achieve this.

Finally, there is provision for the Secretary of State to make regulations (s 34(8)). These may govern, inter alia, steps to be taken by an authority refusing contact in an emergency, the basis upon which the parties may by agreement depart from the terms of an order allowing or authorising refusal of contact, and notification of any variation or suspension of voluntary contact arrangements (i.e. not made under a court order).

5. Supervision

5.42 Reference has already been made to the distinction between the ordinary form of supervision order and the novel education supervision order which the Act introduces. Section 35 and Parts I and II of Sch 3 govern the former while s 36 and Part III of Sch 3 deal with the latter.

(a) Supervision orders

5.43 As an alternative to a care order the court may make a supervision order (s 31(1)(*b*)). It may also make a supervision order when discharging a care order (s 39(4)). It should be emphasised that the basis for making a supervision order is identical to that for a care order (s 31(2)). It was felt that nothing less than this could justify compulsory state intervention even at the lower level of supervision (Review, para 18.18).

The making of a supervision order automatically terminates any earlier care or supervision order (Sch 3, para 10). Supervision orders, like care orders, last until the child attains eighteen unless brought to an end earlier (s 91(12) and (13)). In the first instance an order will last for one year (Sch 3, para 6(1)). The court may extend this on the application of the supervisor for a period of up to three years from the date on which it was made (Sch 3, para 6(3) and (4)). The purpose of the initial time limit is to preserve court scrutiny of the workings of the order.

5.44 The Act recasts the duties of the supervisor (s 35(1)). It reiterates the general duty to advise, assist and befriend the supervised child, but it goes on to create two additional duties. The first is to take such steps as are reasonably necessary to give effect to the order. The second is to consider whether or not to apply for variation or discharge of the order. This duty arises where the order is not wholly complied with or where the supervisor considers that the order may no longer be necessary. These two additional duties are designed to prevent an unsatisfactory situation from drifting. This could happen under the old law where the duty of the supervisor was rather vague and generalised. Supervisors will now be required in law to keep the effectiveness of the order under review and take positive action where the order is proving ineffective.

All other matters relating to supervision are consigned to Sch 3. The following is a summary of these provisions concentrating on those which represent a change in the law.

5.45   Paragraph 2 specifies the powers which the order may confer on the supervisor to give directions to the supervised child. They include directing where the child is to live for specified periods, requiring the child to present himself to a named person or to participate in specified activities at particular times. It is for the supervisor and not the court to decide whether, and to what extent, directions should be given to the child and it is for him to determine at his discretion what they should be in any individual case. This was broadly the position under the 1969 Act.

5.46   Paragraph 3 empowers the court for the first time to impose obligations on any 'responsible person'. This expression is defined in paragraph 1 to include any person with parental responsibility for the child and any other person with whom the child is living. The most obvious category will be parents. It must be said at once that these requirements may only be imposed *with the consent* of the responsible person concerned. Prima facie, it might seem contradictory that the court should be given power to impose requirements only with consent. Yet the essence of supervision is that this sort of order depends for its effectiveness on the degree of cooperation between the supervisor and the family. The child's consent is not required except in relation to psychiatric and medical examinations (see below).

5.47   A supervision order may require the responsible person:

(a)   to take all reasonable steps to ensure that the supervised child complies with any direction given by the supervisor;

(b)   to take all reasonable steps to ensure that the child complies with any requirement in the order concerning psychiatric or medical examination or treatment; and

(c)   to comply with any directions given by the supervisor requiring him to attend at a specified place to take part in specified activities (para 3(1)).

The order may also require any responsible person to keep the supervisor informed of his address where it differs from the child's (para 3(3)). The purpose of these requirements is to prevent supervision being frustrated by the parents or other adults with the care of the child. Without them, it is possible that the supervisor might be refused access to the child or a parent might refuse to allow the medical examination of the child. Requirement (c) above is designed to secure the more active participation of parents in specified activities such as classes in child care or mother and toddler groups. Paragraph 8 provides that a supervision order may require the child to keep the supervisor informed of any change in his address and to allow the supervisor to visit him at the place where he is living. Comparable duties are placed on the responsible person who must inform the supervisor of the child's address where this is requested and is known to him and must allow the supervisor reasonable contact with the child where he is living with him.

5.48 Paragraph 7 limits the duration of any directions which may be given to the child or to a responsible person. The total number of days during which either may be required to comply with directions must not exceed ninety days or a lesser number specified in the order. In arriving at this calculation any days in which directions in the order were not complied with may be disregarded.

5.49 Paragraphs 4 and 5 relate to psychiatric and medical examinations and treatment respectively.

Under s 12(4) of the 1969 Act supervision orders could require the child to submit to psychiatric treatment. The 1989 Act expands the powers of the court to enable it to require the child to submit also to medical treatment. The order may require the child to submit to a medical or psychiatric *examination* or to do so from time to time as directed by the supervisor (para 4(1)). The examination must be carried out by or under the direction of a registered medical practitioner specified in the order (para 4(2)). The court may also include a requirement that the child submit to psychiatric or medical *treatment*. It can only do so on the evidence of a registered medical practitioner (para 5(1)). In the case of psychiatric treatment a practitioner approved for the purposes of the Mental Health Act 1983 must take the view that the mental condition of the child requires and may be susceptible to treatment but is not such as to require the child's detention under an hospital order. With regard to medical treatment there must be the evidence of a practitioner that the physical condition of the child requires and may be susceptible to treatment. The respective examinations and treatment must be carried out by or under the direction of a registered medical practitioner (paras 4(2), 5(2) and 5(4)).

None of these requirements may be included in supervision orders unless the court is satisfied as to two matters. The first is that the child consents to the requirement where he has sufficient understanding to make an informed decision. The second is that satisfactory arrangements have been, or can be, made for the examination or treatment (paras 4(4) and 5(5)).

5.50 The requirement of the child's consent is an interesting one. This provision should be contrasted with others in the Act which merely require the child's wishes to be ascertained and given due consideration. The present requirement operates at a higher level. Provided that the child is able to make an informed decision his wishes are *conclusive*. The court may not include the requirement in these circumstances. The position under the old law was that a requirement relating to psychiatric treatment could not be made in relation to a child who had attained fourteen without his consent.

The Act prefers a test of the individual child's capacity rather than the former arbitrary age-related rule.

(b) Education supervision orders

5.51 Parents have statutory obligations under s 36 of the Education Act 1944 to ensure that their child receives suitable full-time education. They commit an offence under s 37 if they fail to register the child at a school following the service of a school attendance order, and under s 39 if they fail to secure his regular attendance at the school where he is registered. Under s 40(2) of the 1944 Act the authority, as an alternative to prosecuting the parents for these offences, had to consider whether to bring care proceedings instead. A care order might be made under s 1(2)(*e*) of the 1969 Act where it was established that the child was of compulsory school age, was not receiving suitable education and was in need of care and control. It was established by the Court of Appeal in *Re S (A Minor)* [1978] QB 120 that the latter test would be satisfied where the child was not receiving a suitable education even though he was otherwise properly looked after in satisfactory home conditions. The result was that a care order could be made where the only problem was an educational one and the sole purpose of the order was in effect to combat truancy.

5.52 The Review (see paras 12.21 to 12.23) considered that a care order was not appropriate for this limited purpose and that it was not desirable that local education authorities should be qualified applicants in care proceedings. It was in favour of drawing a sharper distinction between cases in which the sole objective was to enforce compliance with the 1944 Act and those in which absence from school formed part of a wider risk to the child's immediate or long-term welfare.

In the former instance it recommended that care orders should not be available and that instead the local education authority should apply for an 'education supervision order'. This would be binding on the child and his parents and for the limited purpose of ensuring that the child attended school. The proceedings would be distinct from care proceedings and the order could be made simply on proof of non-compliance with a school attendance order or failure to secure the child's regular attendance at school. The more complex 'harm' condition for a care or ordinary supervision order would not have to be proved. In the latter instance, where truancy was symptomatic of some wider social problem, a care order would continue to be available provided that the statutory ground was proved. It was considered that the proper applicant here should be the local authority's social services department since it would have responsibility for implementing the order. At the same time the hope was expressed that there would continue to be co-operation between the education and social services departments of local authorities in such cases.

5.53 The Act gives effect to these recommendations. The truancy condition has been swept away along with the other freestanding conditions and *Re S* has been impliedly overruled.

The court may make an education supervision order (ESO) on the application of a local education authority (s 36(1)). The effect is to put the child under the supervision of a designated local education authority. This will be the authority within whose area the child is living or will live or, where the child is a registered pupil at a school, the authority within whose area the school is situated provided that the two authorities agree to this (s 36(7)). Before making an application the local education authority is required to consult the social services committee of the appropriate authority (s 36(8)). The appropriate authority is any authority which is accommodating the child, or in any other case, the authority within whose area the child lives or will live (s 36(9)).

5.54 The court may make an ESO on the sole ground that the child is of compulsory school age and is not being properly educated (s 36(3)). A child is properly educated for these purposes only if he is receiving full-time education suitable to his age, ability and aptitude and any special educational needs he may have (s 36(4)). These two provisions together re-enact the condition in s 1(2)(*e*) of the 1969 Act but without the care and control test. Where there has been a breach of a school attendance order under s 37 of the 1944 Act or failure to attend school regularly as required by s 39, it will be assumed that the child is not being properly educated unless the contrary is proved (s 36(5)). The parental duty under s 36 of the 1944 Act is to educate their child 'either by regular attendance at school or otherwise'. Some parents choose to educate their child at home and might be able to resist an ESO on this basis. It is unlikely that many such attempts would succeed since the local education authority would be certain to challenge the adequacy of the education offered outside school. The onus will be on the parent to rebut the legal presumption that failure to secure the child's attendance at school amounts to a breach of the statutory obligations.

An ESO may not be made where the child is in the care of a local authority (s 36(6)). In these circumstances the authority will itself be responsible for ensuring the proper education of the child.

5.55 Part III of Sch 3 contains the details relating to ESOs. Many of the provisions are analogous to those which apply to ordinary supervision orders but adapted to reflect the specific educational context in which the ESOs apply.

The supervisor is to advise, assist and befriend, and give directions to the child, his parents and in such a way as will in his opinion secure that the child is properly educated (para 12). Before giving any directions, the supervisor is required to ascertain the wishes and feelings of the child and his parents, particularly as regards the place at which the child should be educated, and give due consideration to them. The child's age and understanding is as usual, to be taken into account.

While an ESO is in force the statutory duties of parents under ss 36 and 39 of the 1944 Act are superseded by their duty to comply with any directions made by the supervisor (para 13). Likewise, an ESO will bring about the automatic termination of any existing school attendance orders and will render inapplicable to the child the statutory provisions governing school attendance (1944 Act, s 37), parental wishes (1944 Act, s 76) and parental preference and appeal against admission decisions (ss 6 and 7 of the Education Act 1980).

5.56 Initially, an ESO (like an ordinary supervision order) runs for one year with the possibility of an extension or more than one extension for a period of up to three years. No application for an extension may be made earlier than three months before the expiration of the original order. The order will terminate on the child attaining school-leaving age or if a care order is made (para 15).

The court may discharge an ESO on the application of the child, his parent, or the local education authority concerned. In doing so it may direct the local authority within whose area the child lives or will live, to investigate his circumstances (para 17).

Where a parent persistently fails to comply with a direction in an ESO he commits an offence unless he can show that he took all reasonable steps to comply with it, that the direction itself was unreasonable, or that in certain circumstances he had complied with other directions in an ordinary supervision order (para 18). Where there has been a persistent failure on the part of the child to comply with the directions in an ESO, the LEA must notify the appropriate local authority which is then obliged to investigate the child's circumstances (para 19).

6.   Other Powers of the Court

(a)   Directions to investigate

5.57 We noted above that the power of the courts in family proceedings to give directions to a local authority concerning the treatment of a child committed to its care by them has been removed by the Act. Section 37, however, gives the court a new power in any family proceedings to direct an authority to investigate the circumstances of a child. This reflects the general policy orientation of the reforms that the final decision on whether to seek care or supervision orders should (with the exception of the NSPCC) rest solely with local authorities. At the same time it was recognised by the Law Commission that there would occasionally be circumstances in which the court, in the course of family proceedings, might feel that a care application would be appropriate. While it would not be right for the court to direct the authority to apply for an order which it might not want, it would be appropriate for the court to direct the authority to investigate the child's case. (Report No.172, paras 5.4 to 5.5). This is in line with another important feature of the reforms which is the need to strengthen the investigative duties of local authorities (see Chapter 6). Section 37 allows the court to take the lead in triggering the authority's investigations where it is concerned for the well-being of a child before it. Although this power applies in any family proceedings we are clearly concerned here with those in which a care or supervision order is not sought since, ex hypothesi, where such orders are sought the authority will already have investigated the child's circumstances.

5.58 The court may make a direction in any family proceedings in which a question arises as to the welfare of a child and it appears to the court that it may be appropriate for a care or supervision order to be made (s 37(1)). The court has a complete discretion and there is no question of it being obliged to direct an investigation. If, however, it does decide to do so, the authority concerned is obliged to comply with the direction. The authority must also specifically investigate whether it should:

(i)   apply for a care or supervision order;
(ii)   provide services or assistance for the child or his family; or
(iii)   take any other action with respect to the child (s 37(2)).

5.59 If, following its investigation, the authority decides not to apply for a care or supervision order it must inform the court of:

(i)   the reasons for its decision;
(ii)   any service or assistance which it has provided or intends to provide for the child and his family; and
(iii)   any other action which it has taken or proposes to take in relation to the child (s 37(3)).

It must do so within eight weeks beginning with the date of the court's direction unless the court otherwise directs (s 37(4)). The authority must also apply its mind to whether it should review the child's case at a later date and, if so, determine the date on which the review is to begin. This duty applies at the conclusion of the authority's initial investigation and after any subsequent review (s 37(6)).

5.60 In conducting its investigations the authority will have to consider a number of options. In particular, it will have to reach a view on whether compulsory intervention is necessary or whether the child's welfare can be adequately protected by voluntary arrangements or forms of assistance dependent on the cooperation of the person or persons with parental responsibility. The eight-week timetable for reporting back to the court is consistent with the Act's other provisions which aim at eliminating delay and with the usual period for an interim care order.

5.61 Where the court disagrees with the authority's view that an order should not be sought there is nothing that it can do. It cannot make a compulsory order of its own motion or direct that one should be sought. It is just entitled to be informed that the authority does not intend to bring proceedings for a care or supervision order (or, indeed, take any action at all). This inability of the court to act of its own volition may be seen by some as a potentially serious defect in the legislation which reposes too much faith in authorities and attaches too little importance to the court's protective role. This is compounded by the restriction on the use of the wardship jurisdiction. The basic policy of the Act is nonetheless that final responsibility for these matters should rest with authorities and not the courts.

(b) Interim orders

5.62 A three-stage procedure has traditionally been followed by local authorities wishing to intervene compulsorily in the family. This has been to apply for a place of safety order (see Chapter 6), follow this with one or more interim care orders and, finally, obtain a full care order. The law and practice relating to interim care orders was considered defective in several important respects (see generally the Review, Chapter 17 and *R v Birmingham Juvenile Court, ex parte P and S* [1984] FLR 343).

First, although the duration of each interim care order was limited to twenty-eight days, successive orders might be made. Thus the *maximum* length of interim care was unlimited. Research conducted by the University of Bristol disclosed disturbing evidence of protracted delays occasioned by the excessive use of interim orders. It showed that in 63% of cases studied there were at least two interim orders, in 38% at least three, in 10% four and in one case fourteen such orders (Review, para 17.2). These practices could not stand with the concern to eliminate delay and procrastination in providing for the care of children.

Secondly, there were no standardised grounds for interim orders and this led to considerable variation in what courts required. In general it had to be shown that a prima facie case for a care order was made out but this criterion was criticised as imprecise (Review, para 17.7).

Thirdly, despite the obvious importance of such orders in sanctioning state intervention in family life, they could be made by a single justice without adequate opportunity for parents and others affected to be heard (Review, para 17.11).

5.63 The Act now provides that courts should have power to make an interim care order only after care proceedings have been initiated and under strict rules as to grounds and duration (see White Paper, para 61). In keeping with the new-found emphasis on supervision rather than care the Act introduces interim supervision orders to enable a degree of control to be exerted short of removal from home. It was thought that this was just as important at the interim stage as it was on final disposal of the case (Review, para 17.28).

It will be appreciated that interim orders are only one, admittedly crucial, part of the care process. The changes to the basis on which they may be made should therefore be evaluated alongside the equally significant changes to emergency procedures (see Chapter 6), rights to participation in proceedings, rights to appeal and apply for discharge or variation of orders (see Chapter 8) and the ground for care and supervision orders (discussed earlier in this chapter).

5.64 An interim care or supervision order may now only be made in two sets of circumstances.

These are:

(i)   where the court adjourns applications for care or supervision orders; or
(ii) where it gives a direction under s 37(1) (s 38(1)).

This does away with the power of a single justice to make interim orders. They may now only be made by a full court where there is already an application before it for a care or supervision order or where the court itself considers, in other family proceedings, that it may be appropriate for such an order to be made and directs the authority to investigate the child's situation.

5.65 An interim care or supervision order may only be made on the ground that the court is satisfied that there are reasonable grounds for believing that the child's circumstances fall within those prescribed by s 31(2) i.e. those which suffice for a care or supervision order (s 38(2)). Although there is no reference to the child's welfare again it should be remembered that the principles in s 1 apply. The court should not therefore make an interim care or supervision order unless it considers that doing so would be better for the child than making no order (s 1(5)). This boils down to a purposive criterion restricting intervention to cases of need (Review, para 17.9). If the order contemplates the removal or detention of the child, this power should only be exercised where it is necessary to safeguard the child's welfare during the interim period (White Paper, para 61). It should be emphasised that the test to be satisfied is *reasonable grounds for believing* and not that the ground for a care order is actually established. The Review recognised that, especially in cases following emergency protection orders, it is unrealistic to expect a full forensic inquiry and proof of the care ground at the early stage (Review, para 17.8).

5.66 We noted that one of the aims of the Act is to increase the use of supervision. One aspect of this is that where the court makes a residence order on an application for a care or supervision order, it must also make an interim supervision order unless it is satisfied that the child's welfare will be satisfactorily safeguarded without an interim order (s 38(3)). This power to make residence orders in the course of care proceedings follows the recommendation in the Review that the court should be able to make 'custody' orders in those proceedings (Review, paras 19.7 et seq).

5.67 Section 38(4) governs the duration of interim orders. It provides that an interim order (whether for care or supervision) will terminate on whichever of the following events first occurs:

(a) eight weeks from the date of the order;
(b) in the case of second or subsequent orders, on the expiry of the 'relevant period'. This is defined as four weeks from the date of the order or eight weeks from the date of the original interim order, whichever is the later (s 38(5));
(c) where the order was made on the adjournment of an application for a care or supervision order, the disposal of that application;
(d) where the order was made on giving directions under s 37(1) (i.e. to investigate the child's circumstances), on the disposal of any application for a care or supervision order which resulted from the authority's investigations;
(e) where the court has extended the period in which the authority must report the result of its investigations, the expiry of the period fixed by that direction.

5.68 The effect of these provisions is to bring about for the first time a *maximum* period for interim care. Needless to say interim orders can be made for periods shorter than the maximum. In determining what is the appropriate period the court must 'consider whether any party who was, or might have been, opposed to the making of the order was in a position to argue his case against the order in full' (s 38(10)).

5.69 The power of the court to direct medical or psychiatric examinations of the child when making interim orders is a contentious issue. The Act gives the court a general discretion to give such directions (if any) as it considers appropriate regarding medical or psychiatric examinations or other assessment of the child. Where, however, the child is of sufficient understanding to make an informed decision he may refuse to submit to the examination or assessment (s 38(6)). It is expressly provided that the court may, as well as sanction such examinations or assessments, prohibit them by directing that there is to be no examination or assessment unless it directs otherwise (s 38(7)).

5.70 The above provision relating to the child's views is the result of a Commons' amendment following concern that examinations or assessments could be directed at the interim stage against the wishes of a 'mature' child. Some argued that this would emasculate the rights of young people who at sixteen and seventeen have a statutory right to refuse a medical examination (s 8 of the Family Law Reform Act 1969) and those under sixteen who satisfy the test propounded in *Gillick*. It was also argued that in cases of suspected sexual abuse of a mature child it was inappropriate that there should be a compulsory medical examination. It was said that this should only take place where that child could be persuaded to consent to it. The spectre was raised of doctors strapping down screaming fifteen-year-olds or knocking them out under sedatives. Moreover it was suggested that doctors would in practice consider themselves bound by the law on consent and would not comply with a court order directing an examination if satisfied that a young person was of sufficient understanding to refuse to be examined. (Baroness David, *House of Lords, Official Report*, 19 January 1989, col 405).

There was some doubt as to whether a court order would be capable of superseding the child's common law right arising under *Gillick* or the statutory right of the sixteen or seventeen-year-old to consent. These concerns are now academic in view of the amendment.

(c) Discharge and variations of care and supervision orders

5.71 Before the Act a care order might be discharged by the juvenile court on the application of the authority or the child himself. For these purposes the child's parents could apply for the order to be discharged *on the child's behalf* (1969 Act, s 21(2)). The grounds for discharge were vague in that the court simply had to be satisfied that it was 'appropriate'. An amendment was later introduced which imposed the requirement that the court should not discharge the order where the child was still in need of care and control unless it was satisfied that on discharge the child would receive it.

5.72 These provisions were found lacking in two principal respects. First, they were too restrictive as to the persons qualified to make a discharge application. In particular, although parents might apply on behalf of the child they had no *independent* right to do so, despite the fact that this type of application is exactly the sort of situation in which there may be a conflict of interest between parent and child. This conflict was eventually recognised by providing for separate representation of parent and child where the court perceived a conflict to exist. Where a separate representation order was made the parents' position was somewhat uncertain. It was not clear how far they might continue to pursue a discharge application in the face of opposition by the child's guardian ad litem (*R v Wandsworth West Juvenile Court* [1984] FLR 713). Moreover, it had been held that they had no right to appeal on the child's behalf against refusal to discharge where the guardian refused to do so (*A-R v Avon County Council* [1985] Fam. 150). Relatives or other interested persons had no right to apply for discharge. Secondly, it was thought that the existing ground for discharge resulted in practice in too much significance being attached to the fitness of parents and not enough to the welfare of the child concerned. In short, making the parents rather than the child the focus of attention created a risk of premature or mistaken discharge from care and generated uncertainty over the weight to be attached to the welfare of the child on discharge applications (Review, paras 20.11 et seq).

5.73 The Act addresses both these problems by giving parents and others with parental responsibility an independent right to apply for discharge and by making the welfare of the child the basis for determining whether an order should be discharged.

Section 39(1) and (2) gives the court power to vary or discharge care and supervision orders respectively. In each case the child himself and any person with parental responsibility are qualified applicants. The only difference is that in relation to care orders the authority may also apply, whereas in relation to the supervision orders the supervisor may do so. Thus, married parents, unmarried mothers and others who have acquired parental responsibility by legal process now have an independent right to bring discharge or variation applications. Others without parental responsibility, most notably the unmarried father and wider relatives, are not qualified to apply. The appropriate course for them will be to apply for a residence order under s 8. If they succeed in obtaining it, the effect will be the same since the order will automatically discharge any existing care order (s 91(1) and see Chapter 3). An application for discharge under s 39 rather than a residence order under s 8 will be appropriate in the case of united parents or a person with sole parental responsibility since in these cases it will be inappropriate to seek an order regulating disputes over where a child is to live. By definition there is no such dispute.

5.74 A person with whom the child is living but who is not entitled to apply for discharge may nonetheless apply for variation of a supervision order in so far as it imposes a requirement which affects that person (s 39(3)). This is a more restricted right of application than that enjoyed by those with parental responsibility. It only extends to the variation of specific requirements imposed on the adult concerned and only applies to variation, as opposed to discharge, of the order.

5.75 The reader will search in vain in s 39 for the grounds upon which care or supervision orders may be discharged or varied. All that is clear from the section itself is that the court when considering whether to substitute a care order for a supervision order or vice-versa, or when considering whether to make any other order on discharging a care or supervision order, does not have to be satisfied as to the grounds in s 31(2) (s 39(5)). The reason for the apparent omission is, again, that the principles in Part I apply. This means that the determination of variation or discharge applications will be governed by the welfare of the child (s 1(1)) and by the principle that an order should not be discharged or varied unless the court considers that this would be better for the child than leaving the existing order in operation (s 1(5)). In view of the application of this explicit welfare test, it was considered that the existing statutory requirement that the child would receive the care and control which he needed if the order was discharged was rendered redundant. This former requirement has therefore been removed by the legislation (Review, para 20.21).

5.76 We have seen that the Act shifts the emphasis from parental fitness and the quality of care which parents can provide and makes the welfare of the child a mandatory, indeed the sole, consideration. Inevitably, in practice, the child's welfare will be inextricably bound up with an assessment of the parental position. The point which perhaps ought to be emphasised is that the welfare principle will apply here in its undiluted form. Welfare will be the 'paramount' and not simply the 'first' consideration or just a factor in the court's decision (see Chapter 2). Thus, the absence of a risk of harm to the child on returning home would not, it appears, be a good enough reason for discharging a care order if on balance the child would be better off in care (Review, para 20.17). There is no question where the welfare principle applies, of balancing the child's welfare against other considerations such as parental claims. This should be contrasted with the narrower basis for obtaining compulsorily parental responsibility for a child in the first place, i.e. by proving the ground in s 31(2).

5.77 These changes to the basis for the discharge or variation of orders and those qualified to apply should also be assessed with other procedural and substantive changes brought about by the Act. The vastly improved rights to challenge contact decisions in the courts (s 34) should result in less discharge applications motivated primarily by the desire to ensure contact with the child. The modification of supervision orders should also make this a more appropriate option in some circumstances in which discharge was previously sought. One defect may, however, be thought to remain. This is that the court still has no power to order a phased return of the child in an effort to produce a satisfactory transition from care to the parental home. Neither is it at all likely that wardship will be available for this purpose. Before the Act the Court of Appeal had taken the view that the statutory access code had filled the 'lacuna' which previously existed in the legislation (*Re M (A Minor)* [1985] Fam. 60). A fortiori, this must be the case with the greater judicial control of contact decisions introduced by the Act. Nevertheless, control of contact by the courts is not the same as directing positive planning for rehabilitation. The failure of the legislation to vest this power in the courts reflects the general philosophy of non-intervention which dictates that the essential strategy for the child's future should be a matter for the authority. It would appear that parents or others with parental responsibility who are unhappy with the pace of a rehabilitative programme may have to resort to the 'all or nothing' remedy of a discharge application. It is regrettable that the Act does not address this problem as well as it might.

(d) Orders pending appeals in care and supervision cases

5.78 Section 40 is concerned with the child's position pending an appeal against the court's refusal to make, or decision to discharge, a care or supervision order. In order to avoid the risk of unnecessary disruption to the child, the court may order that he remain in care or under supervision provided that he is already subject to an interim order. The court may include in its order such directions as it thinks fit. The order will not, however, last beyond the 'appeal period' which will terminate either with the conclusion of any appeal or the end of the period within which an appeal may be brought. The intention is to strike a balance between the risk of disruption to the child and the principle that an authority should not be able to keep the child away from his parents where it has not proved the existence of the statutory grounds for care and supervision.

5.79 Section 41 deals with the appointment of guardians ad litem and representation of the child. This is more appropriately considered in Chapter 8 where we discuss jurisdictional and procedural issues.

7. Care in Criminal Cases

5.80 It is appropriate to conclude this chapter with a brief word about care orders in criminal proceedings. We have already referred to the abolition of the 'offence condition' whereby a child might be committed to care in care proceedings on the basis of the commission of a criminal offence. Instead of bringing care proceedings the police might, and usually did, prefer to prosecute in criminal proceedings. Where such a prosecution succeeded, one of the disposals open to the juvenile court was a care order provided that the offence was one which was punishable with imprisonment if committed by an adult (1969 Act, s 7(7)). There had been concern about this for some time since it was felt that it was wrong to use a care order as a form of punishment rather than a mechanism for safeguarding and promoting a child's welfare. Accordingly, the Act abolishes the power of the court to make a care order as a disposal in criminal proceedings (s 90(2)). It is replaced by a power to add a residence requirement to supervision orders which will remain a disposal in these proceedings (s 90(3) and Sch 12, para 23). When making a supervision order with respect to a juvenile offender the court may now require him to live for a specified period in accommodation provided by or on behalf of the local authority within whose area he is ordinarily resident.

CHAPTER SIX

Emergency Protection of Children

1. Introduction

6.1 Nowhere is the tension between child protection and family privacy felt more intensely than where the issue is whether a child should be summarily removed from home under an order for emergency protection. If the state, through social services, does not intervene where abuse or neglect is suspected the child's health or even life may be seriously jeopardised. Yet, if it does intervene and it later transpires that the child was not being ill-treated there may have been an equally serious infringement of parental 'rights'. That both of these scenarios occur is self-evident. Over the years there has been a succession of inquiries into the deaths of children whose lives might have been saved if more decisive action had been taken. Particularly influential on the current reforms were the reports relating to Kimberley Carlile and Jasmine Beckford (op cit, Chapter 1). Conversely, the events in Cleveland graphically revealed the opposite danger of precipitous action by social welfare agencies in cases of suspected sexual abuse which can lead to a denial of natural justice both to parents and the children themselves. It hardly needs stating that no law, however good, can completely eradicate errors of judgement which lead to too little or too much intervention. What it can do is provide a framework of substantive and procedural rules which give adequate recognition to these conflicting claims and considerations.

6.2 The strenuous attempts to arrive at the right balance are epitomised by the debate which took place concerning the inclusion or omission of the so-called 'child assessment order' (hereafter CAO) from the legislation. While there was universal agreement about the introduction of the new 'emergency protection order' (hereafter EPO), there was a genuine difference of opinion, not least between the NSPCC and the Association of the Directors of Social Services, about whether this order would need to be complemented by the introduction of the allegedly less intrusive CAO. The central point was whether there should be provision for the courts to order the assessment including medical or psychiatric examination of a child without, at that stage, going so far as to authorise the removal or detention of the child under an EPO.

[125]

Those in favour of CAOs argued that, without the lesser order, social services might have to resort to the more draconian EPO where they were concerned about a child's welfare but were not yet convinced that the removal or detention of the child was necessary. They argued that a CAO would allow action to be taken where there was 'serious, but not urgent, concern for the child'. Parents, it was said, would be happy to take their children for a medical examination as a normal and routine part of bringing them up. Moreover it was suggested that they would feel less threatened since parental responsibility would remain solely vested in them (see Lord Mottistone, *House of Lords, Official Report*, 19 January 1989, col 427).

Those against CAOs argued that to introduce another order for dealing with emergencies, with different grounds to those prescribed for EPOs, would lead to confusion and would add nothing since the power to direct examinations would be part and parcel of the EPO scheme. It was also argued that to obtain a court order directing a medical examination was liable in practice to 'upset an enormous number of good parents who have a finger pointed at them' and that this result could be better achieved by voluntary cooperation between parents and social services. In the absence of this an EPO would, in any event, be justified (Baroness Faithfull, *House of Lords, Official Report*, 19 January 1989, col 429).

6.3 In the event, those in favour of CAOs have won the day but this debate revealed just how difficult a business it is to formulate a basis for intervention which respects *both* the protective needs of children and the interests of parents. Having said that, there can be little doubt that the fundamental orientation of this part of the Act is to strengthen the legal position of parents where emergency action is thought necessary. This is not because there is a greater concern for parents than for children, but because the most glaring inadequacies of the existing law were those which deprived parents (and other carers) of elementary procedural fairness where their child was taken from them at short notice. Before turning briefly to these inadequacies the point should be made that it must not be assumed that the reforms in this part of the Act are designed *purely* to meet parental claims to natural justice. It is not only parents who lose where this is denied. Children also lose since it cannot be in their best interests that they should be removed and kept away from home without adequate legal mechanisms to scrutinise the necessity of such action.

6.4 Under the old law there were two main legal procedures for taking emergency action. These were Place of Safety Orders and detention under police powers. Place of Safety Orders might be obtained by 'any person' on an application to the juvenile court, but more commonly to a single magistrate (s 28(1), 1969 Act). It was in essence necessary to satisfy the justice that the applicant had 'reasonable cause to believe' that one of the conditions for a care order was satisfied in relation to the child or that the child was about to leave the UK as a juvenile entertainer contrary to s 25 of the Children and Young Persons Act 1933. The test was therefore one of the applicant's belief and not that of the magistrate. The order authorised the removal and detention of the child in a place of safety for up to twenty-eight days. Beyond this basic authorisation, the precise legal effects of the order were unclear especially concerning the powers and obligations of the person looking after the child under it.

6.5 The most serious criticism of this procedure was that the parents affected had little or no input into the process. They were not entitled to be informed or consulted about the proposal to remove the child from them and they had no right of appeal from the order. They were just entitled to an explanation of the reasons for the order as soon as practicable after it was made. If they wished to dispute the order, the only option open to them was to challenge its essential legality through judicial review which would scarcely ever be a realistic course of action. They were also able to apply for an interim care order before the expiration of the Place of Safety Order (*R v Lincoln (Kesteven) County Justices, ex p M* [1974] QB 957). The attraction of doing so lay in the possiblity that the court might refuse the application and return the child to their care. The device was in essence a disguised form of appeal against the Place of Safety Order and this was in due course held to be an illegitimate use of the procedure (*Nottinghamshire County Council v Q* [1982] Fam. 94).

6.6 Detention by the police was probably the most useful power where immediate action was required since a police constable could remove a child without warrant where he had reasonable cause to believe that one of the specified conditions for a care order was satisfied with respect to the child (s 28(2), 1969 Act). With the authority of a senior officer the child could then be detained in a place of safety for up to eight days (s 28(4)). Again, the child's parents or guardian had to be informed of the reasons for the detention as soon as was practicable (s 28(3)). In addition, they did in this context have a right to challenge the detention by applying to a magistrate for release of the child (s 28(4) and (5)). After the expiration of the eight day period, the child had to be released unless proceedings for an interim or full care order had been instigated (s 28(6)).

The Review found that these powers were valuable where it was essential to act without delay and it was impracticable to obtain a magistrates' order owing to the unavailability of social workers, magistrates or their clerks. The main defect was seen to be the period of detention which was considered unnecessarily long, bearing in mind that it had not been authorised by a court (Review, para 3.31, et seq).

6.7 The other way in which the police might become involved in cases of suspected abuse or neglect was in pursuance of a search warrant obtained to assist social services in investigating such cases. Clearly, if force was required to secure entry to a home the police would need to be in attendance. The applicant for a search warrant had to show that there was reasonable cause to suspect that a child was or was being assaulted, ill-treated or neglected

in a manner likely to cause him unnecessary suffering or injury to health
or that an offence in Sch 1 to the Children and Young Persons Act 1933
had been or was being committed (s 40, 1933 Act). A magistrate might then
issue a search warrant in favour of a constable authorising him to enter
specified premises, by force if necessary. It would also authorise him to
take and detain a child for up to twenty-eight days if one was found in
relation to whom the above conditions were satisfied.

6.8   The Review concluded that the magistrates' power to authorise detention
in a place of safety under s 28 of the 1969 Act and s 40 of the 1933 Act
ought to be assimilated by the adoption of common grounds. It proposed
that the single power should be accompanied by a power to attach a search
warrant.

2.   Child Assessment Orders

(a)   General

6.9   Section 43 introduces the new CAO. In essence, the CAO is an order
to enable an assessment of a child's health and welfare to be made where
there is concern about him, but there is doubt about whether emergency
action is warranted. The intention is that the assessment which the order
authorises should enable this determination to be made. In particular, it
is hoped that it will help to overcome the social worker's dilemma. Where
social services are refused access to a home or to a child they may suspect
that all is not well. At the same time, they may have insufficient information
to feel confident about applying for an order to remove the child. The new
order provides a 'half-way house' between compulsory removal and doing
nothing at all.

(b)   Grounds for a CAO

6.10   Unlike EPOs (where anyone can in principle apply) CAOs may only
be sought by a local authority or 'authorised person'. As we have seen,
this category is currently limited to the NSPCC. The reasoning is presumably
that there ought to be no restriction on anyone seeking to help a child in
an emergency but that this consideration does not apply where there is no
need for urgent action. The court may make the order where it is satisfied
that:

'(a)   the applicant has reasonable cause to suspect that the child is suffering, or
is likely to suffer, significant harm;

(b)   an assessment of the state of the child's health or development, or of the
way in which he has been treated, is required to enable the applicant to
determine whether or not the child is suffering, or is likely to suffer, significant
harm; and

(c) it is unlikely that such an assessment will be made, or be satisfactory, in the absence of an order under this section' (s 43(1)).

The test, therefore, contains three elements, the first of which requires the court to be satisfied of the reasonableness of the *applicant's* belief regarding the risk of harm to the child. This should be contrasted with the principal ground for an EPO where the *court itself* must be satisfied about the risk to the child. The second two elements involve the court in an evaluation of the factual circumstances. This boils down to the court having to be satisfied that there are grounds for genuine concern about the child's health or well-being and that proper investigation of the child's situation will be unlikely to take place unless it intervenes.

6.11 'The court', for these purposes, means a full court conducting an inter partes hearing and not 'a magistrate sitting at home in his pyjamas', to borrow the graphic phrase of Stuart Bell MP (*Hansard*, 23 October 1989, col 594). Again this should be contrasted with the position in relation to EPOs, where the emergency nature of those orders sometimes necessitates access to single justices on an *ex parte* basis. The applicant for a CAO must take such steps as are reasonably practicable to ensure that prior notice of the application is given to the parents, anyone else with parental responsibility or who is caring for the child, any person with the benefit of a contact order under s 8 or s 34 and the child himself (s 43(11)). Rules of Court may allow applications for CAOs to be varied or discharged (s 43(12)).

(c) The legal effects of the CAO

6.12 The CAO creates a new legal duty to produce a child which is imposed on anyone who is in a position to do so. The child must be produced to the person named in the order. There is a further duty to comply with any directions the court has made in the order regarding assessment of the child (s 43(6). The most obvious directions are likely to be for medical or psychiatric examinations. The effect of the order is to authorise these and any other necessary action forming part of the child's assessment (s 43(7)). These steps must be taken in accordance with the terms of the order and the Act appears to envisage that the court should spell out with some particularity what may or may not be done. All of this is subject to the qualification that a child with sufficient understanding to make an informed decision may refuse to submit to any examination or any other form of assessment (s 43(8)). This is in line with other provisions in the Act recognising the personal integrity of mature adolescents following the principles of the *Gillick* case.

(d) Contact

6.13 The child may be kept away from home under a CAO but only in accordance with the court's directions, where it is necessary for the assessment and for the period or periods specified in the order (s 43(9)). Where this is allowed, the order must contain directions regarding the contact which the child is to have with other persons while away from home (s 43(10)).

These circumstances for removal from home under a CAO are obviously more restrictive than those which apply to EPOs and reflect the fundamental differences between the two orders. It is manifestly not the purpose of a CAO to enable a child to be removed from the home environment. It is simply to allow an assessment of the situation to be made. In practice, therefore, the court should only authorise removal and detention to the limited extent that is necessary to allow the assessments to be made. Nonetheless, it will need to be realistic about allowing sufficient time in which to make a proper assessment. In keeping with this, it is suggested that the court should allow liberal contact between the child and his parents (and others where appropriate). Restrictions on this should be justified only in so far as contact is likely to interfere with the assessment process.

(e) Duration of CAOs

6.14 The CAO must specify the date by which the assessment is to be given. The order will have effect for the period specified in it, but this must not exceed seven days, beginning with the date on which it is made (s 43(5)). Unlike EPOs, there is no power for the court to extend the maximum duration beyond the seven-day period.

(f) CAO or EPO?

6.15 It will be apparent that CAOs and EPOs are two different ways of taking action to meet anxiety over a child. The relationship between them, since they are alternative and not complementary orders, is clearly crucial. From the point of view of social services, the choice of order ought to depend on the level of concern and the degree of urgency which is felt. The greater the concern and feeling of urgency, the more likely it will be that an EPO will be sought. If, however, the authority decides to apply for a CAO and it later becomes apparent that the situation is more serious or urgent than was originally thought, the court is empowered to treat the application as an application for an EPO (s 43(3)). Indeed, where it is satisfied that there are grounds for making an EPO, and that it ought to make this rather than a CAO, it is precluded from making the latter order (s 43(4)). This obviously recognises the inherent difficulties faced by authorities in deciding between the two orders and is intended to give maximum flexibility to the court to authorise the level of action which it deems necessary in order to protect the child.

3. Emergency Protection Orders

(a) General

6.16 The principal change to emergency procedures introduced by the Act is the replacement of Place of Safety Orders by the new Emergency Protection Orders. The change in nomenclature is intended to underline the emergency nature of the order and to counteract the trend of using Place of Safety Orders almost routinely as the first stage of care proceedings (see Review, para 13.8).

(b) Grounds for EPOs

6.17 EPOs may be granted in any of three sets of circumstances set out in s 44(1). In the first instance the applicant may be anyone. The second and third situations are concerned exclusively with applications by local authorities and authorised persons (i.e. the NSPCC) respectively and deal specifically with the problem of obtaining access to a child.

6.18 The main ground for obtaining an EPO is that the court is satisfied that there is reasonable cause to believe that the child is likely to suffer significant harm if:

'(i) he is not removed to accommodation provided by or on behalf of the applicant; or

(ii) he does not remain in the place in which he is then being accommodated' (s 44(1)(*a*)).

In contrast, therefore, to other orders under the Act the class of applicants entitled to apply for an EPO is wholly unrestricted. Anyone with a real concern about a child may apply for an order, although in practice the vast majority are likely to be sought by local authority social workers. This was the position under the old law relating to Place of Safety Orders. The Review found no evidence that emergency procedures were abused by unmeritorious applications and did not think it desirable or necessary to restrict the range of applicants (para 13.7). The class of children who may be protected is also unrestricted. Any child may be the subject of an EPO and wherever practicable the order should name the child. Where it does not name him it should describe him as clearly as possible (s 44(14)). There will obviously be reported instances of suspected child abuse or neglect in which the name of the child is not known to the applicant. In these cases it is important that the order should identify the child as clearly as possible in view of its draconian effects on family life.

6.19 The court will continue to include a single magistrate. The need for this is self-evident since it is clearly necessary that authorisation of emergency action should be available outside normal court hours. There has, nonetheless, been some disquiet that too many applications for the former Place of Safety

Orders, which could have been made to a full court, were made to the homes of magistrates. The correct procedure for obtaining an EPO will be to apply through the clerk of the court where possible and only to a magistrate at home where this is strictly necessary.

6.20   The new criteria which the court must apply require it to be satisfied that there is reasonable cause to believe that the child is 'likely to suffer significant harm' unless he is *removed* from his present accommodation or, alternatively, *kept* there.

The first alternative relates to the situation where the child is currently in the care of an individual or individuals and is either being abused or neglected already, or is likely to be unless emergency action is taken. The second alternative covers the situation where the child is presently in a safe environment, but is at risk of being removed to an unsafe one. Examples include the plight of the new-born baby in hospital or the child in a settled foster home. In either case there may be real concern that immediate removal of the child by his parents will, in certain circumstances, expose him to an unacceptable risk of significant harm. For these purposes 'harm' has the same meaning as in s 31(9) and whether it is 'significant' is to be determined in accordance with s 31(10) (s 105(1)).

Regarding the first alternative, it is not necessary (contrary to the view taken at para 13.8 of the Review) to prove that the need for the child's removal is *immediate*. A Lords' amendment which would have required this was withdrawn. This is because it is intended that an EPO should be flexible enough to embrace the situation where, on investigation of the child's circumstances, the applicant concludes that immediate removal is unnecessary. This could arise, for example, because a suspected abuser undertakes to leave the home or because the allegations are found to be unsubstantiated. In such cases immediate removal would not be warranted, but the power to remove the child would remain for the duration of the order. A subsequent removal might therefore be justified if circumstances changed (see Lord Mackay LC, *House of Lords, Official Report*, 19 January 1989, col 426).

6.21   The new ground has a *prospective* element in that it is wide enough to embrace the situation where the child has not yet suffered harm, but there is reason to believe that he is *likely* to unless the order is made. The obvious question is: 'How likely does likely have to be?' This is something about which the Act is silent, but which may prove to be an important issue in practice. Does the term imply that the risk of harm materialising must be more probable than not, or simply that there is a realistic chance of it occurring? Commonsense suggests that, in applying the test, the court should make some attempt to relate the chance of harm occurring to the gravity of that harm if it should occur. It would, for example, be dangerously negligent to refuse an order where the child appears to be exposed to the risk of death at the hands of a potentially homicidal individual, even though the chances of that occurring might be considered significantly less than fifty-fifty. On the other hand, where the threatened harm is less grave, it might be necessary for the court to be satisfied that it is more likely than not that it will occur.

6.22 The grounds for EPOs are considerably less restrictive than those for care or supervision orders in s 31(2). It is not necessary for the applicant to show that the risk of harm is attributable to a lack of parental care. The reasoning is obvious. While there may be a strong suspicion, for example, that a child's injuries are non-accidental, it may not be possible to establish this conclusively without a full medical and forensic inquiry. To impose a causative requirement at this initial stage of emergency action would be unrealistic and might, in some cases, deny the child essential protection.

6.23 As an alternative to the normal basis for seeking EPOs, local authorities and authorised persons (the NSPCC) may apply for the order as a means of obtaining access to a child where this is refused (s 44(1)(*b*) and (*c*)). In each case it must be shown that the applicants, in the course of their inquiries into the child's welfare, have reasonable cause to suspect the child is suffering or is likely to suffer, significant harm. It must also be shown that their inquiries are being frustrated by an unreasonable refusal of access to the child and that the applicants have reasonable cause to believe that access is required as a matter of urgency. Clearly, there is an issue as to the overlap between EPOs and CAOs in non-access cases. The distinction seems to hinge on the perception of how urgent the child's situation may be. In order to obtain an EPO the applicant will have to convince the court that he has reasonable cause for thinking that the situation demands urgent action. Where there is no immediate fear for the child's safety but the authority wishes to make an assessment of this situation, the CAO will be the preferred option.

(b)   The Legal effects of EPOs

6.24 Section 44(4) and (5) spells out the legal effects of EPOs and deals in particular with the responsibility of the successful applicant towards the child. An EPO has three legal effects while it remains in force. They are:

(a) to direct any person who is in a position to produce the child to the applicant to do so;

(b) to authorise

 (i) the removal of the child at any time to accommodation provided by, or on behalf of, the applicant and his detention there, or

 (ii) the prevention of the child's removal from a hospital or other place in which he was being accommodated immediately before the order was made, and

(c) to give the applicant parental responsibility for the child (s 44(4)).

In essence, therefore, an EPO transfers the physical care of a child and the concomitant parental responsibility to the applicant. The present 'carer' of the child must cooperate in disclosing the whereabouts of the child and in handing him over at the applicant's request.

6.25 Section 44 (5) governs the exercise of parental responsibility under an EPO. It provides that the applicant:

(*a*) shall only exercise parental responsibility in order to safeguard the welfare of the child; and

(*b*) shall take, and shall only take, such action in meeting this responsibility as is reasonably required to safeguard or promote the welfare of the child (having regard in particular to the duration of the order); and

(*c*) shall comply with the requirements of any regulations made by the Secretary of State regarding this matter.

It appears that the combined effect of s 44(4) and (5) is to impose legal responsibility on the applicant to look after the child. He will have the same sort of statutory duties to accommodate and maintain the child as are placed on local authorities where children are looked after by them under Part III or are in care under Part IV. The Act makes it clear that the applicant has parental responsibility which, as we have seen, is non-transferable. This does not, of course, mean that day-to-day care cannot be delegated. It would be perfectly proper, for example, for a local authority to arrange for the child's accommodation by a foster parent or voluntary organisation. The important point is that the applicant is under a statutory duty either to provide accommodation himself or arrange suitable accommodation for the child elsewhere. He cannot divest himself of this legal responsibility by 'palming it off' on someone else.

At the same time the duty to discharge parental responsibility is limited to taking only such action as is necessary to safeguard or promote the child's welfare while the emergency lasts and the order is in force. This reflects the transitory nature of the order which is no more than a short-term protective expedient. If the applicant wishes to acquire more extensive responsibility for the child, an application would have to be made for a care order.

(c) Contact

6.26 In line with the new statutory presumption of reasonable contact which applies where a child is in care, a similar presumption is introduced where a child is subject to an EPO (s 44(13)). Subject to any directions by the court, the applicant must allow the child reasonable contact with:

(a) his parents;

(b) any other person with parental responsibility for him;

(c) any person with whom he was living immediately before the making of the order;

(d) any person in whose favour a contact order is in force;

(e) any person who is allowed to have contact with the child by virtue of an order under s34; and

(f) any person acting on behalf of any of those persons.

6.27 The court may give directions regarding contact between the child and any named person (s 44(6)(*a*)). It may do so either when it makes the order, or at any time while it is in force (s 44(9)(*a*)). In either case it may impose conditions (s 44(8)). The court therefore has flexible powers to control or prohibit contact. In many (if not most) cases, the court making the EPO will need to exercise them. The very existence of an EPO is predicated on the assumption that the child is at risk, and the danger of allowing unsupervised contact between the child and the various adults involved is obvious. But, equally, Cleveland showed the dangers of denying contact to parents who might subsequently prove to be the victims of unsubstantiated allegations. The Review took the point that, in many cases, limited contact in the presence of a third party would be the only reasonable solution in the child's interests (Review, para 3.17).

6.28 Before leaving the question of contact it should be said that the drastic reduction in the length of time during which children may be kept apart from their parents which the Act brings about (s 45, discussed below), should in itself take some of the heat out of this issue. Much of the discontent generated by the old law related to the length of time during which parents and others might be denied contact under Place of Safety Orders. Finally, it should be observed that there is no right to challenge contact decisions. Section 34 does not apply to the situation of a child being looked after under an EPO in view of its limited duration.

(d) Medical and psychiatric examinations and assessments

6.29 One of the arguments against the introduction of CAOs was that the court when making an EPO, or while it remains in force, has power to direct medical or psychiatric examinations or assessments of the child (s 44(6)(*b*)). It may also prohibit them until it directs otherwise (s 44(8)). One use of an EPO may therefore be to obtain authorisation for such examinations or assessments before a decision is taken to remove a child from home where social services are unable to negotiate with the parents for them to produce the child voluntarily for examination or assessment. If so, they may conclude that there is an emergency, and by applying for an EPO obtain directions for the examination or assessment. If, then, the parent fails to comply with these directions, the authority will have an *automatic* right to remove the child under the continuing EPO and will not have to apply for a separate order. In non-urgent cases the authority may instead apply for similar directions by seeking a CAO.

Any direction either as to contact, examination or assessment may be varied at any time on the application of any person falling within a class prescribed by rules of court (s 44(9)(*b*)).

(e) Returning or releasing the child

6.30 Where a child has been removed or detained the Act embodies the principle that he should not be kept away from parental care for longer than is strictly necessary. Accordingly, the applicant is required to return the child, or allow him to be removed (as the case may be) where it appears to him to be safe to do so, even though the EPO is still in force (s 44(10)). This duty arises automatically and does not necessitate a discharge of the EPO or a return to court. Where it arises, the applicant must return the child to the care of the person from whose care he was removed. Where that is not reasonably practicable the child must be returned to:

(a)   his parent;

(b)   any person with parental responsibility for him; or

(c)   such other person as the applicant (with the agreement of the court) considers appropriate (s 44(11)).

In the event of further change of circumstances, the applicant may again exercise his power under the EPO at any time while it remains in force if it appears to him that it is necessary to do so (s 44(12)). This includes, of course, the power to remove the child again from the parent or other carer to whom he was returned. These provisions illustrate the ongoing nature of an EPO. Although comparatively short in duration, EPOs are not rigid 'one-off' directives, but are flexible enough to allow the child's circumstances to be monitored over a short period and to authorise such action as proves necessary.

(f) The court's discretion

6.31 EPOs, like care and other orders under the Act, are discretionary. Even where the statutory grounds in s 44(1) are found to be proved, the court is not obliged to make an order, but *may* do so. There may be circumstances under which the child's protection can be achieved without an order, as where a suspected abuser undertakes to leave the home and does so immediately. Accepting such an undertaking might go some way towards meeting the concern of the Butler-Sloss report that removing the abuser should always be considered as an alternative to removing the abused child from his home and family. It should also be remembered that the general orientation of the Act (enshrined in s 1(5)) is that an order should not be made unless it can achieve something which making no order could not achieve.

(g) Duration of EPOs and related matters

6.32 Section 45 governs the duration of EPOs. The maximum length of the order is limited initally to *eight days*. This is a drastic reduction from the twenty-eight days which represented the maximum period of the former Place of Safety Orders. The court can also specify a shorter period where appropriate (s 45(1)). Where the court is contemplating an eight-day order but the last day would fall on a public holiday (Christmas Day, Good Friday, a bank holiday or a Sunday), the court may specify a period which ends at noon on the first later day which is not such a holiday (s 45(2)). Where the application is made following the child's detention by the police, the eight-day period commences on the first day that the child was taken into police protection (s 45(3)). The eight-day period follows the recommendation in the Review which rejected suggestions for a shorter seventy-two hour maximum for the initial *ex parte* order to be followed by a full court hearing for renewal of up to twenty-one days. It felt that this would be too short a period to enable the parties to prepare for the hearing and might lead to routine renewals. This could give rise to the danger that an initially short order might precipitate more extensive intervention (Review, para 13.23).

6.33 The expectation is that a local authority with eight days at its disposal should normally have enough time to conduct its investigations and decide whether or not to commence care proceedings. It should have enough time to obtain sufficient evidence for the court to decide whether to make an interim care order. The Act does cater for the minority of cases in which this period will not be long enough by making limited provision for an EPO to be extended. The only applicant entitled to seek an extension is a person with parental responsibility for a child as a result of an EPO and who is entitled to apply for a care order (s 45(4)). This means that local authorities and authorised persons (the NSPCC) alone are entitled to ask for an EPO to be extended. The court is empowered to extend the order for a further seven days, but only if it has reasonable cause to believe that the child concerned is otherwise likely to suffer significant harm (s 45(5)).

It should be incumbent on a local authority when applying for an extension to state in its application why it is not ready to proceed with an application for a care order. A possible example might be where the authority is awaiting the result of a medical or psychiatric examination of the child. But whatever difficulties are facing the authority, only one extension may be granted (s 45(6)). The position was taken in the White Paper that within fifteen days it should always be possible for the court to reach a decision on an interim care order (para 46). The court has an unfettered discretion to allow an extension 'as it thinks fit'. It is not confined to allowing extensions in 'exceptional circumstances' as initially proposed in the Review. The Act adopts instead the position taken in the Butler-Sloss report which thought this criterion too restrictive. Having said that, extensions ought to be relatively uncommon and certainly not granted on a routine basis.

6.34 An EPO may be challenged on its merits by an application to discharge it. Those entitled to bring an application for this purpose are the child himself, his parent, any person having parental responsibility and any person with whom he was living immediately before the order was made (s 45(8)). No application may be heard by the court before the expiration of seventy-two hours from the time when the order was made (s 45(9)). No one who was given proper notice of the original hearing for an EPO and was present at it is entitled to apply for it to be discharged and no discharge application may be made in respect of an EPO which has been extended (s 45(11)). The reasoning here is that, in each case, the person aggrieved by the order will have had a proper opportunity to challenge it in court at a full inter partes hearing and should not, therefore, be given a further opportunity to do so. It should also be remembered that an EPO is designed to have continuing effect over what is a short period and it would be unnecessarily disruptive of the authority's plans to allow two challenges within this time-scale.

6.35 Section 45 deals with two further matters relating to EPOs. First, it allows the court hearing an application relating to an EPO to take account of any statement contained in any report in the course of, or in connection with, the hearing and any evidence given during the hearing which in the court's opinion is relevant to the application (s 45(7)). This is a similarly worded provision to s 7(4) governing evidence in family proceedings. (For a full discussion of this see Chapter 2.)

Secondly, it is provided that a court making an EPO 'may direct that the applicant may, in exercising any powers which he has by virtue of the order, be accompanied by a registered medical practitioner, registered nurse or registered health visitor, if he so chooses' (s 45(12)). The relationship between a direction under this provision and a direction under s 44(6) is somewhat obscure. It would appear that the present provision is intended to cover in particular the initial investigation of the child's home circumstances. Section 44(6) relates more specifically to directions for medical and psychiatric examinations. But it is not clear what a doctor would be authorised to do by virtue of a direction under s 45(12). In general terms, he should be able to do whatever is reasonable in the circumstances, but he should probably not carry out an examination of the child purely for forensic, as opposed to diagnostic, purposes. Examinations of the child specifically for evidential purposes probably need to be authorised by the court under s 44(6).

4. Police Powers for Removal and Accommodation of Children in Emergencies

6.36 Section 46 enacts with modifications the emergency powers of the police to remove and accommodate children. The essence of these powers is that the police are able to act *immediately*, without the necessity of obtaining a court order, in cases of real urgency. As soon as possible after doing so, steps should be taken to pass responsibility for the child to the local authority. The function of the police in this area is essentially to act as a stopgap until the authority, which has primary responsibility for the child's welfare, can be brought in.

6.37 The Act gives a police constable power to remove a child to suitable accommodation and keep him there, or take reasonable steps to ensure that a child's removal from a hospital or other place in which he is being accommodated is prevented. He must himself have reasonable cause to believe that the child would otherwise be likely to suffer significant harm (s 46(1)). This power of removal does not carry with it a right of entry. Where it appears to the police that entry is likely to be refused, an EPO should be sought and a warrant may be attached to this (s 48). The child may be kept in police protection under these powers for up to seventy-two hours (s 46(6)). It will be recalled that this is also the maximum period for which a child may be detained under an ex parte EPO. Detention for a longer period must be authorised by an EPO, failing which the child must be released. This period is a significant reduction in the maximum period allowed for police protection under the old law which was eight days.

6.38 As soon as reasonably practicable after taking control of the child, the constable concerned is required to take certain action. He must contact the authority within whose area the child was found and must inform it of the steps which have been, and are proposed to be, taken and the reasons for taking them. Where the child is ordinarily resident in the area of a different authority, he must also give that authority notice of where the child is being accommodated. If the child has not already been placed in accommodation provided by or on behalf of a local authority, or as a refuge, on arriving in police protection, he must secure that the child is removed to such accommodation. He must also take reasonably practicable steps to discover the wishes and feelings of the child (s 46(3)).

These duties reflect the overriding responsibility of the local authority and the consequent need for the police to involve it as soon as possible in the arrangements for the child's care. The officer must also inform the child (if he appears capable of understanding), the parents, persons with parental responsibility or with whom the child was living before being taken into police protection, of the steps taken or proposed to be taken together with reasons (s 46(4)). Finally, he must secure that an inquiry into the child's circumstances is undertaken by a senior officer designated for this purpose by the chief officer ('the designated officer'). It is then the responsibility of the officer to determine whether the child should be released from protection. He must be released unless the officer considers that there is still reasonable cause for believing that the child would be likely to suffer significant harm if released (s 46(5)). Where, following his inquiries, the officer considers that continuing protection is warranted, he may apply on behalf of the appropriate local authority for an EPO under s 44 (s 46(7)). It would be more accurate to say that he *must* apply since without an EPO the police will lack lawful authority to detain the child beyond seventy-two hours. The application, although on behalf of the authority, may be made whether or not the authority knows of it or agrees to it being made (s 46(8)). Again, the reasoning is that, if the application should succeed, responsibility for the care of the child should shift from the police to the authority as soon as possible. The police are, in effect, acting as agents for the authority in the immediate crisis period. Where the court grants an EPO following police protection the effect is to allow an extension of protection for up to eight days from the initial removal of the child. Thereafter, a further extension or an interim care order would need to be sought by the local authority.

6.39 The legal position of the police under an EPO where the child is in their protection, is somewhat different from that of a local authority or other applicant with the care of a child under an EPO. The Act provides that neither the constable nor the designated officer is to have parental responsibility for the child. Nevertheless, the designated officer is (like the holder of an EPO) required to do what is reasonable in all the circumstances for the purpose of safeguarding or promoting the child's welfare (having regard in particular to the length of time during which the child will remain under police protection) (s 46(9)).

Technically, therefore, the police have no legal powers going beyond removal and detention. The wider decision-making powers which go with parental responsibility do not vest in the police, but for practical purposes they are authorised, indeed required, to take necessary action to protect the child's welfare. In practical terms there may not be much difference between what the police and the local authority may do immediately after acquiring control of the child. The withholding of parental responsibility from the police is really to underline the extremely transitory nature of their involvement and the need to transfer effective control to a local authority (which will gain parental responsibility under an EPO). The police have no more than the basic power which they need to protect the child and the statutory duties under s 46 which are on top of those which anyone with physical control of a child has under the criminal and civil law.

6.40 The legal position regarding contact with a child in police protection also differs from the position where an EPO has been made. The designated officer is required to allow specified individuals 'such contact (if any) with the child as, in the opinion of the designated officer, is both reasonable and in the child's best interests' (s 46(10)). Where a child is by this time accommodated by or on behalf of the local authority, this provision applies to the relevant officer of the authority and not the police (s 46(11)).

In this context there is no presumption of reasonable contact. There would be obvious dangers in creating an obligation to allow contact within the first seventy-two hours of an emergency removal by the police and before the court has had an opportunity of considering what contact should be allowed. Nevertheless, the effect of the above provision appears to be that the police or authority are required to apply their minds to the question of whether contact would be reasonable even at this early stage. It should be remembered that while seventy-two hours does not seem a long time in the abstract, it may feel like a lifetime to parents or children who have been unceremoniously separated. Again, if it is allowed at all, contact under supervision would seem to be the only realistic option in many cases.

6.41 Finally, it should be noted that s 21 places on local authorities a duty to receive and accommodate children who are removed or kept away from home under the emergency procedures in Part V (s 21(1)). They must do the same for children who are in police protection or whom they are requested to receive under s 38(6) of the Police and Criminal Evidence Act 1984. They must also accommodate children who are on remand under s 23(1) of the Children and Young Persons Act 1969 or the subject of a supervision order under s 12AA of the Act which imposes a residence requirement, in each case where they are the designated authority (s 21(2)). Where a child who has been removed under Part V or detained under s 38 (supra) is not being provided with accommodation by a local authority or in a hospital vested in the Secretary of State, the reasonable expenses of accommodating him are recoverable from the authority in whose area he is ordinarily resident (s 21(3)).

5. Abduction of Children

(a) General

6.42 The exercise of emergency powers by the police in the case of adolescents is a controversial and complex issue. It is understood that older children are commonly picked up by the police where there is concern for their welfare, although no crime may have been committed by them. They might be found on the streets late at night, in areas of prostitution or under the influence of drink, drugs or solvent abuse (see Lord Elwyn-Jones, *House of Lords, Official Report*, 19 January 1989, col 443). The legal position of such 'children' is not entirely clear. Do the police have a duty to return them immediately to their parents (where known) or to consult with the local authority? Must they return them to the authority where they are in care? Do the police have power to pick them up in the first place where no crime is suspected? These issues are particularly complicated in the case of so-called 'runaways', either from care or from the parental home. A number of organisations, notably the Children's Society, provide assistance and temporary accommodation. The legal position of these voluntary organisations was precarious since it was feared that this type of assistance might constitute the criminal offence of abduction or a related offence.

6.43   The principal change brought about by the Act is to give the Secretary of State power to exempt organisations like the Children's Society from criminal liability where they give bona fide assistance to runaways, particularly by providing 'safe houses' for them. Apart from these exemptions, the various criminal offences are re-enacted. The Act also introduces changes to the law on the recovery of children who are abducted, run away or stay away from care. It repeals the former power to arrest without warrant, gives the court power to order disclosure of a child's whereabouts and spells out more clearly the legal effects of a recovery order.

6.44   An important issue which has not been entirely resolved by the Act relates to the relevance of the young person's own views on where he or she should live. The Act does not deal directly with the question of when a child is lawfully entitled to leave home. At common law the matter was determined by the so-called 'age of discretion' fixed at 14 for a boy and 16 for a girl (see *R v Howes* (1860) 3 E & E 332). This rigid age-related rule was criticised by the House of Lords in *Gillick* and it is at least arguable that the question is now to be resolved by an assessment of the child's maturity and understanding which was a central principle in that case. It may therefore be that *any* third party assisting a runaway teenager (and not simply those bodies and individuals exempt from criminal liability under the Act) would have a defence to criminal prosecution based on *Gillick*. Such a person would have to argue that he was of the opinion that the child was mature enough to take his own decision on where he wished to live, which was capable of overriding the wishes of his parents or other carers. It is a moot point whether this would constitute a 'reasonable excuse' for the purposes of the new offence in s 49 (discussed at 6.45 below). The argument against allowing such a defence might be that the *Gillick* principles are not intended to apply at all where the matter in issue is governed by statute. Although the 1989 Act does not expressly resolve the issue of when a child may decide to live independently, it may by implication determine that no such right exists where the child is in care, police protection or subject to an EPO. Any common law right which the child might have may in that context be abrogated by statute.

(b)   The new statutory offences

6.45   Section 49(1) provides:

'A person shall be guilty of an offence if, knowingly and without lawful authority or reasonable excuse, he:–

(*a*)   takes a child to whom this section applies away from the responsible person;

(*b*)   keeps such a child away from the responsible person; or

(*c*)   induces, assists or incites such a child to run away from the responsible person.'

The offence applies to children who are in care, subject to an EPO or in police protection and the responsible person is in each case the person having the care of the child under these arrangements, eg foster parents or the managers of a children's home (s 49(2)). There is no corresponding offence applying to children who are merely being voluntarily accommodated by a local authority under Part III.

The *mens rea* required for the offence is 'knowingly and without lawful authority or reasonable excuse'. The defence of reasonable excuse has been added by the present legislation and, as noted above, the most interesting question in practice is likely to be the relevance of the child's own views to this defence.

(c) Recovery Orders

6.46 Section 50(1) is concerned with the recovery of children falling within the offence in s 49. It provides:

'Where it appears to the court that there is reason to believe that a child to whom this section applies:–

(a) has been unlawfully taken away or is being unlawfully kept away from the responsible person;

(b) has run away or is staying away from the responsible person; or

(c) is missing,

the court may make an order under this section ("a recovery order").'

Recovery orders can only be made in relation to children covered by s 49 (s 50(2)).

6.47 Where an order is made its legal effects are spelled out in s 50(3). They are as follows.

(a) It operates as a direction to any person who is in a position to do so to produce the child on request to any authorised person.

(b) It authorises the removal of the child by that person. ('Authorised person' for both of these purposes is defined to include any person specified by the court, any constable and any person authorised to exercise any power under the recovery order by a person with parental responsibility under a care order or EPO.) (s 50(7)).

(c) It requires any person with information as to the child's whereabouts to disclose it if requested to do so, to a constable.

(d) It authorises a constable to enter specified premises and to search for the child. The court may only specify premises in this way, where it appears to it that there are reasonable grounds for believing the child to be on them (s 50(6)).

6.48 Applications for recovery orders may be made by any person with parental responsibility for the child under a care order or EPO or by the designated officer where the child is in police protection (s 50(4)). The order must name the child and the applicant (s 50(5)).

(d) Refuges for Children at Risk

6.49 Section 51 is designed to meet a specific anxiety concerning the provision of so-called 'safe houses' for runaways by voluntary organisations such as the Children's Society. The fear was that the provision of such accommodation might have been deemed by the courts to amount to inducing young people to stay away from home in circumstances which might amount to a criminal offence.

6.50 The Act empowers the Secretary of State to issue a certificate where persons or voluntary organisations propose to provide a refuge for children who appear to be at risk of harm (s 51(1)). The certificate relates to the *home* and while it remains in force, anyone providing a refuge for a child in the home is exempt from criminal prosecution for various statutory offences relating to the abduction or harbouring of children (s 51(5) and (7)). The certificate may be granted in relation to a foster parent who has been requested to provide a refuge by a local authority or voluntary organisation (s 51(2)). 'Foster parent', in this case, means a local authority foster parent or a foster parent with whom children are placed by a voluntary organisation (s 51(3)). The foster parent will also be exempt from criminal prosecution in providing the refuge (s 51(6)). The Secretary of State may make regulations governing the manner in which certificates are issued, imposing requirements to be complied with while the certificates are in force and providing for circumstances in which they may be withdrawn (s 51(4)). This power will no doubt be used to provide the means of discriminating between wholesome bona fide organisations with a genuine concern to help children and more unsavoury individuals who might wish to exploit them for commercial or other ends. It was recognised in Parliament that not everyone coming into contact with vulnerable adolescents is as well-intentioned as the Children's Society and that regulations would need to be drafted in a way which enables separation of 'the sheep' from 'the goats'.

6.   The Investigative Duties of Local Authorities

6.51 English law contains no duty to report cases of suspected child abuse or neglect and the Review decided against introducing a mandatory reporting law (Review, para 12(4)). Under s 2(1) of the 1969 Act local authorities were, however, under a legal duty to make inquiries on receiving information suggesting that there were grounds for bringing care proceedings unless satisfied that this was unnecessary. The 1989 Act recasts this investigative duty by imposing a broader and more positive obligation to conduct inquiries. The new duty is embodied in s 47(1) which provides:

'Where a local authority:

(a) are informed that a child who lives, or is found, in their area:

(i) is the subject of an emergency protection order; or
(ii) is in police protection; or

(b) have reasonable cause to suspect that a child who lives, or is found, in their area is suffering, or is likely to suffer, significant harm,

the authority shall make, or cause to be made, such inquiries as they consider necessary to enable them to decide whether they should take any action to safeguard or promote the child's welfare.'

6.52 The new duty to make inquiries is therefore focused on the risk of harm to the child rather than on the more technical and limited question of whether there are grounds for proceedings, which was the focus of the old law. At the same time there is also a subtle change of wording. The former provision which relieved authorities of the duty to make inquiries where satisfied that they were unnecessary has been replaced by the more positive duty in every case to make such inquiries as are necessary to enable the authority to decide whether any action is required. How much difference this will make in practice remains to be seen. The newly formulated duty is prima facie a broader and more active one. The authority must make inquiries wherever it suspects that a child is suffering significant harm or is likely to do so. In effect this is taken for granted where the child is the subject of an EPO or in police protection since satisfaction of the same 'harm' criterion is a prerequisite to the use of these procedures.

6.53 Section 47(3) specifies the nature of the inquiries which are to be made by the authority. The duty to make these inquiries applies equally to an authority which has obtained an EPO in relation to a child (s 47(2)). The inquiries must, in particular, be directed towards establishing:

(a) Whether the authority should make any application to the court, or exercise any of its other powers under the Act. (This is very wide and will involve consideration of whether to apply for an EPO (where this has not already been done), a care or supervision order or whether to offer voluntary assistance under Part III.)

(b) whether it would be in the best interests of a child who is subject to an EPO , but not in local authority accommodation, to be in such accommodation while the EPO, remains in force.

(c) whether it would be in the best interest of a child who has been taken into police protection for the authority to ask for an application to be made under s 46(7) (i.e. for an EPO which has the effect of extending the period of protection).

We saw that the designated officer also has to make inquiries and take action to safeguard and promote the welfare of a child in police protection. Perhaps the most important aspect of this is deciding whether to apply for an EPO, or to release the child. Section 47(3) ensures that this is not purely an issue for the police. The authority has an equivalent duty to consider whether an EPO is necessary. It is conceivable that there may be instances in which the authority will wish to take action itself where the police are in favour of returning the child home.

6.54 Section 47 goes on to deal with the authority's duty to consider and execute follow-up action arising from its inquiries. Where, in the course of its inquiries, any officer of the authority is refused access to the child concerned or is denied information as to the child's whereabouts, the authority must apply for an EPO, care order, or supervision order, unless satisfied that the child's welfare can be satisfactorily safeguarded without this (s 47(6)).

Where, having concluded its inquiries, the authority decides not to seek any of the above orders, it must consider whether there should be a later review of the child's circumstances and, if so, must fix a date on which the review is to begin (s 47(7)). Where, alternatively, it considers that it should take some action to safeguard or promote the child's welfare, it is obliged to take that action in so far as it is within its power and it is reasonably practicable for it to do so (s 47(8)). This is another provision designed to emphasise the positive duties of local authorities and to avoid delay which, especially in the emergency context, may be extremely detrimental to the child.

6.55 The remaining provisions of s 47 attempt to promote the inter-agency cooperation which was a central feature both of the Jasmine Beckford and Butler-Sloss reports. The former stated, in particular, that there were powerful reasons why the duty on local authorities or health authorities to co-operate under s 22 of the National Health Service Act 1977 should be more specific in the context of child abuse. It was said that it should include the duty to consult and assist by advice and the supply of information in order to help with the management of such cases. The report argued that this would be a positive and practical step to promote multi-disciplinary working in the area. This was thought to be important both at the stage of identification of abuse and in subsequent follow-up action. These views were accepted in the White Paper (para 43), and the Act accordingly makes provision for co-operation between various statutory and voluntary agencies in the investigation of suspected harm and the protection of children at risk.

6.56 A local authority is required to consult with another local authority where it has been making inquiries in relation to a child who appears to be ordinarily resident in the area of that other authority. That authority may then take over the necessary inquiries (s 47(12)). Secondly, where as a result of its inquiries it appears to the authority that there is an educational issue which should be investigated, it must consult the relevant local education authority (s 47(5)). Thirdly, the Act specifies a range of persons who must assist an authority with its inquiries if called upon to do so by providing relevant information and advice (s 47(9)). The duty does not arise where rendering the assistance would be unreasonable in all the circumstances of the case (s 47(10)). The 'persons' are another local authority, any local education authority, any local housing authority, any health authority and 'any person authorised by the Secretary of State for the purposes of this section' (s 47(11)). Presumably the latter category would include voluntary agencies.

7. Powers of the Court to Assist in the Discovery of Children who may be in Need of Emergency Protection

6.57 Section 48 enables the court, on making an EPO, to incorporate other orders to assist in the enforcement of the main order. They may cover disclosure of the whereabouts of children in need of protection, authority to either enter and search premises for children, and warrants authorising assistance by the police where this appears to be necessary.

(a) Disclosure of a child's whereabouts

6.58 Where it appears to a court making an EPO that adequate information as to the child's whereabouts is not available to the applicant, but is available to another person, it may order that other person to disclose any information that he may have as to the child's whereabouts if ordered to do so by the applicant (s 48(1)).

Since the discovery of children is so vital to effective emergency procedures there was some support in Parliament for an automatic duty of disclosure to be part and parcel of the legal effects of an EPO along with the duty to produce the child. This was resisted by the Government on the basis that an order requiring people to do something ought to be justified to the court's satisfaction on proof of evidence of need. It was also thought that the provision preventing someone from relying on the privilege against self-incrimination (s 48(2)) would need to be applied to a particular named individual and could not sensibly apply in the abstract (see Lord Mackay LC, *House of Lords, Official Report*, 19 January, col 435). What this means in practice is that a separate and specific order will have to be requested where this is required. Both the applicant and the court will need to consider at the time when the EPO is made whether there is likely to be a problem in ascertaining the child's whereabouts. If there is any doubt about this it would be wise for special provision to be made to avoid having to return to the court later.

(b) Search warrants

6.59 The Act draws a distinction between entry and search by the applicant alone, and entry and search by the police with or without the applicant in attendance. If police assistance is desired, this should be specifically sought and provision for it incorporated in the EPO.

The court may, on making an EPO, authorise the applicant to enter specified premises and search for the child who is the subject of the order (s 48(3)). Where it is satisfied that there is reasonable cause to believe that there may be *another* child on those premises, with respect to whom an EPO ought to be made, the court may also authorise the applicant to search for that child on the same premises (s 48(4)). If, then, a second child is found on the premises and the applicant is satisfied that the grounds for making an EPO exist with respect to that child, the above order will operate as if it were an EPO (s 48(5)). The reasoning is obvious. The applicant should have power to take immediate action in the circumstances postulated. His right to do so is subject to an obligation to notify the court that another child has been found who is, in accordance with these provisions, now also the subject of the EPO (s 48(6)).

6.60 The above powers authorise entry and search by the applicant. It is a moot point whether they include power to force entry where this is refused. In any event, where it looks like force may be necessary, the applicant would be well advised to enlist the help of the police by applying for a warrant. Anyone (not simply the applicant for the EPO) may apply for a warrant authorising any constable to assist in the exercise of powers under an EPO, *using reasonable force if necessary.* The court may issue the warrant where it appears to it that a person attempting to exercise these powers has been, or is likely to be, prevented from doing so by being refused entry to specified premises or access to the child concerned (s 48(9)). The warrant must be addressed to, and executed by, a police constable who must allow the applicant to accompany him if he desires and the court does not direct otherwise (s 48(10). The court may also direct that the constable be accompanied by a registered medical practitioner, registered nurse or registered health visitor if he so chooses (s 48(11)). Applications for warrants will have to be made in the manner and form prescribed by rules of court (s 48(12)).

6.61 The child must be named in orders authorising entry and search, applications for warrants and the warrants themselves. Where he is not named he should be identified as clearly as possible (s 48(13)). This corresponds with a similar provision relating to children subject to EPOs (s 44(14), supra).

6.62 It should be emphasised again that these powers of entry and search are not automatic when an EPO is granted. The court must also be satisfied that they are necessary to enable proper enforcement of the order. The intention in this part of the Act was evidently to separate the question of whether an EPO should be granted from the question of what enforcement powers are appropriate. It should therefore be borne in mind in practice that either an EPO or a search warrant on its own may not be enough to achieve the dual objectives of discovering a child in need of protection and removing him from danger. Just as an EPO may not confer power to force entry, so a search warrant does not carry with it the authority to remove a child once discovered. The applicant for either order should therefore be alive to the possible need to obtain both orders simultaneously.

8. Procedural and Related Matters

6.63 As elsewhere in the Act, it is difficult to describe procedural matters relating to EPOs and other orders under Part V since they will largely be governed by rules of court which are not available at the time of writing (s 52(1)). Nonetheless, the central features of what is to be embodied in the rules became apparent during the passage of the Bill.

It is clear from the Act itself that the rules may in particular make provision:

(a) as to the form in which any application is to be made or direction to be given;

(b) prescribing the persons who are to be notified of:

    (i) the making or extension of an EPO; or

    (ii) the making of an application under s 45(4) (extension of an EPO), s 45(8) (discharge of an EPO) or s 46(7) (EPO following police protection); and

(c) as to the content of such notification and the manner in which, and person by whom, it is to be given (s 52(2)).

6.64 The notification provisions will be exceptionally important. Many felt that it would have been better if rights of notification had been written into the Act, rather than relegated to rules of court. As we have seen, they are spelled out where a child is in police protection. Failure to observe the fundamental rules of natural justice, both in relation to parents and children, was very much a feature of what happened in Cleveland. Complaints were widespread there and elsewhere, that parents under the existing procedures received either inadequate or no information about the meaning of Place of Safety Orders. The Review recommended that applications for EPOs be made in writing and that magistrates should record their reasons for making the order. It also recommended that these documents should be supplied after the hearing to the parents, the child and the local authority (where it is not the applicant) and that parents should be given information about their right to seek legal advice (paras 13.27–13.28). The reason given for leaving these matters to rules of court is to preserve flexibility. It seems likely that, in addition to parents and children, the list of those entitled to notification will extend to persons with parental responsibility, persons with whom the child was living when the order was made, unmarried fathers and any person who had the benefit of a contact order with respect to the child (see Lord Mackay LC, *House of Lords, Official Report,* 19 January 1989, at col 477).

Apart from the notification provisions, the Review favoured procedural changes which would produce 'a more consistent, fair and thorough scheme which acknowledges the seriousness of making an emergency protection order' (para 13.26). The rules are therefore likely to provide for relatively more formal requirements than were required for Place of Safety Orders.

6.65 Section 52(3) enables the Secretary of State to make regulations where a child is the subject of an EPO which was not applied for by the authority within whose area he is ordinarily resident. The regulations will provide for that other authority to take over responsibility for the child where it is of the opinion that that would be in the child's best interests. Where this occurs, the regulations will provide for the authority to be treated as if it was the original applicant for the EPO and will govern the time when responsibility is transferred (s 52(4)).

CHAPTER SEVEN

The Legal Regulation of Substitute Care

1. Introduction

7.1 This chapter is concerned with the regulation of the many different arrangements for substitute care which are provided for children in care and for other children who are looked after outside the family home. We are concerned both with day care and full-time care in their various manifestations. Much of the law considered in this chapter is a re-enactment with modifications of the position before the Act. Nonetheless, the Act introduces some significant reforms, particularly in relation to child-minding and other day-care services (Part X). The subject matter of this chapter is largely covered by Parts VI to XI and Schs 4 to 10 inclusive. For the sake of completeness we also consider new notification requirements relating to certain children accommodated by health and local education authorities, or in residential care, nursing or mental nursing homes (ss 85 and 86) and new controls relating to independent boarding schools (s 87). We also mention briefly the amendments to the adoption legislation (s 88 and Sch 10).

2. Community Homes

7.2 Part VI and Sch 4 deal with the provision, organisation, conduct and cessation of community homes. They replace Part IV of the Child Care Act 1980 and the Community Homes Regulations 1972.

(a) Provision of community homes

7.3 All local authorities must provide community homes for children who are looked after by them and for the welfare of other children who are not looked after by them. They may do so either alone or jointly with one or more other local authorities (s 53(1)). They must ensure that different types of accommodation are available which are suitable for the different purposes and requirements of the children for whom they are provided (s 53(2)). This would entail, for example, the provision of residential nurseries for younger children as well as homes for older children.

7.4 'Community homes' includes homes provided, managed, equipped and maintained by local authorities themselves, as well as certain homes provided by voluntary organisations. Where a local authority and a voluntary organisation have agreed that, in accordance with an instrument of management, the management, equipment and maintenance of a home will be the responsibility of either the authority or the organisation, the home will be a community home (s 53(3)). Where the managerial function is performed by the authority the home is designated a 'controlled community home' (s 53(4)). Where it rests with the organisation it is known as an 'assisted community home' (s 53(5)). The significance of either designation is that both types of home are exempted from the normal controls over voluntary homes in Part VII and Sch 5. Although the Act obliges authorities to provide a range of homes, individual authorities may make 'such arrangements as they consider appropriate', the effect of which is to confer on them a very wide discretion.

(b)   The management and conduct of community homes

7.5   Schedule 4 contains the details on the management and conduct of community homes. The Secretary of State may make instruments of management providing for the constitution of the body of managers for controlled or assisted community homes. The proportion of managers appointed by the local authority must be two-thirds for the former and one-third for the latter. The remaining managers are appointed by the organisation concerned to represent its interests and to secure, so far as is practicable, preservation of the character of the home and compliance with the terms of any trust deed relating to it (para 1). Where there is a conflict between the terms of the trust deed and the instrument of management, the latter will prevail. The Secretary of State may, after consultation with the organisation and the authority, vary or revoke any provisions of the instrument of management (para 2).

7.6   The managerial functions of the 'responsible body' (the authority in the case of a controlled home and the organisation in the case of an assisted home) are performed by the managers of the respective homes as their agents. They must submit annual accounts to the responsible body. The employment of staff at a home is decided by the responsible body itself, except that the local authority may overrule decisions of the organisation relating to the employment or termination of employment of persons at an assisted community home (para 3).

7.7   The Secretary of State is empowered to make regulations to govern a host of matters relating to the conduct of community homes (para 4). The former Community Homes Regulations 1972 provided a framework within which responsible bodies enjoyed a wide discretion and it is expected that the new regulations will adopt this approach. In general terms they will deal with placement, the conduct of the homes and securing the welfare of the children in them. Specifically, they may cover the standard of premises, health care, discipline and control, religious instruction, the use of secure accommodation and the keeping of records. They may empower the Secretary of State to exert some control over the appointment of the person in charge of a home. They may also allow him to give or revoke directions requiring the responsible body to accommodate a particular child looked after by a local authority for whom no places are made available in that home, or to take other specified action in relation to a child accommodated in the home. It appears that this power may be used in order to protect the public.

(c) Determination of disputes relating to controlled or assisted community homes

7.8   Section 55 gives the Secretary of State power to determine disputes between local authorities and voluntary organisations relating to controlled or assisted community homes where they are referred to him by either party. This power exists notwithstanding the normal allocation of responsibility by the instrument of management for the matter in issue. He may give such directions as he thinks fit to the authority or the organisation. By way of exception, he has no jurisdiction over disputes concerning religious instruction where these have been reserved to an ecclesiastical or denominational authority under the trust deed relating to the home.

(d) The cessation of community homes

7.9   A community home may cease to be used as such for a number of different reasons. The Secretary of State may decide that it is unsuitable, a voluntary organisation may wish to discontinue its provision of a controlled or assisted home, or the local authority may wish to extricate itself from its involvement with such a home by revoking its designation. The Act deals expressly with all these contingencies.

7.10   The Secretary of State may, by written notice to the responsible body, direct that from a specified date premises may no longer be used as a community home. He may do so where they are unsuitable, or where the conduct of the home is in breach of the regulations made under Sch 4, para 4 (supra) or is otherwise unsatisfactory (s 54).

7.11   Before a voluntary organisation discontinues the running of a controlled or assisted community home, it must give at least two years' notice of its intention to the local authority and the Secretary of State. Where the managers of the home give written notice to the Secretary of State that they are unwilling or unable to continue to manage the home during the period of notice, the Secretary of State may require the local authority to conduct the home as if it were a community home provided by itself (s 56). Apart from the lengthy notice requirement, a voluntary organisation may suffer financial disadvantages in deciding to cease to operate a home as a community home. Section 44 of the Child Care Act 1980 provided that, when premises or parts of premises were disposed of, the proportion of their value which was attributable to the expenditure of public money was to be repaid by the organisation providing the home or the trustees in whom it was vested. These provisions have been re-enacted, but the Act goes further and now requires payment of a similar proportion where a controlled or assisted community home is put to *alternative use* during the period before the home's designation has been withdrawn. With the agreement of the responsible authority or the Secretary of State, the liability to repay may be discharged, in whole or in part, by the transfer of premises (s 58). The reality may be that, in view of the extent of the financial burden, a voluntary organisation discontinuing a community home may find itself obliged to transfer all or part of its premises or property to the local authority.

7.12 A local authority may, by at least two years' written notice to the Secretary of State and the voluntary organisation by which the home is provided, withdraw its designation of the home as a controlled or assisted community home. Where the home's managers give written notice to the Secretary of State that they are unable or unwilling to continue as managers until the date specified by the local authority for withdrawal of the designation, he may revoke the home's instrument of management from an earlier date specified by him. Before doing so, he must consult both the organisation and the authority. When either of the above periods of notice expires, the instrument of management ceases to have effect and the home will from that date cease to be a community home (s 57).

3. Voluntary Homes and Voluntary Organisations

7.13 Part VII and Sch 5 are concerned with the regulation of voluntary homes and the statutory obligations of voluntary organisations towards children looked after by them. They replace Part VI of the Child Care Act 1980 and the Voluntary Homes (Registration) Regulations 1948.

(a) Voluntary homes

(i) Definition

7.14 Voluntary homes are essentially homes run by voluntary organisations which are not controlled or assisted community homes. In other words, there is no direct involvement of the local authority in the management or conduct of these homes. They are instead subject to registration requirements and controls exercised by the Secretary of State. They include homes provided by well-known organisations such as Barnardo's and the Church of England Children's Society.

A voluntary home is defined by the Act as 'any home or other institution providing care and accommodation for children which is carried on by a voluntary organisation' (s 60(3)). Some institutions are specifically excluded from this definition. The first exclusions are 'a nursing home, mental nursing home or residential care home', which have the same meaning as that attributed to them in the Registered Homes Act 1984 (s 105(1)). The effect is to exclude from the legal controls on voluntary homes those homes which have a primary medical purpose. Also excluded are schools, health service hospitals, community homes or other institutions provided, equiped and maintained by the Secretary of State and any home specifically exempted by regulations. The purpose of the last category is to enable the Secretary of State to exempt those establishments where registration as voluntary homes would be considered inappropriate. Examples which have been cited include day nurseries and homes which would otherwise be required to register simply because of their use for holiday play schemes.

(ii) Registration

7.15 The basic regulatory mechanism is that no voluntary home may be carried on unless it is registered in the appropriate register kept by the Secretary of State (s 60(1)). The detailed requirements on registration procedures are contained in Part I of Sch 5. An application for registration must be made in prescribed form by those intending to carry on the home. The Secretary of State may grant or refuse it or grant it subject to conditions (para 1). Where he takes either of the last two courses he must give written notice to the applicant including the reasons for his decision (para 2). He also has power to cancel the registration of a home which is not conducted in accordance with regulations made under para 7, or is otherwise unsatisfactory. Where he does so he may require the local authority to remove all or any of the children accommodated in the home and look after them itself. He may also vary the conditions subject to which a home is run or impose additional conditions (para 1). In all of these instances, the person carrying on the home must be informed of his right to make representations to the Secretary of State within fourteen days of the receipt of the notice (para 3). Where these representations do not have the desired effect, the Secretary of State must serve notice in writing of his intention to adopt his proposal (para 4). There is then a right of appeal, within twenty-eight days of receiving the notice, to a Registered Homes Tribunal. The Tribunal has power to confirm the decision or direct that it shall not have effect, vary any condition to which the appeal relates or direct that it shall cease to have effect, or impose any condition itself (para 5).

The person in charge of a voluntary home is required to provide the Secretary of State with certain particulars relating to the home within three months of its establishment and annually thereafter. The particulars prescribed under the Voluntary Homes (Return of Particulars) Regulations 1949 (as amended) related to such matters as the persons running the voluntary organisation providing the home, the children in the home and charges made to local authorities with respect to the accommodation in voluntary homes of children in care. Failure to provide particulars, without reasonable excuse, constitutes an offence (para 6).

(iii)   Conduct of voluntary homes

7.16   Part II of Sch 5 empowers the Secretary of State to make regulations as to the conduct of voluntary homes. The original regulations were the Administration of Children's Homes Regulations 1951, which applied both to homes run by local authorities and voluntary organisations. Since 1972, community homes have been governed by their own regulations and the Act has preserved the two independent sets of regulations. Not surprisingly, the matters which may be covered by each are very similar (see Part III of Sch 4, *supra*).

7.17   One matter which did cause some debate in Parliament relates to the suggested use of secure accommodation by voluntary organisations. We considered this issue in connection with local authorities in Chapter 4. The Bill originally contemplated the possibility that the Secretary of State might wish to provide by regulation for circumstances in which secure accommodation could be used by voluntary organisations subject to his approval and any requirements imposed by him (Sch 5, para 7(2)(*f*)). The view was vigorously pressed in Parliament that voluntary organisations should never be empowered to lock up children (see particularly Baroness David, *House of Lords, Official Report*, 23 January 1989, col 498, et seq). It was argued that this was tantamount to imprisonment which should be the responsibility of the state alone. It was clear from the responses of the Lord Chancellor that the Government had no immediate intention of granting its approval for the use of this type of accommodation by voluntary organisations. In the event, an amendment was accepted which enables the Secretary of State to prohibit the use of secure accommodation by voluntary organisations.

(b)   Voluntary organisations

(i)   The duties of voluntary organisations

7.18   Section 59 is concerned with the ways in which voluntary organisations may accommodate children looked after by them. The provisions are equivalent to those which apply where a local authority is looking after a child. The intention is to produce parity of treatment for children looked after in the public and voluntary sectors respectively. With this in mind, the Secretary of State may also make regulations requiring voluntary organisations to review the cases of children looked after by them and consider representations from prescribed individuals in the manner envisaged for local authorities by s 26. We have already considered these matters in Chapter 4.

7.19   Section 61 places on voluntary organisations the same broad statutory duties that local authorities have where a child is looked after by them. Those relating to promotion of the child's welfare, provision of services and facilities to a child being looked after by his parents, taking into account the wishes and feelings of specified individuals before taking decisions, and providing advice and assistance to the child on ceasing to be accommodated by the organisation, correspond precisely (see s 22(3) to (5) and s 24(1) discussed in Chapter 4). Again the policy here is that these children are in much the same position and should not be treated differently whether they are being looked after in the public or voluntary sector. The only significant difference is that the duty to protect the public, which can allow a local authority to derogate from its general duties to children, has no counterpart in the context of voluntary organisations.

(ii)   The duties of local authorities

7.20   Local authorities are required to satisfy themselves that voluntary organisations accommodating children within their area, or outside their area on their behalf, are satisfactorily safeguarding or promoting their welfare (s 62(1)). Where they are not satisfied they must, unless they consider that it would not be in the best interests of any child concerned, take reasonably practicable steps to secure that the care and accommodation of the child is undertaken by a parent, person with parental responsibility, or relative. They must also consider the extent to which (if at all) they should exercise any of their statutory functions (s 62(5)). A 'relative' for these purposes includes a grandparent, brother, sister, uncle or aunt (whether of the full blood or half blood or by affinity) or stepparent (s 105(1)). In addition to this broad duty, and with a view to discharging it, authorities are specifically required to arrange for children accommodated by voluntary organisations to be visited 'from time to time' in the interests of their welfare (s 62(2)). This was a rather vague obligation, as originally drafted, leaving the nature and frequency of the visits entirely to the discretion of individual authorities. Accordingly, the Secretary of State is now given power to make regulations prescribing more closely the visiting obligations of the authorities (s 62(3)).

7.21   Authorities' duties are backed up with rights of entry and inspection. Any person authorised by an authority may enter, at a reasonable time, any premises in which children are accommodated, may inspect the premises themselves and the children on them and may require any person to co-operate by allowing him to inspect records and by providing information when requested (s 62(6)). Anyone intentionally obstructing this process commits an offence (s 62(9)). As with EPOS, these powers of entry and search do not extend to forced entry. Where this proves necessary, a search warrant, authorising the assistance of the police, must be sought (see s 102(6) and Chapter 6).

7.22   It should be recalled that the duties of local authorities to offer advice and assistance to a young person who was, but is no longer, looked after by them, also apply to those who were accommodated by or on behalf of a voluntary organisation. This is only the case where an authority is satisfied that the organisation concerned does not have the necessary facilities for advising or befriending him (see s 24 and Chapter 4).

4.   Registered Children's Homes

(a)   General

7.23   Part VIII and Sch 6 govern registered children's homes and replace the Children's Homes Act 1982. These homes are, in essence, private children's homes not run by voluntary organisations, but carried on for profit. It is the absence of profit-making which characterises voluntary organisations (s 105(1)). Before the Act children's homes were not subject to any form of regulation apart from the general powers of inspection exercised in relation to all homes by the Secretary of State (discussed below). The Children's Homes Act 1982 introduced a requirement that private children's homes be registered with local authorities, but this legislation has remained unimplemented. Some individual children in private homes were, however, protected to some extent by the legislation governing private fostering (below).

Placement in a private home is another option for local authorities looking after children (whether in care or not). It is understood that some of these homes offer facilities which are not available in community homes or elsewhere, and are able in certain instances to cater for the special needs of some children.

7.24   The Act repeals the 1982 Act in its entirety, but substantially reproduces its provisions. The essential difference between the regulation of voluntary homes and registered homes is that the registration authority for the former is the Secretary of State, while for the latter it is the local authority. The Government mooted the possibility of introducing a comprehensive registration scheme for both kinds of home with the local authority as the sole registration authority (White Paper, para 81) but the Act has preserved the dual registration system. Nonetheless, the registration requirements and procedures and the regulations governing the conduct of homes under the respective regimes are very similar.

(b)   Definition

7.25   Section 63 contains the definition of 'a children's home' for the purposes of Part VIII. It is a complex definition because it is subject to a number of significant exclusions of premises which would otherwise fall within the basic meaning of the term. The starting point is s 63(3) which states that a children's home

(a) means a home which provides (or usually provides or is intended to provide) care and accommodation wholly or mainly for more than three children at any one time; but

(b) does not include a home which is exempted by or under any of the following provisions of this Section or by regulations made for the purposes of this subsection by the Secretary of State.

'Home' for these purposes includes any institution (s 63(9)). Where a private home caters for three children or less at any one time, the children concerned may well fall within the provisions regulating private fostering. The power of the Secretary of State to exempt certain homes from regulation corresponds with his powers to exempt homes which would otherwise be regarded as voluntary homes (see s 60(3), supra). Similar considerations apply. The specific exemptions in the Act are wide-ranging. They include a home in which the child is cared for and accommodated by a parent, person with parental responsibility for him or relative (s 63(4)), a community home, voluntary home, residential care home, nursing home, health service hospital, home provided, equipped and maintained by the Secretary of State, and (subject to exceptions) a school (s 63(5)). An independent school may be treated as a children's home where it provides accommodation for not more than fifty children, and is not a home approved by the Secretary of State under s 11(3)(a) of the Education Act 1981 (s 63(7)).

(c) Registration

7.26 As with voluntary homes the basic statutory requirement is registration. No child may be cared for or provided with accommodation in a children's home unless the home is registered with the local authority (s 63(1)). Where this requirement is not observed, the person carrying on the home is guilty of an offence unless he has a reasonable excuse (s 63(10)). The details of the registration procedure are set out in Part I of Sch 6. The provisions relating to requirements for registration, cancellation of registration, representations and appeals, etc correspond closely with those governing voluntary homes in Sch 5. Although not identical in every respect, there would be little to be gained by repeating what was said in that context.

(d) Conduct of registered children's homes

7.27 Although registration is with the local authority, the conduct of registered children's homes is a matter for regulations to be made by the Secretary of State. Part II of Sch 6 prescribes what the regulations may cover and that content is, again, so similar to that relating to both community homes (Part III, Sch 4) and voluntary homes (Part II, Sch 5) that further discussion is not required.

(e) Protection of the welfare of children in registered children's homes

7.28 The person carrying on a registered children's home has identical general duties towards children being looked after in it, to those placed on local authorities (s 22(3) to (5) and s 24(1)), and voluntary organisations (s.61) towards children looked after by them. Similarly, the statutory duties of local authorities towards children being accommodated by voluntary organisations, together with their powers of entry and inspection (s 62) apply equally in relation to children looked after in a registered children's home (s 64(4)).

7.29 The Act prohibits certain persons disqualified from fostering a child privately under s 68 (below) from carrying on, or being concerned in the management of, or having any financial interest in, a registered children's home, unless they have disclosed the fact of their disqualification to the local authority and obtained its written consent (s 65(1)). It also prohibits the employment of such persons in a registered children's home unless the employer has disclosed the disqualification to the authority and obtained its written consent to employment of the person concerned (s 65(2)). Anyone contravening either requirement commits an offence (s 65(4)). Where the authority refuses to give its consent, it must inform the applicant by written notice stating the reasons for the refusal, the applicant's right to appeal to a Registered Homes Tribunal and the time within which he may do so (s 65(3)).

The policy here is clearly to extend the restrictions on unsuitable persons being involved in private foster care to the employment, or other involvement of such persons in private children's homes. The basis of disqualification is considered below. It is interesting to note in passing that the Law Commission at one time sought views on whether these disqualifications should apply to privately appointed guardians (Law Com Working Paper No 91 on *Guardianship* (1985)), but there was little support for the idea.

(f) Relationship between children's homes and foster care

7.30 Schedule 7 is concerned with limits on the number of foster children and with the relationship between the legal controls relating to children's homes and those relating to foster care.

7.31 The Schedule applies to *all* foster children whether boarded with local authority foster parents, foster parents chosen by a voluntary organisation, or private foster parents (para 1). The general rule is that no foster parent may foster more than three children ('the usual fostering limit') (para 2), unless the children concerned are all siblings of each other (para 3) or the local authority has exempted him from the usual limit (para 4). In considering whether to grant an exemption, the authority must have regard, in particular, to the number of children it is proposed to foster, the arrangements proposed for their care and the period of time envisaged for the arrangement, the intended and likely relationship between the foster parent and the children and whether the welfare of the fostered children (and of any other children who are or will be living in the accommodation) will be safeguarded and promoted (para 4(2)). Where the exemption is granted, the authority must inform the person concerned by written notice which must also name the children whom he may foster and specify any condition to which the exemption is subject (para 4(3)). The authority may, by written notice, vary or cancel the exemption or impose, vary or cancel a condition to which it is subject, having regard to the above considerations (para 4(4)). These provisions may be amplified or modified by the Secretary of State to cater for children who need to be placed with foster parents urgently (para 4(5)).

Where the usual fostering limit is exceeded (including the situation in which this arises because non-exempted children are fostered), the person will cease to be treated as fostering and will instead be treated as carrying on a children's home. As such he will be subject to the controls in Part VIII and Sch 6 (para 5). Local authorities are required to establish complaints procedures for considering representations by those affected by the exemption provisions (para 6).

5. Private Fostering Arrangements

(a) General

7.32 Part IX and Schs 7 and 8 regulate private fostering arrangements and replace the Foster Children Act 1980. We noted earlier (in Chapter 2) that the prohibition on parents transferring parental responsibility does not prevent them from *delegating* its exercise to others. Hence, there is nothing to prevent parents from arranging privately with foster parents for the full-time care of their child. What distinguishes this type of placement from public fostering is that it is not paid for or arranged by a local authority. The absence of initial involvement by social services obviously creates a risk of unsuitable placement. Legal regulation of these private arrangements centres on the requirement of *notification* rather than registration which is the characteristic feature of voluntary and private homes. The purpose of notification is to enable the local authority to satisfy itself as to the welfare of the child, primarily by visits and inspection. Where it is not satisfied, it may prohibit a placement or remove a child already placed in unsatisfactory circumstances.

7.33 This was essentially the system under the 1980 Act. The Act preserves this system, with modifications, and repeals the 1980 Act in toto. The opportunity is taken to redefine 'foster parents'. The old definition was complex and confusing and may have led to some doubt in practice about which children were covered by the fostering legislation. It should be emphasised again that the controls on private fostering are complementary to those governing private children's homes (supra).

(b) Definition of foster child

7.34 The definition of 'foster child' under the old law extended to children under sixteen whose care and maintenance were undertaken by someone other than a 'relative, guardian or custodian' (s 1, 1980 Act). There was a complicated list of exclusions. These included children who were fostered for not more than six days (s 2(3)(*b*)) and children who were fostered for not more than twenty-seven days by someone who was not a regular foster parent (s 2(3)(*a*)). Most of the remaining exclusions related to children who fell within the protective regulation of other pieces of legislation.

The new definition of a 'privately fostered child', which the Act introduces, is detailed if not complicated. To ascertain definitively which children are covered by it we must pick through the provisions of s 66 and Sch 8. The principal change is that, in the interests of simplicity, the exemptions are restricted to those placements lasting or intended to last for less than twenty-eight days (White Paper, para 80).

7.35 The children falling within the definition are those who are:

  (a) under the age of sixteen (s 66(1)), unless they are disabled, in which case they must be under eighteen (s 66(4));

  (b) cared for and provided with accommodation by someone other than a parent, another person with parental responsibility, or a relative (s 66(1));

  (c) cared for and accommodated (or intended to be accommodated) for at least twenty-eight days (s 66(2)). It is not clear whether this is referring to aggregate periods or a single continuous period. The intention was to provide for the former (White Paper, para 80) but the wording of the Act suggests the latter;

  (d) not within the many exemptions contained in Sch 8. These include, inter alia, children looked after by local authorities, those in premises in which any parent, relative (who has assumed responsibility for them), or person with parental responsibility is currently living, those detained or subject to guardianship under the Mental Health Act 1983 and those placed for adoption or within the definition of 'protected child' under the adoption legislation. Other exclusions relate generally to children already protected by other forms of legal regulation.

(c) Notification of placement and related matters

7.36 The Secretary of State may make regulations requiring notification to local authorities of placements or intended placements of children with private foster parents (Sch 8, para 7(1)). The notification requirements may be imposed upon any person arranging or involved in the arrangement of a placement, the parent or person with parental responsibility, the foster parent, or intended foster parent. The regulations may also provide for notification of changes of address and termination of fostering arrangements

(Sch 8, para 7(2)). The notification requirements are intended to be more comprehensive than those which have hitherto applied. In particular, *parents* as well as foster parents will be subject to them. These dual obligations may go some way towards assisting local authorities in detecting private placements. Where a private placement, or intended placement, has been notified, the local authority may impose requirements as to the number, age and sex of the children who may be privately fostered by the person concerned, the standard of the accommodation and equipment to be provided for them, the arrangements for their health and safety and particular arrangements for their care. These may be limited to a particular child or class of child (Sch 8, para 6).

7.37 Advertisements for private fostering are not to be published unless they state the name and address of the person offering to undertake or arrange for the child to be fostered (Sch 8, para 10). A person privately fostering a child is prohibited from having an insurance interest in the life of the child (Sch 8, para 11).

(d) Supervisory duties of local authorities

7.38 Local authorities have a general duty to satisfy themselves that the welfare of privately fostered children in their area is being satisfactorily safeguarded and promoted and to give such advice to foster parents as appears to them to be needed (s 67(1)). This advice-giving function should not be underestimated since it should be remembered that private, as opposed to public, foster parents are not selected, prepared or supported by professional social workers. There is evidence that some of them are uncertain about their role as temporary carers and may have difficulty in not viewing the child as their own. Social work support can do much to alleviate these difficulties.

7.39 Regulations may be made requiring visits by officers of the authority in prescribed circumstances or on specified occasions within specified periods (s 67(2)). The criticism of the visiting requirements under the old law was that they were too vague, particularly as to the frequency of visiting. It is hoped and expected that the new regulations will impose more concrete obligations on authorities. The authority is authorised to inspect premises where there is reasonable cause to believe that a private foster child is being, or is proposed to be, accommodated (s 6 (3)). This power may, again, be backed up by a search warrant where necessary (s 102(6)). The authority has identical duties to those owed to children in voluntary and registered children's homes, where it is not satisfied that the welfare of a privately fostered child is being satisfactorily safeguarded or promoted (s 67(5) and see the discussion of s 62(5), supra). Where the authority wishes to remove a child from an unsatisfactory foster placement, it will need to invoke the emergency procedures in Part V or, in non-urgent cases (and in the absence of voluntary cooperation), care or supervision proceedings in Part IV.

(e) Control of placements – disqualification and prohibition

7.40 Some control over undesirable placements is provided by two mechanisms. First, certain persons are automatically disqualified from taking foster children unless they have obtained the local authority's prior consent. Secondly, the authority itself may specifically prohibit certain placements.

7.41 Section 68 governs disqualifications. It provides generally that no person is to foster a child privately if he is disqualified from doing so under regulations made by the Secretary of State, unless he has disclosed the fact of his disqualification to the local authority and obtained its written consent (s 68(1)). The regulations may provide for disqualification where, inter alia, he has committed specified offences (usually those relating to children), is prohibited from private fostering under s 69, or where his rights and powers with respect to the child have at any time been vested in a specific authority (s 68(2)). The last disqualification relates to those whose parental rights were assumed by resolution under s 3 of the Child Care Act 1980. All of these disqualifications extend to a person living in the same household as the primary disqualified person or living in a household in which that person is employed, unless the authority has been notified of the circumstances and has given its consent (s 68(3)). The purpose behind this is obviously to prevent the child from having any contact with a disqualified person, even though that person is not the proposed foster parent. Where the authority refuses to give its consent, it must give written notice to the applicant with reasons, advising him of his right of appeal and the time within which it must be made (s 68(4)). The appropriate authority is that within whose area it is proposed to foster the child (s 68(5)).

7.42 Section 69 deals with prohibitions on private fostering. The prohibitions apply both where someone is proposing to foster a child privately or where he is already doing so. In the latter instance, following a Commons' Amendment, it is no longer necessary that there should have been a failure to notify the authority of the placement. The authority will have power to intervene even where it deemed the original placement suitable if there is a subsequent change of circumstances (s 69(1)). The authority may prohibit the arrangement where it is of the opinion that the person concerned is not suitable to foster a child, the premises are unsuitable, or it would be prejudicial the welfare of the child for him to be, or continue to be, accommodated by that person in those premises (s 69(2)). Thus, the authority may prohibit someone from fostering a specific child in specified premises, fostering *any* child in specified premises or fostering *any* child in *any* premises within its area. The precise nature of any prohibition will depend on whether it is the foster parent or the premises which are unsuitable, or whether it is the particular needs or characteristics of an individual child which render a particular placement unsatisfactory. The authority may later cancel any prohibition it has made, either of its own motion or on application by the person affected, where it is satisfied that it is no longer justified (s 69(4)). A prohibition may be imposed pending compliance with a requirement laid down by the authority under Sch 8, para 6 (supra). The same rules on notice and rights of appeal apply (s 69(7)).

(f) Appeals and offences

7.43 A person aggrieved by the imposition of a requirement, refusal of consent to or prohibition of a fostering arrangement, refusal to cancel a prohibition, or an adverse decision relating to exemption has a right of appeal to the court (Sch 8, para 8). It must be made within fourteen days of receiving notice of the authority's adverse decision. The court has power to cancel or vary a requirement or prohibition.

7.44 Section 70 specifies the offences which may be committed in connection with private fostering. In general, failure to comply with any of the obligations imposed by this part of the Act will amount to an offence. The mens rea for individual offences does, however, differ. Some require absence of a reasonable excuse, others require knowledge or intention with respect to the breach. The most significant offence is to fail, without reasonable excuse, to give any notice or information required by the Act within a reasonable time, or to be responsible for any statement in such notice or information which is known to be false or misleading (s 70(1)(*a*)). Where it is alleged that s 68(3) has been contravened (fostering a child in a household where a disqualified person is living or employed), it is a defence to show that the accused did not know, and had no reasonable ground for believing, that a disqualified person was living or employed on the premises (s 70(2)).

6. Child-Minding and Day Care for Young Children

(a) General

7.45 Part X and Sch 9 repeal the Nurseries and Child-Minders Regulation Act 1948. They introduce a new unified registration system for child-minders and others providing day care for young children to replace the former separate registers for child-minders and nurseries. The new scheme has many features in common with the old scheme, and is in essence a revamping of it. The modifications are intended to improve the effectiveness of the control by local authorities of private and voluntary day care provision. In recent years there has been a rapid increase in the variety and range of such services. In part, this is a reflection of the inadequacy of public services, especially the absence of comprehensive nursery provision. Day care has traditionally been the least regulated form of substitute care and there is ample evidence of large variations in the practice of individual local authorities and of the general ineffectiveness of the registration system under the 1948 Act. The changes in Part X are complementary to the new duty of authorities to keep day care provision under review in their areas (s 19, discussed in Chapter 4).

The basic objectives of the new scheme are to ensure that individuals who provide services to young children comply with acceptable standards and that where they do not, the local authority is able to deal effectively with them. The scheme principally affects pre-school children, but also extends to out-of-school and holiday provision for children up to the age of eight.

(b) Registration

7.46 Section 71 deals with the principles of registration and further details are contained in Sch 9.

(i) *The duty to register*

7.47 Every local authority is required to keep a register of
- (a) persons who act as child-minders on domestic premises within its area and
- (b) persons who provide day care for children under the age of eight on premises (other than domestic premises) within that area (s 71(1)).

The register may be kept by computer and must be open to inspection by members of the public at all reasonable times (s 71(15)).

7.48 A 'child-minder' is defined as someone who looks after one or more children under the age of eight, *for reward* and the period, or the total of periods, spent looking after the children in any day exceeds *two hours*. This period also applies to persons providing day care (s 71(2). Where a person provides day care on different premises in the authority's area, separate registration of the person is required with respect to each premises (s 71(3)).

The essential distinction between child-minders and other providers of day care is that the former care is for children on 'domestic premises', which are those used wholly or mainly as a private dwelling (s 71(12)). In most cases, they will be either the home of the child-minder, or that of the person engaging the child-minder. Other day care providers subject to registration are those who care for children on non-domestic premises, which can include vehicles (s 71(12)). Most obviously this category includes private nurseries and playgroups. A person is not a child-minder unless operating for reward and it is expressly provided that parents, relatives, persons with parental responsibility and foster parents are not child-minders when they look after the child in relation to whom they have those respective relationships (s.71(4)). They may, of course, be child-minders if they look after *other* children (which will frequently be the case).

Persons employed as 'nannies' are not child-minders and do not, consequently, have to register when looking after a child wholly or mainly in the home of their employer (s 71(5)). Where two employers use the same nanny, she will continue to be exempt, provided that she looks after any of the children wholly or mainly in the home of either of them (s 71(6)). If more than two employers are involved, registration is required. A nanny is defined as someone employed to look after a child by a parent, person with parental responsibility, or a relative who has assumed responsibility for the care of the child (s.71(13)).

7.49   The age limit of eight for children protected by this registration system is an arbitrary one and replaces the previous inconsistent age limits of *five* (which applied to children looked after by child-minders) and *sixteen* (which applied to children otherwise provided with day care). The Government's original intention was to restrict registration to day care for the under-fives, but it yielded to pressure for this age limit to be raised. The higher limit will enable authorities to exert some control, through inspection, of out-of-school and holiday provision for younger schoolchildren. At the same time there has been a deliberate attempt to set a limit which will give a better chance of enforcement than has been previously achieved.

(ii)   Refusal of registration

7.50   In addition to the exemptions and disqualifications discussed below, a local authority may refuse to register an applicant where a person or the intended premises are unfit. Registration may be refused where the authority is satisfied that the applicant, or any person looking after, or likely to be looking after, the children is not fit to look after children under the age of eight. This applies to applications both by child-minders (s 71(7)) and other day carers (s 71(9)). It may also be refused, in either case, where any person living or employed, or likely to be living or employed, on the premises to which the application relates, is not fit to be in the proximity of children of this age (s 71(8) and (10)). An application may also be refused where the authority is satisfied that the premises concerned are not fit to be used for looking after children under eight, whether because of their condition, or the condition of any equipment, or for any reason connected with their situation, construction or size (s 71(11)).

No indication is given in the Act as to what constitutes unfitness, but it is expected that information on this will be issued as part of the general guidance to authorities on implementation of the Act (Mr David Mellor, *Hansard*, 6 June 1989, col 393).

(iii)   Exemptions

7.51   Schedule 9 contains a long list of exemptions from the registration requirements. In general, it includes most schools, children's homes and health facilities. The common factor is that they are all establishments which are provided or assisted by local authorities, education authorities, or are subject to some other form of legal regulation. It should be said, however, that the use of such facilities by independent people, such as the organisers of a play group, necessitates registration. The 'occasional facilities' exemption is worth mentioning specifically, since it will affect a large number of people who provide day care for children on an ad hoc basis. Where day care is provided in particular premises on less than six days in any year, registration is not required, provided that the authority is given written notice before the first occasion on which the premises are used (Sch 9, para 5(1)). This exemption will be particularly useful to people providing the occasional crèche for conferences, training courses and other events.

(iv) Disqualifications

7.52 A person may be disqualified from registering as a child-minder or day care provider in accordance with regulations (Sch 9, para 2(1)). Disqualifications may be imposed on a similar basis to those for private foster parents. Indeed, disqualification from fostering a child privately is itself a reason for disqualification from involvement in day care provision (para 2(2)(*f*)). Nothing need be added here to what was said earlier about disqualification from fostering.

(v) The Formalities of Registration

7.53 Schedule 9 also governs the mechanics of registration and, in particular, the procedure and fees for making applications (para 1), the granting of certificates of registration (para 6) and subsequent inspection of premises (para 7). The local authority is obliged to register the applicant if the application is properly made and it is not otherwise entitled to refuse to do so (para 1).

The introduction of fees for registration is a new and controversial aspect of the scheme. The Government's argument in favour of fees was that local authorities would need to generate more income in order to operate a more effective registration system and cope with the large increase in applications. The opposition argued strongly against the imposition of fees which they felt could operate as a disincentive to registration. They argued that positive support and encouragement should be given to those offering day care services, often on a shoestring budget.

(c) Conditions on registration

7.54 Under the 1948 Act, local authorities had the power to attach certain conditions specified in the Act as requirements of registration. But they were not under a legal obligation to do so and such conditions as they could impose were limited to those listed in the legislation.

The Act introduces two changes here. First, authorities now have a *duty* to impose such reasonable requirements as they consider appropriate in individual cases (s 72(1) and s 73(1)). Certain conditions *must* now be imposed. These relate to the maximum number of children (or the maximum number within particular age-groups) who may be looked after; the obligation to maintain the premises and equipment and to ensure that safety standards are met; the duty to keep records of children looked after, assistants and persons living on the premises; the requirement to notify the authority of any changes in this respect; and (in the case of day care providers) the number of assistants required to look after the children on the premises (s 72(2)) and s 73(3)). The Secretary of State may exert some control over local authorities by obliging them to impose specified requirements or prohibiting them from doing so in specified circumstances (s 72(4)).

In determining the maximum number of children to be specified, authorities are required to take into account the number of other children who may at any time be on the relevant premises (s 72(4) and s 73(6)). Authorities may add to these requirements at their discretion provided that they are not incompatible with any of the above mandatory requirements (s 72(5) and s 73(7)). They may also remove any of them or impose additional requirements at any time (s 72(6) and s 73(8)). It is anticipated that this will give authorities the flexibility to tailor conditions to the applicant's individual circumstances.

(d)   Cancellation of registration

7.55   Under the 1948 Act, it was possible for authorities to cancel the registration of a child-minder or day care provider. The new Act confirms this power and specifies more clearly the circumstances in which cancellation is allowed (s 74). The conditions for cancellation are:

(a)   where it appears to the authority that there are circumstances which would justify refusing to register the individual concerned;

(b)   where the care provided by that person is, in the authority's opinion, seriously inadequate, having regard to the needs of that child;

(c)   where that person has contravened or failed to comply with any requirement imposed by the authority or failed to pay the annual inspection fee (s 74(1) and (2)).

Cancellations must be in writing (s 74(5)). In the case of a day care provider, all separate registrations may be cancelled where a refusal to register would be justified in relation to *any* of the premises concerned (s 74(3)). Failure to comply with requirements relating to premises will not constitute a ground for cancellation unless the time for complying with them has expired (s 74(4)).

7.56   The most problematic of the grounds for cancellation is that which relies on the standard of care being 'seriously inadequate'. The Act gives no further guidance on this, but clearly it is again a matter of degree. The implication must be that some imperfections in the quality of care may have to be tolerated. Nonetheless, there was concern in Parliament about the difference between inadequate and *seriously* inadequate. It was pointed out that the latter was a long way, and possibly too far, along the spectrum. The fear is that it may lead to authorities being obliged to register people with whom they are less than happy – a phenomenon which certainly existed before the Act (See Ms Hilary Armstrong, *Hansard*, 6 June 1989, col 402).

What is certain from the Act itself is that in determining whether the standard of care has fallen below the acceptable level, the authority must have regard to the child's religious persuasion, racial origin and cultural and linguistic background (s 74(6)). This raises similar problems to those discussed in relation to care proceedings (Chapter 5).

(e) Emergency cancellations

7.57 Where a local authority wishes to take emergency action to protect a child against a child-minder or other day care provider it may apply to the court for an order (s 75). The court has power to cancel a registration, vary or remove a requirement, or impose an additional requirement. It may do so where it appears to it that a child who is being, or may be, looked after by a named individual is suffering, or is likely to suffer, significant harm (s 75(1)). It will be recalled that this criterion also governs orders for care and supervision and EPOS (Chapters 5 and 6).

An application for an order may be made ex parte and must be supported by a written statement of the authority's reasons for making it (s 75(3)). If granted, the order takes effect immediately (s 75(2)). As soon as reasonably practicable after the order has been made, the registered person must be served with notice of it, its terms and a copy of the authority's statement of reasons in support of its application (s 75(4)).

(f) Inspection

7.58 The authority's powers of inspection under the Act are essentially those which existed previously with one significant modification. Every authority is now required to carry out inspections of relevant premises at least once a year (s 76(4)). Annual inspection is a *minimum* requirement and it is hoped and expected that many authorities will exercise their powers more frequently. But there was evidence that some authorities sent inspectors less often or not at all and it is at these authorities that the new duty is aimed.

7.59 Any authorised person may enter domestic or non-domestic premises where child-minding or day care is at any time carried on or provided (s 76(1)). He may also enter premises in relation to which the local authority has reasonable cause to believe that a child is being looked after (s 76(2)). He may then inspect the premises themselves, any children being looked after on them, the arrangements made for the children's welfare and any records kept in accordance with the legislation (s 76(3)). In doing so, he is entitled to have access to any computer, apparatus or material used for this purpose and the reasonable assistance of the person having their charge or concerned with their operation (s 76(5)). It is an offence to obstruct intentionally any authorised person (s 76(7)).

(g) Appeals

7.60 Section 70 governs the procedure where a person is aggrieved by a decision of the local authority. The authority must give at least fourteen days' notice of its intention to refuse or cancel a registration, to impose, remove or vary any requirement or to refuse to grant any application for variation or removal of a requirement (s 77(1)). The notice must give the authority's reasons and must inform the person affected of his rights to object to the proposed step (s 77(2)). Where that person indicates in writing that he wishes to object, the authority must give him the opportunity to do so, either in person or through a representative (s 77(3) and (4)). If the authority then decides to press ahead it must give further notice of its decision (s 77(5)). There is then a right of appeal (s 77(6)). No cancellation of registration or imposition, removal or variation of a requirement may be made until the determination of the appeal or the expiration of the time allowed for the appeal (s 77(11)).

(h) Offences

7.61 As before the Act, it continues to be an offence to provide day care for children (under eight) without being registered with respect to the premises on which the care is provided (s 78(1) and (2)).

7.62 The Act introduces a novel procedure for enforcement of the registration requirements affecting child-minders. It maintains the mandatory requirement of registration as a child-minder (s 78(3)), but contravention of this no longer *automatically* constitutes an offence. Instead, the authority may issue an 'enforcement notice' on the person concerned which will be effective for the period of one year from the date of service (s 78(4) and (5)). Only those subject to enforcement notices commit criminal offences by continuing to engage in unregistered child-minding (s 78(6)). It is not necessary, for these purposes, that the activity should be carried on in the area of the authority which served the notice (s 78(7)).

The purpose of this change is to exempt from criminal liability the occasional baby-sitter who would otherwise technically commit an offence. Such a person will now be liable to prosecution only where a local authority is concerned enough about her activities to take action. The overall objective is to achieve a balance between effective enforcement and support for casual arrangements which work well and do not require the superintendence of the authority.

7.63 It should finally be noted that it is an offence to fail to comply, without reasonable excuse, with any registration requirement imposed by the authority (s 78(8)). Other offences in connection with child-minding relate to contravention of the disqualification provisions in Sch 9 (s 78(9) to (11)).

7. Children Accommodated in Health and Educational Establishments and Independent Schools

(a) Health and educational establishments

7.64 Sections 85 and 86 are the result of Commons' Amendments. They are designed to protect the welfare of children who spend long periods in accommodation provided by health or education authorities, or as long-stay residents or patients in private care homes and hospitals. Section 85 covers those who are placed by health authorities or LEAs in NHS hospitals and state-maintained special schools and those placed by statutory agencies in private hospitals, care homes or schools offering special education. Section 86 applies to children in private homes and hospitals who are there to receive treatment, specialised care or education because they are handicapped, chronically ill or have special educational needs.

There was concern that these groups of children often have little or no contact with their families and that their position has not been reviewed systematically enough, or with sufficient attention paid to their welfare needs. The Act imposes on the statutory agency effecting a placement, and the person carrying on a private home, a new duty to notify the local authority of such placement. The authority is then required to ensure that the welfare needs of the child are properly met and that contact and rehabilitation with his family is provided wherever possible.

7.65 Where a health authority, LEA or person carrying on a residential care home, nursing home or mental nursing home accommodates (or intends to accommodate) a child for a consecutive period of at least three months, the authority or person concerned must notify the local authority (s 85(1) and s 86(1)). They must then notify the authority when they cease to accommodate the child (s 85(2) and s 86(2)). The responsible authority, in the case of children accommodated by health authorities or LEAs, is that within whose area the child is ordinarily resident, or (where the child is not ordinarily resident in the area of any authority) the one within whose area the accommodation is situated (s 85(3)). The relevant authority where a child is accommodated in a private home is the one within whose area the home is situated (s 86(1)).

7.66 On receiving notification of the child's position, the authority must take such steps as are reasonably practicable to enable it to determine whether the child's welfare is adequately safeguarded and promoted in his present accommodation and must consider the extent to which (if at all) it should exercise any of its functions under the Act in relation to the child (s 85(4) and s 86(3)). Any person carrying on a private home who fails, without reasonable excuse, to comply with the notification requirements commits an offence (s 86(4)). A person authorised by the local authority may enter any of the private homes mentioned above to establish whether there has been compliance with the statutory requirements (s 86(5)) and it is an offence to obstruct him intentionally (s 86(6)).

(b) Independent schools

7.67 Section 87 is the result of a late Commons' Amendment. It is designed to deal with particular problems relating to allegations of sexual abuse of children in independent boarding schools exposed in the BBC television programme 'That's Life'. Before the Act the only statutory duties regarding inspection of such schools were exercised by HM Inspectorate of Schools and were restricted to the question of educational and other standards. The Act now gives a corresponding power and duty to social services departments who must satisfy themselves as to the social, as opposed to educational, welfare of the children accommodated at these schools. Previously this form of intervention was limited to situations in which specific allegations of child abuse had already been made.

7.68 The Act places the proprietor of an independent school which provides accommodation for a child, or anyone who is responsible for running it, under a duty to safeguard and promote the child's welfare (s 87(1)). This does not apply to schools which cater for less than fifty pupils since they fall within the definition of a 'children's home' or 'residential care home' and are protected by the controls appropriate to those establishments (s 87(2)). The local authority within whose area the school is situated must take reasonably practicable steps to determine whether the child's welfare is adequately safeguarded and promoted while he is accommodated at the school (s 87(3)). Where the authority takes the view that the proprietor or person running the school has failed to discharge his welfare duty, it must notify the Secretary of State. The purpose of this is to enable 'notice of complaint' action to be taken under the Education Act 1944. In a serious case, this could lead to closure and removal of the school from the register of independent schools. Provision is made for powers of entry and inspection by persons authorised by the local authority (s 87(5) to (8)), which approximate to those applying to the control of other establishments regulated by the local authority. Again, it is an offence to obstruct intentionally anyone exercising these powers (s 87(9)).

8. Changes to Adoption Law

7.69 Adoption is the one legal procedure affecting children which has been substantially unaffected by the new legislation. It is understood that the Lord Chancellor's department intends to embark on a full review of adoption law as part of a 'rolling programme' of reform of family law of which the 1989 Act forms a part (see Mr David Mellor, *Hansard*, 6 June 1989, col 379). The Act nonetheless does bring about some comparatively minor changes and makes substantial technical amendments to the Adoption Act 1976 and the Adoption (Scotland) Act 1978 (s 88 and Sch 10).

7.70 The more important changes are as follows:

(a) A first group of amendments is designed to harmonise adoption law within the UK. In particular, they take account of the introduction of new adoption provisions in Northern Ireland by amending existing adoption legislation to include references to Northern Ireland adoption agencies and to orders made by Northern Irish courts. The changes are intended to facilitate cooperation between agencies in different parts of the UK where children move from one part of the country to another and, generally, to produce an integrated and mutually compatible adoption law within the UK.

(b) Another set of amendments is consequential on the changes brought about by the Act and updates the terminology in the adoption legislation to ensure consistency with the new legislation. The best example is the revision of the numerous references to 'parental rights and duties' and 'actual custody' to embrace the new concept of 'parental responsibility'.

(c) Perhaps the most significant amendment is the establishment of an 'Adoption Contact Register' (Sch 10, para 21, adding a new s 51A to the Adoption Act 1976). The Registrar General is required to establish a register consisting of two parts. Part I is to contain the names of adopted persons while Part II is to contain the names of relatives. 'Relative' for these purposes includes 'any person (other than an adoptive relative) who is related to the adopted person by blood (including half-blood) or marriage'. The registrar must register (subject to specified conditions) the name and address of any adopted person who gives notice that he wishes to contact a relative of his. He must also, inter alia, transmit to a registered adopted person the name and address of any relative whose name appears in Part II of the register.

These new provisions are complementary to the right of an adopted person to obtain a copy of his birth certificate on attaining majority (s 51 of the Adoption Act 1976). There is at present no provision for counselling which is a feature of the procedure relating to disclosure of birth records. The new system of registration may be useful, even where there is no prospect of establishing a meaningful relationship between the relative and adopted person, in order to explore the medical history of the natural family. This may serve, in some instances, to reduce the risk of hereditary diseases and other medical problems.

9. The Secretary of State's Supervisory Functions and Responsibilities

(a) General

7.71 Part XI is concerned with the general supervisory functions of the Secretary of State in the child care sphere. These include the power to authorise the inspection of all kinds of premises in which children are provided with substitute care and the power to direct inquiries into the discharge of the child-care functions of social services departments, voluntary organisations and other agencies. His other functions include providing financial support for child-care training and grants to voluntary organisations, the instigation and support of research and reporting to Parliament on the discharge of the statutory functions of local authorities and voluntary organisations relating to children.

The support of Government for adequate training of social workers has been a recurrent theme in the reports of public inquiries into child abuse cases, the most recent being the Butler-Sloss report. Clearly, this has major resource implications and is, in the final analysis, a matter of political will. But the point should be made that without adequate training of social workers the effectiveness of many of the reforms introduced by the Act is likely to be seriously undermined. Criticism has centred on the shortage of numbers and the short duration of training. We must confine ourselves here to the legal framework under which the Secretary of State's support is provided.

(b) Inspection of accommodation

7.72 The Secretary of State may direct the inspection of a wide range of homes in which children are accommodated (s 80(1)). These include children's homes; premises provided by or on behalf of local authorities, voluntary organisations or LEAs or health authorities; placements by adoption agencies and premises in which a 'protected child' is living; private foster homes; premises used for child-minding; residential care homes, nursing homes or mental nursing homes and independent schools in which children are accommodated. Inspections will normally be carried out by the Social Services Inspectorate, although they may be conducted by an officer of the local authority with its consent (s 80(3)). Specified individuals and organisations are required to co-operate by providing information and allowing the Secretary of State's representative to inspect records relating to specified premises, the children living in them, or the discharge of the functions of the Secretary of State or local authority under the Act (s 80(4)).

The list of those required to cooperate is a long one, but essentially includes all those responsible for the various homes in which children are accommodated (s 80(5)). The inspector has a right of entry at any reasonable time (s 80(8)). He may inspect any children on the premises and examine the state of or management of the home or premises and the treatment of children there (s 80(6)). Again, it is an offence to obstruct intentionally the exercise of any of these powers (s 80(10)).

(c) Inquiries

7.73 The Secretary of State may cause an inquiry to be held into the child care functions of, inter alia, social services committees of local authorities, adoption agencies, voluntary organisations, voluntary homes and registered children's homes (s 81(1)). He, or the person conducting the inquiry, may determine that it should be held in private (s 81(2) and (3)). We have already noted the importance of public inquiries in child abuse cases in assisting the process of reform.

(d) Financial support

7.74 The Secretary of State may defray or contribute financially to various costs relating to the child care system (s 82). These include fees, expenses and maintenance costs of those undergoing child care training (s 82(1)), expenditure of local authorities on the provision of secure accommodation in non-assisted community homes (s 82(2)) and expenditure incurred by voluntary organisations in connection with assisted community homes (s 82(4)). He may also arrange for the provision, equipment and maintenance of homes with particular facilities needed by children and which are unlikely to be readily available in community homes (s 82(5)). The amount of any grant is at the complete discretion of the Secretary of State and subject to the consent of the Treasury (s 82(7)). How much money is provided, especially for the training of social workers, may be expected to have a substantial bearing on the operation of the Act in practice. It will be an acid test of the level of real commitment to the paramountcy of children's welfare trumpeted by the legislation.

(e) Research and returns of information

7.75 Both the Secretary of State and local authorities may conduct research, or assist others in conducting research, into their respective statutory functions relating to children (s 83(1), (2) and (9)).

7.76 Local authorities, voluntary organisations, and clerks of court dealing with children's proceedings are required to comply with requests made by the Secretary of State for particulars relating to the discharge of their functions under the child-care legislation (s 83(3), (4) and (5)). This is to enable him to make an annual report to Parliament consisting of a consolidated and classified abstract of information (s 83(6)). He is also required to keep under review the adequacy of child-care training and, in doing so, consider any information or representations by the Central Council for Education and Training in Social Work, representatives of local authorities and such other persons or organisations as appear to him to be appropriate (s 83(8)).

(f) The default power

7.77 We saw that the principal anxiety about the new complaints procedures to be introduced by local authorities under s.26 is whether they will be sufficiently objective and independent, given that they operate within the authority itself (see Chapter 4). In an effort to meet this concern a Commons' Amendment added to the Bill a new default power enabling the Secretary of State to intervene in limited circumstances to secure the proper performance of the authority's statutory duties. Where he is satisfied that any local authority has failed, without reasonable excuse, to comply with any of its duties under the Act, he may make an order, supported by reasons, declaring it to be in default with respect to that duty (s 84(1) and (2)). The order may contain directions for the purpose of ensuring compliance with the duty within a specified period (s 84(3)). In the event of further default, the directions in the order are enforceable through the judicial review procedure, specifically by mandamus (s 84(4)).

7.78 It is unlikely that this power will be exercised very often. It is more likely that the complaints procedure will dispose of the bulk of grievances relating to the treatment of children in care. It should also be remembered that there is judicial control over contact decisions which are perhaps the most frequent and serious subject of complaint. It may be that the default power will be exercised where an authority's failure to discharge its statutory duties affects a *class*, as opposed to individual children. It may prove possible through this mechanism to test the legality of an authority's established policy. Only rarely is it likely to be of any assistance in individual cases.

CHAPTER EIGHT

Jurisdiction, Procedure and the Place of Wardship in the Statutory Scheme

1. Introduction

8.1 This chapter considers the jurisdictional and procedural changes brought about by the Act. One of the most controversial and uncertain aspects of the reforms is the future relationship between the new code and the wardship jurisdiction. The Act provides for concurrent jurisdiction in family proceedings to be exercised by the magistrates' court, the county court and the High Court. One of the avowed reasons for the increased use of wardship under the old law was to secure the benefits of the High Court, particularly in complex cases. At least in theory, these benefits are now available under the statutory regime itself. Hence, it will be possible for the first time for care proceedings (hitherto confined to the juvenile court) to be heard in the High Court.

At the same time it is clear that care proceedings will be allocated in the first instance to the magistrates' court and the ability of local authorities to resort to wardship will be severely curtailed. It will no longer be possible to use it as a means of taking children into care since the Act requires the statutory ground for care orders to be established. Wardship will be available to authorities only to the limited extent that they can demonstrate that the result which they are seeking to achieve cannot be achieved under the statutory procedures. This does not, however, extend to taking a child into care and it has been suggested that the result (in local authority cases) will be to turn wardship into a 'special issues jurisdiction'.

8.2 No comparable restrictions are placed on private individuals wishing to use wardship, but this must be seen in the light of the judicially-imposed restrictions where the child is in care (*A v Liverpool City Council* [1982] AC 363 and *Re W (A Minor)* [1985] AC 791). The Act is silent about these and must be taken to have left the existing law intact. The net result may well be that wardship, in so far as it survives the reforms, will be mainly utilised in non-authority cases to resolve sensitive disputes over children between private individuals. If this is right, the use of the jurisdiction is bound to decline dramatically since the recent escalation in wardship proceedings has been largely attributable to applications by or against local authorities. The more fundamental question of whether wardship should exist at all as an independent jurisdiction is left unresolved by the Act. It seems that to some extent a 'wait and see' policy is likely to operate. If the Act lives up to its promise and embraces effectively all the situations previously covered by wardship, then the question of its total abolition (mooted in Law Com Working Paper No 101 on *Wards of Court* (1987)) is likely to be resurrected. If, on the other hand, it becomes apparent that *lacunae* remain in the statutory scheme and that there is a continuing need for an extra-statutory safety net, wardship may remain alongside the statutory jurisdictions for the foreseeable future. It should be remembered in this respect that wardship proceedings are now within the definition of 'family proceedings' in s 8(3). Thus, all the orders under the Act, including care and supervision orders, may be made in wardship, *but only on the basis of the statutory criteria*. There is, therefore, a clear interrelationship between s 100 (which restricts the use of wardship) and other provisions in the Act, especially s 31 (which prescribes the new statutory ground for care and supervision orders).

8.3 The legislation will bring about substantial procedural changes to allow, inter alia, for wider rights of participation in proceedings and better rights of appeal for those whose legal position is affected in proceedings under the Act. Although most of the detail is left to rules of court (which are unavailable at the time of writing) the general content of the rules can be fairly accurately gleaned from the Review, the White Paper and proceedings in Parliament. As we have seen, many of the technical qualifications for bringing different kinds of proceedings relating to children have been swept away by the Act (see Chapter 3) and this is to be accompanied by a more 'open-door' policy regarding participation by non-parties in proceedings. Nowhere is this approach more evident than in the context of care proceedings where the thrust of the Act is to remove all the remaining vestiges of the quasi-criminal procedure which has hitherto characterised these proceedings and to align procedure with ordinary civil proceedings. The centrepiece of these reforms is the granting of party status to all those whose legal position is likely to be affected by the outcome of the proceedings. Others who may have evidence or views to contribute will be allowed to participate at the court's discretion, but will not enjoy party status as such (White Paper, paras 55-56).

8.4 In the following section we consider the principal jurisdictional changes brought about by s 92 and Sch 11. We then consider the procedural changes which are likely to be brought about by rules of court made under s 93 and the significant changes to the rules governing the appointment of guardians ad litem in s 40. Finally, we conclude with an appraisal of the future role of wardship. It is inevitable that some of the comment in this chapter is conjectural. The position will not become entirely clear at least until all the rules of court have appeared and probably not until the Act has been in operation for some time.

2. Jurisdiction

8.5 We noted above that the Act establishes a concurrent jurisdiction in all proceedings under it. Accordingly, it provides that for the purposes of the Act 'the Court' means the High Court, a county court or a magistrates' court (s 92(7)). Yet, it is clear that the allocation of cases between these courts is not to be a matter of the choice of the parties but is to be determined in accordance with orders made by the Lord Chancellor under Sch 11 (s 92(6)). The normal rule of concurrent jurisdiction will, therefore, more often than not, be effectively displaced by express provision that proceedings may only be commenced in particular courts. The Lord Chancellor is empowered to specify proceedings under the Act and under the Adoption Act 1976 which may only be commenced in:

(a) a specified level of court;

(b) a court which falls within a specified class of court; or

(c) a particular court determined in accordance with, or specified in, the order (Sch 11, para 1(1)).

8.6 The aim of this jurisdictional scheme is to produce flexibility by allocating cases to the appropriate level of court bearing in mind their complexity. The Lord Chancellor outlined, both in Parliament and in the Joseph Jackson memorial lecture on 12 April 1989, how the new jurisdictional arrangements are intended to operate (see (1989) 139 NLJ 505, at 506–507).

Concurrent jurisdiction means that all proceedings affecting children could, prima facie, take place in the magistrates' court, county court or High Court. The reality is that some cases will be self-allocating since any orders in relation to children will be made as part of proceedings instituted for a wider purpose. We may usefully refer to these types of proceedings as 'adult proceedings'. The obvious example of this form of self-allocation is divorce, which will take place in the divorce county court. The Act itself provides expressly that the magistrates' court is to have no jurisdiction over the administration or application of any property belonging to or held in trust for a child or the income of any such property (s 92(4)). Where cases are not self-allocating they will be allocated in accordance with the orders of the Lord Chancellor. Where a court is already seised of proceedings under the Act, the Adoption Act 1976 or the inherent jurisdiction of the High Court in relation to children he may make provision by order for any other family proceedings affecting or connected with the child to be commenced in the same court (Sch 11, para 1(3)).

8.7 The most significant category of cases which require specific allocation are those relating to care and supervision orders. For the first time it will be theoretically possible for these cases to be heard in the county court or High Court. In another significant change, care proceedings in the magistrates' court will now be heard in the 'family proceedings court' by the 'family panel'. It is hoped that this will remove the criminal overtones associated with the juvenile court, whose jurisdiction will henceforth be confined to criminal cases. At the same time it is intended that there should be a properly trained panel of specialist justices with appropriate expertise in children cases.

There has been a clear indication in Parliament that the Lord Chancellor will exercise his powers to determine that classes of proceedings are commenced in a particular court to require *all* care and supervision cases to be commenced at the magistrates' court level, subject to the possibility of a subsequent transfer to the county court or High Court where the nature of the particular proceedings is thought to justify this. The reasoning is that magistrates are competent to handle the majority of care cases and that it would be wasteful and productive of delay if cases which could be dealt with at the lowest level were allowed to be started in a higher court only to be transferred down. It was thought desirable to minimise the number of such transfers. The Government nevertheless acknowledged the experimental nature of the new arrangements and indicated that, if it should transpire that a large number of care cases are not suitable for magistrates' determination, the power exists to require the proceedings to be commenced at the higher level, or to make provision for the parties themselves to have some choice in the matter.

8.8   An important element in the new scheme is clearly the power to transfer cases from one court to another and the circumstances in which (in practice) this will be done. There was an existing power to transfer family business between the High Court and county court under the Matrimonial and Family Proceedings Act 1984. The innovation in the Act is to extend this system of transfers to cover the magistrates' court. Schedule 11 states that the Lord Chancellor may by order provide that in specified circumstances the whole, or any specified part of, specified proceedings shall be transferred to:

'(a)   a specified level of court;

(b)   a court which falls within a specified class of court; or

(c)   a particular court determined in accordance with, or specified in, the order' (para 2(1)).

Any such order may provide for transfers to be made at any stage, or specified stage, of the proceedings irrespective of whether any part of the proceedings has already been transferred (para 2(2)). These provisions apply to any proceedings under the Act, the Adoption Act 1976 and any other 'family proceedings' (other than the inherent jurisdiction of the High Court) which 'may affect, or are otherwise connected with, the child concerned' (para 2(3)). In the case of the latter, the proceedings (which as we have noted will be primarily concerned with 'adult' issues) may only be transferred for the purpose of consolidating them with proceedings under the Act, the Adoption Act 1976 or the inherent jurisdiction of the High Court with respect to children (para 2(4)). Obviously the intention behind such a transfer is that all issues affecting children should be heard together.

8.9 Where the case starts in the magistrates' court, the decision to transfer the case up will rest with the clerk to the magistrates and will be taken in accordance with the criteria laid down by the Lord Chancellor. Although it is not yet entirely clear what these will be, it has been indicated that three of the criteria will be the forensic or legal complexity of a case, the need to expedite a case or avoid unreasonable delay and the desirability of consolidating cases relating to the same child and his family. Where the magistrates refuse to order a transfer the aggrieved party will be given a right of appeal in certain circumstances to a county court registrar who will have the power to order a transfer applying the same criteria. The Act gives the Lord Chancellor power to determine the circumstances in which appeals from transfer decisions may be made (s 94(10)). Where a case is transferred a decision will then have to be taken as to whether the High Court or the county court is the more suitable forum.

8.10 In order to implement these arrangements an administrative machinery will be established. The Butler-Sloss report recommended that there should be an 'Office of Child Protection' which would, inter alia, be responsible for the allocation of cases between courts. This proposal has been rejected following the response to a consultation paper entitled 'Improvements in the Arrangements for Care Proceedings' issued by the Lord Chancellor's department in 1988. Instead, the responsibility will be left to the courts themselves. The precise details of the administration of the new arrangements are not available at the time of writing, but they will undoubtedly entail close co-operation and liaison between courts, particularly between county courts and magistrates' courts. There will also be a central advisory and monitoring committee structure under the President of the Family Division and through local committees. A feature of this administration will be an attempt to strengthen the links between local courts so that, for example, a magistrates' court which found itself unable to give an early hearing might transfer the case to a neighbouring magistrates' court or county court with a view to expediting it. Judge Bracewell has been asked by the Lord Chancellor to be responsible to the President of the Family Division for advising on the administration involving the allocation and transfer of cases.

8.11 Considerable anxiety has been expressed, both in Parliament and by commentators, about the likely practical effect of these changes. The principal objection has been that there ought not to be restrictions on access to the High Court, especially if these are motivated (as some have suspected) by considerations of cost reduction. The argument has been put forward that the approach taken in the Act is not consistent with the all-embracing welfare principle in s 1. The Butler-Sloss report, which was strongly in favour of access to the High Court in difficult or lengthy care cases set out some of the features of a case which might fall into this category. They included the complexity of the dispute, difficult medical or psychiatric evidence, unusual features, special difficulties affecting the parent or child, international or competing jurisdictions, the length of the projected hearing and analysis of expert evidence.

8.12 The alleged benefits of the High Court in cases like this have led some commentators to argue that if they are not to be available to local authorities in wardship by virtue of the restrictions in s 100, they should instead have 'an unfettered right to initiate proceedings in a court of their choosing' (see Nigel Lowe, 'Caring for Children' (1989) 139 NLJ 87). Those who take this view are wholly unimpressed by the transfer provisions. They point out that the experience with other transfer powers has been that lower courts are reluctant to divest themselves of a case, that transfers usually involve delay and that key decisions such as this should not be left to the officials of lower courts. Lowe's solution would be to give authorities a free hand in taking their own decisions on where to commence proceedings and leave it to the higher courts to transfer down cases which they think can be appropriately handled at the lower level. Alternatively, he suggests that control could be effectively exercised by requiring authorities to apply to the High Court for leave to bring cases before that court. Leave could be granted, he suggests, on the basis of an application of the welfare principle with particular reference, possibly, to the factors set out in the Butler-Sloss report.

8.13 Not everyone agrees with this view. In a reply to Lowe's article, John Eekelaar and Robert Dingwall point out that 'forum shopping' in child care cases through the wardship mechanism has been a major cause for concern ('The role of the courts under the Children Bill' (1989) 139 NLJ 217). Although they acknowledge that initiation of care proceedings in the High Court would not bypass the statutory scheme (since the Act itself enables care cases to be heard in the High Court), they argue that it would be undesirable to give authorities choice over the point of access into the system. They reason that in order to facilitate the administrative machinery set up under the Act to allocate cases, it will be necessary 'to create an adequate information base on which decisions about case allocation can be seriously made' and that, for these purposes, the initiation of all cases through a simple channel is desirable. That channel, they argue, should be the magistrates' court, since most cases will continue to be heard there.

8.14 Only time will tell whether the fears of Lowe and others concerning restricted access to the High Court, coupled with the curtailment of wardship, are justified. A great deal is going to depend on attitudes taken in practice. The interpretation by magistrates of the conditions for care and supervision orders and the willingness of the lower courts to consider transfers are going to be key components in assessing the working of the Act. However well the system works, there will be many who will conclude that it is a poor substitute for the specialised 'family court' over which there has been much debate in recent years. It was the Government's position that the new jurisdictional arrangements should be seen as an important stage in the development of the family court in England.

3. Procedure

8.15 Procedural matters are left almost entirely to rules of court. Section 93(1) is really just an enabling provision which specifies that an authority having power to make rules of court may, inter alia, make rules for giving effect to the Act. Section 93(2) goes on to specify in some detail the matters which the rules may cover. All of the discussion in this section is somewhat speculative but the gist of the procedural changes which the Act is seeking to bring about is reasonably clear. An attempt is made here to identify some of the more important changes. During the passage of the Bill, a number of specific procedural issues gave rise to concern and this resulted in some late amendments to the legislation. There is no particular harmony or unity between these various single reforms which we simply consider in the order in which they appear in the Act.

(a) Participation in care proceedings

8.16 One striking manifestation of the quasi-criminal procedure which characterised care proceedings under the 1969 Act was that only the local authority and the child had party status. Although in reality the contest was almost invariably between the local authority and the child's parents, the parents themselves were not parties in the proceedings. This was a serious defect since it was usually parental behaviour or their standard of care which was directly in issue. Initially, the lack of party status meant that parents were not even entitled to legal aid in relation to their limited rights of participation in the proceedings (*R v Worthing Justices, ex p Stevenson* [1976] 2 All ER 194). Ironically the parents *were* able to represent the child in care proceedings except in defined circumstances. This was wholly inappropriate given the obvious conflict of interest which would exist in most cases between the parents and the child.

This conflict of interest was eventually recognised by the Children Act 1975 which made provision for the court to order separate representation of parent and child in defined circumstances. These provisions were not completely brought into force for some years. The 1975 Act also provided that where a separation order was made parents might be granted legal aid separately from the child (s 65, introducing s 28A into the Legal Aid Act 1974).

These reforms did not address the fundamental problem of party status, nor did they deal with the problem of relatives and non-parents who wished to participate in care proceedings, but had no right to do so. The extent to which parents were allowed to take part at all was at first limited to receiving notice of the hearing, attending it and meeting allegations against them by calling and cross-examining witnesses (Magistrates' Courts (Children and Young Persons) Rules 1970). Subsequently, under the Children and Young Persons (Amendment) Act 1986, parents became entitled to party status but only where a separate representation order had been made. The same legislation allowed grandparents to apply to be made parties in the proceedings but did not extend this right to other non-parents.

8.17 The failure of the old law to recognise the independent claims of parent and child was particularly well illustrated by the highly unsatisfactory position relating to appeals. Only the child had a right of appeal (s 2(12) of the 1969 Act). Logically, since parents were allowed to represent the child in the first instance they were also entitled to appeal on his behalf (*B v Gloucestershire County Council* [1980] 2 All ER 746). This was again wholly unsuitable since they might well be arguing an appeal that the justices were wrong in accepting allegations of abuse or neglect on their part and that a care order should not have been made. Yet it was probably the case that this right of appeal might be exercised by parents even where the child had been separately represented in the juvenile court (*Southwark London Borough Council v C (A Minor)* [1982] 2 All ER 636. They were, however, precluded from exercising the child's right of appeal where a formal order for separate representation had been made (*A–R v Avon County Council* [1985] Fam. 150). One effect of the separation order was therefore to deprive aggrieved parents of the only available avenue of redress. As for the local authority, it had no right of appeal at all against, for example, the refusal to make a care order or the decision to discharge an existing care order. There is no better illustration of the criminal flavour of care proceedings than the authority, in effect, being cast in the role of a public prosecutor. Not surprisingly some authorities attempted to use wardship (occasionally successfully) to provide an unofficial appeal mechanism (see, for example, *Re C (A Minor) (Justices' Decision Review)* (1981) 2 FLR 62; *Hertfordshire County Council v Dolling* (1982) 3 FLR 423; and *Re R (A Minor) (Care: Wardship)* (1987) 2 FLR 400).

8.18 The recognition that the child should in some circumstances be separately represented in care proceedings necessitated the appointment of a guardian ad litem to represent the child's independent interests. The court was therefore obliged to appoint a guardian ad litem (GAL) when making a separate representation order where it appeared to it that it was in the interests of the child to do so (r 14A(1) of the Magistrates' Courts (Children and Young Persons) Rules 1970). The court could also order legal representation for the child (r 14A(4)(*b*)). The salient feature of the position before the 1989 Act was that the court enjoyed a wide discretion in deciding whether to appoint a GAL when making an order for separate representation. This led to considerable regional variation in practice in the number of appointments made, which in some areas was only done in a small proportion of cases (see *R v Plymouth Juvenile Court, ex p F and F* [1987] 1 FLR 169).

8.19 The Act provides that one of the matters which may be covered by rules of court relates to 'the persons entitled to participate in any relevant proceedings, whether as parties to the proceedings or by being given the opportunity to make representations to the court' (s 93(2)). There is no doubt that the rules will tackle most of the procedural problems in care proceedings head-on by giving party status to parents and others 'whose legal position could be affected by the proceedings' (White Paper, para 55). This expression should extend to a guardian and anyone who, at the time of the proceedings, has parental responsibility for the child. The unmarried father would also be included as a 'parent'. In addition it is thought that it would include 'anyone who is permitted to seek and is seeking legal responsibility for the child in the proceedings'. Thus, anyone seeking a residence order would automatically be a party. It also goes without saying that the child and the local authority, as applicant, will continue to be parties.

8.20 The Government recognised the advantages of involving in care proceedings anyone else who has a proper interest in the child's future and his welfare. The rules will also therefore make provision for these people to take such part in the proceedings as the court directs, short of giving them full party status. The intention is that the court should be able to allow them to make representations or call them as witnesses and, where the court thinks fit, allow them to receive some or all of the documents or reports in the case (White Paper, para 56). The position of grandparents caused some concern in Parliament since there was anxiety that the hard won gains in the Children and Young Persons (Amendment) Act 1986 should not be lost. In fact, these fears would appear to be unfounded. Those grandparents who are seeking to take over the physical care of a child will be entitled, under the rules, to be joined as parties since their legal position might be affected in the proceedings. Those who do not wish to have the care of the child, but wish to present their views to the court, will almost certainly be allowed to do so under the more flexible powers to allow representations from non-parents. Exactly the same considerations will now apply to other relatives or other non-parents. One of the effects of the legislation is therefore to remove the *preferential* treatment for grandparents, which was brought about by the 1986 Act, by according equal procedural and substantive rights to others with a genuine interest in the child.

(b) Attendance of the child

8.21 In care proceedings under the 1969 Act the child was 'brought before the court'. In accordance with the general thrust of the Act towards decriminalisation of care proceedings, the court is now merely empowered to order the attendance of the child at any stage of proceedings relating to care or supervision orders under Part IV or emergency orders under Part V (s 95(1)) in accordance with rules of court (s 95(2)). Where it does so, the court may authorise a constable to take charge of the child and bring him to court and to enter and search premises where he has reasonable cause to believe that the child is on them (s 95(4)). It may also order anyone who is in a position to do so to bring the child to court (s 95(5)) and anyone who is thought to have information about the child's whereabouts to divulge it (s 95(6)).

8.22   In most cases it is unlikely that the child will be required to attend in view of the more comprehensive provision for representation by GALs (see s 41, discussed infra). But it is envisaged that in a minority of cases the court may be assisted by hearing the child's account first hand. This might be so where there are contradictions in the arguments put forward by either the child's legal representative or GAL (see Sir Nicholas Lyell, The Solicitor-General, *Hansard*, 23 October 1989, col 640). It is, of course, the case that the child by virtue of his party status is *entitled* to attend if he so chooses. This may be an important procedural right in the case of adolescents.

(c)   Appeals

8.23   Section 94 introduces at a stroke the single change which was required to resolve most of the unsatisfactory aspects of appeals relating to care proceedings. All those entitled to party status in the proceedings are now given an automatic right of appeal against the decisions of the magistrates' court (s 94(1)). An exception relates to a decision of the magistrates' court to decline jurisdiction, because it considers that the case can be more conveniently dealt with by another court. In this instance there is no right of appeal (s 94(2)).

8.24   The effect of this reform is that parents will be able in all cases to appeal in their own right and there will no longer be any need to consider whether they should be able to exercise the child's right of appeal. The local authority will also have a right of appeal against, in particular, the refusal to make a care order. The Review would have stopped here, but the White Paper went further and accepted that anyone who was a party in the original proceedings should be able to appeal (White Paper, para 66). The Act gives effect to this.

8.25   The other major change relates to the venue for appeals. In keeping with other reforms which attempt to bring care proceedings into line with civil, rather than criminal, procedure, appeal will henceforth lie to the Family Division of the High Court and not to the crown court as before (s 94(1)). These appeal rights extend to *all* orders made by magistrates under the Act or refusals to make such orders and not just those relating to care and supervision. By way of exception these appeal rights do not extend to interim orders for periodical payments made under Sch 1 (s 94(3)). The High Court will have a complete discretion to make such orders as may be necessary to give effect to its determination of the appeal (s 94(4) and such incidental or consequential orders as appear to it to be just (s 94(5)).

(d) Advance disclosure and discovery

8.26 The Act envisages that the rules may make provision 'with respect to the documents and information to be furnished and notices to be given, in connection with any relevant proceedings' (s 93(2)). The Review and White Paper took the position that there should be more advance disclosure and discovery of documents to enable, in particular, children and parents to know in advance the elements of the case for a care order. Discovery was the subject of proposals in the Review (Chapter 16) which were accepted, with two modifications, in the White Paper. There was concern that the automatic disclosure of the local authority's case would not be balanced by a similar requirement in the case of respondents who, on the Review's proposals, would only have to disclose their case on the direction of the court. The White Paper proposed a minimum requirement that, where practicable, respondents should give an outline of their reasons for contesting the application. The second modification relates to discovery. The Review had recommended that consideration be given to the introduction of full discovery of documents which would have given parties access to all parties' documents including those which would not be produced in court. The White Paper concluded that this was not practicable at present but that it was none the less important that the child's GAL should have access to all records as a statutory right.

8.27 The Act gives effect to this recommendation by allowing the child's GAL the right to examine and take copies of any records of, or held by, the local authority with regard to applications under the Act and other records compiled in connection with any of the functions of its social services committee under the Local Authority Social Services Act 1970. In each case, the records must, of course, relate to the child concerned (s 42(1)). The copies taken will then be admissible as evidence in the proceedings (s 42(2)). The reasoning behind these provisions is that if the GAL is to represent the child, and advise the court properly, he must have access to *all* information held by the authority. In particular, he must have access to information upon which the authority is not intending to rely and which therefore would not come to light in the process of advance disclosure. Under these provisions, the GAL will have total freedom to decide what is relevant and what is not.

(e) Evidence in children cases

8.28 Section 96 deals with two quite distinct aspects of the law of evidence as it applies to children cases. First, it provides that the unsworn evidence of a child may be heard by a court in civil proceedings, provided that the court is of the opinion that the child understands that it is his duty to speak the truth and that he has sufficient understanding to justify his evidence being heard (s 96(2)). The child's evidence may be heard notwithstanding his inability to understand the nature of the oath (s 96(1)). This is already the position in criminal proceedings and the Act is simply bringing civil proceedings into line with this.

8.29   The other aspect relates to the unfortunate decision of the Court of Appeal in *Re H (A Minor); Re K (Minors) (Child Abuse Evidence)* [1989] 2 FLR 313, that in proceedings relating to custody and access in the county court, hearsay evidence was generally inadmissible unless the case was covered by one of the recognised statutory or common law exceptions. Before this case it had been the practice of the courts to relax the strict rules of evidence in children cases, but the Court of Appeal took the view that this was mistaken except in wardship cases. In that context the inquisitorial nature of the jurisdiction has always meant that the technical rules of evidence would be moderated.

It was thought that this decision could give rise to several adverse consequences. First, the courts would be deprived of a valuable source of evidence in their quest to ascertain the welfare of children before them. Secondly, more children might be forced to undergo the trauma of giving direct oral evidence. Thirdly, wardship would have been seen as a preferable procedure and a means of circumventing the evidential restrictions applying elsewhere. This might have caused a drift towards wardship in direct opposition to what the Act is trying to achieve.

Accordingly, the Act gives the Lord Chancellor power to make provision for the admissibility of hearsay evidence in such civil proceedings as he may prescribe and in proceedings relating to the upbringing, maintenance and welfare of a child (s 96(4)). The order may extend to both oral and written statements (s 96(5)). Such was the urgency of the problem produced by *Re H*; *Re K*, that these provisions, by way of exception, came into effect immediately on Royal Assent and it is understood (at the time of writing) that the Lord Chancellor will shortly exercise the necessary power to bring the provisions into practical operation.

(f) Privacy for children

8.30   Section 97 is concerned with privacy for children in cases which come before magistrates' courts. The existing rules governing when magistrates may sit in private, or restrict publication of material relating to the proceedings were inconsistent, especially as between proceedings relating to custody and access and care proceedings. The Act replaces these rules with more coherent and consistent provisions. Rules may be made under s 144 of the Magistrates' Court Act 1980 providing for hearings in private in any proceedings in which the powers under the Act may be exercised (s 97(1)). It becomes a criminal offence (s 97(6)) to publish any material which is intended, or likely to identify a child as being involved in proceedings in a magistrates' court under the Act or disclose the child's address or school in a way which connects this information with the proceedings (s 97(2)). It is a defence to prove, inter alia, that the accused did not know and had no reason to suspect that the published material was intended, or likely to identify the child (s 97(3)).

The court or the Secretary of State may lift these restrictions by order where satisfied that the welfare of the child requires it (s 97(4)). This is only likely to be justified in rare cases, possibly to put an end to unwanted speculation and rumour. These provisions only relate to magistrates' courts since the higher courts already have power to deal with these issues under the law of contempt.

(g) Self-incrimination

8.31 Section 98 removes the privilege against self-incrimination in proceedings under Parts IV and V of the Act, i.e. proceedings relating to care and supervision or emergency proceedings. It provides that no person shall be excused from giving evidence on any matter or answering any question put to him in the course of giving evidence, on the ground that doing so might incriminate him or his spouse of an offence (s 98(1)). But any statement or admission made in the proceedings may not then be used against him or his spouse in proceedings for any offence other than perjury (s 98(2)).

The rationale of these provisions is similar to that for the admissibility of hearsay evidence. It is that the court should not be deprived of any evidence which could assist in arriving at its determination of the best interests of the children before it. This is considered sufficiently important that someone who might otherwise be liable to prosecution is granted an indemnity, at least in relation to statements made in family proceedings.

(h) Paternity tests

8.32 The Act amends s 20 of the Family Law Reform Act 1969 which gives the court power to order tests to determine paternity. It requires the proposed 'tester' to be named in any application for a direction to be made under this section (s 89(1)). If the court then decides to make the direction, it must specify the person named in the application as the person who is to carry out the tests unless it considers that it would be inappropriate to do so. In that case, it must decline to give the direction (s 89(2)). This provision is designed to meet an urgent need for a mechanism to enable a choice to be made between testers in individual cases. It comes into force on Royal Assent (see Lord Mackay LC, *House of Lords, Official Report*, 8 November 1989, col 850).

(i) Legal aid

8.33 The Act amends the Legal Aid Act 1988 to ensure that civil legal aid is available for all proceedings under it, including those in the magistrates' court (Sch 12, para 45). Previously only those proceedings in the High Court and county court would automatically have attracted civil legal aid without express provision.

(j) The appointment of guardians ad litem

8.34 Section 41(1) contains one of the Act's most significant procedural changes. It provides:

> 'For the purpose of any specified proceedings, the court shall appoint a guardian ad litem for the child concerned unless satisfied that it is not necessary to do so in order to safeguard his interests.'

This provision changes the emphasis on the appointment of guardians to place a more positive duty on the court. In effect it creates a legal presumption in favour of the appointment of a GAL in the 'specified proceedings' which are listed in s 41(6). They are:

(a) applications for care or supervision orders;

(b) proceedings in which the court has directed an investigation of a child's circumstances under s 37(1) or has made, or is considering whether to make, an interim care order;

(c) applications for variation or discharge of care or supervision orders;

(d) applications under s 39(4) (substitution of supervision order for care order);

(e) proceedings in which the court is considering whether to make a residence order in relation to a child who is the subject of a care order;

(f) proceedings under s 34 relating to contact between a child in care and another person;

(g) proceedings under Part V (emergency protection);

(h) appeals relating to care orders, supevision orders, s 34 orders or residence orders relating to children in care (or the refusal to make such orders) or the variation or discharge (or refusal to vary or discharge) any of those orders;

(i) any other proceedings specified by rules of court.

8.35 In general terms, the principle of separate representation of the child by a GAL therefore applies in 'public' proceedings where a local authority is involved, but does not generally apply in 'private' proceedings in which the dispute is confined to individual adults. It is an interesting example of the application of distinct and separate principles in public and private law, contrary to the principal orientation of the Act, which as we have seen, is to bring the two closer together. In the specified proceedings, a guardian should be appointed, unless there is good reason for not doing so. The Lord Chancellor has accepted that the courts will be unlikely to find many cases in which it will not be appropriate to make an appointment, but it was still thought desirable to stop short of creating a mandatory requirement of appointment in all cases in case suitable instances for not appointing a GAL should arise (*Hansard*, 19 January 1989, col 408). It could arise where an older child has sufficient capacity and inclination to instruct a solicitor on his own behalf.

8.36 The GAL will be appointed in accordance with rules of court and will have the general duty 'to safeguard the interests of the child in the manner prescribed by such rules' (s 41(2)). The point is worth emphasising that the GAL is more than a mouthpiece for the child. While his duties undoubtedly include ascertaining and presenting the child's views his overriding duty is a protective one, ie to safeguard the *interests* of the child. It has been observed many times that a child's *interests* may not be synonymous with his *views* and the need to protect a child against his wishes may be a distinct necessity in certain cases of alleged abuse or neglect.

The precise duties of GALs will not be clear until the new rules are available, but the Act makes it clear that they may specify, *inter alia*, what assistance the GAL may be required to give the court, what consideration is to be given by the GAL to applying for variation or discharge of various orders made under the Act and the extent to which he is required to participate in reviews conducted by the court (s 41(10)).

8.37 One significant issue, both before and after the Act, is whether a solicitor should also be appointed to represent the child and, if so, what the relationship between the GAL and the solicitor should be. Under the Act, the court may appoint a solicitor for an unrepresented child where no GAL has been appointed, where the child has sufficient understanding to instruct a solicitor and wishes to do so or where it appears to the court that to do so would be in the child's best interests (s 41(3) and (4)). Any of these alternative sets of circumstances will do, but where they exist, the appointment of a solicitor is not mandatory and there is no presumption in favour of appointment of a solicitor such as applies to the appointment of GALs. Where a solicitor is appointed his duty is to represent the child in accordance with rules of court (s 41(5)). It is understood that the rules will also provide for the GAL, in certain circumstances, to appoint and instruct a solicitor where the court has not appointed one. In these circumstances, the rules will require the solicitor to represent the child in accordance with the GAL's instructions. An older child who is able to instruct his own solicitor will be allowed to do so, and in those circumstances the solicitor should take his instructions from the child. This is quite simply because the child is a party to the proceedings and is therefore entitled to legal representation. This may be important where the child disagrees with the GAL's view of his best interests and wishes to have his independent views presented effectively to the court. It may, however, entail the unfortunate consequence that the GAL will be left without legal representation.

8.38   The Act empowers the Secretary of State to make regulations providing for the establishment of panels of persons from whom GALs appointed under s 41 must be selected (s 41(7)). It goes on to specify some of the matters which may be governed by the regulations (s 41(9)). The panels will be constituted by experienced local authority social workers as before the Act. The chosen person must be independent of the authority involved in the proceedings. The new legislation is in part designed to meet anxieties which were expressed about the need to ensure that this independence is properly secured in practice. One of the problems which occurred in the early years of the operation of the panels, was that GALs often represented children in cases in which the local authority managing the panel from which the GAL was appointed also appeared as applicant in the proceedings. This could give the appearance of a conflict of interest and cast doubt on the independence of the GAL. The problem was to some extent overcome where several authorities continued to operate a joint panel and employed a joint manager who did not also have responsibilities for care management in the social services department.   The Act attempts to build on this approach and provides that the regulations may, inter alia, require two or more local authorities to make arrangements for the joint management of a panel and co-operate in the provision of panels in specified areas (s 41(9)). The expectation is that there will be a framework for regional, if not national, co-ordination of arrangements. Moves to set up a national administration or administration by the courts were resisted in Parliament. Other matters which will be covered by the regulations include the constitution, administration and procedures of panels and the qualifications and training of panel members.

8.39   One matter which is in some doubt is the relationship between the court's power to appoint GALs and the role of the Official Solicitor. This has become an issue, since it will be appreciated that the High Court will now have jurisdiction in care cases and will deal with some of the cases which were previously the subject of wardship proceedings. The Official Solicitor, of course, frequently represents wards of court. The Act preserves the power of the Lord Chancellor to confer or impose duties on the Official Solicitor under s 90(3) of the Supreme Court Act 1981 (s 41(8)). This does not answer the question of when precisely the Official Solicitor will represent a child rather than a GAL. The intention is not, however, to reserve representation in the High Court to the Official Solicitor's department. The Lord Chancellor indicated in Parliament that an important consideration would be that the roles and duties of GALs under the Act should be as similar as possible, no matter which court the proceedings are heard in. Moreover, it is intended that the transfer of cases between courts should not delay proceedings unnecessarily by requiring a GAL who is already involved in a case to be removed and a new one substituted as a matter of course (see *Hansard*, 19 January, col 421). It may be that the result of this will be some diminution in the work of the Official Solicitor's department but this will only become clear after the Act has been in operation for some time.

(k) Participation in other family proceedings

8.40   We have been concentrating on the special procedural considerations which apply to care proceedings. We must now look briefly at some procedural features of other 'family proceedings' as defined by the Act. The position of adults is comparatively straightforward. The general position before the Act, which is likely to be preserved by the rules, is that anyone whose legal position might be affected by an order should be joined as a party or at least given an automatic right to participate in the proceedings. The rules may also be expected to follow the recommendation of the Law Commission that, as in care proceedings, there should be provision for more limited participation by people with an interest in the child's welfare and whose participation is likely to be relevant to the proceedings (Report No 172, para 6.30).

The standing of children themselves in proceedings other than those relating to care and supervision is more problematic as recognised by the Commission (paras 6.22–6.29). Party status and independent representation for the child is not generally the norm in those other proceedings. The Commission took the position that this distinction between 'public' and 'private' proceedings could continue to be justified. In its view, intervention by the state was different in kind from choosing between two parents and the case for recognising the child's own point of view was much stronger in the former instance (para 6.28). In most ordinary family disputes the child will not therefore be a party and his views will be represented through the medium of the welfare officer's report. The Commission nevertheless felt that the child has a vital interest in the outcome of private family disputes, especially where non-parents are involved. Thus, it recommended that the courts should be able to make the child a party in *all* proceedings. It is thought that this is most likely to be appropriate where older children are concerned. Clearly, where an older child has been given leave to make his own application for an order, he will automatically be a party.

4. The Place of Wardship in the Statutory Scheme

8.41   Wardship proceedings, it will be recalled, are 'family proceedings' for the purpose of the Act, since the definition includes proceedings under the inherent jurisdiction of the High Court in relation to children. All the orders which may be made under the Act may therefore (subject to express exceptions) be made in wardship proceedings. The issue which needs to be addressed is the extent to which it should be possible to obtain orders in wardship proceedings which are wider or different from those available under the legislation or which are granted on the basis of extra-statutory criteria.

8.42 The Law Commission considered the whole question of the relationship between wardship and the statutory jurisdictions relating to children (Law Com Working Paper No 101, 'Wards of Court' (1987)). It canvassed three options for redefinition of the role of wardship following implementation of the present reforms.

Option A proposed that wardship should be retained as a separate independent jurisdiction alongside the statutory scheme (paras 4.6–4.14). The principal advantage of this was thought to be that wardship could continue to exist as a safety net, making good any deficiencies which might have crept into the reformed statutory code. Under this option wardship would retain its existing form. The main counter-argument was that the continued existence of a universal jurisdiction might make a nonsense of the statutory code. As the Commission put it:

> 'If careful consideration has been given by all those responsible for framing legislation to the circumstances in which, for example, children should be committed to local authority care or non-parents be able to apply for custody or access, it is difficult to justify retaining an *independent* jurisdiction in which those circumstances can be ignored.'

Option B would also entail retaining wardship, but only as a residuary jurisdiction (paras 4.15–4.20). Wardship would then exist *solely* to make good deficiencies in the statutory code. Its use would be justified only to support and add to the powers and solutions which were available under legislation and not to supplant them. The difficulty with this option was acknowledged to be that it might prove very difficult to distinguish between inadvertent *lacunae* in the statutory scheme and gaps which were deliberately left by Parliament. The problem was graphically described by the Commission thus:

> 'It may be possible to recognise the difference between a hole in a blanket which needs to be patched, and a hole in a Swiss cheese, which is part of the fabric and virtue of the cheese itself, but it is difficult to describe it in legislative language.'

Option C was the most radical and would involve the total abolition of wardship as a separate jurisdiction. In its place its most satisfactory features would be incorporated in, and form part of, the statutory code itself (paras 4.21–4.26). The principal advantage of this option was thought to be that it would 'preclude people or authorities from acquiring rights in relation to children which they could not acquire under the statutes, while improving the machinery available under those statutes for the protection of children'. Against this it was argued that the abolition of wardship would place a burden on the statutory schemes to be flexible enough to cover all the situations in which a child might require the court's protection. Throughout the passage of the Bill many doubts were expressed about whether the new legislation will indeed be broad or flexible enough to cover every eventuality in which a child may need protection.

8.43 In its final report the Commission decided to postpone making any substantial recommendations for reform of the court's inherent power in wardship. Instead, the aim of the Act is to incorporate most of the valuable features of wardship into the new statutory scheme and thus reduce the need to resort to it, but the jurisdiction itself remains intact. Having said that, to the surprise (and dismay) of many people, the Act does introduce severe restrictions on the use of wardship by local authorities. The cumulative effect of these restrictions and the greater flexibility in other family proceedings brought about by the Act, should inevitably result in a vastly reduced rôle for wardship. But it should be emphasised that the new restrictions do *not* apply to family disputes between private individuals. These individuals will continue to be able to bring wardship proceedings whether or not they could have achieved their objectives under the statutory scheme. The overall effect of the Act may be to bring about a situation which combines Options B and C. Most of the desirable features of wardship, such as the prospective ground for care orders, are contained in the new scheme, but a residual rôle for it is at the same time being retained, at least for the foreseeable future, by preserving the jurisdiction itself.

8.44 The restrictions which the Act imposes on local authorities will bring about a certain symmetry in the respective positions of authorities and private individuals since parents and others have, for some years, been subjected to judicially-imposed restrictions where the child is the subject of care proceedings. They do, however, create something of an imbalance between public and private law. Where the state (as represented by the local authority) is involved, wardship may fast become a thing of the past, while it is likely to perform a continuing rôle in purely private disputes. In attempting to assess the Act it is therefore vital to distinguish between local authority cases and purely private disputes.

(a) Local authority cases

8.45 The all important provision is s 100. It severely curtails the circumstances under which local authorities may resort to wardship. There is nothing in the Act about the use of wardship *against* local authorities and it must be assumed that the Act did not intend to interfere with the restrictions established by case law, despite the view of Butler-Sloss that they could be lifted. Let us first consider the position where an individual is trying to challenge a local authority in wardship and the likely impact of the Act on this.

(i) Wardship against the local authorities

8.46 It is now a settled rule that the courts will not allow wardship to be used as a means of reviewing the merits of local authorities' decisions relating to children in their care. In the leading case of *A v Liverpool City Council* [1982] AC 363, the House of Lords held that while the existing statutory scheme for child care could not oust completely the prerogative jurisdiction of the court in wardship proceedings, the exercise of that jurisdiction was circumscribed by the statutory code. It held that wardship should not be used to interfere with the proper discharge of a local authority's statutory discretions (in this case relating to access). It was not accepted that Parliament had reserved any general reviewing power to the courts in this matter. There is nothing in the Act to contradict this. The very reform of the legislation will also mean that many of the grievances which caused people to invoke wardship will, in any event, disappear. This is surely the case with respect to the much-improved procedures for challenging contact (access) decisions under s 34. The standing of non-parents in care proceedings will also be immeasurably improved and this should go a long way towards meeting the difficulties which caused an uncle, aunt and grandparents to take wardship proceedings (unsuccessfully) as far as the House of Lords in *Re W (A Minor) (Wardship: Jurisdiction)* [1985] AC 791. The new appeal rights are also likely to account for some cases in which wardship was invoked.

8.47 An important question must be whether this embargo on the use of wardship is going to apply under the new law to the situation where the child is not 'in care', but is merely being looked after by an authority under a voluntary arrangement envisaged by Part III of the Act. We noted that a central purpose of the Act is to draw a much sharper distinction between compulsory and voluntary arrangements. An authority looking after a child will not have 'parental responsibility' and will only have such legal powers of upbringing as are delegated to it by the parents or others having this responsibility. Prima facie, therefore, it could be argued that a court in exercising wardship would not be interfering with the exercise of an authority's statutory power since the legal powers relating to upbringing remain formally vested in the parents or others concerned. At one time this kind of argument was persuasive. In 1965 Lord Denning MR thought that there was no objection to the exercise of wardship where a child was in voluntary care because the power of the authority was transient (*Re S (An Infant)* [1965] 1 WLR 483, at 487). But, in due course, it became clear that the restraints on wardship would be applied to voluntary situations. In *W v Nottinghamshire County Council* [1986] 1 FLR 565, Purchas LJ took the view that the mere existence of a local authority's statutory powers and duties precluded intervention by the courts. If this is right, the better view is that the restrictions will apply to the voluntary arrangements under Part III. Again, given the clarification of the respective powers and duties of parents and authorities and the strengthening of the legal position of parents under such arrangements, it is unlikely that many will feel the need to resort to wardship. The simplest solution for an aggrieved parent will surely be to demand the return of the child which would force the authority to seek compulsory powers in the court.

8.48 Where an authority was guilty of impropriety, or in some way exceeded its statutory powers, it used to be possible to seek redress in wardship (see for example, *Re L (AC)* [1971] 3 All ER 743; and *D v X City Council (No 1)* [1985] FLR 275). It is now clear that the appropriate means of challenge is by way of judicial review under the Order 53 procedure (see *Re RM and LM (Minors)* [1986] 2 FLR 205; and *Re DM (A Minor) (Wardship): Jurisdiction)* [1986] 2 FLR 122). Judicial review has been used to attack decisions of local authorities said to have been taken in breach of the rules of natural justice (see *R v Bedfordshire County Council, ex p C; R v Hertfordshire County Council, ex p B* [1987] 1 FLR 239). It should be emphasised that judicial review is an extremely narrow legal basis for objecting to action taken by an authority. It will succeed only where *ultra vires* action can be shown to have taken place, applying the orthodox principles of administrative law. Where a parent or someone else wishes to challenge the *merits,* as opposed to basic legality, of what an authority is doing, this will now have to be done under the new complaints procedures to be established by authorities under the Act. It is anyone's guess how effective these will be, but we are virtually certain to see some regional variation in the adequacy of these procedures, bearing in mind the latitude given to authorities under s 26.

8.49   Can it therefore be said with total confidence that it will never be possible to invoke wardship successfully against local authorities following the Act? We are certainly getting close to this position, but it may yet be possible in a very unusual case to rely on the so-called *lacuna* principle. If an applicant in wardship is able to convince the court that there is an inadvertent gap or deficiency in the statutory scheme which Parliament could not possibly have intended and that it is operating to the detriment of the child, it is just about possible that the court might be persuaded to exercise jurisdiction. It is difficult to visualise such circumstances and it has been judicially doubted whether the *lacuna* principle has survived the House of Lords' decision in *Re W (A Minor) (supra)* at all (see Bush J in *Re Y (A Minor) (Wardship: Access Challenge* [1988] 1 FLR 299).

Nevertheless, the day may come (sooner or later) when it becomes apparent that the statutory code *is not* perfect and the court may find the *lacuna* principle to be the only basis upon which it can act. Critics of the reforms, while finding it difficult to visualise circumstances in which the new code will be deficient, would preserve wardship as a safety net or insurance policy.

These considerations apply equally to the new restrictions on the use of wardship *by* authorities.

(ii)   Wardship by local authorities

8.50   Traditionally, the courts have encouraged local authorities to seek their assistance in wardship proceedings where they feel that the powers under the statutory code are inadequate. In *Re D (Justices' Decision Review)* [1977] Fam. 158, Dunn J said that:

'far from local authorities being discouraged from applying to the court in wardship ... they should be encouraged to do so, because in very many cases it is the

only way in which orders can be made in the interests of the child, untrammelled
by the statutory provisions.'

It will be apparent by now that the need for authorities to use wardship
will be substantially diminished under the reformed legislation which provides
prospective grounds for care proceedings, rights of appeal and at least the
possibility of access to the High Court in care proceedings. Nonetheless,
Parliament has gone out of its way to impose severe restrictions on the
circumstances in which authorities may step outside the statutory scheme
and use wardship. It would not be an exaggeration to describe the policy
of the Act as a volte-face, bearing in mind the 'open-door' policy previously
pursued by the courts. The underlying philosophy is that where an authority
wishes to take compulsory action in relation to a child it ought to satisfy
the criteria laid down in s 31. It should not be able to justify public intervention
by some different and more open ended criterion such as the welfare or
best interests of the child.

8.51   The crucial provision is s 100. This abolishes the statutory jurisdiction
to place a ward of court in care, or under supervision of a local authority
in exceptional circumstances (see s 7(2) of the Family Law Reform Act 1969)
s 100(1)). It goes on to prevent the court from exercising the inherent
jurisdiction of the High Court to place the child in care or under supervision,
to keep the child in local authority accommodation, to make a child in care
a ward of court or to confer on the authority any power to determine any
question which has arisen or which may arise, in connection with any aspect
of parental responsibility for a child (s 100(2)).

The broad effect of these provisions is to prevent an authority from using
wardship to take a child into care or to keep him there. This will only
be allowed where the new criteria in s 31(2) are satisfied. The legislation
does not therefore permit wardship to be used where the authority cannot
prove the new ground, but is none the less suspicious about parental behaviour
or concerned for the welfare of a child in the family (for an example of
this use of wardship based on suspected sexual abuse of a child see *Re
P (A Minor) (Child Abuse: Evidence)* [1987] 2 FLR 467). The effect of making
the statutory criteria the *sole* ground for compulsory action is to remove
the safety net function of wardship, at least as far as taking children into
care or keeping them there is concerned. The other effect of these provisions
is to preclude the court from conferring parental powers on an authority
under the inherent jurisdiction. This means that where the court is resolving
a dispute about a particular aspect of upbringing, it must take the decision
itself and cannot authorise the authority to take it. This is in line with the
policy that the authority should only be able to acquire parental responsibility
by court order on satisfaction of the statutory criteria.

8.52   However, the Act does provide that the inherent jurisdiction of the
court over children may be invoked by an authority with leave of the court
(s 100(3)). Leave will only be granted where the court is satisfied that the

result which the authority wishes to achieve could not be achieved through any order which the authority is entitled to apply for under the Act. It is assumed for these purposes that the authority would have obtained leave to apply for any order (where required). Secondly, the court must be satisfied that there is reasonable cause to believe that if the court's inherent jurisdiction is not exercised the child is likely to suffer significant harm (s 100(4) and (5)).

The effect of all this is that wardship may continue to be used by local authorities as a kind of 'special issues jurisdiction'. The purpose of the leave requirement is again to act as a filter to prevent unmeritorious applications. The onus will be squarely on the authority to demonstrate why the statutory code does not enable it to achieve what it wishes to achieve and what harm will be likely to befall the child, unless the jurisdiction is exercised. It should be remembered that where a child is formally 'in care' under s 31, the court may not make any s 8 order other than a residence order (s 9(1), and see Chapter 3). If, therefore, an authority wishes to obtain the court's ruling on a specific matter of upbringing, it will not be able to do so by applying for a prohibited steps or special issues order. With leave, it may be able to secure the court's assistance in wardship. An example might be where the authority is seeking an injunction preventing an undesirable adult from having contact with the child.

8.53 These restrictions have already evoked strong feelings, both positive and negative. Nigel Lowe (supra) takes the view that the legislation has gone unnecessarily far in curtailing wardship. He argues against the removal of the safety net underpinning the statutory grounds for care and supervision. He points out that this could give rise to the danger that if the new grounds are interpreted strictly, a child may be left without protection where there is concern that he should be in care or under supervision. He gives the example of a child who is well settled with foster parents under a voluntary arrangement and is threatened with sudden removal by parents who have hitherto shown little interest in him. In this situation, any risk of harm to the child would result from the *move* and would not be attributable to the standard of parental care. Hence, the grounds in s 31(2) would probably not be satisfied. Lowe feels that it ought to be possible in these circumstances to preserve the child's existing home in wardship proceedings.

Eekelaar and Dingwall (supra) take a different view. They hold the position:

'that it remains right that if parents are to be deprived of their legal status over their children, something more than the fears of the harm that may be caused by moving the child back to them should be shown.'

8.54 Another of Lowe's anxieties is that the courts will no longer have the power to commit a child into care of their own motion where they disagree with local authorities about the necessity for compulsory action. The new statutory code makes no provision for this and at the same time removes the court's power to achieve this result in wardship. Eekelaar and

Dingwall's response to this is that if the statutory grounds are not satisfied there is no proper basis on which the court should be able to act.

8.55 A final criticism of Lowe, shared by Eekelaar and Dingwall, is that the basis for granting leave in 'special issues' cases is too narrow. They argue that the criterion for leave should be the welfare of the child and not the significant harm test since the authority is not seeking to acquire full parental responsibility (which would be governed by the harm test), but is seeking to have some specific matter of upbringing determined.

There is considerable force in this view. The criteria in s 31 govern the basis upon which a child is taken into care and parental responsibility is transferred to the local authority. It is right that this should not take place other than on satisfaction of the statutory grounds, but it is surely inappropriate to require these to be satisifed where a single issue of upbringing is concerned. The welfare principle should govern all decisions on upbringing, and this would have been a much better determinant of whether leave should be granted.

(b) Wardship and private disputes

8.56 The rationale of the restrictions on the use of wardship by local authorities is that if a statutory mechanism exists to achieve certain results, that mechanism should be used. To allow a different legal basis for achieving the same objectives would be to defeat the purpose of defining by statute the circumstances in which the state may intervene in the family. This logic is equally applicable to private family disputes which do not involve the state at all. The new legislation has, again, defined the circumstances in which various orders may be sought by, and granted to, particular individuals and has spelt out the legal effects of these orders. It is therefore certainly arguable that this code should provide the definitive basis for the resolution of private disputes affecting children. The Law Commission, in considering the abolition of wardship as an independent jurisdiction, was evidently sympathetic to this view. Apart from this, the substantial relaxation in the rules of *locus standi* for non-parents and the much greater flexibility in the orders which the court can make ought to go a long way towards obviating the necessity for private individuals to resort to wardship.

8.57 It was apparent from the Law Commission's consultation process that there was substantial opposition to the notion that wardship be abolished, not least from practitioners. The result is that the Act does not contain any restrictions on the use of wardship in non-authority cases. For the moment at least, wardship will continue to operate alongside other family proceedings and there appears to be no principle that individuals should be obliged to use these other statutory procedures and seek the orders provided by the Act, rather than have recourse to wardship. It seems that a genuine applicant will be able to by-pass the primary statutory scheme by initiating wardship proceedings. The true significance of not placing restrictions on wardship is that the *wider* aspects of the jurisdiction are preserved. It is impossible at this stage to be definite about when it might be advantageous for an applicant to utilise the inherent jurisdiction in wardship, but what follows are some tentative suggestions about what might happen in practice.

8.58   The first advantage of wardship might be to overcome the requirement of leave which non-qualified individuals have to obtain before seeking s 8 orders. It might be that the orders available in wardship would not achieve any more than the flexible s 8 orders, but access to the court in wardship is as of right (provided the application is not vexatious) and might be more attractive than having to seek leave. It must, however, be acknowledged that leave is unlikely to be refused where someone does have a genuine interest in the child's welfare. It is also doubtful whether the court would be prepared to allow wardship to operate as an avenue of appeal where leave is refused.

A second reason for resorting to wardship may be in an attempt to gain immediate access to the High Court and its superior remedies. As we have noted, this is not normally left to the parties to decide under the new concurrent jurisdiction.

A third, and possibly the most substantial, reason for continuing to use wardship may be where it is considered desirable to preserve a measure of *continuing* judicial control over a child's situation. Here there does appear to be a significant difference in the nature of proceedings in wardship from those of other family proceedings under the statutory code. The legal effect of wardship is that custody (or parental responsibility in the new terminology) vests in the court. This means that all major issues of upbringing must be referred back to the court for its decision. The court may even decide to order a course of action which has not been contemplated by the parties themselves (see particularly *Re E (SA) (A Minor) (Wardship)* [1984] 1 All ER 289). The nature of this ongoing supervision is not always well understood and led in one case to the court issuing a rebuke to a local authority for having arranged an abortion for an adolescent girl who was in their care but was also a ward of court (*Re G–U (A Minor) (Wardship)* [1984] FLR 811). With all its flexibility, the rôle of the court under the new scheme is different in kind from this continuing supervisory rôle which characterises wardship. The essential difference is that under the statutory scheme the onus is on the individual to go back to the court to seek, for example, a prohibited steps or special issues order in an attempt to prevent a person from taking a course of action in relation to the child. In wardship the onus is on the person wishing to take the action to seek the court's approval for it, and this is, at least in theory, a mandatory requirement. It must be conceded, nonetheless, that in practice major issues of upbringing will usually be brought back to the court because someone is objecting to what is proposed. But, in the final analysis, if it is thought desirable that this form of continuing control should be exerted, wardship would be the most effective way of achieving it.

8.59   These observations are, of necessity, speculative, and it will be some time before it becomes clear whether wardship has a continuing rôle to play or whether the new scheme is so comprehensive and flexible that the independent jurisdiction is redundant. Much time and effort has been spent in recent months in attempting to foresee the circumstances in which the legislation may prove to be deficient. In one sense this is wasted effort. For if the statutory scheme itself incorporates wardship as a safety net, it does not matter that it is difficult or impossible to predict in advance what might fall into it. As far as private family proceedings are concerned, the Act secures this. Wardship remains as an alternative to the other statutory procedures. The relationship between wardship and the statutory procedures for care and supervision is, on the contrary, a cause for concern. The safety net has been removed entirely for compulsory action. While preserved for certain issues, it is unnecessarily trammelled with technical restrictions. The argument in favour of requiring authorities and others to demonstrate that the carefully remodelled statutory scheme is unable to protect adequately the welfare of an individual child, before using wardship, is a compelling one. But there will be many who will feel that this would have been sufficient protection against unjustified state interference. It may be argued that it is wrong in principle that a court wishing to offer protection to a child, which it finds it is unable to offer under the legislation, should *ever* find its hands tied. After all, the cardinal principle that the welfare of the child is paramount is supposed to inform and influence every decision made under the new law.

APPENDIX

Text of the Children Act 1989

ARRANGEMENT OF SECTIONS

PART I

INTRODUCTORY

PART II

ORDERS WITH RESPECT TO CHILDREN IN FAMILY PROCEEDINGS

General

Financial relief

Family assistance orders

Part III

Local Authority Support for Children and Families

Provision of services for children and their families

Provision of accommodation for children

Duties of local authorities in relation to children looked after by them

Advice and assistance for certain children

Secure accommodation

Supplemental

Part IV

Care and Supervision

General

Care orders

Supervision orders

Powers of court

Guardians ad litem

PART V
PROTECTION OF CHILDREN

PART VI
COMMUNITY HOMES

PART VII
VOLUNTARY HOMES AND VOLUNTARY ORGANISATIONS

PART VIII
REGISTERED CHILDREN'S HOMES

PART IX
PRIVATE ARRANGEMENTS FOR FOSTERING CHILDREN

PART X
CHILD MINDING AND DAY CARE FOR YOUNG CHILDREN

PART XI
SECRETARY OF STATE'S SUPERVISORY FUNCTIONS AND RESPONSIBILITIES

Part XII

Miscellaneous and General

Notification of children accommodated in certain establishments

Adoption

Paternity tests

Criminal care and supervision orders

Effect and duration of orders etc.

Jurisdiction and procedure etc.

Search warrants

General

SCHEDULES:

An Act to reform the law relating to children; to provide for local authority services for children in need and others; to amend the law with respect to children's homes, community homes, voluntary homes and voluntary organisations; to make provision with respect to fostering, child minding and day care for young children and adoption; and for connected purposes.

BE IT ENACTED by the Queen's most Excellent Majesty, by and with the advice and consent of the Lords Spiritual and Temporal, and Commons, in this present Parliament assembled, and by the authority of the same, as follows:

PART I

INTRODUCTORY

1 Welfare of the child

(1) When a court determines any question with respect to—
  (*a*) the upbringing of a child; or
  (*b*) the administration of a child's property or the application of any income arising from it,
the child's welfare shall be the court's paramount consideration.

(2) In any proceedings in which any question with respect to the upbringing of a child arises, the court shall have regard to the general principle that any delay in determining the question is likely to prejudice the welfare of the child.

(3) In the circumstances mentioned in subsection (4), a court shall have regard in particular to—
  (*a*) the ascertainable wishes and feelings of the child concerned (considered in the light of his age and understanding);
  (*b*) his physical, emotional and educational needs;
  (*c*) the likely effect on him of any change in his circumstances;
  (*d*) his age, sex, background and any characteristics of his which the court considers relevant;
  (*e*) any harm which he has suffered or is at risk of suffering;
  (*f*) how capable each of his parents, and any other person in relation to whom the court considers the question to be relevant, is of meeting his needs;
  (*g*) the range of powers available to the court under this Act in the proceedings in question.

(4) The circumstances are that—
  (*a*) the court is considering whether to make, vary or discharge a section 8 order, and the making, variation or discharge of the order is opposed by any party to the proceedings; or
  (*b*) the court is considering whether to make, vary or discharge an order under Part IV.

(5) Where a court is considering whether or not to make one or more orders under this Act with respect to a child, it shall not make the order or any of the orders unless it considers that doing so would be better for the child than making no order at all.

2 Parental responsibility for children

(1) Where a child's father and mother were married to each other at the time of his birth, they shall each have parental responsibility for the child.

(2) Where a child's father and mother were not married to each other at the time of his birth—
  (*a*)   the mother shall have parental responsibility for the child;
  (*b*)   the father shall not have parental responsibility for the child, unless he acquires it in accordance with the provisions of this Act.

(3) References in this Act to a child whose father and mother were, or (as the case may be) were not, married to each other at the time of his birth must be read with section 1 of the Family Law Reform Act 1987 (which extends their meaning).

(4) The rule of law that a father is the natural guardian of his legitimate child is abolished.

(5) More than one person may have parental responsibility for the same child at the same time.

(6) A person who has parental responsibility for a child at any time shall not cease to have that responsibility solely because some other person subsequently acquires parental responsibility for the child.

(7) Where more than one person has parental responsibility for a child, each of them may act alone and without the other (or others) in meeting that responsibility; but nothing in this Part shall be taken to affect the operation of any enactment which requires the consent of more than one person in a matter affecting the child.

(8) The fact that a person has parental responsibility for a child shall not entitle him to act in any way which would be incompatible with any order made with respect to the child under this Act.

(9) A person who has parental responsibility for a child may not surrender or transfer any part of that responsibility to another but may arrange for some or all of it to be met by one or more persons acting on his behalf.

(10) The person with whom any such arrangement is made may himself be a person who already has parental responsibility for the child concerned.

(11) The making of any such arrangement shall not affect any liability of the person making it which may arise from any failure to meet any part of his parental responsibility for the child concerned.

3 Meaning of "parental responsibility"

(1) In this Act "parental responsibility" means all the rights, duties, powers, responsibilities and authority which by law a parent of a child has in relation to the child and his property.

(2) It also includes the rights, powers and duties which a guardian of the child's estate (appointed, before the commencement of section 5, to act generally) would have had in relation to the child and his property.

(3) The rights referred to in subsection (2) include, in particular, the right of the guardian to receive or recover in his own name, for the benefit of the child, property of whatever description and wherever situated which the child is entitled to receive or recover.

(4) The fact that a person has, or does not have, parental responsibility for a child shall not affect—

(*a*)   any obligation which he may have in relation to the child (such as a statutory duty to maintain the child); or

(*b*)   any rights which, in the event of the child's death, he (or any other person) may have in relation to the child's property.

(5) A person who—
  (*a*)   does not have parental responsibility for a particular child; but
  (*b*)   has care of the child,
may (subject to the provisions of this Act) do what is reasonable in all the circumstances of the case for the purpose of safeguarding or promoting the child's welfare.

4   Acquisition of parental responsibility by father

(1) Where a child's father and mother were not married to each other at the time of his birth—
  (*a*)   the court may, on the application of the father, order that he shall have parental responsibility for the child; or
  (*b*)   the father and mother may by agreement ("a parental responsibility agreement") provide for the father to have parental responsibility for the child.

(2) No parental responsibility agreement shall have effect for the purposes of this Act unless—
  (*a*)   it is made in the form prescribed by regulations made by the Lord Chancellor; and
  (*b*)   where regulations are made by the Lord Chancellor prescribing the manner in which such agreements must be recorded, it is recorded in the prescribed manner.

(3) Subject to section 12(4), an order under subsection (1)(*a*), or a parental responsibility agreement, may only be brought to an end by an order of the court made on the application—
  (*a*)   of any person who has parental responsibility for the child, or
  (*b*)   with leave of the court, of the child himself.

(4) The court may only grant leave under subsection (3)(*b*) if it is satisfied that the child has sufficient understanding to make the proposed application.

5   Appointment of guardians

(1) Where an application with respect to a child is made to the court by any individual, the court may by order appoint an individual to be the child's guardian if—
  (*a*)   the child has no parent with parental responsibility for him; or
  (*b*)   a residence order has been made with respect to the child in favour of a parent or guardian of his who has died while the order was in force.

(2) The power conferred by subsection (1) may also be exercised in any family proceedings if the court considers that the order should be made even though no application has been made for it.

(3) A parent who has parental responsibility for his child may appoint another individual to be the child's guardian in the event of his death.

(4) A guardian of a child may appoint another individual to take his place as the child's guardian in the event of his death.

(5) An appointment under subsection (3) or (4) shall not have effect unless it is made in writing, is dated and is signed by the person making the appointment or—
  (*a*)   in the case of an appointment made by a will which is not signed by the

testator, is signed at the direction of the testator in accordance with the requirements of section 9 of the Wills Act 1837; or

(b)   in any other case, is signed at the direction of the person making the appointment, in his presence and in the presence of two witnesses who each attest the signature.

(6) A person appointed as a child's guardian under this section shall have parental responsibility for the child concerned.

(7) Where—

(a)   on the death of any person making an appointment under subsection (3) or (4), the child concerned has no parent with parental responsibility for him; or

(b)   immediately before the death of any person making such an appointment, a residence order in his favour was in force with respect to the child,

the appointment shall take effect on the death of that person.

(8) Where, on the death of any person making an appointment under subsection (3) or (4)—

(a)   the child concerned has a parent with parental responsibility for him; and

(b)   subsection (7)(b) does not apply,

the appointment shall take effect when the child no longer has a parent who has parental responsibility for him.

(9) Subsections (1) and (7) do not apply if the residence order referred to in paragraph (b) of those subsections was also made in favour of a surviving parent of the child.

(10) Nothing in this section shall be taken to prevent an appointment under subsection (3) or (4) being made by two or more persons acting jointly.

(11) Subject to any provision made by rules of court, no court shall exercise the High Court's inherent jurisdiction to appoint a guardian of the estate of any child.

(12) Where the rules of court are made under subsection (11) they may prescribe the circumstances in which, and conditions subject to which, an appointment of such a guardian may be made.

(13) A guardian of a child may only be appointed in accordance with the provisions of this section.

6   Guardians: revocation and disclaimer

(1) An appointment under section 5(3) or (4) revokes an earlier such appointment (including one made in an unrevoked will or codicil) made by the same person in respect of the same child, unless it is clear (whether as the result of an express provision in the later appointment or by any necessary implication) that the purpose of the later appointment is to appoint an additional guardian.

(2) An appointment under section 5(3) or (4) (including one made in an unrevoked will or codicil) is revoked if the person who made the appointment revokes it by a written and dated instrument which is signed—

(a)   by him; or

(b)   at his direction, in his presence and in the presence of two witnesses who each attest the signature.

(3) An appointment under section 5(3) or (4) (other than one made in a will or codicil) is revoked if, with the intention of revoking the appointment, the person who made it—

(a)   destroys the instrument by which it was made; or

(b)   has some other person destroy that instrument in his presence.

(4) For the avoidance of doubt, an appointment under section 5(3) or (4) made in a will or codicil is revoked if the will or codicil is revoked.

(5) A person who is appointed as a guardian under section 5(3) or (4) may disclaim his appointment by an instrument in writing signed by him and made within a reasonable time of his first knowing that the appointment has taken effect.

(6) Where regulations are made by the Lord Chancellor prescribing the manner in which such disclaimers must be recorded, no such disclaimer shall have effect unless it is recorded in the prescribed manner.

(7) Any appointment of a guardian under section 5 may be brought to an end at any time by order of the court—
- (*a*) on the application of any person who has parental responsibility for the child;
- (*b*) on the application of the child concerned, with leave of the court; or
- (*c*) in any family proceedings, if the court considers that it should be brought to an end even though no application has been made.

7 Welfare reports

(1) A court considering any question with respect to a child under this Act may—
- (*a*) ask a probation officer; or
- (*b*) ask a local authority to arrange for—
  - (i) an officer of the authority; or
  - (ii) such other person (other than a probation officer) as the authority considers appropriate,

to report to the court on such matters relating to the welfare of that child as are required to be dealt with in the report.

(2) The Lord Chancellor may make regulations specifying matters which, unless the court orders otherwise, must be dealt with in any report under this section.

(3) The report may be made in writing, or orally, as the court requires.

(4) Regardless of any enactment or rule of law which would otherwise prevent it from doing so, the court may take account of—
- (*a*) any statement contained in the report; and
- (*b*) any evidence given in respect of the matters referred to in the report,

in so far as the statement or evidence is, in the opinion of the court, relevant to the question which it is considering.

(5) It shall be the duty of the authority or probation officer to comply with any request for a report under this section.

PART II
ORDERS WITH RESPECT TO CHILDREN IN FAMILY PROCEEDINGS

General

8 Residence, contact and other orders with respect to children

(1) In this Act—

"a contact order" means an order requiring the person with whom a child lives, or is to live, to allow the child to visit or stay with the person named in the order, or for that person and the child otherwise to have contact with each other;

"a prohibited steps order" means an order that no step which could be taken by a parent in meeting his parental responsibility for a child, and which is of a kind specified in the order, shall be taken by any person without the consent of the court;

"a residence order" means an order settling the arrangements to be made as to the person with whom a child is to live; and

"a specific issue order" means an order giving direction for the purpose of determining a specific question which has arisen, or which may arise, in connection with any aspect of parental responsibility for a child.

(2) In this Act "a section 8 order" means any of the orders mentioned in subsection (1) and any order varying or discharging such an order.

(3) For the purposes of this Act "family proceedings" means any proceedings—
    (*a*)   under the inherent jurisdiction of the High Court in relation to children; and
    (*b*)   under the enactments mentioned in subsection (4),
but does not include proceedings on an application for leave under section 100(3).

(4) The enactments are—
    (*a*)   Parts I, II and IV of this Act;
    (*b*)   the Matrimonial Causes Act 1973;
    (*c*)   the Domestic Violence and Matrimonial Proceedings Act 1976;
    (*d*)   the Adoption Act 1976;
    (*e*)   the Domestic Proceedings and Magistrates' Courts Act 1978;
    (*f*)   sections 1 and 9 of the Matrimonial Homes Act 1983;
    (*g*)   Part III of the Matrimonial and Family Proceedings Act 1984.

9   Restrictions on making section 8 orders

(1) No court shall make any section 8 order, other than a residence order, with respect to a child who is in the care of a local authority.

(2) No application may be made by a local authority for a residence order or contact order and no court shall make such an order in favour of a local authority.

(3) A person who is, or was at any time within the last six months, a local authority foster parent of a child may not apply for leave to apply for a section 8 order with respect to the child unless—
    (*a*)   he has the consent of the authority;
    (*b*)   he is relative of the child; or
    (*c*)   the child has lived with him for at least three years preceding the application.

(4) The period of three years mentioned in subsection (3)(*c*) need not be continuous but must have begun not more than five years before the making of the application.

(5) No court shall exercise its powers to make a specific issue order or prohibited steps order—

    (*a*)   with a view to achieving a result which could be achieved by making a residence or contact order; or
    (*b*)   in any way which is denied to the High Court (by section 100(2)) in the exercise of its inherent jurisdiction with respect to children.

(6) No court shall make any section 8 order which is to have effect for a period which will end after the child has reached the age of sixteen unless it is satisfied that the circumstances of the case are exceptional.

(7) No court shall make any section 8 order, other than one varying or discharging such an order, with respect to a child who has reached the age of sixteen unless it is satisfied that the circumstances of the case are exceptional.

10 Power of court to make section 8 orders

(1) In any family proceedings in which a question arises with respect to the welfare of any child, the court may make a section 8 order with respect to the child if—
- (a) an application for the order has been made by a person who—
  - (i) is entitled to apply for a section 8 order with respect to the child; or
  - (ii) has obtained the leave of the court to make the application; or
- (b) the court considers that the order should be made even though no such application has been made.

(2) The court may also make a section 8 order with respect to any child on the application of a person who—
- (a) is entitled to apply for a section 8 order with respect to the child; or
- (b) has obtained the leave of the court to make the application.

(3) This section is subject to the restrictions imposed by section 9.

(4) The following persons are entitled to apply to the court for any section 8 order with respect to a child—
- (a) any parent or guardian of the child;
- (b) any person in whose favour a residence order is in force with respect to the child.

(5) The following persons are entitled to apply for a residence or contact order with respect to a child—
- (a) any party to a marriage (whether or not subsisting) in relation to whom the child is a child of the family;
- (b) any person with whom the child has lived for a period of at least three years;
- (c) any person who—
  - (i) in any case where a residence order is in force with respect to the child, has the consent of each of the persons in whose favour the order was made;
  - (ii) in any case where the child is in the care of a local authority, has the consent of that authority; or
  - (iii) in any other case, has the consent of each of those (if any) who have parental responsibility for the child.

(6) A person who would not otherwise be entitled (under the previous provisions of this section) to apply for the variation or discharge of a section 8 order shall be entitled to do so if—
- (a) the order was made on his application; or
- (b) in the case of a contact order, he is named in the order.

(7) Any person who falls within a category of person prescribed by rules of court is entitled to apply for any such section 8 order as may be prescribed in relation to that category of person.

(8) Where the person applying for leave to make an application for a section 8 order is the child concerned, the court may only grant leave if it is satisfied that he has sufficient understanding to make the proposed application for the section 8 order.

(9) Where the person applying for leave to make an application for a section 8 order is not the child concerned, the court shall, in deciding whether or not to grant leave, have particular regard to—

    (*a*)   the nature of the proposed application for the section 8 order;

    (*b*)   the applicant's connection with the child;

    (*c*)   any risk there might be of that proposed application disrupting the child's life to such an extent that he would be harmed by it; and

    (*d*)   where the child is being looked after by a local authority—

        (i)   the authority's plans for the child's future; and

        (ii)   the wishes and feelings of the child's parents.

(10) The period of three years mentioned in subsection (5)(*b*) need not be continuous but must not have begun more than five years before, or ended more than three months before, the making of the application.

11   General principles and supplementary provisions

(1) In proceedings in which any question of making a section 8 order, or any other question with respect to such an order, arises, the court shall (in the light of any rules made by virtue of subsection (2))—

    (*a*)   draw up a timetable with a view to determining the question without delay; and

    (*b*)   give such directions as it considers appropriate for the purpose of ensuring, so far as is reasonably practicable, that that timetable is adhered to.

(2) Rules of court may—

    (*a*)   specify periods within which specified steps must be taken in relation to proceedings in which such questions arise; and

    (*b*)   make other provision with respect to such proceedings for the purpose of ensuring, so far as is reasonably practicable, that such questions are determined without delay.

(3) Where a court has power to make a section 8 order, it may do so at any time during the course of the proceedings in question even though it is not in a position to dispose finally of those proceedings.

(4) Where a residence order is made in favour of two or more persons who do not themselves all live together, the order may specify the periods during which the child is to live in the different households concerned.

(5) Where—

    (*a*)   a residence order has been made with respect to a child; and

    (*b*)   as a result of the order the child lives, or is to live, with one of two parents who each have parental responsibility for him,

the residence order shall cease to have effect if the parents live together for a continuous period of more than six months.

(6) A contact order which requires the parent with whom a child lives to allow the child to visit, or otherwise have contact with, his other parent shall cease to have effect if the parents live together for a continuous period of more than six months.

(7) A section 8 order may—

    (*a*)   contain directions about how it is to be carried into effect;

    (*b*)   impose conditions which must be complied with by any person—

        (i)   in whose favour the order is made;

        (ii)   who is a parent of the child concerned;

    (iii)   who is not a parent of his but who has parental responsibility for him; or

    (iv)   with whom the child is living,

and to whom the conditions are expressed to apply;

  (c)   be made to have effect for a specified period, or contain provisions which are to have effect for a specified period;

  (d)   make such incidental, supplemental or consequential provision as the court thinks fit.

12 Residence orders and parental responsibility

(1) Where the court makes a residence order in favour of the father of a child it shall, if the father would not otherwise have parental responsibility for the child, also make an order under section 4 giving him that responsibility.

(2) Where the court makes a residence order in favour of any person who is not the parent or guardian of the child concerned that person shall have parental responsibility for the child while the residence order remains in force.

(3) Where a person has parental responsibility for a child as a result of subsection (2), he shall not have the right—

  (a)   to consent, or refuse to consent, to the making of an application with respect to the child under section 18 of the Adoption Act 1976;

  (b)   to agree, or refuse to agree, to the making of an adoption order, or an order under section 55 of the Act of 1976, with respect to the child; or

  (c)   to appoint a guardian for the child.

(4) Where subsection (1) requires the court to make an order under section 4 in respect of the father of a child, the court shall not bring that order to an end at any time while the residence order concerned remains in force.

13 Change of child's name or removal from jurisdiction

(1) Where a residence order is in force with respect to a child, no person may—

  (a)   cause the child to be known by a new surname; or

  (b)   remove him from the United Kingdom;

without either the written consent of every person who has parental responsibility for the child or the leave of the court.

(2) Subsection (1)(b) does not prevent the removal of a child, for a period of less than one month, by the person in whose favour the residence order is made.

(3) In making a residence order with respect to a child the court may grant the leave required by subsection (1)(b), either generally or for specified purposes.

14 Enforcement of residence orders

(1) Where—

  (a)   a residence order is in force with respect to a child in favour of any person; and

  (b)   any other person (including one in whose favour the order is also in force) is in breach of the arrangements settled by that order,

the person mentioned in paragraph (a) may, as soon as the requirement in subsection (2) is complied with, enforce the order under section 63(3) of the Magistrates' Courts Act 1980 as if it were an order requiring the other person to produce the child to him.

(2) The requirement is that a copy of the residence order has been served on the other person.

(3) Subsection (1) is without prejudice to any other remedy open to the person in whose favour the residence order is in force.

Financial relief

15   Orders for financial relief with respect to children

(1) Schedule 1 (which consists primarily of the re-enactment, with consequential amendments and minor modifications, of provisions of the Guardianship of Minors Acts 1971 and 1973, the Children Act 1975 and of sections 15 and 16 of the Family Law Reform Act 1987) makes provision in relation to financial relief for children.

(2) The powers of a magistrates' court under section 60 of the Magistrates' Courts Act 1980 to revoke, revive or vary an order for the periodical payment of money shall not apply in relation to an order made under Schedule 1.

Family assistance orders

16   Family assistance orders

(1) Where, in any family proceedings, the court has power to make an order under this Part with respect to any child, it may (whether or not it makes such an order) make an order requiring—
  (*a*)   a probation officer to be made available; or
  (*b*)   a local authority to make an officer of the authority available,
to advise, assist and (where appropriate) befriend any person named in the order.

(2) The persons who may be named in an order under this section ("a family assistance order") are—
  (*a*)   any parent or guardian of the child;
  (*b*)   any person with whom the child is living or in whose favour a contact order is in force with respect to the child;
  (*c*)   the child himself.

(3) No court may make a family assistance order unless—
  (*a*)   it is satisfied that the circumstances of the case are exceptional; and
  (*b*)   it has obtained the consent of every person to be named in the order other than the child.

(4) A family assistance order may direct—
  (*a*)   the person named in the order; or
  (*b*)   such of the persons named in the order as may be specified in the order,
to take such steps as may be so specified with a view to enabling the officer concerned to be kept informed of the address of any person named in the order and to be allowed to visit any such person.

(5) Unless it specifies a shorter period, a family assistance order shall have effect for a period of six months beginning with the day on which it is made.

(6) Where—
  (*a*)   a family assistance order is in force with respect to a child; and
  (*b*)   a section 8 order is also in force with respect to the child,
the officer concerned may refer to the court the question whether the section 8 order should be varied or discharged.

(7) A family assistance order shall not be made so as to require a local authority to make an officer of theirs available unless—
  (*a*)   the authority agree; or
  (*b*)   the child concerned lives or will live within their area.

(8) Where a family assistance order requires a probation officer to be made available, the officer shall be selected in accordance with arrangements made by the probation committee for the area in which the child lives or will live.

(9) If the selected probation officer is unable to carry out his duties, or dies, another probation officer shall be selected in the same manner.

PART III
LOCAL AUTHORITY SUPPORT FOR CHILDREN AND FAMILIES
Provision of services for children and their families

17   Provision of services for children in need, their families and others

(1) It shall be the general duty of every local authority (in addition to the other duties imposed on them by this Part)—
   (a)   to safeguard and promote the welfare of children within their area who are in need; and
   (b)   so far as is consistent with that duty, to promote the upbringing of such children by their families,
by providing a range and level of services appropriate to those children's needs.

(2) For the purpose principally of facilitating the discharge of their general duty under this section, every local authority shall have the specific duties and powers set out in Part 1 of Schedule 2.

(3) Any service provided by an authority in the exercise of functions conferred on them by this section may be provided for the family of a particular child in need or for any member of his family, if it is provided with a view to safeguarding or promoting the child's welfare.

(4) The Secretary of State may by order amend any provision of Part I of Schedule 2 or add any further duty or power to those for the time being mentioned there.

(5) Every local authority—
   (a)   shall facilitate the provision by others (including in particular voluntary organisations) of services which the authority have power to provide by virtue of this section, or section 18, 20, 23 or 24; and
   (b)   may make such arrangements as they see fit for any person to act on their behalf in the provision of any such service.

(6) The services provided by a local authority in the exercise of functions conferred on them by this section may include giving assistance in kind or, in exceptional circumstances, in cash.

(7) Assistance may be unconditional or subject to conditions as to the repayment of the assistance or of its value (in whole or in part).

(8) Before giving any assistance or imposing any conditions, a local authority shall have regard to the means of the child concerned and of each of his parents.

(9) No person shall be liable to make any repayment of assistance or of its value at any time when he is in receipt of income support or family credit under the Social Security Act 1986.

(10) For the purposes of this Part a child shall be taken to be in need if—
   (a)   he is unlikely to achieve or maintain, or to have the opportunity of achieving

or maintaining, a reasonable standard of health or development without the provision for him of services by a local authority under this Part;

(b)   his health or development is likely to be significantly impaired, or further impaired, without the provision for him of such services; or

(c)   he is disabled,

and "family", in relation to such a child, includes any person who has parental responsibility for the child and any other person with whom he has been living.

(11) For the purposes of this Part, a child is disabled if he is blind, deaf or dumb or suffers from mental disorder of any kind or is substantially and permanently handicapped by illness, injury or congenital deformity or such other disability as may be prescribed; and in this Part—

   "development" means physical, intellectual, emotional, social or behavioural development; and

   "health" means physical or mental health.

18   Day care for pre-school and other children

(1) Every local authority shall provide such day care for children in need within their area who are—

(a)   aged five or under; and

(b)   not yet attending schools,

as is appropriate.

(2) A local authority may provide day care for children within their area who satisfy the conditions mentioned in subsection (1)(a) and (b) even though they are not in need.

(3) A local authority may provide facilities (including training, advice, guidance and counselling) for those—

(a)   caring for children in day care; or

(b)   who at any time accompany such children while they are in day care.

(4) In this section "day care" means any form of care or supervised activity provided for children during the day (whether or not it is provided on a regular basis).

(5) Every local authority shall provide for children in need within their area who are attending any school such care or supervised activities as is appropriate—

(a)   outside school hours; or

(b)   during school holidays.

(6) A local authority may provide such care or supervised activities for children within their area who are attending any school even though those children are not in need.

(7) In this section "supervised activity" means an activity supervised by a responsible person.

19   Review of provision for day care, child minding etc

(1) Every local authority in England and Wales shall review—

(a)   the provision which they make under section 18;

(b)   the extent to which the services of child minders are available within their area with respect to children under the age of eight; and

(c)   the provision for day care within their area made for children under the age of eight by persons other, than the authority, required to register under section 71(1)(b).

(2) A review under subsection (1) shall be conducted—

(a) together with the appropriate local education authority; and
(b) at least once in every review period.

(3) Every local authority in Scotland shall, at least once in every review period, review—
(a) the provision for day care within their area made for children under the age of eight by the local authority and by persons required to register under section 71(1)(*b*); and
(b) the extent to which the services of child minders are available within their area with respect to children under the age of eight.

(4) In conducting any such review, the two authorities or, in Scotland, the authority shall have regard to the provision made with respect to children under the age of eight in relevant establishments within their area.

(5) In this section—
"relevant establishment" means any establishment which is mentioned in paragragraphs 3 and 4 of Schedule 9 (hospitals, schools and other establishments exempt from the registration requirements which apply in relation to the provision of day care); and
"review period" means the period of one year beginning with the commencement of this section and each subsequent period of three years beginning with an anniversary of that commencement.

(6) Where a local authority have conducted a review under this section they shall publish the result of the review—
(a) as soon as is reasonably practicable;
(b) in such form as they consider appropriate; and
(c) together with any proposals they may have with respect to the matters reviewed.

(7) The authorities conducting any review under this section shall have regard to—
(a) any representations made to any one of them by any relevant health authority or health board; and
(b) any other representations which they consider to be relevant.

(8) In the application of this section to Scotland, "day care" has the same meaning as in section 79 and "health board" has the same meaning as in the National Health Service (Scotland) Act 1978.

Provision of accommodation for children

20 Provision of accommodation for children: general

(1) Every local authority shall provide accommodation for any child in need within their area who appears to them to require accommodation as a result of—
(a) there being no person who has parental responsibility for him;
(b) his being lost or having been abandoned; or
(c) the person who has been caring for him being prevented (whether or not permanently, and for whatever reason) from providing him with suitable accommodation or care.

(2) Where a local authority provide accommodation under subsection (1) for a child who is ordinarily resident in the area of another local authority, that other local authority may take over the provision of accommodation for the child within—
(a) three months of being notified in writing that the child is being provided with accommodation; or
(b) such other longer period as may be prescribed.

(3) Every local authority shall provide accommodation for any child in need within their area who has reached the age of sixteen and whose welfare the authority consider is likely to be seriously prejudiced if they do not provide him with accommodation.

(4) A local authority may provide accommodation for any child within their area (even though a person who has parental responsibility for him is able to provide him with accommodation) if they consider that to do so would safeguard or promote the child's welfare.

(5) A local authority may provide accommodation for any person who has reached the age of sixteen but is under twenty-one in any community home which takes children who have reached the age of sixteen if they consider that to do so would safeguard or promote his welfare.

(6) Before providing accommodation under this section, a local authority shall, so far as is reasonably practicable and consistent with the child's welfare—
  (a)   ascertain the child's wishes regarding the provision of accommodation; and
  (b)   give due consideration (having regard to his age and understanding) to such wishes of the child as they have been able to ascertain.

(7) A local authority may not provide accommodation under this section for any child if any person who—
  (a)   has parental responsibility for him; and
  (b)   is willing and able to—
        (i)   provide accommodation for him; or
        (ii)   arrange for accommodation to be provided for him,
objects.

(8) Any person who has parental responsibility for a child may at any time remove the child from accommodation provided by or on behalf of the local authority under this section.

(9) Subsections (7) and (8) do not apply while any person—
  (a)   in whose favour a residence order is in force with respect to the child; or
  (b)   who has care of the child by virtue of an order made in the exercise of the High Court's inherent jurisdiction with respect to children,
agrees to the child being looked after in accommodation provided by or on behalf of the local authority.

(10) Where there is more than one such person as is mentioned in subsection (9), all of them must agree.

(11) Subsections (7) and (8) do not apply where a child who has reached the age of sixteen agrees to being provided with accommodation under this section.

21 Provision of accommodation for children in police protection or detention or on remand, etc

(1) Every local authority shall make provision for the reception and accommodation of children who are removed or kept away from home under Part V.

(2) Every local authority shall receive, and provide accommodation for, children—
  (a)   in police protection whom they are requested to receive under section 46(3)(*f*);
  (b)   whom they are requested to receive under section 38(6) of the Police and Criminal Evidence Act 1984;
  (c)   who are—
        (i)   on remand under section 23(1) of the Children and Young Persons Act 1969; or

(ii)   the subject of a supervision order imposing a residence requirement under section 12AA of that Act,

and with respect to whom they are the designated authority.

(3) Where a child has been—

(a)   removed under Part V; or

(b)   detained under section 38 of the Police and Criminal Evidence Act 1984,

and he is not being provided with accommodation by a local authority or in a hospital vested in the Secretary of State, any reasonable expenses of accommodating him shall be recoverable from the local authority in whose area he is ordinarily resident.

Duties of local authorities in relation to children looked after by them

22   General duties of local authority in relation to children looked after by them

(1) In this Act, any reference to a child who is looked after by a local authority is a reference to a child who is—

(a)   in their care; or

(b)   provided with accommodation by the authority in the exercise of any functions (in particular those under this Act) which stand referred to their social services committee under the Local Authority Social Services Act 1970.

(2) In subsection (1) "accommodation" means accommodation which is provided for a continuous period of more than 24 hours.

(3) It shall be the duty of a local authority looking after any child—

(a)   to safeguard and promote his welfare; and

(b)   to make such use of services available for children cared for by their own parents as appears to the authority reasonable in his case.

(4) Before making any decision with respect to a child whom they are looking after, or proposing to look after, a local authority shall, so far as is reasonably practicable, ascertain the wishes and feelings of—

(a)   the child;

(b)   his parents;

(c)   any person who is not a parent of his but who has parental responsibility for him; and

(d)   any other person whose wishes and feelings the authority consider to be relevant,

regarding the matter to be decided.

(5) In making any such decision a local authority shall give due consideration—

(a)   having regard to his age and understanding, to such wishes and feelings of the child as they have been able to ascertain;

(b)   to such wishes and feelings of any person mentioned in subsection (4)(b) to (d) as they have been able to ascertain; and

(c)   to the child's religious persuasion, racial origin and cultural and linguistic background.

(6) If it appears to a local authority that it is necessary, for the purposes of protecting members of the public from serious injury, to exercise their powers with respect to a child whom they are looking after in a manner which may not be consistent with their duties under this section, they may do so.

(7) If the Secretary of State considers it necessary, for the purpose of protecting members of the public from serious injury, to give directions to a local authority

with respect to the exercise of their powers with respect to a child whom they are looking after, he may give such directions to the authority.

(8) Where any such directions are given to an authority they shall comply with them even though doing so is inconsistent with their duties under this section.

23 Provision of accommodation and maintenance by local authority for children whom they are looking after

(1) It shall be the duty of any local authority looking after a child—
>   (a)   when he is in their care, to provide accommodation for him; and
>   (b)   to maintain him in other respects apart from providing accommodation for him.

(2) A local authority shall provide accommodation and maintenance for any child whom they are looking after by—
>   (a)   placing him (subject to subsection (5) and any regulations made by the Secretary of State) with—
>   (i)   a family;
>   (ii)   a relative of his; or
>   (iii)   any other suitable person,
>   on such terms as to payment by the authority and otherwise as the authority may determine;
>   (b)   maintaining him in a community home;
>   (c)   maintaining him in a voluntary home;
>   (d)   maintaining him in a registered children's home;
>   (e)   maintaining him in a home provided by the Secretary of State under section 82(5) on such terms as the Secretary of State may from time to time determine; or
>   (f)   making such other arrangements as—
>   (i)   seem appropriate to them; and
>   (ii)   comply with any regulations made by the Secretary of State.

(3) Any person with whom a child has been placed under subsection (2)(a) is referred to in this Act as a local authority foster parent unless he falls within subsection (4).

(4) A person falls within this subsection if he is—
>   (a)   a parent of the child;
>   (b)   a person who is not a parent of the child but who has parental responsibility for him; or
>   (c)   where the child is in care and there was a residence order in force with respect to him immediately before the care order was made, a person in whose favour the residence order was made.

(5) Where a child is in the care of a local authority, the authority may only allow him to live with a person who falls within subsection (4) in accordance with regulations made by the Secretary of State.

(6) Subject to any regulations made by the Secretary of State for the purposes of this subsection, any local authority looking after a child shall make arrangements to enable him to live with—
>   (a)   a person falling within subsection (4); or
>   (b)   a relative, friend or other person connected with him,
unless that would not be reasonably practicable or consistent with his welfare.

(7) Where a local authority provide accommodation for a child whom they are looking after, they shall, subject to the provisions of this Part and so far as is reasonably practicable and consistent with his welfare, secure that—
  (a) the accommodation is near his home; and
  (b) where the authority are also providing accommodation for a sibling of his, they are accommodated together.

(8) Where a local authority provide accommodation for a child whom they are looking after and who is disabled, they shall, so far as is reasonably practicable, secure that the accommodation is not unsuitable to his particular needs.

(9) Part II of Schedule 2 shall have effect for the purposes of making further provision as to children looked after by local authorities and in particular as to the regulations that may be made under subsections (2)(a) and (f) and (5).

Advice and assistance for certain children

24 Advice and assistance for certain children

(1) Where a child is being looked after by a local authority, it shall be the duty of the authority to advise, assist and befriend him with a view to promoting his welfare when he ceases to be looked after by them.

(2) In this Part "a person qualifying for advice and assistance" means a person within the area of the authority who is under twenty-one and who was, at any time after reaching the age of sixteen but while still a child—
  (a) looked after by a local authority;
  (b) accommodated by or on behalf of a voluntary organisation;
  (c) accommodated in a registered children's home;
  (d) accommodated—
        (i)   by any health authority or local education authority; or
        (ii) in any residential care home, nursing home or mental nursing home, for a consecutive period of at least three months; or
  (e) privately fostered,
but who is no longer so looked after, accommodated or fostered.

(3) Subsection (2)(d) applies even if the period of three months mentioned there began before the child reached the age of sixteen.

(4) Where—
  (a) a local authority know that there is within their area a person qualifying for advice and assistance;
  (b) the conditions in subsection (5) are satisfied; and
  (c) that person has asked them for help of a kind which they can give under this section,
they shall (if he was being looked after by a local authority or was accommodated by or on behalf of a voluntary organisation) and may (in any other case) advise and befriend him.

(5) The conditions are that—
  (a) it appears to the authority that the person concerned is in need of advice and being befriended;
  (b) where that person was not being looked after by the authority, they are satisfied that the person by whom he was being looked after does not have the necessary facilities for advising or befriending him.

(6) Where as a result of this section a local authority are under a duty, or are empowered, to advise and befriend a person, they may also give him assistance.

(7) Assistance given under subsections (1) to (6) may be in kind or, in exceptional circumstances, in cash.

(8) A local authority may give assistance to any person who qualifies for advice and assistance by virtue of subsection (2)(*a*) by—
  - (*a*) contributing to expenses incurred by him in living near the place where he is, or will be—
    - (i)   employed or seeking employment; or
    - (ii)   receiving education or training; or
  - (*b*) making a grant to enable him to meet expenses connected with his education or training.

(9) Where a local authority are assisting the person under subsection (8) by making a contribution or grant with respect to a course of education or training, they may—
  - (*a*) continue to do so even though he reaches the age of twenty-one before completing the course; and
  - (*b*) disregard any interruption in his attendance on the course if he resumes it as soon as is reasonably practicable.

(10) Subsections (7) to (9) of section 17 shall apply in relation to assistance given under this section (otherwise than under subsection (8)) as they apply in relation to assistance given under that section.

(11) Where it appears to a local authority that a person whom they have been advising and befriending under this section as a person qualifying for advice and assistance, proposes to live, or is living, in the area of another local authority, they shall inform that other local authority.

(12) Where a child who is accommodated—
  - (*a*) by a voluntary organisation or in a registered children's home;
  - (*b*) by any health authority or local education authority; or
  - (*c*) in any residential care home, nursing home or mental nursing home,
    ceases to be so accommodated, after reaching the age of sixteen, the organisation, authority or (as the case may be) person carrying on the home shall inform the local authority within whose area the child proposes to live.

(13) Subsection (12) only applies, by virtue of paragraph (*b*) or (*c*), if the accommodation has been provided for a consecutive period of at least three months.

Secure accommodation

25 Use of accommodation for restricting liberty

(1) Subject to the following provisions of this section, a child who is being looked after by a local authority may not be placed, and, if placed, may not be kept, in accommodation provided for the purpose of restricting liberty ("secure accommodation") unless it appears—
  - (*a*) that—
    - (i)   he has a history of absconding and is likely to abscond from any other description of accommodation; and
    - (ii)   if he absconds, he is likely to suffer significant harm; or
  - (*b*) that if he is kept in any other description of accommodation he is likely to injure himself or other persons.

(2) The Secretary of State may by regulations—
  - (*a*) specify a maximum period—
    - (i)   beyond which a child may not be kept in secure accommodation without the authority of the court; and

(ii)   for which the court may authorise a child to be kept in secure accommodation;

(b)   empower the court from time to time to authorise a child to be kept in secure accommodation for such further period as the regulations may specify; and

(c)   provide that applications to the court under this section shall be made only by local authorities.

(3) It shall be the duty of a court hearing an application under this section to determine whether any relevant criteria for keeping a child in secure accommodation are satisfied in his case.

(4) If a court determines that any such criteria are satisfied, it shall make an order authorising the child to be kept in secure accommodation and specifying the maximum period for which he may be so kept.

(5) On any adjournment of the hearing of an application under this section, a court may make an interim order permitting the child to be kept during the period of the adjournment in secure accommodation.

(6) No court shall exercise the powers conferred by this section in respect of a child who is not legally represented in that court unless, having been informed of his right to apply for legal aid and having had the opportunity to do so, he refused or failed to apply.

(7) The Secretary of State may by regulations provide that—
    (a)   this section shall or shall not apply to any description of children specified in the regulations;
    (b)   this section shall have effect in relation to children of a description specified in the regulations subject to such modifications as may be so specified;
    (c)   such other provisions as may be so specified shall have effect for the purpose of determining whether a child of a description specified in the regulations may be placed or kept in secure accommodation.

(8) The giving of an authorisation under this section shall not prejudice any power of any court in England and Wales or Scotland to give directions relating to the child to whom the authorisation relates.

(9) This section is subject to section 20(8).

Supplemental

26   Review of cases and inquiries into representations

(1) The Secretary of State may make regulations requiring the case of each child who is being looked after by a local authority to be reviewed in accordance with the provisions of the regulations.

(2) The regulations may, in particular, make provision—
    (a)   as to the manner in which each case is to be reviewed;
    (b)   as to the considerations to which the local authority are to have regard in reviewing each case;
    (c)   as to the time when each case is first to be reviewed and the frequency of subsequent reviews;
    (d)   requiring the authority, before conducting any review, to seek the views of—
        (i)   the child;
        (ii)   his parents;
        (iii)   any person who is not a parent of his but who has parental responsibility for him; and

> (iv)   any other person whose views the authority consider to be relevant, including, in particular, the views of those persons in relation to any particular matter which is to be considered in the course of the review;

(*e*)   requiring the authority to consider, in the case of a child who is in their care, whether an application should be made to discharge the care order;

(*f*)   requiring the authority to consider, in the case of a child in accommodation provided by the authority, whether the accommodation accords with the requirements of this Part;

(*g*)   requiring the authority to inform the child, so far as is reasonably practicable, of any steps he may take under this Act;

(*h*)   requiring the authority to make arrangements, including arrangements with such other bodies providing services as it considers appropriate, to implement any decision which they propose to make in the course, or as a result, of the review;

(*i*)   requiring the authority to notify details of the result of the review and of any decision taken by them in consequence of the review to—

> (i)   the child;
> (ii)   his parents;
> (iii)   any person who is not a parent of his but who has had parental responsibility for him; and
> (iv)   any other person whom they consider ought to be notified;

(*j*)   requiring the authority to monitor the arrangements which they have made with a view to ensuring that they comply with the regulations.

(3) Every local authority shall establish a procedure for considering any representations (including any complaint) made to them by—

(*a*)   any child who is being looked after by them or who is not being looked after by them but is in need;

(*b*)   a parent of his;

(*c*)   any person who is not a parent of his but who has parental responsibility for him;

(*d*)   any local authority foster parent;

(*e*)   such other person as the authority consider has a sufficient interest in the child's welfare to warrant his representations being considered by them,

about the discharge by the authority of any of their functions under this Part in relation to the child.

(4) The procedure shall ensure that at least one person who is not a member or officer of the authority takes part in—

(*a*)   the consideration; and

(*b*)   any discussions which are held by the authority about the action (if any) to be taken in relation to the child in the light of the consideration.

(5) In carrying out any consideration of representations under this section a local authority shall comply with any regulations made by the Secretary of State for the purpose of regulating the procedure to be followed.

(6) The Secretary of State may make regulations requiring local authorities to monitor the arrangements that they have made with a view to ensuring that they comply with any regulations made for the purposes of subsection (5).

(7) Where any representation has been considered under the procedure established by a local authority under this section, the authority shall—

(*a*)   have due regard to the findings of those considering the representation; and

(*b*)   take such steps as are reasonably practicable to notify (in writing)—

> (i)   the person making the representation;

(ii) the child (if the authority consider that he has sufficient understanding); and

(iii) such other persons (if any) as appear to the authority to be likely to be affected,

of the authority's decision in the matter and their reasons for taking that decision and of any action which they have taken, or propose to take.

(8) Every local authority shall give such publicity to their procedure for considering representations under this section as they consider appropriate.

27 Co-operation between authorities

(1) Where it appears to a local authority that any authority or other person mentioned in subsection (3) could, by taking any specified action, help in the exercise of any of their functions under this Part, they may request the help of that other authority or person, specifying the action in question.

(2) An authority whose help is so requested shall comply with the request if it is compatible with their own statutory or other duties and obligations and does not unduly prejudice the discharge of any of their functions.

(3) The persons are—
   (*a*) any local authority;
   (*b*) any local education authority;
   (*c*) any local housing authority;
   (*d*) any health authority; and
   (*e*) any person authorised by the Secretary of State for the purposes of this section.

(4) Every local authority shall assist any local education authority with the provision of services for any child within the local authority's area who has special educational needs.

28 Consultation with local education authorities

(1) Where—
   (*a*) a child is being looked after by a local authority; and
   (*b*) the authority propose to provide accommodation for him in an establishment at which education is provided for children who are accommodated there,

they shall, so far as is reasonably practicable, consult the appropriate local education authority before doing so.

(2) Where any such proposal is carried out, the local authority shall, as soon as is reasonably practicable, inform the appropriate local education authority of the arrangements that have been made for the child's accommodation.

(3) Where the child ceases to be accommodated as mentioned in subsection (1)(*b*), the local authority shall inform the appropriate local education authority.

(4) In this section "the appropriate local education authority" means—
   (*a*) the local education authority within whose area the local authority's area falls; or
   (*b*) where the child has special educational needs and a statement of his needs is maintained under the Education Act 1981, the local education authority who maintain the statement.

29 Recoupment of cost of providing services etc.

(1) Where a local authority provide any service under section 17 or 18, other than advice, guidance or counselling, they may recover from a person specified in subsection (4) such charge for the service as they consider reasonable.

(2) Where the authority are satisfied that that person's means are insufficient for it to be reasonably practicable for him to pay the charge, they shall not require him to pay more than he can reasonably be expected to pay.

(3) No person shall be liable to pay any charge under subsection (1) at any time when he is in receipt of income support or family credit under the Social Security Act 1986.

(4) The persons are—
   (a) where the service is provided for a child under sixteen, each of his parents;
   (b) where it is provided for a child who has reached the age of sixteen, the child himself; and
   (c) where it is provided for a member of the child's family, that member.

(5) Any charge under subsection (1) may, without prejudice to any other method of recovery, be recovered summarily as a civil debt.

(6) Part III of Schedule 2 makes provision in connection with contributions towards the maintenance of children who are being looked after by local authorities and consists of the re-enactment with modifications of provisions in Part V of the Child Care Act 1980.

(7) Where a local authority provide any accommodation under section 20(1) for a child who was (immediately before they began to look after him) ordinarily resident within the area of another local authority, they may recover from that other authority any reasonable expenses incurred by them in providing the accommodation and maintaining him.

(8) Where a local authority provide accommodation under section 21(1) or (2)(a) or (b) for a child who is ordinarily resident within the area of another local authority and they are not maintaining him in—
   (a) a community home provided by them;
   (b) a controlled community home; or
   (c) a hospital vested in the Secretary of State,
they may recover from that other authority any reasonable expenses incurred by them in providing the accommodation and maintaining him.

(9) Where a local authority comply with any request under section 27(2) in relation to a child or other person who is not ordinarily resident within their area, they may recover from the local authority in whose area the child or person is ordinarily resident any expenses reasonably incurred by them in respect of that person.

30 Miscellaneous

(1) Nothing in this Part shall affect any duty imposed on a local authority by or under any other enactment.

(2) Any question arising under section 20(2), 21(3) or 29(7) to (9) as to the ordinary residence of a child shall be determined by agreement between the local authorities concerned or, in default of agreement, by the Secretary of State.

(3) Where the functions conferred on a local authority by this Part and the functions of a local education authority are concurrent, the Secretary of State may by regulations provide by which authority the functions are to be exercised.

(4) The Secretary of State may make regulations for determining, as respects any local education authority functions specified in the regulations, whether a child who is being looked after by a local authority is to be treated, for purposes so specified, as a child of parents of sufficient resources or as a child of parents without resources.

PART IV

CARE AND SUPERVISION

General

31 Care and supervision orders

(1) On the application of any local authority or authorised person, the court may make an order—
  (a) placing the child with respect to whom the application is made in the care of a designated local authority; or
  (b) putting him under the supervision of a designated local authority or of a probation officer.

(2) A court may only make a care order or supervision order if it is satisfied—
  (a) that the child concerned is suffering, or is likely to suffer, significant harm; and
  (b) that the harm, or likelihood of harm, is attributable to—
    (i) the care given to the child, or likely to be given to him if the order were not made, not being what it would be reasonable to expect a parent to give to him; or
    (ii) the child's being beyond parental control.

(3) No care order or supervision order may be made with respect to a child who has reached the age of seventeen (or sixteen, in the case of a child who is married).

(4) An application under this section may be made on its own or in any other family proceedings.

(5) The court may—
  (a) on an application for a care order, make a supervision order;
  (b) on an application for a supervision order, make a care order.

(6) Where an authorised person proposes to make an application under this section he shall—
  (a) if it is reasonably practicable to do so; and
  (b) before making the application,
consult the local authority appearing to him to be the authority in whose area the child concerned is ordinarily resident.

(7) An application made by an authorised person shall not be entertained by the court if, at the time when it is made, the child concerned is—
  (a) the subject of an earlier application for a care order, or supervision order, which has not been disposed of; or
  (b) subject to—
    (i) a care order or supervision order;
    (ii) an order under section 7(7)(b) of the Children and Young Persons Act 1969; or
    (iii) a supervision requirement within the meaning of the Social Work (Scotland) Act 1968.

(8) The local authority designated in a care order must be—

(a)   the authority within whose area the child is ordinarily resident; or

(b)   where the child does not reside in the area of a local authority, the authority within whose area any circumstances arose in consequence of which the order is being made.

(9) In this section—

"authorised person" means—

(a)   the National Society for the Prevention of Cruelty to Children and any of its officers; and

(b)   any person authorised by order of the Secretary of State to bring proceedings under this section and any officer of a body which is so authorised;

"harm" means ill-treatment or the impairment of health or development;

"development" means physical, intellectual, emotional, social or behavioural development;

"health" means physical or mental health; and

"ill-treatment" includes sexual abuse and forms of ill-treatment which are not physical.

(10) Where the question of whether harm suffered by a child is significant turns on the child's health or development, his health or development shall be compared with that which could reasonably be expected of a similar child.

(11) In this Act—

"a care order" means (subject to section 105(1)) an order under subsection (1)(a) and (except where express provision to the contrary is made) includes an interim care order made under section 38; and

"a supervision order" means an order under subsection (1)(b) and (except where express provision to the contrary is made) includes an interim supervision order made under section 38.

32   Period within which application for order under this Part must be disposed of

(1) A court hearing an application for an order under this Part shall (in the light of any rules made by virtue of subsection (2))—

(a)   draw up a timetable with a view to disposing of the application without delay; and

(b)   give such directions as it considers appropriate for the purpose of ensuring, so far as is reasonably practicable, that that timetable is adhered to.

(2) Rules of court may—

(a)   specify periods within which specified steps must be taken in relation to such proceedings; and

(b)   make other provision with respect to such proceedings for the purpose of ensuring, so far as is reasonably practicable, that they are disposed of without delay.

Care orders

33   Effect of care order

(1) Where a care order is made with respect to a child it shall be the duty of the local authority designated by the order to receive the child into their care and to keep him in their care while the order remains in force.

(2) Where—

(a)   a care order has been made with respect to a child on the application of an authorised person; but

(b)   the local authority designated by the order was not informed that that person proposed to make the application,

the child may be kept in the care of that person until received into the care of the authority.

(3) While a care order is in force with respect to a child, the local authority designated by the order shall—

(a)   have parental responsibility for the child; and

(b)   have the power (subject to the following provisions of this section) to determine the extent to which a parent or guardian of the child may meet his parental responsibility for him.

(4) The authority may not exercise the power in subsection (3)(b) unless they are satisfied that it is necessary to do so in order to safeguard or promote the child's welfare.

(5) Nothing in subsection (3)(b) shall prevent a parent or guardian of the child who has care of him from doing what is reasonable in all the circumstances of the case for the purpose of safeguarding or promoting his welfare.

(6) While a care order is in force with respect to a child, the local authority designated by the order shall not—

(a)   cause the child to be brought up in any religious persuasion other than that in which he would have been brought up if the order had not been made; or

(b)   have the right—

    (i)   to consent or refuse to consent to the making of an application with respect to the child under section 18 of the Adoption Act 1976;

    (ii)   to agree or refuse to agree to the making of an adoption order, or an order under section 55 of the Act of 1976, with respect to the child; or

    (iii) to appoint a guardian for the child.

(7) While a care order is in force with respect to a child, no person may—

(a)   cause the child to be known by a new surname; or

(b)   remove him from the United Kingdom,

without either the written consent of every person who has parental responsibility for the child or the leave of the court.

(8) Subsection (7)(b) does not—

(a)   prevent the removal of such a child, for a period of less than one month, by the authority in whose care he is; or

(b)   apply to arrangements for such a child to live outside England and Wales (which are governed by paragraph 19 of Schedule 2).

(9) The power in subsection (3)(b) is subject (in addition to being subject to the provisions of this section) to any right, duty, power, responsibility or authority which a parent or guardian of the child has in relation to the child and his property by virtue of any other enactment.

34   Parental contact etc. with children in care

(1) Where a child is in the care of a local authority, the authority shall (subject to the provisions of this section) allow the child reasonable contact with—

(a)   his parents;

(b)   any guardian of his;

(c) where there was a residence order in force with respect to the child immediately before the care order was made, the person in whose favour the order was made; and

(d) where, immediately before the care order was made, a person had care of the child by virtue of an order made in the exercise of the High Court's inherent jurisdiction with respect to children, that person.

(2) On an application made by the authority or the child, the court may make such order as it considers appropriate with respect to the contact which is to be allowed between the child and any named person.

(3) On an application made by—
(a) any person mentioned in paragraphs (a) to (c) of subsection (1); or
(b) any person who has obtained the leave of the court to make the application, the court may make such order as it considers appropriate with respect to the contact which is to be allowed between the child and that person.

(4) On an application made by the authority or the child, the court may make an order authorising the authority to refuse to allow contact between the child and any person who is mentioned in paragraphs (a) to (c) of subsection (1) and named in the order.

(5) When making a care order with respect to a child, or in any family proceedings in connection with a child who is in the care of a local authority, the court may make an order under this section, even though no application for such an order has been made with respect to the child, if it considers that the order should be made.

(6) An authority may refuse to allow the contact that would otherwise be required by virtue of subsection (1) or an order under this section if—
(a) they are satisfied that it is necessary to do so in order to safeguard or promote the child's welfare; and
(b) the refusal—
(i) is decided upon as a matter of urgency; and
(ii) does not last for more than seven days.

(7) An order under this section may impose such conditions as the court considers appropriate.

(8) The Secretary of State may by regulations make provision as to—
(a) the steps to be taken by a local authority who have exercised their powers under subsection (6);
(b) the circumstances in which, and conditions subject to which, the terms of any order under this section may be departed from by agreement between the local authority and the person in relation to whom the order is made;
(c) notification by a local authority of any variation or suspension of arrangements made (otherwise than under an order under this section) with a view to affording any person contact with a child to whom this section applies.

(9) The court may vary or discharge any order made under this section on the application of the authority, the child concerned or the person named in the order.

(10) An order under this section may be made either at the same time as the care order itself or later.

(11) Before making a care order with respect to any child the court shall—
(a) consider the arrangements which the authority have made, or propose to make, for affording any person contact with a child to whom this section applies; and

(*b*) invite the parties to the proceedings to comment on those arrangements.

Supervision orders

35 Supervision orders

(1) While a supervision order is in force it shall be the duty of the supervisor—
- (*a*) to advise, assist and befriend the supervised child;
- (*b*) to take such steps as are reasonably necessary to give effect to the order; and
- (*c*) where—
  - (i) the order is not wholly complied with; or
  - (ii) the supervisor considers that the order may no longer be necessary,

to consider whether or not to apply to the court for its variation or discharge.

(2) Parts I and II of Schedule 3 make further provision with respect to supervision orders.

36 Education supervision orders

(1) On the application of any local education authority, the court may make an order putting the child with respect to whom the application is made under the supervision of a designated local education authority.

(2) In this Act "an education supervision order" means an order under subsection (1).

(3) A court may only make an education supervision order if it is satisfied that the child concerned is of compulsory school age and is not being properly educated.

(4) For the purposes of this section, a child is being properly educated only if he is receiving efficient full-time education suitable to his age, ability and aptitude and any special educational needs he may have.

(5) Where a child is—
- (*a*) the subject of a school attendance order which is in force under section 37 of the Education Act 1944 and which has not been complied with; or
- (*b*) a registered pupil at a school which he is not attending regularly within the meaning of section 39 of that Act,

then, unless it is proved that he is being properly educated, it shall be assumed that he is not.

(6) An education supervision order may not be made with respect to a child who is in the care of a local authority.

(7) The local education authority designated in an education supervision order must be—
- (*a*) the authority within whose area the child concerned is living or will live; or
- (*b*) where—
  - (i) the child is a registered pupil at a school; and
  - (ii) the authority mentioned in paragraph (*a*) and the authority within whose area the school is situated agree,

the latter authority.

(8) Where a local education authority propose to make an application for an education supervision order they shall, before making the application, consult the social services committee (within the meaning of the Local Authority Social Services Act 1970) of the appropriate local authority.

(9) The appropriate local authority is—
- (a) in the case of a child who is being provided with accommodation by, or on behalf of, a local authority, that authority; and
- (b) in any other case, the local authority within whose area the child concerned lives, or will live.

(10) Part III of Schedule 3 makes further provision with respect to education supervision orders.

Powers of court

37   Powers of court in certain family proceedings

(1) Where, in any family proceedings in which a question arises with respect to the welfare of any child, it appears to the court that it may be appropriate for a care or supervision order to be made with respect to him, the court may direct the appropriate authority to undertake an investigation of the child's circumstances.

(2) Where the court gives a direction under this section the local authority concerned shall, when undertaking the investigation, consider whether they should—
- (a) apply for a care order or for a supervision order with respect to the child;
- (b) provide services or assistance for the child or his family; or
- (c) take any other action with respect to the child.

(3) Where a local authority undertake an investigation under this section, and decide not to apply for a care order or supervision order with respect to the child concerned, they shall inform the court of—
- (a) their reasons for so deciding;
- (b) any service or assistance which they have provided, or intend to provide, for the child and his family; and
- (c) any other action which they have taken, or propose to take, with respect to the child.

(4) The information shall be given to the court before the end of the period of eight weeks beginning with the date of the direction, unless the court otherwise directs.

(5) The local authority named in a direction under subsection (1) must be—
- (a) the authority in whose area the child is ordinarily resident; or
- (b) where the child does not reside in the area of a local authority, the authority within whose area any circumstances arose in consequence of which the direction is being given.

(6) If, on the conclusion of any investigation or review under this section, the authority decide not to apply for a care order or supervision order with respect to the child—
- (a) they shall consider whether it would be appropriate to review the case at a later date; and
- (b) if they decide that it would be, they shall determine the date on which that review is to begin.

38   Interim orders

(1) Where—
- (a) in any proceedings on an application for a care order or supervision order, the proceedings are adjourned; or
- (b) the court gives a direction under section 37(1),

the court may make an interim care order or an interim supervision order with respect to the child concerned.

(2) A court shall not make an interim care order or interim supervision order under this section unless it is satisfied that there are reasonable grounds for believing that the circumstances with respect to the child are as mentioned in section 31(2).

(3) Where, in any proceedings on an application for a care order or supervision order, a court makes a residence order with respect to the child concerned, it shall also make an interim supervision order with respect to him unless satisfied that his welfare will be satisfactorily safeguarded without an interim order being made.

(4) An interim order made under or by virtue of this section shall have effect for such period as may be specified in the order, but shall in any event cease to have effect on whichever of the following events first occurs—
- (a) the expiry of the period of eight weeks beginning with the date on which the order is made;
- (b) if the order is the second or subsequent such order made with respect to the same child in the same proceedings, the expiry of the relevant period;
- (c) in a case which falls within subsection (1)(a), the disposal of the application;
- (d) in a case which falls within subsection (1)(b), on the disposal of an application for a care order or supervision order made by the authority with respect to the child;
- (e) in a case which falls within subsection (1)(b) and in which—
  - (i) the court has given a direction under section 37(4), but
  - (ii) no application for a care order or supervision order has been made with respect to the child,
  the expiry of the period fixed by that direction.

(5) In subsection (4)(b) "the relevant period" means—
- (a) the period of four weeks beginning with the date on which the order in question is made; or
- (b) the period of eight weeks beginning with the date on which the first order was made if that period ends later than the period mentioned in paragraph (a).

(6) Where the court makes an interim care order, or interim supervision order, it may give such directions (if any) as it considers appropriate with regard to the medical or psychiatric examination or other assessment of the child; but if the child is of sufficient understanding to make an informed decision he may refuse to submit to the examination or other assessment.

(7) A direction under subsection (6) may be to the effect that there is to be—
- (a) no such examination or assessment; or
- (b) no such examination or assessment unless the court directs otherwise.

(8) A direction under subsection (6) may be—
- (a) given when the interim order is made or at any time while it is in force; and
- (b) varied at any time on the application of any person falling within any class of person prescribed by rules of court for the purposes of this subsection.

(9) Paragraphs 4 and 5 of Schedule 3 shall not apply in relation to an interim supervision order.

(10) Where a court makes an order under or by virtue of this section it shall, in determining the period for which the order is to be in force, consider whether any party who was, or might have been, opposed to the making of the order was in a position to argue his case against the order in full.

39 Discharge and variation etc. of care orders and supervision orders

(1) A care order may be discharged by the court on the application of—
  (a) any person who has parental responsibility for the child;
  (b) the child himself; or
  (c) the local authority designated by the order.

(2) A supervision order may be varied or discharged by the court on the application of—
  (a) any person who has parental responsibility for the child;
  (b) the child himself; or
  (c) the supervisor.

(3) On the application of a person who is not entitled to apply for the order to be discharged, but who is a person with whom the child is living, a supervision order may be varied by the court in so far as it imposes a requirement which affects that person.

(4) Where a care order is in force with respect to a child the court may, on the application of any person entitled to apply for the order to be discharged, substitute a supervision order for the care order.

(5) When a court is considering whether to substitute one order for another under subsection (4) any provision of this Act which would otherwise require section 31(2) to be satisfied at the time when the proposed order is substituted or made shall be disregarded.

40 Orders pending appeals in cases about care or supervision orders

(1) Where—
  (a) a court dismisses an application for a care order; and
  (b) at the time when the court dismisses the application, the child concerned is the subject of an interim care order,
the court may make a care order with respect to the child to have effect subject to such directions (if any) as the court may see fit to include in the order.

(2) Where—
  (a) a court dismisses an application for a care order, or an application for a supervision order; and
  (b) at the time when the court dismisses the application, the child concerned is the subject of an interim supervision order,
the court may make a supervision order with respect to the child to have effect subject to such directions (if any) as the court may see fit to include in the order.

(3) Where a court grants an application to discharge a care order or supervision order, it may order that—
  (a) its decision is not to have effect; or
  (b) the care order, or supervision order, is to continue to have effect but subject to such directions as the court sees fit to include in the order.

(4) An order made under this section shall only have effect for such period, not exceeding the appeal period, as may be specified in the order.

(5) Where—
  (a) an appeal is made against any decision of a court under this section; or
  (b) any application is made to the appellate court in connection with a proposed appeal against that decision,
the appellate court may extend the period for which the order in question is to have effect, but not so as to extend it beyond the end of the appeal period.

(6) In this section "the appeal period" means—
  (a) where an appeal is made against the decision in question, the period between the making of that decision and the determination of the appeal; and
  (b) otherwise, the period during which an appeal may be made against the decision.

Guardians ad litem

41 Representation of child and of his interests in certain proceedings

(1) For the purpose of any specified proceedings, the court shall appoint a guardian ad litem for the child concerned unless satisfied that it is not necessary to do so in order to safeguard his interests.

(2) The guardian ad litem shall—
  (a) be appointed in accordance with rules of court; and
  (b) be under a duty to safeguard the interests of the child in the manner prescribed by such rules.

(3) Where—
  (a) the child concerned is not represented by a solicitor; and
  (b) any of the conditions mentioned in subsection (4) is satisfied,
the court may appoint a solicitor to represent him.

(4) The conditions are that—
  (a) no guardian ad litem has been appointed for the child;
  (b) the child has sufficient understanding to instruct a solicitor and wishes to do so;
  (c) it appears to the court that it would be in the child's best interests for him to be represented by a solicitor.

(5) Any solicitor appointed under or by virtue of this section shall be appointed, and shall represent the child, in accordance with rules of court.

(6) In this section "specified proceedings" means any proceedings—
  (a) on an application for a care order or supervision order;
  (b) in which the court has given a direction under section 37(1) and has made, or is considering whether to make, an interim care order;
  (c) on an application for the discharge of a care order or the variation or discharge of a supervision order;
  (d) on an application under section 39(4);
  (e) in which the court is considering whether to make a residence order with respect to a child who is the subject of a care order;
  (f) with respect to contact between a child who is the subject of a care order and any other person;
  (g) under Part V;
  (h) on an appeal against—
    (i) the making of, or refusal to make, a care order, supervision order or any order under section 34;
    (ii) the making of, or refusal to make, a residence order with respect to a child who is the subject of a care order; or
    (iii) the variation or discharge, or refusal of an application to vary or discharge, an order of a kind mentioned in sub-paragraph (i) or (ii);
    (iv) the refusal of an application under section 39(4);
    (v) the making, or refusal to make, an order under Part V; or
  (i) which are specified for the time being, for the purposes of this section, by rules of court.

(7) The Secretary of State may by regulations provide for the establishment of panels of persons from whom guardians ad litem appointed under this section must be selected.

(8) Subsection (7) shall not be taken to prejudice the power of the Lord Chancellor to confer or impose duties on the Official Solicitor under section 90(3) of the Supreme Court Act 1981.

(9) The regulations may, in particular, make provision—
- (a) as to the constitution, administration and procedures of panels;
- (b) requiring two or more specified local authorities to make arrangements for the joint management of a panel;
- (c) for the defrayment by local authorities of expenses incurred by members of panels;
- (d) for the payment by local authorities of fees and alowances for members of panels;
- (e) as to the qualifications for membership of a panel;
- (f) as to the training to be given to members of panels;
- (g) as to the co-operation required of specified local authorities in the provision of panels in specified areas; and
- (h) for monitoring the work of guardians ad litem.

(10) Rules of court may make provision as to—
- (a) the assistance which any guardian ad litem may be required by the court to give to it;
- (b) the consideration to be given by any guardian ad litem, where an order of a specified kind has been made in the proceedings in question, as to whether to apply for the variation or discharge of the order;
- (c) the participation of guardians ad litem in reviews, of a kind specified in the rules, which are conducted by the court.

(11) Regardless of any enactment or rule of law which would otherwise prevent it from doing so, the court may take account of—
- (a) any statement contained in a report made by a guardian ad litem who is appointed under this section for the purpose of the proceedings in question; and
- (b) any evidence given in respect of the matters referred to in the report,

in so far as the statement or evidence is, in the opinion of the court, relevant to the question which the court is considering.

42   Right of guardian ad litem to have access to local authority records

(1) Where a person has been appointed as a guardian ad litem under this Act he shall have the right at all reasonable times to examine and take copies of—
- (a) any records of, or held by, a local authority which were compiled in connection with the making, or proposed making, by any person of any application under this Act with respect to the child concerned; or
- (b) any other records of, or held by, a local authority which were compiled in connection with any functions which stand referred to their social services committee under the Local Authority Social Services Act 1970, so far as those records relate to that child.

(2) Where a guardian ad litem takes a copy of any record which he is entitled to examine under this section, that copy or any part of it shall be admissible as evidence of any matter referred to in any—
- (a) report which he makes to the court in the proceedings in question; or
- (b) evidence which he gives in those proceedings.

(3) Subsection (2) has effect regardless of any enactment or rule of law which wouuld otherwise prevent the record in question being admissible in evidence.

PART V

PROTECTION OF CHILDREN

43 Child assessment orders

(1) On the application of a local authority or authorised person for an order to be made under this section with respect to a child, the court may make the order if, but only if, it is satisfied that—

   (a)   the applicant has reasonable cause to suspect that the child is suffering, or is likely to suffer, significant harm;

   (b)   an assessment of the state of the child's health or development, or of the way in which he has been treated, is required to enable the applicant to determine whether or not the child is suffering, or is likely to suffer, significant harm; and

   (c)   it is unlikely that such an assessment will be made, or be satisfactory, in the absence of an order under this section.

(2) In this Act "a child assessment order" means an order under this section.

(3) A court may treat an application under this section as an application for an emergency protection order.

(4) No court shall make a child assessment order if it is satisfied—

   (a)   that there are grounds for making an emergency protection order with respect to the child; and

   (b)   that it ought to make such an order rather than a child assessment order.

(5) A child assessment order shall—

   (a)   specify the date by which the assessment is to begin; and

   (b)   have effect for such period, not exceeding 7 days beginning with that date, as may be specified in the order.

(6) Where a child assessment order is in force with respect to a child it shall be the duty of any person who is in a position to produce the child—

   (a)   to produce him to such person as may be named in the order; and

   (b)   to comply with such directions relating to the assessment of the child as the court thinks fit to specify in the order.

(7) A child assessment order authorises any person carrying out the assessment, or any part of the assessment, to do so in accordance with the terms of the order.

(8) Regardless of subsection (7), if the child is of sufficient understanding to make an informed decision he may refuse to submit to a medical or psychiatric examination or other assessment.

(9) The child may only be kept away from home—

   (a)   in accordance with directions specified in the order;

   (b)   if it is necessary for the purposes of the assessment; and

   (c)   for such period or periods as may be specified in the order.

(10) Where the child is to be kept away from home, the order shall contain such directions as the court thinks fit with regard to the contact that he must be allowed to have with other persons while away from home.

(11) Any person making an application for a child assessment order shall take such steps as are reasonably practicable to ensure that notice of the application is given to—

(*a*)   the child's parents;

(*b*)   any person who is not a parent of his but who has parental responsibility for him;

(*c*)   any other person caring for the child;

(*d*)   any person in whose favour a contact order is in force with respect to the child;

(*e*)   any person who is allowed to have contact with the child by virtue of an order under section 34; and

(*f*)   the child,

before the hearing of the application.

(12) Rules of court may make provision as to the circumstances in which—

(*a*)   any of the persons mentioned in subsection (11); or

(*b*)   such other person as may be specified in the rules,

may apply to the court for a child assessment order to be varied or discharged.

(13) In this section "authorised person" means a person who is an authorised person for the purposes of section 31.

44   Orders for emergency protection of children

(1) Where any person ("the applicant') applies to the court for an order to be made under this section with respect to a child, the court may make the order if, but only if, it is satisfied that—

(*a*)   there is reasonable cause to believe that the child is likely to suffer significant harm if—

(i)   he is not removed to accommodation provided by or on behalf of the applicant; or

(ii)   he does not remain in the place in which he is then being accommodated;

(*b*)   in the case of an application made by a local authority—

(i)   enquiries are being made with respect to the child under section 47(1)(*b*); and

(ii)   those enquiries are being frustrated by access to the child being unreasonably refused to a person authorised to seek access and that the applicant has reasonable cause to believe that access to the child is required as a matter of urgency; or

(*c*)   in the case of an application made by an authorised person—

(i)   the applicant has reasonable cause to suspect that a child is suffering, or is likely to suffer, significant harm;

(ii)   the applicant is making enquiries with respect to the child's welfare; and

(iii)   those enquiries are being frustrated by access to the child being unreasonably refused to a person authorised to seek access and the applicant has reasonable cause to believe that access to the child is required as a matter of urgency.

(2) In this section—

(*a*)   "authorised person" means a person who is an authorised person for the purposes of section 31; and

(*b*)   "a person authorised to seek access" means—

(i)   in the case of an application by a local authority, an officer of the local authority or a person authorised by the authority to act on their behalf in connection with the enquiries; or

(ii) in the case of an application by an authorised person, that person.

(3) Any person—
  (a) seeking access to a child in connection with enquiries of a kind mentioned in subsection (1); and
  (b) purporting to be a person authorised to do so,
shall, on being asked to do so, produce some duly authenticated document as evidence that he is such a person.

(4) While an order under this section ("an emergency protection order") is in force it—
  (a) operates as a direction to any person who is in a position to do so to comply with any request to produce the child to the applicant;
  (b) authorises—
    (i) the removal of the child at any time to accommodation provided by or on behalf of the applicant and his being kept there; or
    (ii) the prevention of the child's removal from any hospital, or other place, in which he was being accommodated immediately before the making of the order; and
  (c) gives the applicant parental responsibility for the child.

(5) Where an emergency protection order is in force with respect to a child, the applicant—
  (a) shall only exercise the power given by virtue of subsection (4)(b) in order to safeguard the welfare of the child;
  (b) shall take, and shall only take, such action in meeting his parental responsibility for the child as is reasonably required to safeguard or promote the welfare of the child (having regard in particular to the duration of the order); and
  (c) shall comply with the requirements of any regulations made by the Secretary of State for the purposes of this subsection.

(6) Where the court makes an emergency protection order, it may give such directions (if any) as it considers appropriate with respect to—
  (a) the contact which is, or is not, to be allowed between the child and any named person;
  (b) the medical or psychiatric examination or other assessment of the child.

(7) Where any direction is given under subsection (6)(b), the child may, if he is of sufficient understanding to make an informed decision, refuse to submit to the examination or other assessment.

(8) A direction under subsection (6)(a) may impose conditions and one under subsection (6)(b) may be to the effect that there is to be—
  (a) no such examination or assessment; or
  (b) no such examination or assessment unless the court directs otherwise.

(9) A direction under subsection (6) may be—
  (a) given when the emergency protection order is made or at any time while it is in force; and
  (b) varied at any time on the application of any person falling within any class of person prescribed by rules of court for the purposes of this subsection.

(10) Where an emergency protection order is in force with respect to a child and—
  (a) the applicant has exercised the power given by subsection (4)(b)(i) but it appears to him that it is safe for the child to be returned; or
  (b) the applicant has exercised the power given by subsection (4)(b)(ii) but it appears to him that it is safe for the child to be allowed to be removed from the place in question,

he shall return the child or (as the case may be) allow him to be removed.

(11) Where he is required by subsection (10) to return the child the applicant shall—

  (a)   return him to the care of the person from whose care he was removed; or
  (b)   if that is not reasonably practicable, return him to the care of—
        (i)   a parent of his;
        (ii)   any person who is not a parent of his but who has parental responsibility for him; or
        (iii) such other person as the applicant (with the agreement of the court) considers appropriate.

(12) Where the applicant has been required by subsection (10) to return the child, or to allow him to be removed, he may again exercise his powers with respect to the child (at any time while the emergency protection order remains in force) if it appears to him that a change in the circumstances of the case makes it necessary for him to do so.

(13) Where an emergency protection order has been made with respect to a child, the applicant shall, subject to any direction given under subsection (6), allow the child reasonable contact with—

  (a)   his parents;
  (b)   any person who is not a parent of his but who has parental responsibility for him;
  (c)   any person with whom he was living immediately before the making of the order;
  (d)   any person in whose favour a contact order is in force with respect to him;
  (e)   any person who is allowed to have contact with the child by virtue of an order under section 34; and
  (f)   any person acting on behalf of any of those persons.

(14) Wherever it is reasonably practicable to do so, an emergency protection order shall name the child; and where it does not name him it shall describe him as clearly as possible.

(15) A person shall be guilty of an offence if he intentionally obstructs any person exercising the power under subsection (4)(b) to remove, or prevent the removal of, a child.

(16) A person guilty of an offence under subsection (15) shall be liable on summary conviction to a fine not exceeding level 3 on the standard scale.

45 Duration of emergency protection orders and other supplemental provisions

(1) An emergency protection order shall have effect for such period, not exceeding eight days, as may be specified in the order.

(2) Where—
  (a)   the court making an emergency protection order would, but for this subsection, specify a period of eight days as the period for which the order is to have effect; but
  (b)   the last of those eight days is a public holiday (that is to say, Christmas Day, Good Friday, a bank holiday or a Sunday),
the court may specify a period which ends at noon on the first later day which is not such a holiday.

(3) Where an emergency protection order is made on an application under section 46(7), the period of eight days mentioned in subsection (1) shall begin with the first day on which the child was taken into police protection under section 46.

(4) Any person who—
- (*a*) has parental responsibility for a child as the result of an emergency protection order; and
- (*b*) is entitled to apply for a care order with respect to the child,

may apply to the court for the period during which the emergency protection order is to have effect to be extended.

(5) On an application under subsection (4) the court may extend the period during which the order is to have effect by such period, not exceeding seven days, as it thinks fit, but may do so only if it has reasonable cause to believe that the child concerned is likely to suffer significant harm if the order is not extended.

(6) An emergency protection order may only be extended once.

(7) Regardless of any enactment or rule of law which would otherwise prevent it from doing so, a court hearing an application for, or with respect to, an emergency protection order may take account of—
- (*a*) any statement contained in any report made to the court in the course of, or in connection with, the hearing; or
- (*b*) any evidence given during the hearing,

which is, in the opinion of the court, relevant to the application.

(8) Any of the following may apply to the court for an emergency protection order to be discharged—
- (*a*) the child;
- (*b*) a parent of his;
- (*c*) any person who is not a parent of his but who has parental responsibility for him; or
- (*d*) any person with whom he was living immediately before the making of the order.

(9) No application for the discharge of an emergency protection order shall be heard by the court before the expiry of the period of 72 hours beginning with the making of the order.

(10) No appeal may be made against the making of, or refusal to make, an emergency protection order or against any direction given by the court in connection with such an order.

(11) Subsection (8) does not apply —
- (*a*) where the person who would otherwise be entitled to apply for the emergency protection order to be discharged—
  - (i) was given notice (in accordance with rules of court) of the hearing at which the order was made; and
  - (ii) was present at that hearing; or
- (*b*) to any emergency protection order the effective period of which has been extended under subsection (5).

(12) A court making an emergency protection order may direct that the applicant may, in exercising any powers which he has by virtue of the order, be accompanied by a registered medical practitioner, registered nurse or registered health visitor, if he so chooses.

46   Removal and accommodation of children by police in cases of emergency

(1) Where a constable has reasonable cause to believe that a child would otherwise be likely to suffer significant harm, he may—

    (a)   remove the child to suitable accommodation and keep him there; or

    (b)   take such steps as are reasonable to ensure that the child's removal from any hospital, or other place, in which he is then being accommodated is prevented.

(2) For the purposes of this Act, a child with respect to whom a constable has exercised his powers under this section is referred to as having been taken into police protection.

(3) As soon as is reasonably practicable after taking a child into police protection, the constable concerned shall—

    (a)   inform the local authority within whose area the child was found of the steps that have been, and are proposed to be, taken with respect to the child under this section and the reasons for taking them;

    (b)   give details to the authority within whose area the child is ordinarily resident ("the appropriate authority") of the place at which the child is being accommodated;

    (c)   inform the child (if he appears capable of understanding)—

        (i)   of the steps that have been taken with respect to him under this section and of the reasons for taking them; and

        (ii)   of the further steps that may be taken with respect to him under this section;

    (d)   take such steps as are reasonably practicable to discover the wishes and feelings of the child;

    (e)   secure that the case is inquired into by an officer designated for the purposes of this section by the chief officer of the police area concerned; and

    (f)   where the child was taken into police protection by being removed to accommodation which is not provided—

        (i)   by or on behalf of a local authority; or

        (ii)   as a refuge, in compliance with the requirements of section 51,

secure that he is moved to accommodation which is so provided.

(4) As soon as is reasonably practicable after taking a child into police protection, the constable concerned shall take such steps as are reasonably practicable to inform—

    (a)   the child's parents;

    (b)   every person who is not a parent of his but who has parental responsibility for him; and

    (c)   any other person with whom the child was living immediately before being taken into police protection,

of the steps that he has taken under this section with respect to the child, the reasons for taking them and the further steps that may be taken with respect to him under this section.

(5) On completing any inquiry under subsection (3)(e), the officer conducting it shall release the child from police protection unless he considers that there is still reasonable cause for believing that the child would be likely to suffer significant harm if released.

(6) No child may be kept in police protection for more than 72 hours.

(7) While a child is being kept in police protection, the designated officer may apply on behalf of the appropriate authority for an emergency protection order to be made under section 44 with respect to the child.

(8) An application may be made under subsection (7) whether or not the authority know of it or agree to its being made.

(9) While a child is being kept in police protection—
  (*a*)   neither the constable concerned nor the designated officer shall have parental responsibility for him; but
  (*b*)   the designated officer shall do what is reasonable in all the circumstances of the case for the purpose of safeguarding or promoting the child's welfare (having regard in particular to the length of the period during which the child will be so protected).

(10) Where a child has been taken into police protection, the designated officer shall allow—
  (*a*)   the child's parents;
  (*b*)   any person who is not a parent of the child but who has parental responsibility for him;
  (*c*)   any person with whom the child was living immediately before he was taken into police protection;
  (*d*)   any person in whose favour a contact order is in force with respect to the child;
  (*e*)   any person who is allowed to have contact with the child by virtue of an order under section 34; and
  (*f*)   any person acting on behalf of any of those persons,
to have such contact (if any) with the child as, in the opinion of the designated officer, is both reasonable and in the child's best interests.

(11) Where a child who has been taken into police protection is in accommodation provided by, or on behalf of, the appropriate authority, subsection (10) shall have effect as if it referred to the authority rather than to the designated officer.

47 Local authority's duty to investigate

(1) Where a local authority—
  (*a*)   are informed that a child who lives, or is found, in their area—
    (i)   is the subject of an emergency protection order; or
    (ii)   is in police protection; or
  (*b*)   have reasonable cause to suspect that a child who lives, or is found, in their area is suffering, or is likely to suffer, significant harm,
the authority shall make, or cause to be made, such enquiries as they consider necessary to enable them to decide whether they should take any action to safeguard or promote the child's welfare.

(2) Where a local authority have obtained an emergency protection order with respect to a child, they shall make, or cause to be made, such enquiries as they consider necessary to enable them to decide what action they should take to safeguard or promote the child's welfare.

(3) The enquiries shall, in particular, be directed towards establishing—
  (*a*)   whether the authority should make any application to the court, or exercise any of their other powers under this Act, with respect to the child;
  (*b*)   whether, in the case of a child—
    (i)   with respect to whom an emergency protection order has been made; and
    (ii)   who is not in accommodation provided by or on behalf of the authority, it would be in the child's best interests (while an emergency protection order remains in force) for him to be in such accommodation; and
  (*c*)   whether, in the case of a child who has been taken into police protection,

it would be in the child's best interests for the authority to ask for an application to be made under section 46(7).

(4) Where enquiries are being made under subsection (1) with respect to a child, the local authority concerned shall (with a view to enabling them to determine what action, if any, to take with respect to him) take such steps as are reasonably practicable—

    (a)   to obtain access to him; or

    (b)   to ensure that access to him is obtained, on their behalf, by a person authorised by them for the purpose,

unless they are satisfied that they already have sufficient information with respect to him.

(5) Where, as a result of any such enquiries, it appears to the authority that there are matters connected with the child's education which should be investigated, they shall consult the relevant local education authority.

(6) Where, in the course of enquiries made under this section—

    (a)   any officer of the local authority concerned; or

    (b)   any person authorised by the authority to act on their behalf in connected with those enquiries—

        (i)   is refused access to the child concerned; or

        (ii)   is denied information as to his whereabouts,

the authority shall apply for an emergency protection order, a child assessment order, a care order or a supervision order with respect to the child unless they are satisfied that his welfare can be satisfactorily safeguarded without their doing so.

(7) If, on the conclusion of any enquiries or review made under this section, the authority decide not to apply for an emergency protection order, a care order, a child assessment order or a supervision order they shall—

    (a)   consider whether it would be appropriate to review the case at a later date; and

    (b)   if they decide that it would be, determine the date on which that review is to begin.

(8) Where, as a result of complying with this section, a local authority conclude that they should take action to safeguard or promote the child's welfare they shall take that action (so far as it is both within their power and reasonably practicable for them to do so).

(9) Where a local authority are conducting enquiries under this section, it shall be the duty of any person mentioned in subsection (11) to assist them with those enquiries (in particular by providing relevant information and advice) if called upon by the authority to do so.

(10) Subsection (9) does not oblige any person to assist a local authority where doing so would be unreasonable in all the circumstances of the case.

(11) The persons are—

    (a)   any local authority;

    (b)   any local education authority;

    (c)   any local housing authority;

    (d)   any health authority; and

    (e)   any person authorised by the Secretary of State for the purposes of this section.

(12) Where a local authority are making enquiries under this section with respect to a child who appears to them to be ordinarily resident within the area of another authority, they shall consult that other authority, who may undertake the necessary enquiries in their place.

48 Powers to assist in discovery of children who may be in need of emergency protection

(1) Where it appears to a court making an emergency protection order that adequate information as to the child's whereabouts—

    (*a*)   is not available to the applicant for the order; but

    (*b*)   is available to another person,

it may include in the order a provision requiring that other person to disclose, if asked to do so by the applicant, any information that he may have as to the child's whereabouts.

(2) No person shall be excused from complying with such a requirement on the ground that complying might incriminate him or his spouse of an offence; but a statement or admission made in complying shall not be admissible in evidence against either of them in proceedings for any offence other than perjury.

(3) An emergency protection order may authorise the applicant to enter premises specified by the order and search for the child with respect to whom the order is made.

(4) Where the court is satisfied that there is reasonable cause to believe that there may be another child on those premises with respect to whom an emergency protection order ought to be made, it may make an order authorising the applicant to search for that other child on those premises.

(5) Where—

    (*a*)   an order has been made under subsection (4);

    (*b*)   the child concerned has been found on the premises; and

    (*c*)   the applicant is satisfied that the grounds for making an emergency protection order exist with respect to him,

the order shall have effect as if it were an emergency protection order.

(6) Where an order has been made under subsection (4), the applicant shall notify the court of its effect.

(7) A person shall be guilty of an offence if he intentionally obstructs any person exercising the power of entry and search under subsection (3) or (4).

(8) A person guilty of an offence under subsection (7) shall be liable on summary conviction to a fine not exceeding level 3 on the standard scale.

(9) Where, on an application made by any person for a warrant under this section, it appears to the court—

    (*a*)   that a person attempting to exercise powers under an emergency protection order has been prevented from doing so by being refused entry to the premises concerned or access to the child concerned; or

    (*b*)   that any such person is likely to be so prevented from exercising any such powers,

it may issue a warrant authorising any constable to assist the person mentioned in paragraph (*a*) or (*b*) in the exercise of those powers, using reasonable force if necessary.

(10) Every warrant issued under this section shall be addressed to, and executed by, a constable who shall be accompanied by the person applying for the warrant if—

    (*a*)   that person so desires; and

    (*b*)   the court by whom the warrant is issued does not direct otherwise.

(11) A court granting an application for a warrant under this section may direct that the constable concerned may, in executing the warrant, be accompanied by

a registered medical practitioner, registered nurse or registered health visitor if he so chooses.

(12) An application for a warrant under this section shall be made in the manner and form prescribed by rules of court.

(13) Wherever it is reasonably practicable to do so, an order under subsection (4), an application for a warrant under this section and any such warrant shall name the child; and where it does not name him it shall describe him as clearly as possible.

49 Abduction of children in care etc.

(1) A person shall be guilty of an offence if, knowingly and without lawful authority or reasonable excuse, he—
- (a)   takes a child to whom this section applies away from the responsible person;
- (b)   keeps such a child away from the responsible person; or
- (c)   induces, assists or incites such a child to run away or stay away from the responsible person.

(2) This section applies in relation to a child who is—
- (a)   in care;
- (b)   the subject of an emergency protection order; or
- (c)   in police protection,

and in this section "the responsible person" means any person who for the time being has care of him by virtue of the care order, the emergency protection order, or section 46, as the case may be.

(3) A person guilty of an offence under this section shall be liable on summary conviction to imprisonment for a term not exceeding six months, or to a fine not exceeding level 5 on the standard scale, or to both.

50 Recovery of abducted children etc.

(1) Where it appears to the court that there is reason to believe that a child to whom this section applies—
- (a)   has been unlawfully taken away or is being unlawfully kept away from the responsible person;
- (b)   has run away or is staying away from the responsible person; or
- (c)   is missing,

the court may make an order under this section ("a recovery order").

(2) This section applies to the same children to whom section 49 applies and in this section "the responsible person" has the same meaning as in section 49.

(3) A recovery order—
- (a)   operates as a direction to any person who is in a position to do so to produce the child on request to any authorised person;
- (b)   authorises the removal of the child by any authorised person;
- (c)   requires any person who has information as to the child's whereabouts to disclose that information, if asked to do so, to a constable or an officer of the court;
- (d)   authorises a constable to enter any premises specified in the order and search for the child, using reasonable force if necessary.

(4) The court may make a recovery order on the application of—
- (a)   any person who has parental responsibility for the child by virtue of a care order or emergency protection order; or
- (b)   where the child is in police protection, the designated officer.

(5) A recovery order shall name the child and—
  (a) any person who has parental responsibility for the child by virtue of a care order or emergency protection order; or
  (b) where the child is in police protection, the designated officer.

(6) Premises may only be specified under subsection (3)(d) if it appears to the court that there are reasonable grounds for believing the child to be on them.

(7) In this section—

"an authorised person" means—
  (a) any person specified by the court;
  (b) any constable;
  (c) any person who is authorised—
    (i) after the recovery order is made; and
    (ii) by a person who has parental responsibility for the child by virtue of a care order or an emergency protection order,
    to exercise any power under a recovery order; and
"the designated officer" means the officer designated for the purposes of section 46.

(8) Where a person is authorised as mentioned in subsection (7)(c)—
  (a) the authorisation shall identify the recovery order; and
  (b) any person claiming to be so authorised shall, if asked to do so, produce some duly authenticated document showing that he is so authorised.

(9) A person shall be guilty of an offence if he intentionally obstructs an authorised person exercising the power under subsection (3)(b) to remove a child.

(10) A person guilty of an offence under this section shall be liable on summary conviction to a fine not exceeding level 3 on the standard scale.

(11) No person shall be excused from complying with any request made under subsection (3)(c) on the ground that complying with it might incriminate him or his spouse of an offence; but a statement or admission made in complying shall not be admissible in evidence against either of them in proceedings for an offence other than perjury.

(12) Where a child is made the subject of a recovery order whilst being looked after by a local authority, any reasonable expenses incurred by an authorised person in giving effect to the order shall be recoverable from the authority.

(13) A recovery order shall have effect in Scotland as if it had been made by the Court of Session and as if that court had had jurisdiction to make it.

(14) In this section "the court", in relation to Northern Ireland, means a magistrates' court within the meaning of the Magistrates' Courts (Northern Ireland) Order 1981.

51 Refuges for children at risk

(1) Where it is proposed to use a voluntary home or registered children's home to provide a refuge for children who appear to be at risk of harm, the Secretary of State may issue a certificate under this section with respect to that home.

(2) Where a local authority or voluntary organisation arrange for a foster parent to provide such a refuge, the Secretary of State may issue a certificate under this section with respect to that foster parent.

(3) In subsection (2) "foster parent" means a person who is, or who from time to time is, a local authority foster parent or a foster parent with whom children are placed by a voluntary organisation.

(4) The Secretary of State may by regulations—
  (a)   make provision as to the manner in which certificates may be issued;
  (b)   impose requirements which must be complied with while any certificate is in force; and
  (c)   provide for the withdrawal of certificates in prescribed circumstances.

(5) Where a certificate is in force with respect to a home, none of the provisions mentioned in subsection (7) shall apply in relation to any person providing a refuge for any child in that home.

(6) Where a certificate is in force with respect to a foster parent, none of those provisions shall apply in relation to the provision by him of a refuge for any child in accordance with arrangements made by the local authority or voluntary organisation.

(7) The provisions are—
  (a)   section 49;
  (b)   section 71 of the Social Work (Scotland) Act 1968 (harbouring children who have absconded from residential establishments etc.), so far as it applies in relation to anything done in England and Wales;
  (c)   section 32(3) of the Children and Young Persons Act 1969 (compelling, persuading, inciting or assisting any person to be absent from detention, etc.), so far as it applies in relation to anything done in England and Wales;
  (d)   section 2 of the Child Abduction Act 1984.

52   Rules and regulations

(1) Without prejudice to section 93 or any other power to make such rules, rules of court may be made with respect to the procedure to be followed in connection with proceedings under this Part.

(2) The rules may, in particular make provision—
  (a)   as to the form in which any application is to be made or direction is to be given;
  (b)   prescribing the persons who are to be notified of—
        (i)   the making, or extension, of an emergency protection order; or
        (ii)   the making of an application under section 45(4) or (8) or 46(7); and
  (c)   as to the content of any such notification and the manner in which, and person by whom, it is to be given.

(3) The Secretary of State may by regulations provide that, where—
  (a)   an emergency protection order has been made with respect to a child;
  (b)   the applicant for the order was not the local authority within whose area the child is ordinarily resident; and
  (c)   that local authority are of the opinion that it would be in the child's best interests for the applicant's responsibilities under the order to be transferred to them,
that authority shall (subject to their having complied with any requirements imposed by the regulations) be treated, for the purposes of this Act, as though they and not the original applicant had applied for, and been granted, the order.

(4) Regulations made under subsection (3) may, in particular, make provision as to—
  (a)   the considerations to which the local authority shall have regard in forming an opinion as mentioned in subsection (3)(c); and
  (b)   the time at which responsibility under any emergency protection order is to be treated as having been transferred to a local authority.

PART VI

COMMUNITY HOMES

53 Provision of community homes by local authorities

(1) Every local authority shall make such arrangements as they consider appropriate for securing that homes ("community homes") are available—
  (a) for the care and accommodation of children looked after by them; and
  (b) for purposes connected with the welfare of children (whether or not looked after by them),
and may do so jointly with one or more other local authorities.

(2) In making such arrangements, a local authority shall have regard to the need for ensuring the availability of accommodation—
  (a) of different descriptions; and
  (b) which is suitable for different purposes and the requirements of different descriptions of children.

(3) A community home may be a home—
  (a) provided, managed, equipped and maintained by a local authority; or
  (b) provided by a voluntary organisation but in respect of which a local authority and the organisation—
    (i) propose that, in accordance with an instrument of management, the management, equipment and maintenance of the home shall be the responsibility of the local authority; or
    (ii) so propose that the management, equipment and maintenance of the home shall be the responsibility of the voluntary organisation.

(4) Where a local authority are to be responsible for the management of a community home provided by a voluntary organisation, the authority shall designate the home as a controlled community home.

(5) Where a voluntary organisation are to be responsible for the management of a community home provided by the organisation, the local authority shall designate the home as an assisted community home.

(6) Schedule 4 shall have effect for the purpose of supplementing the provisions of this Part.

54 Directions that premises be no longer used for community home

(1) Where it appears to the Secretary of State that—
  (a) any premises used for the purposes of a community home are unsuitable for those purposes; or
  (b) the conduct of a community home—
    (i) is not in accordance with regulations made by him under paragraph 4 of Schedule 4; or
    (ii) is otherwise unsatisfactory,
he may, by notice in writing served on the responsible body, direct that as from such date as may be specified in the notice the premises shall not be used for the purposes of a community home.

(2) Where—
  (a) the Secretary of State has given a direction under subsection (1); and
  (b) the direction has not been revoked,
he may at any time by order revoke the instrument of management for the home concerned.

(3) For the purposes of subsection (1), the responsible body—

(a)   in relation to a community home provided by a local authority, is that local authority;

(b)   in relation to a controlled community home, is the local authority specified in the home's instrument of management; and

(c)   in relation to an assisted community home, is the voluntary organisation by which the home is provided.

55   Determination of disputes relating to controlled and assisted community homes

(1) Where any dispute relating to a controlled community home arises between the local authority specified in the home's instrument of management and—

(a)   the voluntary organisation by which the home is provided; or

(b)   any other local authority who have placed, or desire or are required to place, in the home a child who is looked after by them,

the dispute may be referred by either party to the Secretary of State for his determination.

(2) Where any dispute relating to an assisted community home arises between the voluntary organisation by which the home is provided and any local authority who have placed, or desire to place, in the home a child who is looked after by them, the dispute may be referred by either party to the Secretary of State for his determination.

(3) Where a dispute is referred to the Secretary of State under this section he may, in order to give effect to his determination of the dispute, give such directions as he thinks fit to the local authority or voluntary organisation concerned.

(4) This section applies even though the matter in dispute may be one which, under or by virtue of Part II of Schedule 4, is reserved for the decision, or is the responsibility, of—

(a)   the local authority specified in the home's instrument of management; or

(b)   (as the case may be) the voluntary organisation by which the home is provided.

(5) Where any trust deed relating to a controlled or assisted community home contains provision whereby a bishop or any other ecclesiastical or denominational authority has power to decide questions relating to religious instruction given in the home, no dispute which is capable of being dealt with in accordance with that provision shall be referred to the Secretary of State under this section.

(6) In this Part "trust deed", in relation to a voluntary home, means any instrument (other than an instrument of management) regulating—

(a)   the maintenance, management or conduct of the home; or

(b)   the constitution of a body of managers or trustees of the home.

56   Discontinuance by voluntary organisation of controlled or assisted community home

(1) The voluntary organisation by which a controlled or assisted community home is provided shall not cease to provide the home except after giving to the Secretary of State and the local authority specified in the home's instrument of management not less than two years' notice in writing of their intention to do so.

(2) A notice under subsection (1) shall specify the date from which the voluntary organisation intend to cease to provide the home as a community home.

(3) Where such a notice is given and is not withdrawn before the date specified in it, the home's instrument of management shall cease to have effect on that date and the home shall then cease to be a controlled or assisted community home.

(4) Where a notice is given under subsection (1) and the home's managers give notice in writing to the Secretary of State that they are unable or unwilling to continue as its managers until the date specified in the subsection (1) notice, the Secretary of State may by order—

(a) revoke the home's instrument of management; and
(b) require the local authority who were specified in that instrument to conduct the home until—
    (i)   the date specified in the subsection (1) notice; or
    (ii) such earlier date (if any) as may be specified for the purposes of this paragraph in the order,
as if it were a community home provided by the local authority.

(5) Where the Secretary of State imposes a requirement under subsection (4)(b)—

(a) nothing in the trust deed for the home shall affect the conduct of the home by the local authority;
(b) the Secretary of State may by order direct that for the purposes of any provision specified in the direction and made by or under any enactment relating to community homes (other than this section) the home shall, until the date or earlier date specified as mentioned in subsection (4)(b), be treated as a controlled or assisted community home;
(c) except in so far as the Secretary of State so directs, the home shall until that date be treated for the purposes of any such enactment as a community home provided by the local authority; and
(d) on the date or earlier date specified as mentioned in subsection (4)(b) the home shall cease to be a community home.

57 Closure by local authority of controlled or assisted community home

(1) The local authority specified in the instrument of management for a controlled or assisted community home may give—

(a) the Secretary of State; and
(b) the voluntary organisation by which the home is provided,
not less than two years' notice in writing of their intention to withdraw their designation of the home as a controlled or assisted community home.

(2) A notice under subsection (1) shall specify the date ("the specified date") on which the designation is to be withdrawn.

(3) Where—

(a) a notice is given under subsection (1) in respect of a controlled or assisted community home;
(b) the home's managers give notice in writing to the Secretary of State that they are unable or unwilling to continue as managers until the specified date; and
(c) the managers' notice is not withdrawn,
the Secretary of State may by order revoke the home's instrument of management from such date earlier than the specified date as may be specified in the order.

(4) Before making an order under subsection (3), the Secretary of State shall consult the local authority and the voluntary organisation.

(5) Where a notice has been given under subsection (1) and is not withdrawn, the home's instrument of management shall cease to have effect on—

(a) the specified date; or
(b) where an earlier date has been specified under subsection (3), that earlier date,
and the home shall then cease to be a community home.

58   Financial provisions applicable on cessation of controlled or assisted community home or disposal etc. of premises

(1) Where—
- (a)   the instrument of management for a controlled or assisted community home is revoked or otherwise ceases to have effect under section 54(2), 56(3) or (4)(a) or 57(3) or (5); or
- (b)   any premises used for the purposes of such a home are (at any time after 13th January 1987) disposed of, or put to use otherwise than for those purposes,

the proprietor shall become liable to pay compensation ("the appropriate compensation") in accordance with this section.

(2) Where the instrument of management in force at the relevant time relates—
- (a)   to a controlled community home; or
- (b)   to an assisted community home which, at any time before the instrument came into force, was a controlled community home,

the appropriate compensation is a sum equal to that part of the value of any premises which is attributable to expenditure incurred in relation to the premises, while the home was a controlled community home, by the authority who were then the responsible authority.

(3) Where the instrument of management in force at the relevant time relates—
- (a)   to an assisted community home; or
- (b)   to a controlled community home which, at any time before the instrument came into force, was an assisted community home,

the appropriate compensation is a sum equal to that part of the value of the premises which is attributable to the expenditure of money provided by way of grant under section 82, section 65 of the Children and Young Persons Act 1969 or section 82 of the Child Care Act 1980.

(4) Where the home is, at the relevant time, conducted in premises which formerly were used as an approved school or were an approved probation hostel or home, the appropriate compensation is a sum equal to that part of the value of the premises which is attributable to the expenditure—
- (a)   of sums paid towards the expenses of the managers of an approved school under section 104 of the Children and Young Persons Act 1933; or
- (b)   of sums paid under section 51(3)(c) of the Powers of Criminal Courts Act 1973 in relation to expenditure on approved probation hostels or homes.

(5) The appropriate compensation shall be paid—
- (a)   in the case of compensation payable under subsection (2), to the authority who were the responsible authority at the relevant time; and
- (b)   in any other case, to the Secretary of State.

(6) In this section—
"disposal" includes the grant of a tenancy and any other conveyance, assignment, transfer, grant, variation or extinguishment of an interest in or right over land, whether made by instrument or otherwise;
"premises" means any premises or part of premises (including land) used for the purposes of the home and belonging to the proprietor;
"the proprietor" means—
- (a)   the voluntary organisation by which the home is, at the relevant time, provided; or
- (b)   if the premises are not, at the relevant time, vested in that organisation, the persons in whom they are vested;

"the relevant time" means the time immediately before the liability to pay arises under subsection (1); and "the responsible authority" means the local authority specified in the instrument of management in question.

(7) For the purposes of this section an event of a kind mentioned in subsection (1)(*b*) shall be taken to have occurred—

    (*a*) in the case of a disposal, on the date on which the disposal was completed or, in the case of a disposal which is effected by a series of transactions, the date on which the last of those transactions was completed;

    (*b*) in the case of premises which are put to different use, on the date on which they first begin to be put to their new use.

(8) The amount of any sum payable under this section shall be determined in accordance with such arrangements—

    (*a*) as may be agreed between the voluntary organisation by which the home is, at the relevant time, provided and the responsible authority or (as the case may be) the Secretary of State; or

    (*b*) in default of agreement, as may be determined by the Secretary of State.

(9) With the agreement of the responsible authority or (as the case may be) the Secretary of State, the liability to pay any sum under this section may be discharged, in whole or in part, by the transfer of any premises.

(10) This section has effect regardless of—

    (*a*) anything in any trust deed for a controlled or assisted community home;

    (*b*) the provisions of any enactment or instrument governing the disposition of the property of a voluntary organisation.

PART VII

VOLUNTARY HOMES AND VOLUNTARY ORGANISATIONS

59 Provision of accommodation by voluntary organisations

(1) Where a voluntary organisation provide accommodation for a child, they shall do so by—

    (*a*) placing him (subject to subsection (2)) with—

        (i)   a family;

        (ii)   a relative of his; or

        (iii) any other suitable person,

        on such terms as to payment by the organisation and otherwise as the organisation may determine;

    (*b*) maintaining him in a voluntary home;

    (*c*) maintaining him in a community home;

    (*d*) maintaining him in a registered children's home;

    (*e*) maintaining him in a home provided by the Secretary of State under section 82(5) on such terms as the Secretary of State may from time to time determine; or

    (*f*) making such other arrangements (subject to subsection (3)) as seem appropriate to them.

(2) The Secretary of State may make regulations as to the placing of children with foster parents by voluntary organisations and the regulations may, in particular, make provision which (with any necessary modifications) is similar to the provision that may be made under section 23(2)(*f*).

(3) The Secretary of State may make regulations as to the arrangements which may be made under subsection (1)(*f*) and the regulations may in particular make provision

which (with any necessary modifications) is similar to the provision that may be made under section 23(2)(*f*).

(4) The Secretary of State may make regulations requiring any voluntary organisation who are providing accommodation for a child—

    (*a*)   to review his case; and

    (*b*)   to consider any representations (including any complaint) made to them by any person falling within a prescribed class of person,

in accordance with the provisions of the regulations.

(5) Regulations under subsection (4) may in particular make provision which (with any necessary modifications) is similar to the provision that may be made under section 26.

(6) Regulations under subsections (2) to (4) may provide that any person who, without reasonable excuse, contravenes or fails to comply with a regulation shall be guilty of an offence and liable on summary conviction to a fine not exceeding level 4 on the standard scale.

60   Registration and regulation of voluntary homes

(1) No voluntary home shall be carried on unless it is registered in a register to be kept for the purposes of this section by the Secretary of State.

(2) The register may be kept by means of a computer.

(3) In this Act "voluntary home" means any home or other institution providing care and accommodation for children which is carried on by a voluntary organisation but does not include—

    (*a*)   a nursing home, mental nursing home or residential care home;

    (*b*)   a school;

    (*c*)   any health service hospital;

    (*d*)   any community home;

    (*e*)   any home or other institution provided, equipped and maintained by the Secretary of State; or

    (*f*)   any home which is exempted by regulations made for the purposes of this section by the Secretary of State.

(4) Schedule 5 shall have effect for the purpose of supplementing the provisions of this Part.

61   Duties of voluntary organisations

(1) Where a child is accommodated by or on behalf of a voluntary organisation, it shall be the duty of the organisation—

    (*a*)   to safeguard and promote his welfare;

    (*b*)   to make such use of the services and facilities available for children cared for by their own parents as appears to the organisation reasonable in his case; and

    (*c*)   to advise, assist and befriend him with a view to promoting his welfare when he ceases to be so accommodated.

(2) Before making any decision with respect to any such child the organisation shall, so far as is reasonably practicable, ascertain the wishes and feelings of—

    (*a*)   the child;

    (*b*)   his parents;

    (*c*)   any person who is not a parent of his but who has parental responsibility for him; and

(*d*)   any other person whose wishes and feelings the organisation consider to be
relevant,
regarding the matter to be decided.

(3) In making any such decision the organisation shall give due consideration—
   (*a*)   having regard to the child's age and understanding, to such wishes and feelings
of his as they have been able to ascertain;
   (*b*)   to such other wishes and feelings mentioned in subsection (2) as they have
been able to ascertain; and
   (*c*)   to the child's religious persuasion, racial origin and cultural and linguistic
background.

62   Duties of local authorities

(1) Every local authority shall satisfy themselves that any voluntary organisation
providing accommodation—
   (*a*)   within the authority's area for any child; or
   (*b*)   outside that area for any child on behalf of the authority,
are satisfactorily safeguarding and promoting the welfare of the children so provided
with accommodation.

(2) Every local authority shall arrange for children who are accommodated within
their area by or on behalf of voluntary organisations to be visited, from time to
time, in the interests of their welfare.

(3) The Secretary of State may make regulations—
   (*a*)   requiring every child who is accommodated within a local authority's area,
by or on behalf of a voluntary organisation, to be visited by an officer of
the authority—
      (i)   in prescribed circumstances; and
      (ii)   on specified occasions or within specified periods; and
   (*b*)   imposing requirements which must be met by any local authority, or officer
of a local authority, carrying out functions under this section.

(4) Subsection (2) does not apply in relation to community homes.

(5) Where a local authority are not satisfied that the welfare of any child who is
accommodated by or on behalf of a voluntary organisation is being satisfactorily
safeguarded or promoted they shall—
   (*a*)   unless they consider that it would not be in the best interests of the child,
take such steps as are reasonably practicable to secure that the care and
accommodation of the child is undertaken by—
      (i)   a parent of his;
      (ii)   any person who is not a parent of his but who has parental responsibility
for him; or
      (iii) a relative of his; and
   (*b*)   consider the extent to which (if at all) they should exercise any of their
functions with respect to the child.

(6) Any person authorised by a local authority may, for the purpose of enabling
the authority to discharge their duties under this section—
   (*a*)   enter, at any reasonable time, and inspect any premises in which children
are being accommodated as mentioned in subsection (1) or (2);
   (*b*)   inspect any children there;
   (*c*)   require any person to furnish him with such records of a kind required to
be kept by regulations made under paragraph 7 of Schedule 5 (in whatever
form they are held), or allow him to inspect such records, as he may at
any time direct.

(7) Any person exercising the power conferred by subsection (6) shall, if asked to do so, produce some duly authenticated document showing his authority to do so.

(8) Any person authorised to exercise the power to inspect records conferred by subsection (6)—

    (*a*)   shall be entitled at any reasonable time to have access to, and inspect and check the operation of, any computer and any associated apparatus or material which is or has been in use in connection with the records in question; and

    (*b*)   may require—

        (i)   the person by whom or on whose behalf the computer is or has been so used; or

        (ii)   any person having charge of, or otherwise concerned with the operation of, the computer, apparatus or material,

        to afford him such assistance as he may reasonably require.

(9) Any person who intentionally obstructs another in the exercise of any power conferred by subsection (6) or (8) shall be guilty of an offence and liable on summary conviction to a fine not exceeding level 3 on the standard scale.

Part VIII

Registered Children's Homes

63 Children not to be cared for and accommodated in unregistered children's homes

(1) No child shall be cared for and provided with accommodation in a children's home unless the home is registered under this Part.

(2) The register may be kept by means of a computer.

(3) For the purposes of this Part, "a children's home"—

    (*a*)   means a home which provides (or usually provides or is intended to provide) care and accommodation wholly or mainly for more than three children at any one time; but

    (*b*)   does not include a home which is exempted by or under any of the following provisions of this section or by regulations made for the purposes of this subsection by the Secretary of State.

(4) A child is not cared for and accommodated in a children's home when he is cared for and accommodated by—

    (*a*)   a parent of his;

    (*b*)   a person who is not a parent of his but who has parental responsibility for him; or

    (*c*)   any relative of his.

(5) A home is not a children's home for the purposes of this Part if it is—

    (*a*)   a community home;

    (*b*)   a voluntary home;

    (*c*)   a residential care home, nursing home or mental nursing home;

    (*d*)   a health service hospital;

    (*e*)   a home provided, equipped and maintained by the Secretary of State; or

    (*f*)   a school (but subject to subsection (6)).

(6) An independent school is a children's home if—

    (*a*)   it provides accommodation for not more than fifty children; and (*b*) it is not approved by the Secretary of State under section 11(3)(*a*) of the Education Act 1981.

(7) A child shall not be treated as cared for and accommodated in a children's home when—

(*a*) any person mentioned in subsection (4)(*a*) or (*b*) is living at the home; or

(*b*) the person caring for him is doing so in his personal capacity and not in the course of carrying out his duties in relation to the home.

(8) In this Act "a registered children's home" means a children's home registered under this Part.

(9) In this section "home" includes any institution.

(10) Where any child is at any time cared for and accommodated in a children's home which is not a registered children's home, the person carrying on the home shall be—

(*a*) guilty of an offence; and

(*b*) liable to a fine not exceeding level 5 on the standard scale,

unless he has a reasonable excuse.

(11) Schedule 6 shall have effect with respect to children's homes.

(12) Schedule 7 shall have effect for the purpose of setting out the circumstances in which a person may foster more than three children without being treated as carrying on a children's home.

64 Welfare of children in children's homes

(1) Where a child is accommodated in a children's home, it shall be the duty of the person carrying on the home to—

(*a*) safeguard and promote the child's welfare;

(*b*) make such use of the services and facilities available for children cared for by their own parents as appears to that person reasonable in the case of the child; and

(*c*) advise, assist and befriend him with a view to promoting his welfare when he ceases to be so accommodated.

(2) Before making any decision with respect to any such child the person carrying on the home shall, so far as is reasonably practicable, ascertain the wishes and feelings of—

(*a*) the child;

(*b*) his parents;

(*c*) any other person who is not a parent of his but who has parental responsibility for him; and

(*d*) any person whose wishes and feelings the person carrying on the home considers to be relevant,

regarding the matter to be decided.

(3) In making any such decision the person concerned shall give due consideration—

(*a*) having regard to the child's age and understanding, to such wishes and feelings of his as he has been able to ascertain;

(*b*) to such other wishes and feelings mentioned in subsection (2) as he has been able to ascertain; and

(*c*) to the child's religious persuasion, racial origin and cultural and linguistic background.

(4) Section 62, except subsection (4), shall apply in relation to any person who is carrying on a children's home as it applies in relation to any voluntary organisation.

65   Persons disqualified from carrying on, or being employed in, children's homes

(1) A person who is disqualified (under section 68) from fostering a child privately shall not carry on, or be otherwise concerned in the management of, or have any financial interest in, a children's home unless he has—
  (*a*)   disclosed to the responsible authority the fact that he is so disqualified; and
  (*b*)   obtained their written consent.

(2) No person shall employ a person who is so disqualified in a children's home unless he has—
  (*a*)   disclosed to the responsible authority the fact that that person is so disqualified; and
  (*b*)   obtained their written consent.

(3) Where an authority refuse to give their consent under this section, they shall inform the applicant by a written notice which states—
  (*a*)   the reason for the refusal;
  (*b*)   the applicant's right to appeal against the refusal to a Registered Homes Tribunal under paragraph 8 of Schedule 6; and
  (*c*)   the time within which he may do so.

(4) Any person who contravenes subsection (1) or (2) shall be guilty of an offence and liable on summary conviction to imprisonment for a term not exceeding six months or to a fine not exceeding level 5 on the standard scale or to both.

(5) Where a person contravenes subsection (2) he shall not be guilty of an offence if he proves that he did not know, and had no reasonable grounds for believing, that the person whom he was employing was disqualified under section 68.

Part IX
Private Arrangements For Fostering Children

66   Privately fostered children

(1) In this Part—
  (*a*)   "a privately fostered child" means a child who is under the age of sixteen and who is cared for, and provided with accommodation by, someone other than—
     (i)   a parent of his;
     (ii)   a person who is not a parent of his but who has parental responsibility for him; or
     (iii) a relative of his; and
  (*b*)   "to foster a child privately" means to look after the child in circumstances in which he is a privately fostered child as defined by this section.

(2) A child is not a privately fostered child if the person caring for and accommodating him—
  (*a*)   has done so for a period of less than 28 days; and
  (*b*)   does not intend to do so for any longer period.

(3) Subsection (1) is subject to—
  (*a*)   the provisions of section 63; and
  (*b*)   the exceptions made by paragraphs 1 to 5 of Schedule 8.

(4) In the case of a child who is disabled, subsection (1)(*a*) shall have effect as if for "sixteen" there were substituted "eighteen".

(5) Schedule 8 shall have effect for the purposes of supplementing the provision made by this Part.

67 Welfare of privately fostered children

(1) It shall be the duty of every local authority to satisfy themselves that the welfare of children who are privately fostered within their area is being satisfactorily safeguarded and promoted and to secure that such advice is given to those caring for them as appears to the authority to be needed.

(2) The Secretary of State may make regulations—
- (a) requiring every child who is privately fostered within a local authority's area to be visited by an officer of the authority—
  - (i) in prescribed circumstances; and
  - (ii) on specified occasions or within specified periods; and
- (b) imposing requirements which are to be met by any local authority, or officer of a local authority, in carrying out functions under this section.

(3) Where any person who is authorised by a local authority to visit privately fostered children has reasonable cause to believe that—
- (a) any privately fostered child is being accommodated in premises within the authority's area; or
- (b) it is proposed to accommodate any such child in any such premises,

he may at any reasonable time inspect those premises and any children there.

(4) Any person exercising the power under subsection (3) shall, if so required, produce some duly authenticated document showing his authority to do so.

(5) Where a local authority are not satisfied that the welfare of any child who is privately fostered within their area is being satisfactorily safeguarded or promoted they shall—
- (a) unless they consider that it would not be in the best interests of the child, take such steps as are reasonably practicable to secure that the care and accommodation of the child is undertaken by—
  - (i) a parent of his;
  - (ii) any person who is not a parent of his but who has parental responsibility for him; or
  - (iii) a relative of his; and
- (b) consider the extent to which (if at all) they should exercise any of their functions under this Act with respect to the child.

68 Persons disqualified from being private foster parents

(1) Unless he has disclosed the fact to the appropriate local authority and obtained their written consent, a person shall not foster a child privately if he is disqualified from doing so by regulations made by the Secretary of State for the purposes of this section.

(2) The regulations may, in particular, provide for a person to be so disqualified where—
- (a) an order of a kind specified in the regulations has been made at any time with respect to him;
- (b) an order of a kind so specified has been made at any time with respect to any child who has been in his care;
- (c) a requirement of a kind so specified has been imposed at any time with respect to any such child, under or by virtue of any enactment;
- (d) he has been convicted of any offence of a kind so specified, or has been

placed on probation or discharged absolutely or conditionally for any such offence;

(e)   a prohibition has been imposed on him at any time under section 69 or under any other specified enactment;

(f)   his rights and powers with respect to a child have at any time been vested in a specified authority under a specified enactment.

(3) Unless he has disclosed the fact to the appropriate local authority and obtained their written consent, a person shall not foster a child privately if—

(a)   he lives in the same household as a person who is himself prevented from fostering a child by subsection (1); or

(b)   he lives in a household at which any such person is employed.

(4) Where an authority refuse to give their consent under this section, they shall inform the applicant by a written notice which states—

(a)   the reason for the refusal;

(b)   the applicant's right under paragraph 8 of Schedule 8 to appeal against the refusal; and

(c)   the time within which he may do so.

(5) In this section—

"the appropriate authority" means the local authority within whose area it is proposed to foster the child in question; and

"enactment" means any enactment having effect, at any time, in any part of the United Kingdom.

69   Power to prohibit private fostering

(1) This section applies where a person—

(a)   proposes to foster a child privately; or

(b)   is fostering a child privately.

(2) Where the local authority for the area within which the child is proposed to be, or is being, fostered are of the opinion that—

(a)   he is not a suitable person to foster a child;

(b)   the premises in which the child will be, or is being, accommodated are not suitable; or

(c)   it would be prejudicial to the welfare of the child for him to be, or continue to be, accommodated by that person in those premises,

the authority may impose a prohibition on him under subsection (3).

(3) A prohibition imposed on any person under this subsection may prohibit him from fostering privately—

(a)   any child in any premises within the area of the local authority; or

(b)   any child in premises specified in the prohibition;

(c)   a child identified in the prohibition, in premises specified in the prohibition.

(4) A local authority who have imposed a prohibition on any person under subsection (3) may, if they think fit, cancel the prohibition—

(a)   of their own motion; or

(b)   on an application made by that person,

if they are satisfied that the prohibition is no longer justified.

(5) Where a local authority impose a requirement on any person under paragraph 6 of Schedule 8, they may also impose a prohibition on him under subsection (3).

(6) Any prohibition imposed by virtue of subsection (5) shall not have effect unless—

(a)   the time specified for compliance with the requirement has expired; and

(b)   the requirement has not been complied with.

(7) A prohibition imposed under this section shall be imposed by notice in writing addressed to the person on whom it is imposed and informing him of—
- (*a*) the reason for imposing the prohibition;
- (*b*) his right under paragraph 8 of Schedule 8 to appeal against the prohibition; and
- (*c*) the time within which he may do so.

70 Offences

(1) A person shall be guilty of an offence if—
- (*a*) being required, under any provision made by or under this Part, to give any notice or information—
  - (i) he fails without reasonable excuse to give the notice within the time specified in that provision; or
  - (ii) he fails without reasonable excuse to give the information within a reasonable time; or
  - (iii) he makes, or causes or procures another person to make, any statement in the notice or information which he knows to be false or misleading in a material particular;
- (*b*) he refuses to allow a privately fostered child to be visited by a duly authorised officer of a local authority;
- (*c*) he intentionally obstructs another in the exercise of the power conferred by section 67(3);
- (*d*) he contravenes section 68;
- (*e*) he fails without reasonable excuse to comply with any requirement imposed by a local authority under this Part;
- (*f*) he accommodates a privately fostered child in any premises in contravention of a prohibition imposed by a local authority under this Part;
- (*g*) he knowingly causes to be published, or publishes, an advertisement which he knows contravenes paragraph 10 of Schedule 8.

(2) Where a person contravenes section 68(3), he shall not be guilty of an offence under this section if he proves that he did not know, and had no reasonable ground for believing, that any person to whom section 68(1) applied was living or employed in the premises in question.

(3) A person guilty of an offence under subsection (1)(*a*) shall be liable on summary conviction to a fine not exceeding level 5 on the standard scale.

(4) A person guilty of an offence under subsection (1)(*b*), (*c*) or (*g*) shall be liable on summary conviction to a fine not exceeding level 3 on the standard scale.

(5) A person guilty of an offence under subsection (1)(*d*) or (*f*) shall be liable on summary conviction to imprisonment for a term not exceeding six months, or to a fine not exceeding level 5 on the standard scale, or to both.

(6) A person guilty of an offence under subsection (1)(*e*) shall be liable on summary conviction to a fine not exceeding level 4 on the standard scale.

(7) If any person who is required, under any provision of this Part, to give a notice fails to give the notice within the time specified in that provision, proceedings for the offence may be brought at any time within six months from the date when evidence of the offence came to the knowledge of the local authority.

(8) Subsection (7) is not affected by anything in section 127(1) of the Magistrates' Courts Act 1980 (time limit for proceedings).

Part X

Child Minding and Day Care for Young Children

71 Registration

(1) Every local authority shall keep a register of—
  (a) persons who act as child minders on domestic premises within the authority's area; and
  (b) persons who provide day care for children under the age of eight on premises (other than domestic premises) within that area.

(2) For the purposes of this Part—
  (a) a person acts as a child minder if—
      (i)   he looks after one or more children under the age of eight, for reward; and
      (ii) the period, or the total of the periods, which he spends so looking after children in any day exceeds two hours; and
  (b) a person does not provide day care for children unless the period, or the total of the periods, during which children are looked after exceeds two hours in any day.

(3) Where a person provides day care for children under the age of eight on different premises situated within the area of the same local authority, that person shall be separately registered with respect to each of those premises.

(4) A person who—
  (a) is the parent, or a relative, of a child;
  (b) has parental responsibility for a child; or
  (c) is a foster parent of a child,
does not act as a child minder for the purposes of this Part when looking after that child.

(5) Where a person is employed as a nanny for a child, she does not act as a child minder when looking after that child wholly or mainly in the home of the person so employing her.

(6) Where a person is so employed by two different employers, she does not act as a child minder when looking after any of the children concerned wholly or mainly in the home or either of her employers.

(7) A local authority may refuse to register an applicant for registration under subsection (1)(a) if they are satisfied that—
  (a) the applicant; or
  (b) any person looking after, or likely to be looking after, any children on any premises on which the applicant is, or is likely to be, child minding,
is not fit to look after children under the age of eight.

(8) A local authority may refuse to register an applicant for registration under subsection (1)(a) if they are satisfied that—
  (a) any person living, or likely to be living, at any premises on which the applicant is, or is likely to be, child minding; or
  (b) any person employed, or likely to be employed, on those premises,
is not fit to be in the proximity of children under the age of eight.

(9) A local authority may refuse to register an applicant for registration under subsection (1)(b) if they are satisfied that any person looking after, or likely to be looking after, any children on the premises to which the application relates is not fit to look after children under the age of eight.

(10) A local authority may refuse to register an applicant for registration under subsection (1)(*b*) if they are satisfied that—
  (*a*) any person living, or likely to be living, at the premises to which the application relates; or
  (*b*) any person employed, or likely to be employed, on those premises,
is not fit to be in the proximity of children under the age of eight.

(11) A local authority may refuse to register an applicant for registration under this section if they are satisfied—
  (*a*) in the case of an application under subsection (1)(*a*), that any premises on which the applicant is, or is likely to be, child minding; or
  (*b*) in the case of an application under subsection (1)(*b*), that the premises to which the application relates,
are not fit to be used for looking after children under the age of eight, whether because of their condition or the condition of any equipment used on the premises or for any reason connected with their situation, construction or size.

(12) In this section—
  "domestic premises" means any premises which are wholly or mainly used as a private dwelling;
  "premises" includes any vehicle.

(13) For the purposes of this Part a person acts as a nanny for a child if she is employed to look after the child by—
  (*a*) a parent of the child;
  (*b*) a person who is not a parent of the child but who has parental responsibility for him; or
  (*c*) a person who is a relative of the child and who has assumed responsibility for his care.

(14) For the purposes of this section, a person fosters a child if—
  (*a*) he is a local authority foster parent in relation to the child;
  (*b*) he is a foster parent with whom the child has been placed by a voluntary organisation; or
  (*c*) he fosters the child privately.

(15) Any register kept under this section—
  (*a*) shall be open to inspection by members of the public at all reasonable times; and
  (*b*) may be kept by means of a computer.

(16) Schedule 9 shall have effect for the purpose of making further provision with respect to registration under this section including, in particular, further provision for exemption from the requirement to be registered and provision for disqualification.

72 Requirements to be complied with by child minders

(1) Where a local authority register a person under section 71(1)(*a*), they shall impose such reasonable requirements on him as they consider appropriate in his case.

(2) In imposing requirements on him, the authority shall—
  (*a*) specify the maximum number of children, or the maximum number of children within specified age groups, whom he may look after when acting as a child minder;
  (*b*) require him to secure that any premises on which he so looks after any child, and the equipment used in those premises, are adequately maintained and kept safe;
  (*c*) require him to keep a record of the name and address of—

> (i)   any child so looked after by him on any premises within the authority's area;
> (ii) any person who assists in looking after any such child; and
> (iii) any person living, or likely at any time to be living, at those premises;
>
> (d) require him to notify the authority in writing of any change in the persons mentioned in paragraph (c)(ii) and (iii).

(3) The Secretary of State may by regulations make provision as to—
  (a) requirements which must be imposed by local authorities under this section in prescribed circumstances;
  (b) requirements of such descriptions as may be prescribed which must not be imposed by local authorities under this section.

(4) In determining the maximum number of children to be specified under subsection (2)(a), the authority shall take account of the number of other children who may at any time be on any premises on which the person concerned acts, or is likely to act, as a child minder.

(5) Where, in addition to the requirements mentioned in subsection (2), a local authority impose other requirements, those other requirements must not be incompatible with any of the subsection (2) requirements.

(6) A local authority may at any time vary any requirement imposed under this section, impose any additional requirement or remove any requirement.

73 Requirements to be complied with by persons providing day care for young children

(1) Where a local authority register a person under section 71(1)(b) they shall impose such reasonable requirements on him as they consider appropriate in his case.

(2) Where a person is registered under section 71(1)(b) with respect to different premises within the area of the same authority, this section applies separately in relation to each registration.

(3) In imposing requirements on him, the authority shall—
  (a) specify the maximum number of children, or the maximum number of children within specified age groups, who may be looked after on the premises;
  (b) require him to secure that the premises, and the equipment used in them, are adequately maintained and kept safe;
  (c) require him to notify the authority of any change in the facilities which he provides or in the period during which he provides them;
  (d) specify the number of persons required to assist in looking after children on the premises;
  (e) require him to keep a record of the name and address of—
    (i)   any child looked after on the registered premises;
    (ii) any person who assists in looking after any such child; and
    (iii) any person who lives, or is likely at any time to be living, at those premises;
  (f) require him to notify the authority of any change in the persons mentioned in paragraph (e)(ii) and (iii).

(4) The Secretary of State may by regulations make provision as to—
  (a) requirements which must be imposed by local authorities under this section in prescribed circumstances;
  (b) requirements of such descriptions as may be prescribed which must now be imposed by local authorities under this section.

(5) In subsection (3), references to children looked after are to children looked after in accordance with the provision of day care made by the registered person.

(6) In determining the maximum number of children to be specified under subsection (3)(*a*), the authority shall take account of the number of other children who may at any time be on the premises.

(7) Where, in addition to the requirements mentioned in subsection (3), a local authority impose other requirements, those other requirements must not be incompatible with any of the subsection (3) requirements.

(8) A local authority may at any time vary any requirement imposed under this section, impose any additional requirement or remove any requirement.

74 Cancellation of registration

(1) A local authority may at any time cancel the registration of any person under section 71(1)(*a*) if—
- (*a*)   it appears to them that the circumstances of the case are such that they would be justified in refusing to register that person as a child minder;
- (*b*)   the care provided by that person when looking after any child as a child minder is, in the opinion of the authority, seriously inadequate having regard to the needs of that child; or
- (*c*)   that person has—
  - (i)   contravened, or failed to comply with, any requirement imposed on him under section 72; or
  - (ii)   failed to pay any annual fee under paragraph 7 of Schedule 9 within the prescribed time.

(2) A local authority may at any time cancel the registration of any person under section 71(1)(*b*) with respect to particular premises if—
- (*a*)   it appears to them that the circumstances of the case are such that they would be justified in refusing to register that person with respect to those premises;
- (*b*)   the day care provided by that person on those premises is, in the opinion of the authority, seriously inadequate having regard to the needs of the children concerned; or
- (*c*)   that person has—
  - (i)   contravened, or failed to comply with, any requirement imposed on him under section 73; or
  - (ii)   failed to pay any annual registration fee under paragraph 7 of Schedule 9 within the prescribed time.

(3) A local authority may at any time cancel all registrations of any person under section 71(1)(*b*) if it appears to them that the circumstances of the case are such that they would be justified in refusing to register that person with respect to any premises.

(4) Where a requirement to carry out repairs or make alterations or additions has been imposed on a registered person under section 72 or 73, his registration shall not be cancelled on the ground that the premises are not fit to be used for looking after children if—
- (*a*)   the time set for complying with the requirements has not expired, and
- (*b*)   it is shown that the condition of the premises is due to the repairs not having been carried out or the alterations or additions not having been made.

(5) Any cancellation under this section must be in writing.

(6) In considering the needs of any child for the purposes of subsection (1)(*b*) or (2)(*b*), a local authority shall, in particular, have regard to the child's religious persuasion, racial origin and cultural and linguistic background.

75 Protection of children in an emergency

(1) If—
- (*a*) a local authority apply to the court for an order—
  - (i)   cancelling a registered person's registration;
  - (ii)   varying any requirement imposed on a registered person under section 72 or 73; or
  - (iii)   removing a requirement or imposing an additional requirement on such a person; and
- (*b*) it appears to the court that a child who is being, or may be, looked after by that person, or (as the case may be) in accordance with the provision for day care made by that person, is suffering, or is likely to suffer, significant harm,

the court may make the order.

(2) Any such cancellation, variation, removal or imposition shall have effect from the date on which the order is made.

(3) An application under subsection (1) may be made *ex parte* and shall be supported by a written statement of the authority's reasons for making it.

(4) Where an order is made under this section, the authority shall serve on the registered person, as soon as is reasonably practicable after the making of the order—
- (*a*) notice of the order and of its terms; and
- (*b*) a copy of the statement of the authority's reasons which supported their application for the order.

(5) Where the court imposes or varies any requirement under subsection (1), the requirement, or the requirement as varied, shall be treated for all purposes, other than those of section 77, as if it had been imposed under section 72 or (as the case may be) 73 by the authority concerned.

76 Inspection

(1) Any person authorised to do so by a local authority may at any reasonable time enter—
- (*a*) any domestic premises within the authority's area on which child minding is at any time carried on; or
- (*b*) any premises within their area on which day care for children under the age of eight is at any time provided.

(2) Where a local authority have reasonable cause to believe that a child is being looked after on any premises within their area in contravention of this Part, any person authorised to do so by the authority may enter those premises at any reasonable time.

(3) Any person entering premises under this section may inspect—
- (*a*) the premises;
- (*b*) any children being looked after on the premises;
- (*c*) the arrangements made for their welfare; and
- (*d*) any records relating to them which are kept as a result of this Part.

(4) Every local authority shall exercise their power to inspect the premises mentioned in subsection (1) at least once every year.

(5) Any person inspecting any records under this section—
  (a) shall be entitled at any reasonable time to have access to, and inspect and check the operation of, any computer and any associated apparatus or material which is, or has been, in use in connection with the records in question; and
  (b) may require—
      (i) the person by whom or on whose behalf the computer is or has been so used; or
      (ii) any person having charge of, or otherwise concerned with the operation of, the computer, apparatus or material,
    to afford him such reasonable assistance as he may require.

(6) A person exercising any power conferred by this section shall, if so required, produce some duly authenticated document showing his authority to do so.

(7) Any person who intentionally obstructs another in the exercise of any such power shall be guilty of an offence and liable on summary conviction to a fine not exceeding level 3 on the standard scale.

77 Appeals

(1) Not less than 14 days before—
  (a) refusing an application for registration under section 71;
  (b) cancelling any such registration;
  (c) refusing consent under paragraph 2 of Schedule 9;
  (d) imposing, removing or varying any requirement under section 72 or 73; or
  (e) refusing to grant any application for the variation or removal of any such requirement,
the authority concerned shall send to the applicant, or (as the case may be) registered person, notice in writing of their intention to take the step in question ("the step").

(2) Every such notice shall—
  (a) give the authority's reasons for proposing to take the step; and
  (b) inform the person concerned of his rights under this section.

(3) Were the recipient of such a notice informs the authority in writing of his desire to object to the step being taken, the authority shall afford him an opportunity to do so.

(4) Any objection made under subsection (3) may be made in person or by a representative.

(5) If the authority, after giving the person concerned an opportunity to object to the step being taken, decide nevertheless to take it they shall send him written notice of their decision.

(6) A person aggrieved by the taking of any step mentioned in subsection (1) may appeal against it to the court.

(7) Where the court imposes or varies any requirement under subsection (8) or (9) the requirement, or the requirement as varied, shall be treated for all purposes (other than this section) as if it had been imposed by the authority concerned.

(8) Where the court allows an appeal against the refusal or cancellation of any registration under section 71 it may impose requirements under section 72 or (as the case may be) 73.

(9) Where the court allows an appeal against such a requirement it may, instead of cancelling the requirement, vary it.

(10) In Scotland, an appeal under subsection (6) shall be by summary application to the sheriff and shall be brought within 21 days from the date of the step to which the appeal relates.

(11) A step of a kind mentioned in subsection (1)(*b*) or (*d*) shall not take effect until the expiry of the time within which an appeal may be brought under this section or, where such an appeal is brought, before its determination.

78 Offences

(1) No person shall provide day care for children under the age of eight on any premises within the area of a local authority unless he is registered by the authority under section 71(1)(*b*) with respect to those premises.

(2) If any person contravenes subsection (1) without reasonable excuse, he shall be guilty of an offence.

(3) No person shall act as a child minder on domestic premises within the area of a local authority unless he is registered by the authority under section 71(1)(*a*).

(4) Where it appears to a local authority that a person has contravened subsection (3), they may serve a notice ("an enforcement notice") on him.

(5) An enforcement notice shall have effect for a period of one year beginning with the date on which it is served.

(6) If a person with respect to whom an enforcement notice is in force contravenes subsection (3) without reasonable excuse, he shall be guilty of an offence.

(7) Subsection (6) applies whether or not the subsequent contravention occurs within the area of the authority who served the enforcement notice.

(8) Any person who without reasonable excuse contravenes, or otherwise fails to comply with, any requirement imposed on him under sections 72 or 73 shall be guilty of an offence.

(9) If any person—
    (*a*)   acts as a child minder on domestic premises at any time when he is disqualified by regulations made under paragraph 2 of Schedule 9; or
    (*b*)   contravenes any of sub-paragraphs (3) to (5) of paragraph 2,
he shall be guilty of an offence.

(10) Where a person contravenes sub-paragraph (3) of paragraph 2 he shall not be guilty of an offence under this section if he proves that he did not know, and had no reasonable grounds for believing, that the person in question was living or employed in the household.

(11) Where a person contravenes sub-paragraph (5) of paragraph 2 he shall not be guilty of an offence under this section if he proves that he did not know, and had no reasonable grounds for believing, that the person whom he was employing was disqualified.

(12) A person guilty of an offence under this section shall be liable on summary conviction—
    (*a*)   in the case of an offence under subsection (8), to a fine not exceeding level 4 on the standard scale;
    (*b*)   in the case of an offence under subsection (9), to imprisonment for a term not exceeding six months, or to a fine not exceeding level 5 on the standard scale, or to both; and
    (*c*)   in the case of any other offence, to a fine not exceeding level 5 on the standard scale.

79 Application of this Part to Scotland

In the application to Scotland of this Part—
- (*a*) "the court" means the sheriff;
- (*b*) "day care" means any form of care or of activity supervised by a responsible person provided for children during the day (whether or not it is provided on a regular basis);
- (*c*) "education authority" has the same meaning as in the Education (Scotland) Act 1980;
- (*d*) "local authority foster parent" means a foster parent with whom a child is placed by a local authority;
- (*e*) for references to a person having parental responsibility for a child there shall be substituted references to a person in whom parental rights and duties relating to the child are vested; and
- (*f*) for references to fostering a child privately there shall be substituted references to maintaining a foster child within the meaning of the Foster Children (Scotland) Act 1984.

PART XI

SECRETARY OF STATE'S SUPERVISORY FUNCTIONS AND RESPONSIBILITIES

80 Inspection of children's homes etc. by persons authorised by Secretary of State

(1) The Secretary of State may cause to be inspected from time to time any—
- (*a*) children's home;
- (*b*) premises in which a child who is being looked after by a local authority is living;
- (*c*) premises in which a child who is being accommodated by or on behalf of a local education authority or voluntary organisation is living;
- (*d*) premises in which a child who is being accommodated by or on behalf of a health authority is living;
- (*e*) premises in which a child is living with a person with whom he has been placed by an adoption agency;
- (*f*) premises in which a child who is a protected child is, or will be, living;
- (*g*) premises in which a privately fostered child, or child who is treated as a foster child by virtue of paragraph 9 of Schedule 8, is living or in which it is proposed that he will live;
- (*h*) premises on which any person is acting as a child minder;
- (*i*) premises with respect to which a person is registered under section 74(1)(*b*);
- (*j*) residential care home, nursing home or mental nursing home required to be registered under the Registered Homes Act 1984 and used to accommodate children.
- (*k*) premises which are provided by a local authority and in which any service is provided by that authority under Part III;
- (*l*) independent school providing accommodation for any child.

(2) An inspection under this section shall be conducted by a person authorised to do so by the Secretary of State.

(3) An officer of a local authority shall not be authorised except with the consent of that authority.

(4)   The Secretary of State may require any person of a kind mentioned in subsection (5) to furnish him with such information, or allow him to inspect such records (in whatever form they are held), relating to—

- (*a*)   any premises to which subsection (1) or, in relation to Scotland, subsection (1)(*h*) or (*i*) applies;
- (*b*)   any child who is living in any such premises;
- (*c*)   the discharge by the Secretary of State of any of his functions under this Act; or
- (*d*)   the discharge by any local authority of any of their functions under this Act,

as the Secretary of State may at any time direct.

(5)   The persons are any—

- (*a*)   local authority;
- (*b*)   voluntary organisation;
- (*c*)   person carrying on a children's home;
- (*d*)   proprietor of an independent school;
- (*e*)   person fostering any privately fostered child or providing accommodation for a child on behalf of a local authority, local education authority, health authority or voluntary organisation;
- (*f*)   local education authority providing accommodation for any child;
- (*g*)   person employed in a teaching or administrative capacity at any educational establishment (whether or not maintained by a local education authority) at which a child is accommodated on behalf of a local authority or local education authority;
- (*h*)   person who is the occupier of any premises in which any person acts as a child minder (within the meaning of Part X) or provides day care for young children (within the meaning of that Part);
- (*i*)   person carrying on any home of a kind mentioned in subsection (1)(*j*).

(6)   Any person inspecting any home or other premises under this section may—

- (*a*)   inspect the children there; and
- (*b*)   make such examination into the state and management of the home or premises and the treatment of the children there as he thinks fit.

(7)   Any person authorised by the Secretary of State to exercise the power to inspect records conferred by subsection (4)—

- (*a*)   shall be entitled at any reasonable time to have access to, and inspect and check the operation of, any computer and any associated apparatus or material which is or has been in use in connection with the records in question; and
- (*b*)   may require—
  - (i)   the person by whom or on whose behalf the computer is or has been so used; or
  - (ii)   any person having charge of, or otherwise concerned with the operation of, the computer, apparatus or material,

  to afford him such reasonable assistance as he may require.

(8)   A person authorised to inspect any premises under this section shall have a right to enter the premises for that purpose, and for any purpose specified in subsection (4), at any reasonable time.

(9)   Any person exercising that power shall, if so required, produce some duly authenticated document showing his authority to do so.

(10) Any person who intentionally obstructs another in the exercise of that power shall be guilty of an offence and liable on summary conviction to a fine not exceeding level 3 on the standard scale.

(11) The Secretary of State may by order provide for subsections (1), (4) and (6) not to apply in relation to such homes, or other premises, as may be specified in the order.

(12) Without prejudice to section 104, any such order may make different provision with respect to each of those subsections.

81 Inquiries

(1) The Secretary of State may cause an inquiry to be held into any matter connected with—
- (a) the functions of the social services committee of a local authority, in so far as those functions relate to children;
- (b) the functions of an adoption agency;
- (c) the functions of a voluntary organisation, in so far as those functions relate to children;
- (d) a registered children's home or voluntary home;
- (e) a residential care home, nursing home or mental nursing home, so far as it provides accommodation for children;
- (f) a home provided by the Secretary of State under section 82(5);
- (g) the detention of a child under section 53 of the Children and Young Persons Act 1933.

(2) Before an inquiry is begun, the Secretary of State may direct that it shall be held in private.

(3) Where no direction has been given, the person holding the inquiry may if he thinks fit hold it, or any part of it, in private.

(4) Subsections (2) to (5) of section 250 of the Local Government Act 1972 (powers in relation to local inquiries) shall apply in relation to an inquiry under this section as they apply in relation to a local inquiry under that section.

(5) In this section "functions" includes powers and duties which a person has otherwise than by virtue of any enactment.

82 Financial support by Secretary of State

(1) The Secretary of State may (with the consent of the Treasury) defray or contribute towards—
- (a) any fees or expenses incurred by any person undergoing approved child care training;
- (b) any fees charged, or expenses incurred, by any person providing approved child care training or preparing material for use in connection with such training; or
- (c) the cost of maintaining any person undergoing such training.

(2) The Secretary of State may make grants to local authorities in respect of expenditure incurred by them in providing secure accommodation in community homes other than assisted community homes.

(3) Where—
- (a) a grant has been made under subsection (2) with respect to any secure accommodation; but

    (*b*)   the grant is not used for the purpose for which it was made or the accommodation is not used as, or ceases to be used as, secure accommodation,
the Secretary of State may (with the consent of the Treasury) require the authority concerned to repay the grant, in whole or in part.

(4)   The Secretary of State may make grants to voluntary organisations towards—
    (*a*)   expenditure incurred by them in connection with the establishment, maintenance or improvement of voluntary homes which, at the time when the expenditure was incurred—
        (i)   were assisted community homes; or
        (ii)   were designated as such; or
    (*b*)   expenses incurred in respect of the borrowing of money to defray any such expenditure.

(5)   The Secretary of State may arrange for the provision, equipment and maintenance of homes for the accommodation of children who are in need of particular facilities and services which—
    (*a*)   are or will be provided in those homes; and
    (*b*)   in the opinion of the Secretary of State, are unlikely to be readily available in community homes.

(6)   In this Part—
       "child care training" means training undergone by any person with a view to, or in the course of—
    (*a*)   his employment for the purposes of any of the functions mentioned in section 83(9) or in connection with the adoption of children or with the accommodation of children in a residential care home, nursing home or mental nursing home; or
    (*b*)   his employment by a voluntary organisation for similar purposes;
       "approved child care training" means child care training which is approved by the Secretary of State; and
       "secure accommodation" means accommodation provided for the purpose of restricting the liberty of children.

(7)   Any grant made under this section shall be of such amount, and shall be subject to such conditions, as the Secretary of State may (with the consent of the Treasury) determine.

83   Research and returns of information

(1)   The Secretary of State may conduct, or assist other persons in conducting, research into any matter connected with—
    (*a*)   his functions, or the functions of local authorities, under the enactments mentioned in subsection (9);
    (*b*)   the adoption of children; or
    (*c*)   the accommodation of children in a residential care home, nursing home or mental nursing home.

(2)   Any local authority may conduct, or assist other persons in conducting, research into any matter connected with—
    (*a*)   their functions under the enactments mentioned in subsection (9);
    (*b*)   the adoption of children; or
    (*c*)   the accommodation of children in a residential care home, nursing home or mental nursing home.

(3)   Every local authority shall, at such times and in such form as the Secretary of State may direct, transmit to him such particulars as he may require with respect to—

(*a*) the performance by the local authority of all or any of their functions—
(i) under the enactments mentioned in subsection (9); or
(ii) in connection with the accommodation of children in a residential care home, nursing home or mental nursing home; and
(*b*) the children in relation to whom the authority have exercised those functions.

(4) Every voluntary organisation shall, at such times and in such form as the Secretary of State may direct, transmit to him such particulars as he may require with respect to children accommodated by them or on their behalf.

(5) The Secretary of State may direct the clerk of each magistrates' court to which the direction is expressed to relate to transmit—
(*a*) to such person as may be specified in the direction; and
(*b*) at such times and in such form as he may direct,
such particulars as he may require with respect to proceedings of the court which relate to children.

(6) The Secretary of State shall in each year lay before Parliament a consolidated and classified abstract of the information transmitted to him under subsections (3) to (5).

(7) The Secretary of State may institute research designed to provide information on which requests for information under this section may be based.

(8) The Secretary of State shall keep under review the adequacy of the provision of child care training and for that purpose shall receive and consider any information from or representations made by—
(*a*) the Central Council for Education and Training in Social Work;
(*b*) such representatives of local authorities as appear to him to be appropriate; or
(*c*) such other persons or organisations as appear to him to be appropriate,
concerning the provision of such training.

(9) The enactments are—
(*a*) this Act;
(*b*) the Children and Young Persons Acts 1933 to 1969;
(*c*) section 116 of the Mental Health Act 1983 (so far as it relates to children looked after by local authorities);
(*d*) section 10 of the Mental Health (Scotland) Act 1984 (so far as it relates to children for whom local authorities have responsibility).

84 Local authority failure to comply with statutory duty: default power of Secretary of State

(1) If the Secretary of State is satisfied that any local authority has failed, without reasonable excuse, to comply with any of the duties imposed on them by or under this Act he may make an order declaring that authority to be in default with respect to that duty.

(2) An order under subsection (1) shall give the Secretary of State's reasons for making it.

(3) An order under subsection (1) may contain such directions for the purpose of ensuring that the duty is complied with, within such period as may be specified in the order, as appear to the Secretary of State to be necessary.

(4) Any such direction shall, on the application of the Secretary of State, be enforceable by mandamus.

Part XII

Miscellaneous and General

Notification of children accommodated in
certain establishments

85 Children accommodated by health authorities and local education authorities

(1) Where a child is provided with accommodation by any health authority or local education authority ("the accommodating authority")—
  (a) for a consecutive period of at least three months; or
  (b) with the intention, on the part of that authority, of accommodating him for such a period,
the accommodating authority shall notify the responsible authority.

(2) Where subsection (1) applies with respect to a child, the accommodating authority shall also notify the responsible authority when they cease to accommodate the child.

(3) In this section "the responsible authority" means—
  (a) the local authority appearing to the accommodating authority to be the authority within whose area the child was ordinarily resident immediately before being accommodated; or
  (b) where it appears to the accommodating authority that a child was not ordinarily resident within the area of any local authority, the local authority within whose area the accommodation is situated.

(4) Where a local authority have been notified under this section, they shall—
  (a) take such steps as are reasonably practicable to enable them to determine whether the child's welfare is adequately safeguarded and promoted while he is accommodated by the accommodating authority; and
  (b) consider the extent to which (if at all) they should exercise any of their functions under this Act with respect to the child.

86 Children accommodated in residential care, nursing or mental nursing homes

(1) Where a child is provided with accommodation in any residential care home, nursing home or mental nursing home—
  (a) for a consecutive period of at least three months; or
  (b) with the intention, on the part of the person taking the decision to accommodate him, of accommodating him for such period,
the person carrying on the home shall notify the local authority within whose area the home is carried on.

(2) Where subsection (1) applies with respect to a child, the person carrying on the home shall also notify that authority when he ceases to accommodate the child in the home.

(3) Where a local authority have been notified under this section, they shall—
  (a) take such steps as are reasonably practicable to enable them to determine whether the child's welfare is adequately safeguarded and promoted while he is accommodated in the home; and
  (b) consider the extent to which (if at all) they should exercise any of their functions under this Act with respect to the child.

(4) If the person carrying on any home fails, without reasonable excuse, to comply with this section he shall be guilty of an offence.

(5) A person authorised by a local authority may enter any residential care home, nursing home or mental nursing home within the authority's area for the purpose of establishing whether the requirements of this section have been complied with.

(6) Any person who intentionally obstructs another in the exercise of the power of entry shall be guilty of an offence.

(7) Any person exercising the power of entry shall, if so required, produce some duly authenticated document showing his authority to do so.

(8) Any person committing an offence under this section shall be liable on summary conviction to a fine not exceeding level 3 on the standard scale.

87   Welfare of children accommodated in independent schools

(1) It shall be the duty of—
  (a)   the proprietor of any independent school which provides accommodation for any child; and
  (b)   any person who is not the proprietor of such a school but who is responsible for conducting it,
to safeguard and promote the child's welfare.

(2) Subsection (1) does not apply in relation to a school which is a children's home or a residential care home.

(3) Where accommodation is provided for a child by an independent school within the area of a local authority, the authority shall take such steps as are reasonably practicable to enable them to determine whether the child's welfare is adequately safeguarded and promoted while he is accommodated by the school.

(4) Where a local authority are of the opinion that there has been a failure to comply with subsection (1) in relation to a child provided with accommodation by a school within their area, they shall notify the Secretary of State.

(5) Any person authorised by a local authority may, for the purpose of enabling the authority to discharge their duty under this section, enter at any reasonable time any independent school within their area which provides accommodation for any child.

(6) Any person entering an independent school in exercise of the power conferred by subsection (5) may carry out such inspection of premises, children and records as in prescribed by regulations made by the Secretary of State for the purposes of this section.

(7) Any person exercising that power shall, if asked to do so, produce some duly authenticated document showing his authority to do so.

(8) Any person authorised by the regulations to inspect records—
  (a)   shall be entitled at any reasonable time to have access to, and inspect and check the operation of, any computer and any associated apparatus or material which is or has been in use in connection with the records in question; and
  (b)   may require—
    (i)   the person by whom or on whose behalf the computer is or has been so used; or
    (ii)   any person having charge of, or otherwise concerned with the operation of, the computer, apparatus or material,
    to afford him such assistance as he may reasonably require.

(9) Any person who intentionally obstructs another in the exercise of any power conferred by this section or the regulations shall be guilty of an offence and liable on summary conviction to a fine not exceeding level 3 on the standard scale.

(10) In this section "proprietor" has the same meaning as in the Education Act 1944.

Adoption

88   Amendments of adoption legislation

(1) The Adoption Act 1976 shall have effect subject to the amendments made by Part I of Schedule 10.

(2) The Adoption (Scotland) Act 1978 shall have effect subject to the amendments made by Part II of Schedule 10.

Paternity tests

89   Tests to establish paternity

In section 20 of the Family Law Reform Act 1969 (power of court to require use of tests to determine paternity), the following subsections shall be inserted after subsection (1)—

"(1A) Where—
   (a)   an application is made for a direction under this section; and
   (b)   the person whose paternity is in issue is under the age of eighteen when the application is made,
the application shall specify who is to carry out the tests.

(1B) In the case of a direction made on an application to which subsection (1A) applies the court shall—
   (a)   specify, as the person who is to carry out the tests, the person specified in the application; or
   (b)   where the court considers that it would be inappropriate to specify that person (whether because to specify him would be incompatible with any provision made by or under regulations made under section 22 of this Act or for any other reason), decline to give the direction applied for."

Criminal care and supervision orders

90   Care and supervision orders in criminal proceedings

(1) The power of a court to make an order under subsection (2) of section 1 of the Children and Young Persons Act 1969 (care proceedings in juvenile courts) where it is of the opinion that the condition mentioned in paragraph (*f*) of that subsection ("the offence condition") is satisfied is hereby abolished.

(2) The powers of the court to make care orders—
   (a)   under section 7(7)(*a*) of the Children and Young Persons Act 1969 (alteration in treatment of young offenders etc.); and
   (b)   under section 15(1) of that Act, on discharging a supervision order made under section 7(7)(*b*) of that Act,
are hereby abolished.

(3) The powers given by that Act to include requirements in supervision orders shall have effect subject to amendments made by Schedule 12.

Effect and duration of orders etc.

91 Effect and duration of orders etc.

(1) The making of a residence order with respect to a child who is the subject of a care order discharges the care order.

(2) The making of a care order with respect to a child who is the subject of any section 8 order discharges that order.

(3) The making of a care order with respect to a child who is the subject of a supervision order discharges that other order.

(4) The making of a care order with respect to a child who is a ward of court brings that wardship to an end.

(5) The making of a care order with respect to a child who is the subject of a school attendance order made under section 37 of the Education Act 1944 discharges the school attendance order.

(6) Where an emergency protection order is made with respect to a child who is in care, the care order shall have effect subject to the emergency protection order.

(7) Any order made under section 4(1) or 5(1) shall continue in force until the child reaches the age of eighteen, unless it is brought to an end earlier.

(8) Any—
    (*a*)   agreement under section 4; or
    (*b*)   appointment under section 5(3) or (4),
shall continue in force until the child reaches the age of eighteen, unless it is brought to an end earlier.

(9) An order under Schedule 1 has effect as specified in that Schedule.

(10) A section 8 order shall, if it would otherwise still be in force, cease to have effect when the child reaches the age of sixteen, unless it is to have effect beyond that age by virtue of section 9(6).

(11) Where a section 8 order has effect with respect to a child who has reached the age of sixteen, it shall, if it would otherwise still be in force, cease to have effect when he reaches the age of eighteen.

(12) Any care order, other than an interim care order, shall continue in force until the child reaches the age of eighteen, unless it is brought to an end earlier.

(13) Any order made under any other provision of this Act in relation to a child shall, if it would otherwise still be in force, cease to have effect when he reaches the age of eighteen.

(14) On disposing of any application for an order under this Act, the court may (whether or not it makes any other order in response to the application) order that no application for an order under this Act of any specified kind may be made with respect to the child concerned by any person named in the order without leave of the court.

(15) Where an application ("the previous application") has been made for—
    (*a*)   the discharge of a care order;
    (*b*)   the discharge of a supervision order;
    (*c*)   the discharge of an education supervision order;
    (*d*)   the substitution of a supervision order for a care order; or
    (*e*)   a child assessment order,

no further application of a kind mentioned in paragraphs (*a*) to (*e*) may be made with respect to the child concerned, without leave of the court, unless the period between the disposal of the previous application and the making of the further application exceeds six months.

(16) Subsection (15) does not apply to applications made in relation to interim orders.

(17) Where—
    (*a*)   a person has made an application for an order under section 34;
    (*b*)   the application has been refused; and
    (*c*)   a period of less than six months has elapsed since the refusal,
that person may not make a further application for such an order with respect to the same child, unless he has obtained the leave of the court.

Jurisdiction and procedure etc.

92 Jurisdiction of courts

(1) The name "domestic proceedings", given to certain proceedings in magistrates' courts, is hereby changed to "family proceedings" and the names "domestic court" and "domestic court panel" are hereby changed to "family proceedings court" and "family panel", respectively.

(2) Proceedings under this Act shall be treated as family proceedings in relation to magistrates' courts.

(3) Subsection (2) is subject to the provisions of section 65(1) and (2) of the Magistrates' Courts Act 1980 (proceedings which may be treated as not being family proceedings), as amended by this Act.

(4) A magistrates' court shall not be competent to entertain any application, or make any order, involving the administration or application of—
    (*a*)   any property belonging to or held in trust for a child; or
    (*b*)   the income of any such property.

(5) The powers of a magistrates' court under section 63(2) of the Act of 1980 to suspend or rescind orders shall not apply in relation to any order made under this Act.

(6) Part I of Schedule 11 makes provision, including provision for the Lord Chancellor to make orders, with respect to the jurisdiction of courts and justices of the peace in relation to—
    (*a*)   proceedings under this Act; and
    (*b*)   proceedings under certain other enactments.

(7) For the purposes of this Act "the court" means the High Court, a county court or a magistrates' court.

(8) Subsection (7) is subject to the provision made by or under Part I of Schedule 11 and to any express provision as to the jurisdiction of any court made by any other provision of this Act.

(9) The Lord Chancellor may by order make provision for the principal registry of the Family Division of the High Court to be treated as if it were a county court for such purposes of this Act, or of any provision made under this Act, as may be specified in the order.

(10) Any order under subsection (9) may make such provision as the Lord Chancellor thinks expedient for the purpose of applying (with or without modifications) provisions

which apply in relation to the procedure in county courts to the principal registry when it acts as if it were a county court.

(11) Part II of Schedule 11 makes amendments consequential on this section.

93 Rules of Court

(1) An authority having power to make rules of court may make such provision for giving effect to—
   (*a*)   this Act;
   (*b*)   the provisions of any statutory instrument made under this Act; or
   (*c*)   any amendment made by this Act in any other enactment,
as appears to that authority to be necessary or expedient.

(2) The rules may, in particular, make provision—
   (*a*)   with respect to the procedure to be followed in any relevant proceedings (including the manner in which any application is to be made or other proceedings commenced);
   (*b*)   as to the persons entitled to participate in any relevant proceedings, whether as parties to the proceedings or by being given the opportunity to make representations to the court;
   (*c*)   with respect to the documents and information to be furnished, and notices to be given, in connection with any relevant proceedings;
   (*d*)   applying (with or without modification) enactments which govern the procedure to be followed with respect to proceedings brought on a complaint made to a magistrates' court to relevant proceedings in such a court brought otherwise than on a complaint;
   (*e*)   with respect to preliminary hearings;
   (*f*)   for the service outside the United Kingdom, in such circumstances and in such manner as may be prescribed, of any notice of proceedings in a magistrates' court;
   (*g*)   for the exercise by magistrates' courts, in such circumstances as may be prescribed, of such powers as may be prescribed (even though a party to the proceedings in question is outside England and Wales);
   (*h*)   enabling the court, in such circumstances as may be prescribed, to proceed on any application even though the respondent has not been given notice of the proceedings;
   (*i*)   authorising a single justice to discharge the functions of a magistrates' court with respect to such relevant proceedings as may be prescribed;
   (*j*)   authorising a magistrates' court to order any of the parties to such relevant proceedings as may be prescribed, in such circumstances as may be prescribed, to pay the whole or part of the costs of all or any of the other parties.

(3) In subsection (2)—

"notice of proceedings" means a summons or such other notice of proceedings as is required; and "given", in relation to a summons, means "served";

"prescribed" means prescribed by the rules; and

"relevant proceedings" means any application made, or proceedings brought, under any of the provisions mentioned in paragraphs (*a*) to (*c*) of subsection (1) and any part of such proceedings.

(4) This section and any other power in this Act to make rules of court are not to be taken as in any way limiting any other power of the authority in question to make rules of court.

(5) When making any rules under this section an authority shall be subject to the same requirements as to consultation (if any) as apply when the authority makes rules under its general rule making power.

94   Appeals

(1) An appeal shall lie to the High Court against—
   (a)   the making by a magistrates' court of any order under this Act; or
   (b)   any refusal by a magistrates' court to make such an order.

(2) Where a magistrates' court has power, in relation to any proceedings under this Act, to decline jurisdiction because it considers that the case can more conveniently be dealt with by another court, no appeal shall lie against any exercise by that magistrates' court of that power.

(3) Subsection (1) does not apply in relation to an interim order for periodical payments made under Schedule 1.

(4) On an appeal under this section, the High Court may make such orders as may be necessary to give effect to its determination of the appeal.

(5) Where an order is made under subsection (4) the High Court may also make such incidental or consequential orders as appear to it to be just.

(6) Where an appeal from a magistrates' court relates to an order for the making of periodical payments, the High Court may order that its determination of the appeal shall have effect from such date as it thinks fit to specify in the order.

(7) The date so specified must not be earlier than the earliest date allowed in accordance with rules of court made for the purposes of this section.

(8) Where, on an appeal under this section in respect of an order requiring a person to make periodical payments, the High Court reduces the amount of those payments or discharges the order—
   (a)   it may order the person entitled to the payments to pay to the person making them such sum in respect of payments already made as the High Court thinks fit; and
   (b)   if any arrears are due under the order for periodical payments, it may remit payment of the whole, or part, of those arrears.

(9) Any order of the High Court made on an appeal under this section (other than one directing that an application be re-heard by a magistrates' court) shall, for the purposes—
   (a)   of the enforcement of the order; and
   (b)   of any power to vary, revive or discharge orders,
be treated as if it were an order of the magistrates' court from which the appeal was brought and not an order of the High Court.

(10) The Lord Chancellor may by order make provision as to the circumstances in which appeals may be made against decisions taken by courts on questions arising in connection with the transfer, or proposed transfer, of proceedings by virtue of any order under paragraph 2 of Schedule 11.

(11) Except to the extent provided for in any order made under subsection (10), no appeal may be made against any decision of a kind mentioned in that subsection.

95   Attendance of child at hearing under Part IV or V

(1) In any proceedings in which a court is hearing an application for an order under Part IV or V, or is considering whether to make any such order, the court may

order the child concerned to attend such stage or stages of the proceedings as may be specified in the order.

(2) The power conferred by subsection (1) shall be exercised in accordance with rules of court.

(3) Subsections (4) to (6) apply where—
  (*a*)   an order under subsection (1) has not been complied with; or
  (*b*)   the court has reasonable cause to believe that it will not be complied with.

(4) The court may make an order authorising a constable, or such person as may be specified in the order—
  (*a*)   to take charge of the child and to bring him to the court; and
  (*b*)   to enter and search any premises specified in the order if he has reasonable cause to believe that the child may be found on the premises.

(5) The court may order any person who is in a position to do so to bring the child to the court.

(6) Where the court has reason to believe that a person has information about the whereabouts of the child it may order him to disclose it to the court.

96   Evidence given by, or with respect to, children

(1) Subsection (2) applies in any civil proceedings where a child who is called as a witness in any civil proceedings does not, in the opinion of the court, understand the nature of an oath.

(2) The child's evidence may be heard by the court if, in its opinion—
  (*a*)   he understands that it is his duty to speak the truth; and
  (*b*)   he has sufficient understanding to justify his evidence being heard.

(3) The Lord Chancellor may by order make provision for the admissibility of evidence which would otherwise be inadmissible under any rule of law relating to hearsay.

(4) An order under subsection (3) may only be made with respect to—
  (*a*)   civil proceedings in general or such civil proceedings, or class of civil proceedings, as may be prescribed; and
  (*b*)   evidence in connection with the upbringing, maintenance or welfare of a child.

(5) An order under subsection (3)—
  (*a*)   may, in particular, provide for the admissibility of statements which are made orally or in a prescribed form or which are recorded by any prescribed method of recording;
  (*b*)   may make different provision for different purposes and in relation to different descriptions of court; and
  (*c*)   may make such amendments and repeals in any enactment relating to evidence (other than in this Act) as the Lord Chancellor considers necessary or expedient in consequence of the provision made by the order.

(6) Subsection (5)(*b*) is without prejudice to section 104(4):

(7) In this section—
"civil proceedings" and "court" have the same meaning as they have in the Civil Evidence Act 1968 by virtue of section 18 of that Act; and
"prescribed" means prescribed by an order under subsection (3).

97 Privacy for children involved in certain proceedings

(1) Rules made under section 144 of the Magistrates' Courts Act 1980 may make provision for a magistrates' court to sit in private in proceedings in which any powers under this Act may be exercised by the court with respect to any child.

(2) No person shall publish any material which is intended, or likely, to identify—
- (a) any child as being involved in any proceedings before a magistrates' court in which any power under this Act may be exercised by the court with respect to that or any other child; or
- (b) an address or school as being that of a child involved in any such proceedings.

(3) In any proceedings for an offence under this section it shall be a defence for the accused to prove that he did not know, and had no reason to suspect, that the published material was intended, or likely, to identify the child.

(4) The court or the Secretary of State may, if satisfied that the welfare of the child requires it, by order dispense with the requirements of subsection (2) to such extent as may be specified in the order.

(5) For the purposes of this section—
"publish" includes—
- (a) broadcast by radio, television or cable television; or
- (b) cause to be published; and
"material" includes any picture or representation.

(6) Any person who contravenes this section shall be guilty of an offence and liable, on summary conviction, to a fine not exceeding level 4 on the standard scale.

(7) Subsection (1) is without prejudice to—
- (a) the generality of the rule making power in section 144 of the Act of 1980; or
- (b) any other power of a magistrates' court to sit in private.

(8) Section 71 of the Act of 1980 (newspaper reports of certain proceedings) shall apply in relation to any proceedings to which this section applies subject to the provisions of this section.

98 Self-incrimination

(1) In any proceedings in which a court is hearing an application for an order under Part IV or V, no person shall be excused from—
- (a) giving evidence on any matter; or
- (b) answering any question put to him in the course of his giving evidence,
on the ground that doing so might incriminate him or his spouse of an offence.

(2) A statement or admission made in such proceedings shall not be admissible in evidence against the person making it or his spouse in proceedings for an offence other than perjury.

99 Legal aid

(1) The Legal Aid Act 1988 is amended as mentioned in subsections (2) to (4).

(2) In section 15 (availability of, and payment for, representation under provisions relating to civil legal aid), for the words "and (3)" in subsection (1) there shall be substituted "to (3B)"; and the following subsections shall be inserted after subsection (3)—

"(3A) Representation under this Part shall not be available—
(a) to any local authority; or

(*b*) to any other body which falls within a prescribed description,

for the purposes of any proceedings under the Children Act 1989.

(3B) Regardless of subsection (2) or (3), representation under this Part must be granted where a child who is brought before a court under section 25 of the 1989 Act (use of accommodation for restricting liberty) is not, but wishes to be, legally represented before the court.''

(3) In section 19(5) (scope of provisions about criminal legal aid), at the end of the definition of ''criminal proceedings'' there shall be added ''and also includes proceedings under section 15 of the Children and Young Persons Act 1969 (variation and discharge of supervision orders) and section 16(8) of that Act (appeals in such proceedings)''.

(4) Sections 27, 28 and 30(1) and (2) (provisions about legal aid in care, and other, proceedings in relation to children) shall cease to have effect.

(5) The Lord Chancellor may by order make such further amendments in the Legal Aid Act 1988 as he considers necessary or expedient in consequence of any provision made by or under this Act.'

100 Restrictions on use of wardship jurisdiction

(1) Section 7 of the Family Law Reform Act 1969 (which gives the High Court power to place a ward of court in the care, or under the supervision, of a local authority) shall cease to have effect.

(2) No court shall exercise the High Court's inherent jurisdiction with respect to children—
  (*a*) so as to require a child to be placed in the care, or put under the supervision, of a local authority;
  (*b*) so as to require a child to be accommodated by or on behalf of a local authority;
  (*c*) so as to make a child who is the subject of a care order a ward of court; or
  (*d*) for the purpose of conferring on any local authority power to determine any question which has arisen, or which may arise, in connection with any aspect of parental responsibility for a child.

(3) No application for any exercise of the court's inherent jurisdiction with respect to children may be made by a local authority unless the authority have obtained the leave of the court.

(4) The court may only grant leave if it is satisfied that—
  (*a*) the result which the authority wish to achieve could not be achieved through the making of any order of a kind to which subsection (5) applies; and
  (*b*) there is reasonable cause to believe that if the court's inherent jurisdiction is not exercised with respect to the child he is likely to suffer significant harm.

(5) This subsection applies to any order—
  (*a*) made otherwise than in the exercise of the court's inherent jurisdiction; and
  (*b*) which the local authority is entitled to apply for (assuming, in the case of any application which may only be made with leave, that leave is granted).

101 Effect of orders as between England and Wales and Northern Ireland, the Channel Islands or the Isle of Man

(1) The Secretary of State may make regulations providing—
  (*a*) for prescribed orders which—

      (i)   are made by a court in Northern Ireland; and
      (ii)   appear to the Secretary of State to correspond in their effect to orders
             which may be made under any provision of this Act,
      to have effect in prescribed circumstances, for prescribed purposes of this
      Act, as if they were orders of a prescribed kind made under this Act;
  (b) for prescribed orders which—
      (i)   are made by a court in England and Wales; and
      (ii)   appear to the Secretary of State to correspond in their effect to orders
             which may be made under any provision in force in Northern Ireland,
      to have effect in prescribed circumstances, for prescribed purposes of the
      law of Northern Ireland, as if they were orders of a prescribed kind made
      in Northern Ireland.

(2) Regulations under subsection (1) may provide for the order concerned to cease
to have effect for the purposes of the law of Northern Ireland, or (as the case may
be) the law of England and Wales, if prescribed conditions are satisfied.

(3) The Secretary of State may make regulations providing for prescribed orders
which—
  (a) are made by a court in the Isle of Man or in any of the Channel Islands;
       and
  (b) appear to the Secretary of State to correspond in their effect to orders which
       may be made under this Act,
to have effect in prescribed circumstances for prescribed purposes of this Act, as
if they were orders of a prescribed kind made under this Act.

(4) Where a child who is in the care of a local authority is lawfully taken to live
in Northern Ireland, the Isle of Man or in any of the Channel Islands, the care
order in question shall cease to have effect if the conditions prescribed in regulations
by the Secretary of State are satisfied.

(5) Any regulations made under this section may—
  (a) make such consequential amendments (including repeals) in—
      (i)   section 25 of the Children and Young Persons Act 1969 (transfers
             between England and Wales and Northern Ireland); or
      (ii)   section 26 (transfers between England and Wales and Channel Islands
             or Isle of Man) of that Act,
      as the Secretary of State considers necessary or expedient; and
  (b) modify any provision of this Act, in its application (by virtue of the regulations)
       in relation to an order made otherwise than in England and Wales.

Search warrants

**102 Power of constable to assist in exercise of certain powers to search
for children or inspect premises**

(1) Where, on an application made by any person for a warrant under this section,
it appears to the court—
  (a) that a person attempting to exercise powers under any enactment mentioned
       in subsection (6) has been prevented from doing so by being refused entry
       to the premises concerned or refused access to the child concerned; or
  (b) that any such person is likely to be so prevented from exercising any such
       powers,
it may issue a warrant authorising any constable to assist that person in the exercise
of those powers using reasonable force if necessary.

(2) Every warrant issued under this section shall be addressed to, and executed by, a constable who shall be accompanied by the person applying for the warrant if—

    (*a*)   that person so desires; and

    (*b*)   the court by whom the warrant is issued does not direct otherwise.

(3) A court granting an application for a warrant under this section may direct that the constable concerned may, in executing the warrant, be accompanied by a registered medical practitioner, registered nurse or registered health visitor if he so chooses.

(4) An application for a warrant under this section shall be made in the manner and form prescribed by rules of court.

(5) Where—

    (*a*)   an application for a warrant under this section relates to a particular child; and

    (*b*)   it is reasonably practicable to do so,

the application and any warrant granted on the application shall name the child; and where it does not name him it shall describe him as clearly as possible.

(6) The enactments are—

    (*a*)   sections 62, 64, 67, 76, 80, 86 and 87;

    (*b*)   paragraph 8(1)(*b*) and (2)(*b*) of Schedule 3;

    (*c*)   section 33 of the Adoption Act 1976 (duty of local authority to secure that protected children are visited from time to time).

General

103 Offences by bodies corporate

(1) This section applies where any offence under this Act is committed by a body corporate.

(2) If the offence is proved to have been committed with the consent or connivance of or to be attributable to any neglect on the part of any director, manager, secretary or other similar officer of the body corporate, or any person who was purporting to act in any such capacity, he (as well as the body corporate) shall be guilty of the offence and shall be liable to be proceeded against and punished accordingly.

104 Regulations and orders

(1) Any power of the Lord Chancellor or the Secretary of State under this Act to make an order, regulations, or rules, except an order under section 54(2), 56(4)(*a*), 57(3), 84 or 97(4) or paragraph 1(1) of Schedule 4, shall be exercisable by statutory instrument.

(2) Any such statutory instrument, except one made under section 17(4), 107 or 108(2), shall be subject to annulment in pursuance of a resolution of either House of Parliament.

(3) An order under section 17(4) shall not be made unless a draft of it has been laid before, and approved by a resolution of, each House of Parliament.

(4) Any statutory instrument made under this Act may—

    (*a*)   make different provision for different cases;

    (*b*)   provide for exemptions from any of its provisions; and

    (*c*)   contain such incidental, supplemental and transitional provisions as the person making it considers expedient.

105 Interpretation

(1) In this Act—

"adoption agency" means a body which may be referred to as an adoption agency by virtue of section 1 of the Adoption Act 1976;

"bank holiday" means a day which is a bank holiday under the Banking and Financial Dealings Act 1971;

"care order" has the meaning given by section 31(11) and also includes any order which by or under any enactment has the effect of, or is deemed to be, a care order for the purposes of this Act; and any reference to a child who is in the care of an authority is a reference to a child who is in their care by virtue of a care order;

"child" means, subject to paragraph 16 of Schedule 1, a person under the age of eighteen;

"child assessment order" has the meaning given by section 43(2);

"child minder" has the meaning given by section 71;

"child of the family", in relation to the parties to a marriage, means—

  (a) a child of both of those parties;

  (b) any other child, not being a child who is placed with those parties as foster parents by a local authority or voluntary organisation, who has been treated by both of those parties as a child of their family;

"children's home", has the same meaning as in section 63;

"community home" has the meaning given by section 53;

"contact order" has the meaning given by section 8(1);

"day care" has the same meaning as in section 18;

"disabled", in relation to a child, has the same meaning as in section 17(11);

"district health authority" has the same meaning as in the National Health Service Act 1977;

"domestic premises" has the meaning given by section 71(12);

"education supervision order" has the meaning given in section 36;

"emergency protection order" means an order under section 44;

"family assistance order" has the meaning given in section 16(2);

"family proceedings" has the meaning given by section 8(3);

"functions" includes powers and duties;

"guardian of a child" means a guardian (other than a guardian of the estate of a child) appointed in accordance with the provisions of section 5;

"harm" has the same meaning as in section 31(9) and the question of whether harm is significant shall be determined in accordance with section 31(10);

"health authority" means any district health authority and any special health authority established under the National Health Services Act 1977;

"health service hospital" has the same meaning as in the National Health Service Act 1977;

"hospital" has the same meaning as in the Mental Health Act 1983, except that it does not include a special hospital within the meaning of that Act;

"ill-treatment" has the same meaning as in section 31(9);

"independent school" has the same meaning as in the Education Act 1944;

"local authority" means, in relation to England and Wales, the council of a county, a metropolitan district, a London Borough or the Common Council of the City of London and, in relation to Scotland, a local authority within the meaning of section 1(2) of the Social Work (Scotland) Act 1968;

"local authority foster parent" has the same meaning as in section 23(3);

"local education authority" has the same meaning as in the Education Act 1944;

"local housing authority" has the same meaning as in the Housing Act 1985;

"mental nursing home" has the same meaning as in the Registered Homes Act 1984;

"nursing home" has the same meaning as in the Act of 1984;

"parental responsibility" has the meaning given in section 3;

"parental responsibility agreement" has the meaning given in section 4(1);

"prescribed" means prescribed by regulations made under this Act;

"privately fostered child" and "to foster a child privately" have the same meaning as in section 66;

"prohibited steps order" has the meaning given by section 8(1);

"protected child" has the same meaning as in Part III of the Adoption Act 1976;

"registered children's home" has the same meaning as in section 63;

"registered pupil" has the same meaning as in the Education Act 1944;

"relative", in relation to a child, means a grandparent, brother, sister, uncle or aunt (whether of the full blood or half blood or by affinity) or step-parent;

"residence order" has the meaning given by section 8(1);

"responsible person", in relation to a child who is the subject of a supervision order, has the meaning given in paragraph 1 of Schedule 3;

"school" has the same meaning as in the Education Act 1944 or, in relation to Scotland, in the Education (Scotland) Act 1980;

"service", in relation to any provision made under Part III, includes any facility;

"signed", in relation to any person, includes the making by that person of his mark;

"special educational needs" has the same meaning as in the Education Act 1981;

"special health authority" has the same meaning as in the National Health Service Act 1977;

"specific issue order" has the meaning given by section 8(1);

"supervision order" has the meaning given by section 31(11);

"supervised child" and "supervisor", in relation to a supervision order or an education supervision order, mean respectively the child who is (or is to be) under supervision and the person under whose supervision he is (or is to be) by virtue of the order;

"upbringing", in relation to any child, includes the care of the child but not his maintenance;

"voluntary home" has the meaning given by section 60;

"voluntary organisation" means a body (other than a public or local authority) whose activities are not carried on for profit.

(2) References in this Act to a child whose father and mother were, or (as the case may be) were not, married to each other at the time of his birth must be read with section 1 of the Family Law Reform Act 1987 (which extends the meaning of such references).

(3) References in this Act to—

    (a)   a person with whom a child lives, or is to live, as the result of a residence order; or

    (b)   a person in whose favour a residence order is in force,

shall be construed as references to the person named in the order as the person with whom the child is to live.

(4) References in this Act to a child who is looked after by a local authority have the same meaning as they have (by virtue of section 22) in Part III.

(5) References in this Act to accommodation provided by or on behalf of a local authority are references to accommodation so provided in the exercise of functions which stand referred to the social services committee of that or any other local authority under the Local Authority Social Services Act 1970.

(6) In determining the "ordinary residence" of a child for any purpose of this Act, there shall be disregarded any period in which he lives in any place—

    (a)   which is a school or other institution;

    (b)   in accordance with the requirements of a supervision order under this Act or an order under section 7(7)(*b*) of the Children and Young Persons Act 1969; or

(*c*)   while he is being provided with accommodation by or on behalf of a local authority.

(7) References in this Act to children who are in need shall be construed in accordance with section 17.

(8) Any notice or other document required under this Act to be served on any person may be served on him by being delivered personally to him, or being sent by post to him in a registered letter or by the recorded delivery service at his proper address.

(9) Any such notice or other document required to be served on a body corporate or a firm shall be duly served if it is served on the secretary or clerk of that body or a partner of that firm.

(10) For the purposes of this section, and of section 7 of the Interpretation Act 1978 in its application to this section, the proper address of a person—

(*a*)   in the case of a secretary or clerk of a body corporate, shall be that of the registered or principal office of that body;

(*b*)   in the case of a partner of a firm, shall be that of the principal office of the firm; and

(*c*)   in any other case, shall be the last known address of the person to be served.

106   Financial provisions

(1) Any—

(*a*)   grants made by the Secretary of State under this Act; and

(*b*)   any other expenses incurred by the Secretary of State under this Act,

shall be payable out of money provided by Parliament.

(2) Any sums received by the Secretary of State under section 58, or by way of the repayment of any grant made under section 82(2) or (4) shall be paid into the Consolidated Fund.

107   Application to the Channel Islands

Her Majesty may by Order in Council direct that any of the provisions of this Act shall extend to any of the Channel Islands with such exceptions and modifications as may be specified in the Order.

108   Short title, commencement extent etc.

(1) This Act may be cited as the Children Act 1989.

(2) Sections 89 and 96(3) to (7), and paragraph 35 of Schedule 12, shall come into force on the passing of this Act and paragraph 36 of Schedule 12 shall come into force at the end of the period of two months beginning with the day on which this Act is passed but otherwise this Act shall come into force on such date as may be appointed by order made by the Lord Chancellor or the Secretary of State, or by both acting jointly.

(3) Different dates may be appointed for different provisions of this Act in relation to different cases.

(4) The minor amendments set out in Schedule 12 shall have effect.

(5) The consequential amendments set out in Schedule 13 shall have effect.

(6) The transitional provisions and savings set out in Schedule 14 shall have effect.

(7) The repeals set out in Schedule 15 shall have effect.

(8) An order under subsection (2) may make such transitional provisions or savings as appear to the person making the order to be necessary or expedient in connection with the provisions brought into force by the order, including—
  (a) provisions adding to or modifying the provisions of Schedule 14; and
  (b) such adaptations—
        (i) of the provisions brought into force by the order; and
        (ii) of any provisions of this Act then in force,
     as appear to him necessary or expedient in consequence of the partial operation of this Act.

(9) The Lord Chancellor may by order make such amendments or repeals, in such enactments as may be specified in the order, as appear to him to be necessary or expedient in consequence of any provision of this Act.

(10) This Act shall, in its application to the Isles of Scilly, have effect subject to such exceptions, adaptations and modifications as the Secretary of State may by order prescribe.

(11) *(Application to Scotland)*

(12) *(Application to Northern Ireland)*

SCHEDULES

SCHEDULE 1

FINANCIAL PROVISION FOR CHILDREN

Orders for financial relief against parents

1—(1) On an application made by a parent or guardian of a child, or by any person in whose favour a residence order is in force with respect to a child, the court may—

    (a)   in the case of an application to the High Court or a county court, make one or more of the orders mentioned in sub-paragraph (2);

    (b)   in the case of an application to a magistrates' court, make one or both of the orders mentioned in paragraphs (a) and (c) of that sub-paragraph.

(2) The orders referred to in sub-paragraph (1) are—

    (a)   an order requiring either or both parents of a child—

        (i)   to make to the applicant for the benefit of the child; or

        (ii)   to make to the child himself,

    such periodical payments, for such term, as may be specified in the order;

    (b)   an order requiring either or both parents of a child—

        (i)   to secure to the applicant for the benefit of the child; or

        (ii)   to secure to the child himself,

    such periodical payments, for such term, as may be so specified;

    (c)   an order requiring either or both parents of a child—

        (i)   to pay to the applicant for the benefit of the child; or

        (ii)   to pay to the child himself,

    such lump sum as may be so specified;

    (d)   an order requiring a settlement to be made for the benefit of the child, and to the satisfaction of the court, of property—

        (i)   to which either parent is entitled (either in possession or in reversion); and

        (ii)   which is specified in the order;

    (e)   an order requiring either or both parents of a child—

        (i)   to transfer to the applicant, for the benefit of the child; or

        (ii)   to transfer to the child himself,

    such property to which the parent is, or the parents are, entitled (either in possession or in reversion) as may be specified in the order.

(3) The powers conferred by this paragraph may be exercised at any time.

(4) An order under sub-paragraph (2)(a) or (b) may be varied or discharged by a subsequent order made on the application of any person by or to whom payments were required to be made under the previous order.

(5) Where a court makes an order under this paragraph—

    (a)   it may at any time make a further such order under sub-paragraph (2)(a), (b) or (c) with respect to the child concerned if he has not reached the age of eighteen;

    (b)   it may not make more than one order under sub-paragraph (2)(d) or (e) against the same person in respect of the same child.

(6) On making, varying or discharging a residence order the court may exercise any of its powers under this Schedule even though no application has been made to it under this Schedule.

Orders for financial relief for persons over eighteen

2—(1) If, on an application by a person who has reached the age of eighteen, it appears to the court —

  (*a*) that the applicant is, will be or (if an order were made under this paragraph) would be receiving instruction at an educational establishment or undergoing training for a trade, profession or vocation, whether or not while in gainful employment; or

  (*b*) that there are special circumstances which justify the making of an order under this paragraph,

the court may make one or both of the orders mentioned in sub-paragraph (2).

(2) The orders are—

  (*a*) an order requiring either or both of the applicant's parents to pay to the applicant such periodical payments, for such term, as may be specified in the order;

  (*b*) an order requiring either or both of the applicant's parents to pay to the applicant such lump sum as may be so specified.

(3) An applicant may not be made under this paragraph by any person if, immediately before he reached the age of sixteen, a periodical payments order was in force with respect to him.

(4) No order shall be made under this paragraph at a time when the parents of the applicant are living with each other in the same household.

(5) An order under sub-paragraph (2)(*a*) may be varied or discharged by a subsequent order made on the application of any person by or to whom payments were required to be made under the previous order.

(6) In sub-paragraph (3) "periodical payments order" means an order made under—

  (*a*) this Schedule;

  (*b*) section 6(3) of the Family Law Reform Act 1969;

  (*c*) section 23 or 27 of the Matrimonial Causes Act 1973;

  (*d*) Part I of the Domestic Proceedings and Magistrates' Courts Act 1978, for the making or securing of periodical payments.

(7) The powers conferred by this paragraph shall be exercisable at any time.

(8) Where the court makes an order under this paragraph it may from time to time while that order remains in force make a further such order.

Duration of orders for financial relief

3—(1) The term to be specified in an order for periodical payments made under paragraph 1(2)(*a*) or (*b*) in favour of a child may begin with the date of the making of an application for the order in question or any later date but—

  (*a*) shall not in the first instance extend beyond the child's seventeenth birthday unless the court thinks it right in the circumstances of the case to specify a later date; and

  (*b*) shall not in any event extend beyond the child's eighteenth birthday.

(2) Paragraph (*b*) of sub-paragraph (1) shall not apply in the case of a child if it appears to the court that—

  (*a*)   the child is, or will be (if an order were made without complying with that paragraph) would be receiving instruction at an educational establishment or undergoing training for a trade, profession or vocation, whether or not while in gainful employment; or

  (*b*)   there are special circumstances which justify the making of an order without complying with that paragraph.

(3) An order for periodical payments made under paragraph 1(2)(*a*) or 2(2)(*a*) shall, notwithstanding anything in the order, cease to have effect on the death of the person liable to make payments under the order.

(4) Where an order is made under paragraph 1(2)(*a*) or (*b*) requiring periodical payments to be made or secured to the parent of a child, the order shall cease to have effect if—

  (*a*)   any parent making or securing the payments; and

  (*b*)   any parent to whom the payments are made or secured,

live together for a period of more than six months.

Matters to which court is to have regard in making orders for financial relief

4—(1) In deciding whether to exercise its powers under paragraph 1 or 2, and if so in what manner, the court shall have regard to all the circumstances including—

  (*a*)   the income, earning capacity, property and other financial resources which each person mentioned in sub-paragraph (3) has or is likely to have in the forseeable future;

  (*b*)   the financial needs, obligations and responsibilities which each person mentioned in sub-paragraph (3) has or is likely to have in the foreseeable future;

  (*c*)   the financial needs of the child;

  (*d*)   the income, earning capacity (if any), property and other financial resources of the child;

  (*e*)   any physical or mental disability of the child;

  (*f*)   the manner in which the child was being, or was expected to be, educated or trained.

(2) In deciding whether to exercise its powers under paragraph 1 against a person who is not the mother or father of the child, and if so in what manner, the court shall in addition have regard to—

  (*a*)   whether that person had assumed responsibility for the maintenance of the child, and, if so, the extent to which and basis on which he assumed that responsibility and the length of the period during which he met that responsibility;

  (*b*)   whether he did so knowing that the child was not his child;

  (*c*)   the liability of any other person to maintain the child.

(3) Where the court makes an order under paragraph 1 against a person who is not the father of the child, it shall record in the order that the order is made on the basis that the person against whom the order is made is not the child's father.

(4) The persons mentioned in sub-paragraph (1) are—
- (a)   in relation to a decision whether to exercise its powers under paragraph 1, any parent of the child;
- (b)   in relation to a decision whether to exercise its powers under paragraph 2, the mother and father of the child;
- (c)   the applicant for the order;
- (d)   any other person in whose favour the court proposes to make the order.

Provisions relating to lump sums

5—(1) Without prejudice to the generality of paragraph 1, an order under that paragraph for the payment of a lump sum may be made for the purpose of enabling any liabilities or expenses—
- (a)   incurred in connection with the birth of the child or in maintaining the child; and
- (b)   reasonably incurred before the making of the order,
to be met.

(2) The amount of any lump sum required to be paid by an order made by a magistrates' court under paragraph 1 or 2 shall not exceed £1000 or such larger amount as the Secretary of State may from time to time by order fix for the purposes of this sub-paragraph.

(3) The power of the court under paragraph 1 or 2 to vary or discharge an order for the making or securing of periodical payments by a parent shall include power to make an order under that provision for the payment of a lump sum by that parent.

(4) The amount of any lump sum which a parent may be required to pay by virtue of sub-paragraph (3) shall not, in the case of an order made by a magistrates' court, exceed the maximum amount that may at the time of the making of the order be required to be paid under sub-paragraph (2), but a magistrates' court may make an order for the payment of a lump sum not exceeding that amount even though the parent was required to pay a lump sum by a previous order under this Act.

(5) An order made under paragraph 1 or 2 for the payment of a lump sum may provide for the payment of that sum by instalments.

(6) Where the court provides for the payment of a lump sum by instalments the court, on an application made either by the person liable to pay or the person entitled to receive that sum, shall have power to vary that order by varying—
- (a)   the number of instalments payable;
- (b)   the amount of any instalment payable;
- (c)   the date on which any instalment becomes payable.

Variation etc of orders for periodical payments

6—(1) In exercising its powers under paragraph 1 or 2 to vary or discharge an order for the making or securing of periodical payments the court shall have regard to all the circumstances of the case, including any change in any of the matters to which the court was required to have regard when making the order.

(2) The power of the court under paragraph 1 or 2 to vary an order for the making

or securing of periodical payments shall include power to suspend any provision of the order temporarily and to revive any provision so suspended.

(3) Where on an application under paragraph 1 or 2 for the variation or discharge of an order for the making or securing of periodical payments the court varies the payments required to be made under that order, the court may provide that the payments as so varied shall be made from such date as the court may specify, not being earlier than the date of the making of the application.

(4) An application for the variation of an order made under paragraph 1 for the making or securing of periodical payments to or for the benefit of a child may, if the child has reached the age of sixteen, be made by the child himself.

(5) Where an order for the making or securing of periodical payments made under paragraph 1 ceases to have effect on the date on which the child reaches the age of sixteen, or at any time after that date but before or on the date on which he reaches the age of eighteen, the child may apply to the court which made the order for an order for its revival.

(6) If on such an application it appears to the court that—
    (*a*)   the child is, will be or (if an order were made under this sub-paragraph) would be receiving instruction at an educational establishment or undergoing training for a trade, profession or vocation, whether or not while in gainful employment; or
    (*b*)   there are special circumstances which justify the making of an order under this paragraph,
the court shall have power by order to revive the order from such date as the court may specify, not being earlier than the date of the making of the application.

(7) Any order which is revived by an order under sub-paragraph (5) may be varied or discharged under that provision, on the application of any person by whom or to whom payments are required to be made under the revived order.

(8) An order for the making or securing of periodical payments made under paragraph 1 may be varied or discharged, after the death of either parent, on the application of a guardian of the child concerned.

Variation of orders for secured periodical payments after death of parent

7—(1) Where the parent liable to make payments under a secured periodical payments order has died, the persons who may apply for the variation or discharge of the order shall include the personal representatives of the deceased parent.

(2) No application for the variation of the order shall, except with the permission of the court, be made after the end of the period of six months from the date on which representation in regard to the estate of that parent is first taken out.

(3) The personal representatives of a deceased person against whom a secured periodical payments order was made shall not be liable for having distributed any part of the estate of the deceased after the end of the period of six months referred to in sub-paragraph (2) on the ground that they ought to have taken into account the possibility that the court might permit an application for variation to be made after that period by the person entitled to payments under the order.

(4) Sub-paragraph (3) shall not prejudice any power to recover any part of the estate so distributed arising by virtue of the variation of an order in accordance with this paragraph.

(5) Where an application to vary a secured periodical payments order is made after the death of the parent liable to make payments under the order, the circumstances to which the court is required to have regard under paragraph 6(1) shall include the changed circumstances resulting from the death of the parent.

(6) In considering for the purposes of sub-paragraph (2) the question when representation was first taken out, a grant limited to settled land or to trust property shall be left out of account and a grant limited to real estate or to personal estate shall be left out of account unless a grant limited to the remainder of the estate has previously been made or is made at the same time.

(7) In this paragraph "secured periodical payments order" means an order for secured periodical payments under paragraph 1(2)(*b*).

Financial relief under other enactments

8—(1) This paragraph applies where a residence order is made with respect to a child at a time when there is in force an order ("the finacial relief order") made under any enactment other than this Act and requiring a person to contribute to the child's maintenance.

(2) Where this paragraph applies, the court may, on the application of—
  (*a*) any person required by the financial relief order to contribute to the child's maintenance; or
  (*b*) any person in whose favour a residence order with respect to the child is in force,
make an order revoking the financial relief order, or varying it by altering the amount of any sum payable under that order or by substituting the applicant for the person to whom any such sum is otherwise payable under that order.

Interim orders

9—(1) Where an application is made under paragraph 1 or 2 the court may, at any time before it disposes of the application, make an interim order—
  (*a*) requiring either or both parents to make such periodical payments, at such times and for such term as the court thinks fit; and
  (*b*) giving any direction which the court thinks fit.

(2) An interim order made under this paragraph may provide for payments to be made from such date as the court may specify, not being earlier than the date of the making of the application under paragraph 1 or 2.

(3) An interim order made under this paragraph shall cease to have effect when the application is disposed of or, if earlier, on the date specified for the purposes of this paragraph in the interim order.

(4) An interim order in which a date has been specified for the purposes of sub-paragraph (3) may be varied by substituting a later date.

Alteration of maintenance agreements

10—(1) In this paragraph and in paragraph 11 "maintenance agreement" means any agreement in writing made with respect to a child, whether before or after the commencement of this paragraph, which—

    (*a*)   is or was made between the father and mother of the child; and

    (*b*)   contains provision with respect to the making or securing of payments, or the disposition or use of any property, for the maintenance or education of the child,

and any such provisions are in this paragraph, and paragraph 11, referred to as "financial arrangements".

(2) Where a maintenance agreement is for the time being subsisting and each of the parties to the agreement is for the time being either domiciled or resident in England and Wales, then, either party may apply for an order under this paragraph.

(3) If the court to which the application is made is satisfied either—

    (*a*)   that, by reason of a change in the circumstances in the light of which any financial arrangements contained in the agreement were made (including a change foreseen by the parties when making the agreement), the agreement should be altered so as to make different financial arrangements; or

    (*b*)   that the agreement does not contain proper financial arrangements with respect to the child,

then that court may by order make such alterations in the agreement by varying or revoking any financial arrangements contained in it as may appear to it to be just having regard to all the circumstances.

(4) If the maintenance agreement is altered by an order under this paragraph, the agreement shall have effect thereafter as if the alteration had been made by agreement between the parties and for valuable consideration.

(5) Where a court decides to make an order under this paragraph altering the maintenance agreement—

    (*a*)   by inserting provision for the making or securing by one of the parties to the agreement of periodical payments for the maintenance of the child; or

    (*b*)   by increasing the rate of periodical payments required to be made or secured by one of the parties for the maintenance of the child,

then, in deciding the term for which under the agreement as altered by the order the payments or (as the case may be) the additional payments attributable to the increase are to be made or secured for the benefit of the child, the court shall apply the provisions of sub-paragraphs (1) and (2) of paragraph 3 as if the order were an order under paragraph 1(2)(*a*) or (*b*).

(6) A magistrates' court shall not entertain an application under sub-paragraph (2) unless both the parties to the agreement are resident in England and Wales and at least one of the parties is resident in the commission area (within the meaning of the Justices of the Peace Act 1979) for which the court is appointed, and shall not have power to make any order on such an application except—

    (*a*)   in a case where the agreement contains no provision for periodical payments by either of the parties, an order inserting provision for the making by one of the parties of periodical payments for the maintenance of the child;

    (*b*)   in a case where the agreement includes provision for the making by one of the parties of periodical payments, an order increasing or reducing the rate of, or terminating, any of those payments.

(7) For the avoidance of doubt it is hereby declared that nothing in this paragraph affects any power of a court before which any proceedings between the parties to a maintenance agreement are brought under any other enactment to make an order containing financial arrangements or any right of either party to apply for such an order in such proceedings.

11—(1) Where a maintenance agreement provides for the continuation, after the death of one of the parties, of payments for the maintenance of a child and that party dies domiciled in England and Wales, the surviving party or the personal representatives of the deceased party may apply to the High Court or a county court for an order under paragraph 10.

(2) If a maintenance agreement is altered by a court on an application under this paragraph, the agreement shall have effect thereafter as if the alteration had been made, immediately before the death, by agreement between the parties and for valuable consideration.

(3) An application under this paragraph shall not, except with leave of the High Court or a county court, be made after the end of the period of six months beginning with the day on which representation in regard to the estate of the deceased is first taken out.

(4) In considering for the purposes of sub-paragraph (3) the question when representation was first taken out, a grant limited to settled land or to trust property shall be left out of account and a grant limited to real estate or to personal estate shall be left out of account unless a grant limited to the remainder of the estate has previously been made or is made at the same time.

(5) A county court shall not entertain an application under this paragraph, or an application for leave to make an application under this paragraph, unless it would have jurisdiction to hear and determine proceedings for an order under section 2 of the Inheritance (Provision for Family and Dependants) Act 1975 in relation to the deceased's estate by virtue of section 25 of the County Courts Act 1984 (jurisdiction under the Act of 1975).

(6) The provisions of this paragraph shall not render the personal representatives of the deceased liable for having distributed any part of the estate of the deceased after the expiry of the period of six months referred to in sub-paragraph (3) on the ground that they ought to have taken into account the possibility that a court might grant leave for an application by virtue of this paragraph to be made by the surviving party after that period.

(7) Sub-paragraph (6) shall not prejudice any power to recover any part of the estate so distributed arising by virtue of the making of an order in pursuance of this paragraph.

Enforcement of orders for maintenance

12—(1) Any person for the time being under an obligation to make payments in pursuance of any order for the payment of money made by a magistrates' court under this Act shall give notice of any change of address to such person (if any) as may be specified in the order.

(2) Any person failing without reasonable excuse to give such a notice shall be guilty of an offence and liable on summary conviction to a fine not exceeding level 2 on the standard scale.

(3) An order for the payment of money made by a magistrates' court under this Act shall be enforceable as a magistrates' court maintenance order within the meaning of section 150(1) of the Magistrates' Courts Act 1980.

Direction for settlement of instrument by conveyancing counsel

13   Where the High Court of a county court decides to make an order under this Act for the securing of periodical payments or for the transfer or settlement of property, it may direct that the matter be referred to one of the conveyancing counsel of the court to settle a proper instrument to be executed by all necessary parties.

Financial provision for child resident in country outside England and Wales

14—(1) Where one parent of a child lives in England and Wales and the child lives outside England and Wales with—
  (*a*)   another parent of his;
  (*b*)   a guardian of his; or
  (*c*)   a person in whose favour a residence order is in force with respect to the child,
the court shall have power, on an application made by any of the persons mentioned in paragraphs (*a*) to (*c*), to make one or both of the orders mentioned in paragraph 1(2)(*a*) and (*b*) against the parent living in England and Wales.

(2) Any reference in this Act to the powers of the court under paragraph 1(2) or to an order made under paragraph 1(2) shall include a reference to the powers which the court has by virtue of sub-paragraph (1) or (as the case may be) to an order made by virtue of sub-paragraph (1).

Local authority contribution to child's maintenance

15—(1) Where a child lives, or is to live, with a person as the result of a residence order, a local authority may make contributions to that person towards the cost of the accommodation and maintenance of the child.

(2) Sub-paragraph (1) does not apply where the person with whom the child lives, or is to live, is a parent of the child or the husband or wife of a parent of the child.

Interpretation

16—(1) In this Schedule "child" includes, in any case where an application is made under paragraph 2 or 6 in relation to a person who has reached the age of eighteen, that person.

(2) In this Schedule except paragraphs 2 and 15, "parent" includes any party to a marriage (whether or not subsisting) in relation to whom the child concerned is a child of the family; and for this purpose any reference to either parent or both parents shall be construed as references to any parent of his and to all of his parents.

SCHEDULE 2

LOCAL AUTHORITY SUPPORT FOR CHILDREN AND FAMILIES

PART I

PROVISION OF SERVICES FOR FAMILIES

Identification of children in need and provision of information

1—(1) Every local authority shall take reasonable steps to identify the extent to which there are children in need within their area.

(2) Every local authority shall—
  (a) publish information—
      (i) about services provided by them under sections 17, 18, 20 and 24; and
      (ii) where they consider it appropriate, about the provision by others (including, in particular, voluntary organisations) of services which the authority have power to provide under those sections; and
  (b) take such steps as are reasonably practicable to ensure that those who might benefit from the services receive the information relevant to them.

Maintenance of a register of disabled children

2—(1) Every local authority shall open and maintain a register of disabled children within their area.

(2) The register may be kept by means of a computer.

Assessment of children's needs

3—Where it appears to a local authority that a child within their area is in need, the authority may assess his needs for the purposes of this Act at the same time as any assessment of his needs is made under—
  (a) the Chronically Sick and Disabled Persons Act 1970;
  (b) the Education Act 1981;
  (c) the Disabled Persons (Services, Consultation and Representation) Act 1986; or
  (d) any other enactment.

Prevention of neglect and abuse

4—(1) Every local authority shall take reasonable steps, through the provision of services under Part III of this Act, to prevent children within their area suffering ill-treatment or neglect.

(2) Where a local authority believe that a child who is at any time within their area—
  (a) is likely to suffer harm; but
  (b) lives or proposes to live in the area of another local authority they shall inform that other local authority.

(3) When informing that other local authority they shall specify—
  (a) the harm that they believe he is likely to suffer; and
  (b) (if they can) where the child lives or proposes to live.

Provision of accommodation in order to protect child

5—(1) Where—
   (a)   it appears to a local authority that a child who is living on particular premises
        is suffering, or is likely to suffer, ill treatment at the hands of another person
        who is living on those premises; and
   (b)   that other person proposes to move from the premises,
the authority may assist that other person to obtain alternative accommodation.

(2) Assistance given under this paragraph may be in cash.

(3) Subsections (7) to (9) of section 17 shall apply in relation to assistance given
under this paragraph as they apply in relation to assistance given under that section.

Provision for disabled children

6 Every local authority shall provide services designed—
   (a)   to minimise the effect on disabled chidren within their area of their disabilities;
        and
   (b)   to give such children the opportunity to lead lives which are as normal as
        possible.

Provision to reduce need for care proceedings etc.

7 Every local authority shall take reasonable steps designed—
   (a)   to reduce the need to bring—
       (i)   proceedings for care or supervision orders with respect to children
            within their area;
       (ii)   criminal proceedings against such children;
       (iii)   any family or other proceedings with respect to such children which
            might lead to them being placed in the authority's care; or
       (iv)   proceedings under the inherent jurisdiction of the High Court with
            respect to children;
   (b)   to encourage children within their area not to commit criminal offences;
        and
   (c)   to avoid the need for children within their area to be placed in secure
        accommodation.

Provision for children living with their families

8 Every local authority shall make such provision as they consider appropriate for
the following services to be available with respect to children in need within their
area while they are living with their families—
   (a)   advice, guidance and counselling;
   (b)   occupational, social, cultural or recreational activities;
   (c)   home help (which may include laundry facilities);
   (d)   facilities for, or assistance with, travelling to and from home for the purpose
        of taking advantage of any other service provided under this Act or of any
        similar service;
   (e)   assistance to enable the child concerned and his family to have a holiday.

Family centres

9—(1) Every local authority shall provide such family centres as they consider appropriate in relation to children within their area.

(2) "Family centre" means a centre at which any of the persons mentioned in sub-paragraph (3) may—
  (a)   attend for occupational, social, cultural or recreational activities;
  (b)   attend for advice, guidance or counselling; or
  (c)   be provided with accommodation while he is receiving advice, guidance or counselling.

(3) The persons are—
  (a)   a child;
  (b)   his parents;
  (c)   any person who is not a parent of his but who has parental responsibility for him;
  (d)   any other person who is looking after him.

Maintenance of the family home

10   Every local authority shall take such steps as are reasonably practicable, where any child within their area who is in need and whom they are not looking after is living apart from his family—
  (a)   to enable him to live with his family; or
  (b)   to promote contact between him and his family,
if, in their opinion, it is necessary to do so in order to safeguard or promote his welfare.

Duty to consider racial groups to which children in need belong

11   Every local authority shall, in making any arrangements—
  (a)   for the provision of day care within their area; or
  (b)   designed to encourage persons to act as local authority foster parents,
have regard to the different racial groups to which children within their area who are in need belong.

PART II

CHILDREN LOOKED AFTER BY LOCAL AUTHORITIES

Regulations as to placing of children with local authority foster parents

12   Regulations under section 23(2)(a) may, in particular, make provision—
  (a)   with regard to the welfare of children placed with local authority foster parents;
  (b)   as to the arrangements to be made by local authorities in connection with the health and education of such children;
  (c)   as to the records to be kept by local authorities;
  (d)   for securing that a child is not placed with a local authority foster parent unless that person is for the time being approved as a local authority foster parent by such local authority as may be prescribed;
  (e)   for securing that where possible the local authority foster parent with whom a child is to be placed is—
      (i)   of the same religious persuasion as the child; or

(ii)   gives an undertaking that the child will be brought up in that religious persuasion;

(*f*)   for securing that children placed with local authority foster parents, and the premises in which they are accommodated, will be supervised and inspected by a local authority and that the children will be removed from those premises if their welfare appears to require it;

(*g*)   as to the circumstances in which local authorities may make arrangements for duties imposed on them by the regulations to be discharged, on their behalf.

Regulations as to arrangements under section 23(2)(f)

13   Regulations under section 23(2)(*f*) may, in particular, make provision as to—

(*a*)   the persons to be notified of any proposed arrangements;

(*b*)   the opportunities such persons are to have to make representations in relation to the arrangements proposed;

(*c*)   the persons to be notified of any proposed changes in arrangements;

(*d*)   the records to be kept by local authorities;

(*e*)   the supervision by local authorities of any arrangements made.

Regulations as to conditions under which child in care is allowed to live with parent, etc.

14   Regulations under section 23(5) may, in particular, impose requirements on a local authority as to—

(*a*)   the making of any decision by a local authority to allow a child to live with any person falling within section 23(4) (including requirements as to those who must be consulted before the decision is made, and those who must be notified when it has been made);

(*b*)   the supervision or medical examination of the child concerned;

(*c*)   the removal of the child, in such circumstances as may be prescribed, from the care of the person with whom he has been allowed to live.

Promotion and maintenance of contact between child and family

15—(1) Where a child is being looked after by a local authority, the authority shall, unless it is not reasonably practicable or consistent with his welfare, endeavour to promote contact between the child and—

(*a*)   his parents;

(*b*)   any person who is not a parent of his but who has parental responsibility for him; and

(*c*)   any relative, friend or other person connected with him.

(2) Where a child is being looked after by a local authority—

(*a*)   the authority shall take such steps as are reasonably practicable to secure that—

(i)   his parents; and

(ii)   any person who is not a parent of his but who has parental responsibility for him,

are kept informed of where he is being accommodated; and

(b) every such person shall secure that the authority are kept informed of his or her address.

(3) Where a local authority ("the receiving authority") take over the provision of accommodation for a child from another local authority ("the transferring authority") under section 20(2)—
 (a) the receiving authority shall (where reasonably practicable) inform—
  (i) the child's parents; and
  (ii) any person who is not a parent of his but who has parental responsibility for him;
 (b) sub-paragraph (2)(a) shall apply to the transferring authority, as well as the receiving authority, until at least one such person has been informed of the change; and
 (c) sub-paragraph (2)(b) shall not require any person to inform the receiving authority of his address until he has been so informed.

(4) Nothing in this paragraph requires a local authority to inform any person of the whereabouts of a child if—
 (a) the child is in the care of the authority; and
 (b) the authority has reasonable cause to believe that informing the person would prejudice the child's welfare.

(5) Any person who fails (without reasonable excuse) to comply with sub-paragraph (2)(b) shall be guilty of an offence and liable on summary conviction to a fine not exceeding level 2 on the standard scale.

(6) It shall be a defence in any proceedings under sub-paragraph (5) to prove that the defendant was residing at the same address as another person who was the child's parent or had parental responsibility for the child and had reasonable cause to believe that the other person had informed the appropriate authority that both of them were residing at that address.

Visits to, or by children: expenses

16—(1) This paragraph applies where—
 (a) a child is being looked after by a local authority; and
 (b) the conditions mentioned in sub-paragraph (3) are satisfied.

(2) The authority may—
 (a) make payments to—
  (i) a parent of the child;
  (ii) any person who is not a parent of his but who has parental responsibility for him; or
  (iii) any relative, friend or other person connected with him,
  in respect of travelling, subsistence or other expenses incurred by that person in visiting the child; or
 (b) make payments to the child, or to any person on his behalf, in respect of travelling, subsistence or other expenses incurred by or on behalf of the child in his visiting—
  (i) a parent of his;
  (ii) any person who has parental responsibility for him; or
  (iii) any relative, friend or other person connected with him.

(3) The conditions are that—
- (a)   it appears to the authority that the visit in question could not otherwise be made without undue financial hardship; and
- (b)   the circumstances warrant the making of the payments.

Appointment of visitor for child who is not being visited

17—(1) Where it appears to a local authority in relation to any child that they are looking after that—
- (a)   communication between the child and—
  - (i)   a parent of his, or
  - (ii)   any person who is not a parent of his but who has parental responsibility for him,

    has been infrequent; or
- (b)   he has not visited or been visited by (or lived with) any such person during the preceding twelve months,

and that it would be in the child's best interests for an independent person to be appointed to be his visitor for the purposes of this paragraph, they shall appoint such a visitor.

(2) A person so appointed shall—
- (a)   have the duty of visiting, advising and befriending the child; and
- (b)   be entitled to recover from the authority who appointed him any reasonable expenses incurred by him for the purposes of his functions under this paragraph.

(3) A person's appointment as a visitor in pursuance of this paragraph shall be determined if—
- (a)   he gives notice in writing to the authority who appointed him that he resigns the appointment; or
- (b)   the authority give him notice in writing that they have terminated it.

(4) The determination of such an appointment shall not prejudice any duty under this paragraph to make a further appointment.

(5) Where a local authority propose to appoint a visitor for a child under this paragraph, the appointment shall not be made if—
- (a)   the child objects to it; and
- (b)   the authority are satisfied that he has sufficient understanding to make an informed decision.

(6) Where a visitor has been appointed for a child under this paragraph, the local authority shall determine the appointment if—
- (a)   the child objects to its continuing; and
- (b)   the authority are satisfied that he has sufficient understanding to make an informed decision.

(7)   The Secretary of State may make regulations as to the circumstances in which a person appointed as a visitor under this paragraph is to be regarded as independent of the local authority appointing him.

Power to guarantee apprenticeship deeds etc.

18—(1) While a child is being looked after by a local authority, or is a person qualifying for advice and assistance, the authority may undertake any obligation by way of guarantee under any deed of apprenticeship or articles of clerkship which he enters into.

(2) Where a local authority have undertaken any such obligation under any deed or articles they may at any time (whether or not they are still looking after the person concerned) undertake the like obligation under any supplemental deed or articles.

Arrangements to assist children to live abroad

19—(1) A local authority may only arrange for, or assist in arranging for, any child in their care to live outside England and Wales with the approval of the court.

(2) A local authority may, with the approval of every person who has parental responsibility for the child arrange for, or assist in arranging for, any other child looked after by them to live outside England and Wales.

(3) The court shall not give its approval under sub-paragraph (1) unless it is satisfied that—
- (a)   living outside England and Wales would be in the child's best interests;
- (b)   suitable arrangements have been, or will be, made for his reception and welfare in the country in which he will live;
- (c)   the child has consented to living in that country; and
- (d)   every person who has parental responsibility for the child has consented to his living in that country.

(4) Where the court is satisfied that the child does not have sufficient understanding to give or withhold his consent, it may disregard sub-paragraph (3)(c) and give its approval if the child is to live in the country concerned with a parent, guardian, or other suitable person.

(5) Where a person whose consent is required by sub-paragraph (3)(d) fails to give his consent, the court may disregard that provision and give its approval if it is satisfied that that person—
- (a)   cannot be found;
- (b)   is incapable of consenting; or
- (c)   is withholding his consent unreasonably.

(6) Section 56 of the Adoption Act 1976 (which requires authority for the taking or sending abroad for adoption of a child who is a British subject) shall not apply in the case of any child who is to live outside England and Wales with the approval of the court given under this paragraph.

(7) Where a court decides to give its approval under this paragraph it may order that its decision is not to have effect during the appeal period.

(8) In sub-paragraph (7) "the appeal period" means—
- (a)   where an appeal is made against the decision, the period between the making of the decision and the determination of the appeal; and
- (b)   otherwise, the period during which an appeal may be made against the decision.

Death of children being looked after by local authorities

20—(1) If a child who is being looked after by a local authority dies, the authority—
- (a)   shall notify the Secretary of State;
- (b)   shall, so far as is reasonably practicable, notify the child's parents and every

person who is not a parent of his but who has parental responsibility for him;

(c)   may, with the consent (so far as it is reasonably practicable to obtain it) of every person who has parental responsibility for the child, arrange for the child's body to be buried or cremated; and

(d)   may, if the conditions mentioned in sub-paragraph (2) are satisfied, make payments to any person who has parental responsibility for the child, or any relative, friend or other person connected with the child, in respect if travelling, subsistence or other expenses incurred by that person in attending the child's funeral.

(2) The conditions are that—

(a)   it appears to the authority that the person concerned could not otherwise attend the child's funeral without undue financial hardship; and

(b)   that the circumstances warrant the making of the payments.

(3) Sub-paragraph (1) does not authorise cremation where it does not accord with the practice of the child's religious persuasion.

(4) Where a local authority have exercised their power under sub-paragraph (1)(c) with respect to a child who was under sixteen when he died, they may recover from any parent of the child any expenses incurred by them.

(5) Any sums so recoverable shall, without prejudice to any other method of recovery, be recoverable summarily as a civil debt.

(6) Nothing in this paragraph affects any enactment regulating or authorising the burial, cremation or anatomical examination of the body of a deceased person.

PART III

CONTRIBUTIONS TOWARDS MAINTENANCE OF CHILDREN
LOOKED AFTER BY LOCAL AUTHORITIES

Liability to contribute

21—(1) Where a local authority are looking after a child (other than in the cases mentioned in sub-paragraph (7)) they shall consider whether they should recover contributions towards the child's maintenance from any person liable to contribute ("a contributor").

(2) An authority may only recover contributions from a contributor if they consider it reasonable to do so.

(3) The persons liable to contribute are—

(a)   where the child is under sixteen, each of his parents;

(b)   where he has reached the age of sixteen, the child himself.

(4) A parent is not liable to contribute during any period when he is in receipt of income support or family credit under the Social Security Act 1986.

(5) A person is not liable to contribute towards the maintenance of a child in the

care of a local authority in respect of any period during which the child is allowed by the authority (under section 23(5)) to live with a parent of his.

(6) A contributor is not obliged to make any contribution towards a child's maintenance except as agreed or determined in accordance with this Part of this Schedule.

(7) The cases are where the child is looked after by a local authority under—
    (*a*)   section 21;
    (*b*)   an interim care order;
    (*c*)   secton 53 of the Children and Young Persons Act 1933.

Agreed contributions

22—(1) Contributions towards a child's maintenance may only be recovered if the local authority have served a notice ("a contribution notice") on the contributor specifying—
    (*a*)   the weekly sum which they consider that he should contribute; and
    (*b*)   arrangements for payment.

(2) The contribution notice must be in writing and dated.

(3) Arrangements for payment shall, in particular, include—
    (*a*)   the date on which liability to contribute begins (which must not be earlier than the date of the notice);
    (*b*)   the date on which liability under the notice will end (if the child has not before that date ceased to be looked after by the authority); and
    (*c*)   the date on which the first payment is to be made.

(4) The authority may specify in a contribution notice a weekly sum which is a standard contribution determined by them for all children looked after by them.

(5) The authority may not specify in a contribution notice a weekly sum greater than that which they consider—
    (*a*)   they would normally be prepared to pay if they had placed a similar child with local authority foster parents; and
    (*b*)   it is reasonably practicable for the contributor to pay (having regard to his means).

(6) An authority may at any time withdraw a contribution notice (without prejudice to their power to serve another).

(7) Where the authority and the contributor agree—
    (*a*)   the sum which the contributor is to contribute; and
    (*b*)   arrangements for payment,
(whether as specified in the contribution notice or otherwise) and the contributor notifies the authority in writing that he so agrees, the authority may recover summarily as a civil debt any contribution which is overdue and unpaid.

(8) A contributor may, by serving a notice in writing on the authority, withdraw his agreement in relation to any period of liability falling after the date of service of the notice.

(9) Sub-paragraph (7) is without prejudice to any other method of recovery.

Contribution orders

23—(1) Where a contributor has been served with a contribution notice and has—
- (a) failed to reach any agreement with the local authority as mentioned in paragraph 22(7) within the period of one month beginning with the day on which the contribution notice was served; or
- (b) served a notice under paragraph 22(8) withdrawing his agreement,

the authority may apply to the court for an order under this paragraph.

(2) On such an application the court may make an order ("a contribution order") requiring the contributor to contribute a weekly sum towards the child's maintenance in accordance with arrangements for payment specified by the court.

(3) A contribution order—
- (a) shall not specify a weekly sum greater than that specified in the contribution notice; and
- (b) shall be made with due regard to the contributor's means.

(4) A contribution order shall not—
- (a) take effect before the date specified in the contribution notice; or
- (b) have effect while the contributor is not liable to contribute (by virtue of paragraph 21); or
- (c) remain in force after the child has ceased to be looked after by the authority who obtained the order.

(5) An authority may not apply to the court under sub-paragraph (1) in relation to a contribution notice which they have withdrawn.

(6) Where—
- (a) a contribution order is in force;
- (b) the authority serve another contribution notice; and
- (c) the contributor and the authority reach an agreement under paragraph 22(7) in respect of that other contribution notice,

the effect of the agreement shall be to discharge the order from the date on which it is agreed that the agreement shall take effect.

(7) Where an agreement is reached under sub-paragraph (6) the authority shall notify the court—
- (a) of the agreement; and
- (b) of the date on which it took effect.

(8) A contribution order may be varied or revoked on the application of the contributor or the authority.

(9) In proceedings for the varition of a contribution order, the authority shall specify—
- (a) the weekly sum which, having regard to paragraph 22, they propose that the contributor should contribute under the order as varied; and
- (b) the proposed arrangements for payment.

(10) Where a contribution order is varied, the order—
- (a) shall not specify a weekly sum greater than that specified by the authority in the proceedings for variation; and
- (b) shall be made with due regard to the contributor's means.

(11) An appeal shall lie in accordance with rules of court from any order made under this paragraph.

Enforcement of contribution orders etc.

24—(1) A contribution order made by a magistrates' court shall be enforceable as a magistrates' court maintenance order (within the meaning of section 150(1) of the Magistrates' Courts Act 1980).

(2) Where a contributor has agreed, or has been ordered, to make contributions to a local authority, any other local authority within whose area the contributor is for the time being living may—

- (a)   at the request of the local authority who served the contribution notice; and
- (b)   subject to agreement as to any sum to be deducted in respect of services rendered,

collect from the contributor any contributions due on behalf of the authority who served the notice.

(3) In sub-paragraph (2) the reference to any other local authority includes a reference to—

- (a)   a local authority within the meaning of section 1(2) of the Social Work (Scotland) Act 1968; and
- (b)   a Health and Social Services Board established under Article 16 of the Health and Personal Social Services (Northern Ireland) Order 1972.

(4) The power to collect sums under sub-paragraph (2) includes the power to—

- (a)   receive and give a discharge for any contributions due; and
- (b)   (if necessary) enforce payment of any contributions,

even though those contributions may have fallen due at a time when the contributor was living elsewhere.

(5) Any contributions collected under sub-paragraph (2) shall be paid (subject to any agreed deduction) to the local authority who served the contribution notice.

(6) In any proceedings under this paragraph, a document which purports to be—

- (a)   a copy of an order made by a court under or by virtue of paragraph 23; and
- (b)   certified as a true copy by the clerk of the court,

shall be evidence of the order.

(7) In any proceedings under this paragraph, a certificate which—

- (a)   purports to be signed by the clerk or some other duly authorised officer of the local authority who obtained the contribution order; and
- (b)   states that any sum due to the authority under the order is overdue and unpaid,

shall be evidence that the sum is overdue and unpaid.

Regulations

25   The Secretary of State may make regulations—

- (a)   as to the considerations which a local authority must take into account in deciding—
  - (i)   whether it is reasonable to recover contributions; and
  - (ii)   what the arrangements for payment should be;
- (b)   as to the procedures they must follow in reaching agreements with—
  - (i)   contributors (under paragraph 22 and 23); and
  - (ii)   any other local authority (under paragraph 23).

SCHEDULE 3

SUPERVISION ORDERS

PART I

GENERAL

Meaning of "responsible person"

1 In this Schedule, "the responsible person", in relation to a supervised child, means—
- (*a*) any person who has parental responsibility for the child; and
- (*b*) any other person with whom the child is living.

Power of supervisor to give directions to supervised child

2—(1) A supervision order may require the supervised child to comply with any directions given from time to time by the supervisor which require him to do all or any of the following things—
- (*a*) to live at a place or places specified in the directions for a period or periods so specified;
- (*b*) to present himself to a person or persons specified in the directions at a place or places and on a day or days so specified;
- (*c*) to participate in activities specified in the directions on a day or days so specified.

(2) It shall be for the supervisor to decide whether, and to what extent, he exercises his power to give directions and to decide the form of any directions which he gives.

(3) Sub-paragraph (1) does not confer on a supervisor power to give directions in respect of any medical or psychiatric examination or treatment (which are matters dealt with in paragraphs 4 and 5).

Imposition of obligations on responsible person

3—(1) With the consent of any responsible person, a supervision order may include a requirement—
- (*a*) that he take all reasonable steps to ensure that the supervised child complies with any direction given by the supervisor under paragraph 2;
- (*b*) that he take all reasonable steps to ensure that the supervised child complies with any requirement included in the order under paragraph 4 or 5;
- (*c*) that he comply with any directions given by the supervisor requiring him to attend at a place specified in the directions for the purpose of taking part in activities so specified.

(2) A direction given under sub-paragraph (1)(*c*) may specify the time at which the responsible person is to attend and whether or not the supervised child is required to attend with him.

(3) A supervision order may require any person who is a responsible person in relation to the supervised child to keep the supervisor informed of his address, if it differs from the child's.

Psychiatric and medical examinations

4—(1) A supervision order may require the supervised child—

    (*a*)   to submit to a medical or psychiatric examination; or

    (*b*)   to submit to any such examination from time to time as directed by the supervisor.

(2) Any such examination shall be required to be conducted—

    (*a*)   by, or under the direction of, such registered medical practitioner as may be specified in the order;

    (*b*)   at a place specified in the order and at which the supervised child is to attend as a non-resident patient; or

    (*c*)   at—

        (i)   a health service hospital; or

        (ii)   in the case of a psychiatric examination, a hospital or mental nursing home,

    at which the supervised child is, or is to attend as, a resident patient.

(3) A requirement of a kind mentioned in sub-paragraph (2)(*c*) shall not be included unless the court is satisfied, on the evidence of a registered medical practitioner, that—

    (*a*)   the child may be suffering from a physical or mental condition that requires, and may be susceptible to, treatment; and

    (*b*)   a period as a resident patient is necessary if the examination is to be carried out properly.

(4) No court shall include a requirement under this paragraph in a supervision order unless it is satisfied that—

    (*a*)   where the child has sufficient understanding to make an informed decision, he consents to its inclusion; and

    (*b*)   satisfactory arrangements have been, or can be, made for the examination.

Psychiatric and medical treatment

5—(1) Where a court which proposes to make or vary a supervision order is satisfied, on the evidence of a registered medical practitioner approved for the purposes of section 12 of the Mental Health Act 1983, that the mental condition of the supervised child—

    (*a*)   is such as requires, and may be susceptible to, treatment; but

    (*b*)   is not such as to warrant his detention in pursuance of a hospital order under Part III of that Act,

the court may include in the order a requirement that the supervised child shall, for a period specified in the order, submit to such treatment as is so specified.

(2) The treatment specified in accordance with sub-paragraph (1) must be—

    (*a*)   by, or under the direction of, such registered medical practitioner as may be specified in the order;

    (*b*)   as a non-resident patient at such a place as may be so specified; or

    (*c*)   as a resident patient in a hospital or mental nursing home.

(3) Where a court which proposes to make or vary a supervision order is satisfied, on the evidence of a registered medical practitioner, that the physical condition of the supervised child is such as requires, and may be susceptible to, treatment, the

court may include in the order a requirement that the supervised child shall, for a period specified in the order, submit to such treatment as is so specified.

(4) The treatment specified in accordance with sub-paragraph (3) must be—
- (a)   by, or under the direction of, such registered medical practitioner as may be specified in the order;
- (b)   as a non-patient at such place as may be so specified; or
- (c)   as a resident patient in a health service hospital.

(5) No court shall include a requirement under this paragraph in a supervision order unless it is satisfied—
- (a)   where the child has sufficient understanding to make an informed decision, that he consents to its inclusion; and
- (b)   that satisfactory arrangements have been, or can be, made for the treatment.

(6) If a medical practitioner by whom or under whose direction a supervised person is being treated in pursuance of a requirement included in a supervision order by virtue of this paragraph is unwilling to continue to treat or direct the treatment of the supervised child or is of the opinion that—
- (a)   the treatment should be continued beyond the period specified in the order;
- (b)   the supervised child needs different treatment;
- (c)   he is not susceptible to treatment; or
- (d)   he does not require further treatment,

the practitioner shall make a report in writing to that effect to the supervisor.

(7) On receiving a report under this paragraph the supervisor shall refer it to the court, and on such a reference the court may make an order cancelling or varying the requirement.

Part II

Miscellaneous

Life of supervision order

6—(1) Subject to sub-paragraph (2) and section 91, a supervision order shall cease to have effect at the end of the period of one year beginning with the date on which it was made.

(2) A supervision order shall also cease to have effect if an event mentioned in section 25(1)(a) or (b) of the Child Abduction and Custody Act 1985 (termination of existing orders) occurs with respect to the child.

(3) Where the supervisor applies to the court to extend, or further extend, a supervision order the court may extend the order for such period as it may specify.

(4) A supervision order may not be extended so as to run beyond the end of the period of three years beginning with the date on which it was made.

Limited life of directions

7—(1) The total number of days in respect of which a supervised child or (as the case may be) responsible person may be required to comply with directions given under paragraph 2 or 3 shall not exceed 90 or such lesser number (if any) as the supervision order may specify.

(2) For the purpose of calculating that total number of days, the supervisor may disregard any day in respect of which directions previously given in pursuance of the order were not complied with.

Information to be given to supervisor etc.

8—(1) A supervision order may require the supervised child—
  (a)   to keep the supervisor informed of any change in his address; and
  (b)   to allow the supervisor to visit him at the place where he is living.

(2) The responsible person in relation to any child with respect to whom a supervision order is made shall—
  (a)   if asked by the supervisor, inform him of the child's address (if it is known to him); and
  (b)   if he is living with the child, allow the supervisor reasonable contact with the child.

Selection of supervisor

9—(1) A supervision order shall not designate a local authority as the supervisor unless—
  (a)   the authority agree; or
  (b)   the supervised child lives or will live within their area.

(2) A court shall not place a child under the supervision of a probation officer unless—
  (a)   the appropriate authority so request; and
  (b)   a probation officer is already exercising or has exercised, in relation to another member of the household to which the child belongs, duties imposed on probation officers—
    (i)   by paragraph 8 of Schedule 3 to the Powers of Criminal Courts Act 1973; or
    (ii)   by rules under paragraph 18(1)(b) of that Schedule.

(3) In sub-paragraph (2) "the appropriate authority" means the local authority appearing to the court to be the authority in whose area the supervised child lives or will live.

(4) Where a supervision order places a person under the supervision of a probation officer, the officer shall be selected in accordance with arrangements made by the probation committee for the area in question.

(5) If the selected probation officer is unable to carry out his duties, or dies, another probation officer shall be selected in the same manner.

Effect of supervision order on earlier orders

10   The making of a supervision order with respect to any child brings to an end
any earlier care or supervision order which—
    (*a*)   was made with respect to that child; and
    (*b*)   would otherwise continue in force.

Local authority functions and expenditure

11—(1) The Secretary of State may make regulations with respect to the exercise
by a local authority of their functions where a child has been placed under their
supervision by a supervision order.

(2) Where a supervision order requires compliance with directions given by virtue
of this section, any expenditure incurred by the supervisor for the purposes of the
directions shall be defrayed by the local authority designated in the order.

Part III

Education Supervision Orders

Effect of orders

12—(1) Where an education supervision order is in force with respect to a child,
it shall be the duty of the supervisor—
    (*a*)   to advise, assist and befriend, and give directions to—
        (i)   the supervised child; and
        (ii)   his parents;
    in such a way as will, in the opinion of the supervisor, secure that he is
    properly educated;
    (*b*)   where any such direction given to—
        (i)   the supervised child; or
        (ii)   a parent of his,
    have not been complied with, to consider what further steps to take in the
    exercise of the supervisor's powers under this Act.

(2) Before giving any directions under sub-paragraph (1) the supervisor shall, so
far as is reasonably practicable, ascertain the wishes and feelings of—
    (*a*)   the child; and
    (*b*)   his parents;
including, in particular, their wishes as to the place at which the child should be
educated.

(3) When settling the terms of any such directions, the supervisor shall give due
consideration—
    (*a*)   having regard to the child's age and understanding, to such wishes and feelings
    of his as the supervisor has been able to ascertain; and
    (*b*)   to such wishes and feelings of the child's parents as he has been able to
    ascertain.

(4) Directions may be given under this paragraph at any time while the education
supervision order is in force.

13—(1) Where an education supervision order is in force with respect to a child,
the duties of the child's parents under sections 36 and 39 of the Education Act
1944 (duty to secure education of children and to secure regular attendance of registered

pupils) shall be superseded by their duty to comply with any directions in force under the education supervision order.

(2) Where an education supervision order is made with respect to a child—
   (*a*) any school attendance order—
      (i)   made under section 37 of the Act of 1944 with respect to the child; and
      (ii)   in force immediately before the making of the education supervision order,
      shall cease to have effect; and
   (*b*) while the education supervision order remains in force, the following provisions shall not apply with respect to the child—
      (i)   section 37 of that Act (school attendance orders);
      (ii)   section 76 of that Act (pupils to be educated in accordance with wishes of their parents);
      (iii) sections 6 and 7 of the Education Act 1980 (parental preference and appeals against admission decisions);
   (*c*) a supervision order made with respect to the child in criminal proceedings, while the education supervision order is in force, may not include an education requirement of the kind which could otherwise be included under section 12C of the Children and Young Persons Act 1969;
   (*d*) any education requirement of a kind mentioned in paragraph (*c*), which was in force with respect to the child immediately before the making of the education supervision order, shall cease to have effect.

Effect where child also subject to supervision order

14—(1) This paragraph applies where an education supervision order and a supervision order, or order under section 7(7)(*b*) of the Children and Young Persons Act 1969, are in force at the same time with respect to the same child.

(2) Any failure to comply with a direction given by the supervisor under the education supervision order shall be disregarded if it would not have been reasonably practicable to comply with it without failing to comply with a direction given under the other order.

Duration of orders

15—(1) An education supervision order shall have effect for a period of one year, beginning with the date on which it is made.

(2) An education supervision order shall not expire if, before it would otherwise have expired, the court has (on the application of the authority in whose favour the order was made) extended the period during which it is in force.

(3) Such an application may not be made earlier than three months before the date on which the order would otherwise expire.

(4) The period during which an education supervision order is in force may be extended under sub-paragraph (2) on more than one occasion.

(5) No one extension may be for a period of more than three years.

(6) An education supervision order shall cease to have effect on—

(*a*)   the child's ceasing to be of compulsory school age; or
(*b*)   the making of a care order with respect to the child;
and sub-paragraphs (1) to (4) are subject to this sub-paragraph.

Information to be given to supervisor etc.

16—(1) An education supervision order may require the child—
(*a*)   to keep the supervisor informed of any change in his address; and
(*b*)   to allow the supervisor to visit him at the place where he is living.

(2) A person who is the parent of a child with respect to whom an education supervision order has been made shall—
(*a*)   if asked by the supervisor, inform him of the child's address (if it is known to him); and
(*b*)   if he is living with the child, allow the supervisor reasonable contact with the child.

Discharge of orders

17—(1) The court may discharge any education supervision order on the application of—
(*a*)   the child concerned;
(*b*)   a parent of his; or
(*c*)   the local education authority concerned.

(2) On discharging an education supervision order, the court may direct the local authority within whose area the child lives, or will live, to investigate the circumstances of the child.

Offences

18—(1) If a parent of a child with respect to whom an education supervision order is in force persistently fails to comply with a direction given under the order he shall be guilty of an offence.

(2) It shall be a defence for any person charged with such an offence to prove that—
(*a*)   he took all reasonable steps to ensure that the direction was complied with;
(*b*)   the direction was unreasonable; or
(*c*)   he had complied with—
(i)   a requirement included in a supervision order made with respect to the child; or
(ii)   directions given under such a requirement,
and that it was not reasonably practicable to comply both with the direction and with the requirement or directions mentioned in this paragraph.

(3) A person guilty of an offence under this paragraph whall be liable on summary conviction to a fine not exceeding level 3 on the standard scale.

Persistent failure of child to comply with directions

19—(1) Where a child with respect to whom an education supervision order is in force persistently fails to comply with any direction given under the order, the local education authority concerned shall notify the appropriate local authority.

(2) Where a local authority have been notified under sub-paragraph (1) they shall investigate the circumstances of the child.

(3) In this paragraph "the appropriate local authority" has the same meaning as in section 36.

Miscellaneous

20   The Secretary of State may by regulations make provision modifying, or displacing, the provisions of any enactment about education in relation to any child with respect to whom an education supervision order is in force to such extent as appears to the Secretary of State to be necessary or expedient in consequence of the provision made by this Act with respect to such orders.

Interpretation

21   In this part of this Schedule "parent" has the same meaning as in the Education Act 1944 (as amended by Schedule 13).

SCHEDULE 4

MANAGEMENT AND CONDUCT OF COMMUNITY HOMES

PART I

INSTRUMENTS OF MANAGEMENT

Instruments of management for controlled and assisted community homes

1—(1) The Secretary of State may by order make an instrument of management providing for the constitution of a body of managers for any voluntary home which is designated as a controlled or assisted community home.

(2) Sub-paragraph (3) applies where two or more voluntary homes are designated as controlled community homes or as assisted community homes.

(3) If—
  (a) those homes are, or are to be, provided by the same voluntary organisations; and
  (b) the same local authority is to be represented on the body of managers for those homes,
a single instrument of management may be made by the Secretary of State under this paragraph constituting one body of managers for those homes or for any two or more of them.

(4) The number of persons who, in accordance with an instrument of management, constitute the body of managers for a voluntary home shall be such number (which must be a multiple of three) as may be specified in the instrument.

(5) The instrument shall provide that the local authority specified in the instrument shall appoint—
  (a) in the case of a voluntary home which is designated as a controlled community home, two-thirds of the managers; and
  (b) in the case of a voluntary home which is designated as an assisted community home, one-third of them.

(6) An instrument of management shall provide that the foundation managers shall be appointed, in such manner and by such persons as may be specified in the instrument—

   (a)   so as to represent the interests of the voluntary organisation by which the home is, or is to be, provided; and

   (b)   for the purpose of securing that—

         (i)   so far as is practicable, the character of the home as a voluntary home will be preserved; and

         (ii)   subject to paragraph 2(3), the terms of any trust deed relating to the home are observed.

(7) An instrument of management shall come into force on such date as it may specify.

(8) If an instrument of management is in force in relation to a voluntary home the home shall be (and be known as) a controlled community home or an assisted community home, according to its designation.

(9) In this paragraph—

"foundation managers", in relation to a voluntary home, means those of the managers of the home who are not appointed by a local authority in accordance with sub-paragraph (5); and

"designated" means designated in accordance with section 53.

2—(1) An instrument of management shall contain such provisions as the Secretary of State considers appropriate.

(2) Nothing in the instrument of management shall affect the purposes for which the premises comprising the home are held.

(3) Without prejudice to the generality of sub-paragraph (1), an instrument of management may contain provisions—

   (a)   specifying the nature and purpose of the home (or each of the homes) to which it relates;

   (b)   requiring a specified number or proportion of the places in that home (or those homes) to be made available to local authorities and to any other body specified in the instrument; and

   (c)   relating to the management of that home (or those homes) and the charging of fees with respect to—

         (i)   children placed there; or

         (ii)   places made available to any local authority or other body.

(4) Subject to sub-paragraphs (1) and (2), in the event of any inconsistency between the provisions of any trust deed and an instrument of management, the instrument of management shall prevail over the provisions of the trust deed in so far as they relate to the home concerned.

(5) After consultation with the voluntary organisation concerned and with the local authority specified in its instrument of management, the Secretary of State may by order vary or revoke any provisions of the instrument.

Part II

Management of Controlled and Assisted Community Homes

3—(1) The management, equipment and maintenance of a controlled community home shall be the responsibility of the local authority specified in its instrument of management.

(2) The management, equipment and maintenance of an assisted community home shall be the responsibility of the voluntary organisation by which the home is provided.

(3) In this paragraph—

"home" means a controlled community home or (as the case may be) assisted community home; and

"the managers", in relation to a home, means the managers constituted by its instrument of management; and

"the responsible body", in relation to a home, means the local authority or (as the case may be) voluntary organisation responsible for its management, equipment and maintenance.

(4) The functions of a home's responsible body shall be exercised through the managers.

(5) Anything done, liability incurred or property acquired by a home's managers shall be done, incurred or acquired by them as agents of the responsible body.

(6) In so far as any matter is reserved for the decision of a home's responsible body by—
  (a)   sub-paragraph (8);
  (b)   the instrument of management;
  (c)   the service by the body on the managers, or any of them, of a notice reserving any matter,
that matter shall be dealt with by the body and not by the managers.

(7) In dealing with any matter so reserved, the responsible body shall have regard to any representations made to the body by the managers.

(8) The employment of persons at a home shall be a matter reserved for the decision of the responsible body.

(9) Where the instrument of management of a controlled community home so provides, the responsible body may enter into arrangements with the voluntary organisation by which that home is provided whereby, in accordance with such terms as may be agreed between them and the voluntary organisation, persons who are not in the employment of the responsible body shall undertake duties at that home.

(10) Subject to sub-paragraph (11)—
  (a)   where the responsible body for an assisted community home proposes to engage any person to work at that home or to terminate without notice the employment of any person at that home, it shall consult the local authority specified in the instrument of management and, if that authority so direct, the responsible body shall not carry out its proposal without their consent; and
  (b)   that local authority may, after consultation with the responsible body, require that body to terminate the employment of any person at that home.

(11) Paragraphs (*a*) and (*b*) of sub-paragraph (10) shall not apply—
- (*a*) in such cases or circumstances as may be specified by notice in writing given by the local authority to the responsible body; and
- (*b*) in relation to the employment of any persons or class of persons specified in the home's instrument of management.

(12) The accounting year of the managers of a home shall be such as may be specified by the responsible body.

(13) Before such date in each accounting year as may be so specified, the managers of a home shall submit to the responsible body estimates, in such form as the body may require, of expenditure and receipts in respect of the next accounting year.

(14) Any expenses incurred by the managers of a home with the approval of the responsible body shall be defrayed by that body.

(15) The managers of a home shall keep—
- (*a*) proper accounts with respect to the home; and
- (*b*) proper records in relation to the accounts.

(16) Where an instrument of management relates to more than one home, one set of accounts and records may be kept in respect of all the homes to which it relates.

PART III
REGULATIONS

4—(1) The Secretary of State may make regulations—
- (*a*) as to the placing of children in community homes;
- (*b*) as to the conduct of such homes; and
- (*c*) for securing the welfare of children in such homes.

(2) The regulations may, in particular—
- (*a*) prescribe standards to which the premises used for such homes are to conform;
- (*b*) impose requirements as to the accommodation, staff and equipment to be provided in such homes, and as to the arrangements to be made for protecting the health of children in such homes;
- (*c*) provide for the control and discipline of children in such homes;
- (*d*) impose requirements as to the keeping of records and giving of notices in respect of children in such homes;
- (*e*) impose requirements as to the facilities which are to be provided for giving religious instruction to children in such homes;
- (*f*) authorise the Secretary of State to give and revoke directions requiring—
  - (i) the local authority by whom a home is provided or who are specified in the instrument of management for a controlled community home, or
  - (ii) the voluntary organisation by which an assisted community home is provided,

  to accommodate in the home a child looked after by a local authority for whom no places are made available in that home or to take such action in relation to a child accommodated in the home as may be specified in the directions;
- (*g*) provide for consultation with the Secretary of State as to applicants for appointment to the charge of a home;
- (*h*) empower the Secretary of State to prohibit the appointment of any particular

applicant in the cases (if any) in which the regulations dispense with such consultation by reason that the person to be appointed possesses such qualifications as may be prescribed;

(*i*) require the approval of the Secretary of State for the provision and use of accommodation for the purpose of restricting the liberty of children in such homes and impose other requirements (in addition to those imposed by section 25) as to the placing of a child in accommodation provided for that purpose, including a requirement to obtain the permission of any local authority who are looking after the child;

(*j*) provide that, to such extent as may be provided for in the regulations, the Secretary of State may direct that any provision of regulations under this paragraph which is specified in the direction and makes any such provision as is referred to in paragraph (*a*) or (*b*) shall not apply in relation to a particular home or the premises used for it, and may provide for the variation or revocation of any such direction by the Secretary of State.

(3) Without prejudice to the power to make regulations under this paragraph conferring functions on—

(*a*) the local authority or voluntary organisation by which a community home is provided; or

(*b*) the managers of a controlled or assisted community home,

regulations under this paragraph may confer functions in relation to a controlled or assisted community home on the local authority named in the instrument of management for the home.

SCHEDULE 5

VOLUNTARY HOMES AND VOLUNTARY ORGANISATIONS

PART I

REGISTRATION OF VOLUNTARY HOMES

General

1—(1) An application for registration under this paragraph shall—

(*a*) be made by the persons intending to carry on the home to which the application relates; and

(*b*) be made in such manner, and be accompanied by such particulars, as the Secretary of State may prescribe.

(2) On an application duly made under sub-paragraph (1) the Secretary of State may—

(*a*) grant or refuse the application, as he thinks fit; or

(*b*) grant the application subject to such conditions as he considers appropriate.

(3) The Secretary of State may from time to time—

(*a*) vary any condition for the time being in force with respect to a voluntary home by virtue of this paragraph; or

(*b*) impose an additional condition,

either on the application of the person carrying on the home or without such an application.

(4) Where at any time it appears to the Secretary of State that the conduct of any voluntary home—

(*a*)   is not in accordance with regulations made under paragraph 7; or
(*b*)   is otherwise unsatisfactory,
he may cancel the registration of the home and remove it from the register.

(5) Any person who, without reasonable excuse, carries on a voluntary home in contravention of—
(*a*)   section 60; or
(*b*)   a condition to which the registration of the home is for the time being subject by virtue of this Part,
shall be guilty of an offence.

(6) Any person guilty of such an offence shall be liable on summary conviction to a fine not exceeding—
(*a*)   level 5 on the standard scale, if his offence is under sub-paragraph (5)(*a*); or
(*b*)   level 4, if it is under sub-paragraph (5)(*b*).

(7) Where the Secretary of State registers a home under this paragraph, or cancels the registration of a home, he shall notify the local authority within whose area the home is situated.

Procedure

2—(1) Where—
(*a*)   a person applies for registration of a voluntary home; and
(*b*)   the Secretary of State proposes to grant his application,
the Secretary of State shall give him written notice of his proposal and of the conditions subject to which he proposes to grant the application.

(2) The Secretary of State need not give notice if he proposes to grant the application subject only to conditions which—
(*a*)   the applicant specified in the application; or
(*b*)   the Secretary of State and the applicant have subsequently agreed.

(3) Where the Secretary of State proposes to refuse such an application he shall give notice of his proposal to the applicant.

(4) The Secretary of State shall give any person carrying on a voluntary home notice of a proposal to—
(*a*)   cancel the registration of the home;
(*b*)   vary any condition for the time being in force with respect to the home by virtue of paragraph 1; or
(*c*)   impose any additional condition.

(5) A notice under this paragraph shall give the Secretary of State's reasons for his proposal.

Right to make representations

3—(1) A notice under paragraph 2 shall state that within 14 days of service of the notice any person on whom it is served may (in writing) require the Secretary of State to give him an opportunity to make representations to the Secretary of State concerning the matter.

(2) Where a notice has been served under paragraph 2, the Secretary of State shall not determine the matter until either—

  (a)   any person on whom the notice was served has made representations to him concerning the matter; or

  (b)   the period during which any such person could have required the Secretary of State to give him an opportunity to make representations has elapsed without the Secretary of State being required to give such an opportunity; or

  (c)   the conditions specified in sub-paragraph (3) are satisfied.

(3) The conditions are that—

  (a)   a person on whom the notice was served has required the Secretary of State to give him an opportunity to make representations to the Secretary of State;

  (b)   the Secretary of State has allowed him a reasonable period to make his representations; and

  (c)   he has failed to make them within that period.

(4) The representations may be made, at the option of the person making them, either in writing or orally.

(5) If he informs the Secretary of State that he desires to make oral representations, the Secretary of State shall give him an opportunity of appearing before, and of being heard by, a person appointed by the Secretary of State.

Decision of Secretary of State

4—(1) If the Secretary of State decides to adopt the proposal, he shall serve notice in writing of his decision on any person on whom he was required to serve notice of his proposal.

(2) A notice under this paragraph shall be accompanied by a notice explaining the right of appeal conferred by paragraph 5.

(3) A decision of the Secretary of State, other than a decision to grant an application for registration subject only to such conditions as are mentioned in paragraph 2(2) or to refuse an application for registration, shall not take effect—

  (a)   if no appeal is brought, until the end of the period of 28 days referred to in paragraph 5(3); and

  (b)   if an appeal is brought, until it is determined or abandoned.

Appeals

5—(1) An appeal against a decision of the Secretary of State under Part VII shall lie to a Registered Homes Tribunal.

(2) An appeal shall be brought by notice in writing given to the Secretary of State.

(3) No appeal may be brought by a person more than 28 days after service on him of notice of the decision.

(4) On an appeal, the Tribunal may confirm the Security of State's decision or direct that it shall not have effect.

(5) A Tribunal shall also have power on an appeal to—

(a)   vary any condition for the time being in force by virtue of Part VII with respect to the home to which the appeal relates;
(b)   direct that any such condition shall cease to have effect; or
(c)   direct that any such condition as it thinks fit shall have effect with respect to the home.

Notification of particulars with respect to voluntary homes

6—(1) It shall be the duty of the person in charge of any voluntary home established after the commencement of this Act to send to the Secretary of State within three months from the establishment of the home such particulars with respect to the home as the Secretary of State may prescribe.

(2) It shall be the duty of the person in charge of any voluntary home (whether established before or after the commencement of this Act) to send to the Secretary of State such particulars with respect to the home as may be prescribed.

(3) The particulars must be sent—
(a)   in the case of a home established before the commencement of this Act, in every year, or
(b)   in the case of a home established after the commencement of this Act, in every year subsequent to the year in which particulars are sent under sub-paragraph (1),
by such date as the Secretary of State may prescribe.

(4) Where the Secretary of State by regulations varies the particulars which are to be sent to him under sub-paragraph (1) or (2) by the person in charge of a voluntary home—
(a)   that person shall send to the Secretary of State the prescribed particulars within three months from the date of the making of the regulations;
(b)   where any such home was established before, but not more than three months before, the making of the regulations, compliance with paragraph (a) shall be sufficient compliance with the requirement of sub-paragraph (1) to send the prescribed particulars within three months from the establishment of the home;
(c)   in the year in which the particulars are varied, compliance with paragraph (a) by the person in charge of any voluntary home shall be sufficient compliance with the requirement of sub-paragraph (2) to send the prescribed particulars before the prescribed date in that year.

(5) If the person in charge of a voluntary home fails, without reasonable excuse, to comply with any of the requirements of this paragraph he shall be guilty of an offence.

(6) Any person guilty of such an offence shall be liable on summary conviction to a fine not exceeding level 2 on the standard scale.

PART II

REGULATIONS AS TO VOLUNTARY HOMES

Regulations as to conduct of voluntary homes

7—(1) The Secretary of State may make regulations—

(a) as to the placing of children in voluntary homes;
(b) as to the conduct of such homes; and
(c) for securing the welfare of children in such homes.

(2) The regulations may, in particular—
(a) prescribe standards to which the premises used for such homes are to conform;
(b) impose requirements as to the accommodation, staff and equipment to be provided in such homes, and as to the arrangements to be made for protecting the health of children in such homes;
(c) provide for the control and discipline of children in such homes;
(d) require the furnishing to the Secretary of State of information as to the facilities provided for—
  (i) the parents of children in the homes; and
  (ii) persons who are not parents of such children but who have parental responsibility for them; and
  (iii) other persons connected with such children,
  to visit and communicate with the children;
(e) authorise the Secretary of State to limit the number of children who may be accommodated in any particular voluntary home;
(f) prohibit the use of accommodation for the purpose of restricting the liberty of children in such homes;
(g) impose requirements as to the keeping of records and giving of notices with respect to children in such homes;
(h) impose requirements as to the facilities which are to be provided for giving religious instruction to children in such homes;
(i) require notice to be given to the Secretary of State of any change of the person carrying on or in charge of a voluntary home or of the premises used by such a home.

(3) The regulations may provide that a contravention of, or failure to comply with, any specified provision of the regulations without reasonable excuse shall be an offence against the regulations.

(4) Any person guilty of such an offence shall be liable to a fine not exceeding level 4 on the standard scale.

Disqualification

8   The Secretary of State may by regulation make provision with respect to the disqualification of persons in relation to voluntary homes of a kind similar to that made in relation to children's homes by section 65.

SCHEDULE 6

REGISTERED CHILDREN'S HOMES

PART I

REGISTRATION

Application for registration

1—(1) An application for the registration of a children's home shall be made—
(a) by the person carrying on, or intending to carry on, the home; and
(b) to the local authority for the area in which the home is, or is to be, situated.

(2) The application shall be made in the prescribed manner and shall be accompanied by—

    (*a*)   such particulars as may be prescribed; and

    (*b*)   such reasonable fee as the local authority may determine.

(3) In this Schedule "prescribed" means prescribed by regulations made by the Secretary of State.

(4) If a local authority are satisfied that a children's home with respect to which an application has been made in accordance with this Schedule complies or (as the case may be) will comply—

    (*a*)   with such requirements as may be prescribed, and

    (*b*)   with such other requirements (if any) as appear to them to be appropriate,

they shall grant the application, either unconditionally or subject to conditions imposed under paragraph 2.

(5) Before deciding whether or not to grant an application a local authority shall comply with any prescribed requirements.

(6) Regulations made for the purposes of sub-paragraph (5) may, in particular, make provision as to the inspection of the home in question.

(7) Where an application is granted, the authority shall notify the applicant that the home has been registered under this Act as from such date as may be specified in the notice.

(8) If the authority are not satisfied as mentioned in sub-paragraph (4), they shall refuse the application.

(9) For the purposes of this Act, an application which has not been granted or refused within the period of twelve months beginning with the date when it is served on the authority shall be deemed to have been refused by them, and the applicant shall be deemed to have been notified of their refusal at the end of that period.

(10) Where a school to which section 63(1) applies is registered it shall not cease to be a registered children's home by reason only of a subsequent change in the number of children for whom it provides accommodation.

Conditions imposed on registration

2—(1) A local authority may grant an application for registration subject to such conditions relating to the conduct of the home as they think fit.

(2) A local authority may from time to time—

    (*a*)   vary any condition for the time being in force with respect to a home by virtue of this paragraph; or

    (*b*)   impose an additional condition,

either on the application of the person carrying on the home or without such an application.

(3) If any condition imposed or varied under this paragraph is not complied with, the person carrying on the home shall, if he has no reasonable excuse, be guilty

of an offence and liable on summary conviction to a fine not exceeding level 4 on the standard scale.

Annual review of registration

3—(1) In this Part "the responsible authority", in relation to a registered children's home means the local authority who registered it.

(2) The responsible authority for a registered children's home shall, at the end of the period of twelve months beginning with the date of registration, and annually thereafter, review its registration for the purpose of determining whether the registration should continue in force or be cancelled under paragraph 4(3).

(3) If on any such annual review the responsible authority are satisfied that the home is being carried on in accordance with the relevant requirements they shall determine that, subject to sub-paragraph (4), the registration should continue in force.

(4) The responsible authority shall give to the person carrying on the home notice of their determination under sub-paragraph (3) and the notice shall require him to pay to the authority with respect to the review such reasonable fee as the authority may determine.

(5) It shall be a condition of the home's continued registration that the fee is so paid before the expiry of the period of twenty-eight days beginning with the date on which the notice is received by the person carrying on the home.

(6) In this Schedule "the relevant requirements" means any requirements of Part VIII and of any regulations made under paragraph 10, and any conditions imposed under paragraph 2.

Cancellation of registration

4—(1) The person carrying on a registered children's home may at any time make an application, in such manner and including such particulars as may be prescribed, for the cancellation by the responsible authority of the registration of the home.

(2) If the authority are satisfied, in the case of a school registered by virtue of section 63(6), that it is no longer a school to which that provision applies, the authority shall give to the person carrying on the home notice that the registration of the home has been cancelled as from the date of the notice.

(3) If on any annual review under paragraph 3, or at any other time, it appears to the responsible authority that a registered home is being carried on otherwise than in accordance with the relevent requirements, they may determine that the registration of the home should be cancelled.

(4) The responsible authority may at any time determine that the registration of a home should be cancelled on the ground—
  (a) that the person carrying on the home has been convicted of an offence under this Part or any regulations made under paragraph 10; or
  (b) that any other person has been convicted of such an offence in relation to the home.

Procedure

5—(1) Where—
    (*a*)   a person applies for the registration of a children's home; and
    (*b*)   the local authority propose to grant his application,
they shall give him written notice of their proposal and of the conditions (if any) subject to which they propose to grant his application.

(2) The authority need not give notice if they propose to grant the application subject only to conditions which—
    (*a*)   the applicant specified in the application; or
    (*b*)   the authority and the applicant have subsequently agreed.

(3) The authority shall give an applicant notice of a proposal to refuse his application.

(4) The authority shall give any person carrying on a registered children's home notice of a proposal—
    (*a*)   to cancel the registration;
    (*b*)   to vary any condition for the time being in force with respect to the home by virtue of Part VIII; or
    (*c*)   to impose any additional condition.

(5) A notice under this paragraph shall give the local authority's reasons for their proposal.

Right to make representations

6—(1) A notice under paragraph 5 shall state that within 14 days of service of the notice any person on whom it is served may in writing require the local authority to give him an opportunity to make representations to them concerning the matter.

(2) Where a notice has been served under paragraph 5, the local authority shall not determine the matter until—
    (*a*)   any person on whom the notice was served has made representations to them concerning the matter;
    (*b*)   the period during which any person could have required the local authority to give him an opportunity to make representations has elapsed without their being required to give such an opportunity; or
    (*c*)   the conditions specified in sub-paragraph (3) below are satisfied.

(3) The conditions are—
    (*a*)   that a person on whom the notice was served has required the local authority to give him an opportunity to make representations to them concerning the matter;
    (*b*)   that the authority have allowed him a reasonable period to make his representations; and
    (*c*)   that he has failed to make them within that period.

(4) The representations may be made, at the option of the person making them, either in writing or orally.

(5) If he informs the local authority that he desires to make oral representations, the authority shall give him an opportunity of appearing before and of being heard by a committee or sub-committee of theirs.

Decision of local authority

7—(1) If the local authority decide to adopt a proposal of theirs to grant an application, they shall serve notice in writing of their decision on any person on whom they were required to serve notice of their proposal.

(2) A notice under this paragraph shall be accompanied by an explanation of the right of appeal conferred by paragraph 8.

(3) A decision of a local authority, other than a decision to grant an application for registration subject only to such conditions as are mentioned in paragraph 5(2) or to refuse an application for registration, shall not take effect—
- (a) if no appeal is brought, until the end of the period of 28 days referred to in paragraph 8(3); and
- (b) if an appeal is brought, until it is determined or abandoned.

Appeals

8—(1) An appeal against a decision of a local authority under Part VIII shall lie to a Registered Homes Tribunal.

(2) An appeal shall be brought by notice in writing given to the local authority.

(3) No appeal shall be brought by a person more than 28 days after service on him of notice of the decision.

(4) On an appeal the Tribunal may confirm the local authority's decision or direct that it shall not have effect.

(5) A Tribunal shall also have power on an appeal—
- (a) to vary any condition in force with respect to the home to which the appeal relates by virtue of paragraph 2;
- (b) to direct that any such condition shall cease to have effect; or
- (c) to direct that any such condition as it thinks fit shall have effect with respect to the home.

(6) A local authority shall comply with any direction given by a Tribunal under this paragraph.

Prohibition on further applications

9—(1) Where an application for the registration of a home is refused, no further application may be made within the period of six months beginning with the date when the applicant is notified of the refusal.

(2) Sub-paragraph (1) shall have effect, where an appeal against the refusal of an application is determined or abandoned, as if the reference to the date when the applicant is notified of the refusal were a reference to the date on which the appeal is determined or abandoned.

(3) Where the registration of a home is cancelled, no application for the registration of the home shall be made within the period of six months beginning with the date of cancellation.

(4) Sub-paragraph (3) shall have effect, where an appeal against the cancellation of the registration of a home is determined or abandoned, as if the reference to the date of cancellation were a reference to the date on which the appeal is determined or abandoned.

Part II

Regulations

10—(1) The Secretary of State may make regulations—
 (*a*)   as to the placing of children in registered children's homes;
 (*b*)   as to the conduct of such homes; and
 (*c*)   for securing the welfare of the children in such homes.

(2) The regulations may in particular—
 (*a*)   prescribe standards to which the premises used for such homes are to conform;
 (*b*)   impose requirements as to the accommodation, staff and equipment to be provided in such homes;
 (*c*)   impose requirements as to the arrangements to be made for protecting the health of children in such homes;
 (*d*)   provide for the control and discipline of children in such homes;
 (*e*)   require the furnishing to the responsible authority of information as to the facilities provided for—
   (i)   the parents of children in such homes;
   (ii)   persons who are not parents of such children but who have parental responsibility for them; and
   (iii) other persons connected with such children, to visit and communicate with the children.
 (*f*)   impose requirements as to the keeping of records and giving of notices with respect to children in such homes;
 (*g*)   impose requirements as to the facilities which are to be provided for giving religious instruction to children in such homes;
 (*h*)   make provision as to the carrying out of annual reviews under paragraph 3;
 (*i*)   authorise the responsible authority to limit the number of children who may be accommodated in any particular registered home;
 (*j*)   prohibit the use of accommodation for the purpose of restricting the liberty of children in such homes;
 (*k*)   require notice to be given to the responsible authority of any change of the person carrying on or in charge of a registered home or of the premises used by such a home;
 (*l*)   make provision similar to that made by regulations under section 26.

(3) The regulations may provide that a contravention of or failure to comply with any specified provision of the regulations, without reasonable excuse, shall be an offence against the regulations.

(4) Any person guilty of such an offence shall be liable on summary conviction to a fine not exceeding level 4 on the standard scale.

SCHEDULE 7

FOSTER PARENTS: LIMITS ON NUMBER OF FOSTER CHILDREN

Interpretation

1   For the purposes of this Schedule, a person fosters a child if—
   (a)   he is a local authority foster parent in relation to the child;
   (b)   he is a foster parent with whom the child has been placed by a voluntary organisation; or
   (c)   he fosters the child privately.

The usual fostering limit

2   Subject to what follows, a person may not foster more than three children ("the usual fostering limit").

Siblings

3   A person may exceed the usual fostering limit if the children concerned are all siblings with respect to each other.

Exemption by local authority

4—(1) A person may exceed the usual fostering limit if he is exempted from it by the local authority within whose area he lives.

(2) In considering whether to exempt a person, a local authority shall have regard, in particular, to—
   (a)   the number of children whom the person proposes to foster;
   (b)   the arrangements which the person proposes for the care and accommodation of the fostered children;
   (c)   the intended and likely relationship between the person and the fostered children;
   (d)   the period of time for which he proposes to foster the children; and
   (e)   whether the welfare of the fostered children (and of any other children who are or will be living in the accommodation) will be safeguarded and promoted.

(3) Where a local authority exempt a person, they shall inform him by notice in writing—
   (a)   that he is so exempted;
   (b)   of the children, described by name, whom he may foster; and
   (c)   of any condition to which the exemption is subject.

(4) A local authority may at any time by notice in writing—
   (a)   vary or cancel an exemption; or
   (b)   impose, vary or cancel a condition to which the exemption is subject,
and, in considering whether to do so, they shall have regard in particular to the considerations mentioned in sub-paragraph (2).

(5) The Secretary of State may make regulations amplifying or modifying the provisions of this paragraph in order to provide for cases where children need to be placed with foster parents as a matter of urgency.

Effect of exceeding fostering limit

5—(1) A person shall cease to be treated as fostering and shall be treated as carrying on a children's home if—
  (*a*) he exceeds the usual fostering limit; or
  (*b*) where he is exempted under paragraph 4,—
    (i)   he fosters any child not named in the exemption; and
    (ii) in so doing, he exceeds the usual fostering limit.

(2) Sub-paragraph (1) does not apply if the children concerned are all siblings in respect of each other.

Complaints etc.

6—(1) Every local authority shall establish a procedure for considering any representations (including any complaint) made to them about the discharge of their functions under paragraph 4 by a person exempted or seeking to be exempted under that paragraph.

(2) In carrying out any consideration of representations under subparagraph (1), a local authority shall comply with any regulations made by the Secretary of State for the purposes of this paragraph.

SCHEDULE 8

Privately Fostered Children

Exemptions

1—A child is not a privately fostered child while he is being looked after by a local authority.

2—(1) A child is not a privately fostered child while he is in the care of any person—
  (*a*) in premises in which any—
    (i)   parent of his;
    (ii)   person who is not a parent of his but who has parental responsibility for him; or
    (iii) person who is a relative of his and who has assumed responsibility for his care,
    is for the time being living;
  (*b*) in any children's home;
  (*c*) in accommodation provided by or on behalf of any voluntary organisation;
  (*d*) in any school in which he is receiving full-time education;
  (*e*) in any health service hospital;
  (*f*) in any residential care home, nursing home or mental nursing home; or
  (*g*) in any home or institution not specified in this paragraph but provided, equipped and maintained by the Secretary of State.

(2) Sub-paragraph (1)(*b*) to (*g*) does not apply where the person caring for the child is doing so in his personal capacity and not in the course of carrying out his duties in relation to the establishment mentioned in the paragraph in question.

3   A child is not a privately fostered child while he is in the care of any person in compliance with—
  (a)   an order under section 7(7)(*b*) of the Children and Young Persons Act 1969; or
  (b)   a supervision requirement within the meaning of the Social Work (Scotland) Act 1968.

4   A child is not a privately fostered child while he is liable to be detained, or subject to guardianship, under the Mental Health Act 1983.

5   A child is not a privately fostered child while—
  (a)   he is placed in the care of a person who proposes to adopt him under arrangements made by an adoption agency within the meaning of—
    (i)   section 1 of the Adoption Act 1976;
    (ii)   section 1 of the Adoption (Scotland) Act 1978; or
    (iii)   Article 3 of the Adoption (Northern Ireland) Order 1987; or
  (b)   he is a protected child.

Power of local authority to impose requirements

6—(1) Where a person is fostering any child privately, or proposes to foster any child privately, the appropriate local authority may impose on him requirements as to—
  (a)   the number, age and sex of the children who may be privately fostered by him;
  (b)   the standard of the accommodation and equipment to be provided for them;
  (c)   the arrangements to be made with respect to their health and safety; and
  (d)   particular arrangements which must be made with respect to the provision of care for them,
and it shall be his duty to comply with any such requirement before the end of such period as the authority may specify unless, in the case of a proposal, the proposal is not carried out.

(2) A requirement may be limited to a particular child, or class of child.

(3) A requirement (other than one imposed under sub-paragraph (1)(*a*)) may be limited by the authority so as to apply only when the number of children fostered by the person exceeds a specified number.

(4) A requirement shall be imposed by notice in writing addressed to the person on whom it is imposed and informing him of—
  (a)   the reason for imposing the requirement;
  (b)   his right under paragraph 8 to appeal against it; and
  (c)   the time within which he may do so.

(5) A local authority may at any time vary any requirement, impose any additional requirement or remove any requirement.

(6) In this Schedule—
  (a)   "the appropriate local authority" means—
    (i)   the local authority within whose area the child is being fostered; or
    (ii)   in the case of a proposal to foster a child, the local authority within whose area it is proposed that he will be fostered;
  and

(b)   "requirement", in relation to any person, means a requirement imposed on him under this paragraph.

Regulations requiring notification of fostering etc.

7—(1) The Secretary of State may by regulations make provision as to—
  (a)   the circumstances in which notification is required to be given in connection with children who are, have been or are proposed to be fostered privately; and
  (b)   the manner and form in which such notification is to be given.

(2) The regulations may, in particular—
  (a)   require any person who is, or proposes to be, involved (whether or not directly) in arranging for a child to be fostered privately to notify the appropriate authority;
  (b)   require any person who is—
      (i)   a parent of a child; or
      (ii)   a person who is not a parent of his but who has parental responsibility for a child,
      and who knows that it is proposed that the child should be fostered privately, to notify the appropriate authority;
  (c)   require any parent of a privately fostered child, or person who is not a parent of such a child but who has parental responsibility for him, to notify the appropriate authority of any change in his address;
  (d)   require any person who proposes to foster a child privately, to notify the appropriate authority of his proposal;
  (e)   require any person who is fostering a child privately, or proposes to do so, to notify the appropriate authority of—
      (i)   any offence of which he has been convicted;
      (ii)   any disqualification imposed on him under section 68; or
      (iii) any prohibition imposed on him under section 69;
  (f)   require any person who is fostering a child privately, to notify the appropriate authority of any change in his address;
  (g)   require any person who is fostering a child privately to notify the appropriate authority in writing of any person who begins, or ceases, to be part of his household;
  (h)   require any person who has been fostering a child privately, but has ceased to do so, to notify the appropriate authority (indicating, where the child has died, that that is the reason).

Appeals

8—(1) A person aggrieved by—
  (a)   a requirement imposed under paragraph 6;
  (b)   a refusal of consent under section 68;
  (c)   a prohibition imposed under section 69;
  (d)   a refusal to cancel such a prohibition;
  (e)   a refusal to make an exemption under paragraph 4 of Schedule 7;
  (f)   a condition imposed in such an exemption; or
  (g)   a variation or cancellation of such an exemption,
may appeal to the court.

(2) The appeal must be made within fourteen days from the date on which the

person appealing is notified of the requirement, refusal, prohibition, condition, variation or cancellation.

(3) Where the appeal is against—
    (a) a requirement imposed under paragraph 6;
    (b) a condition of an exemption imposed under paragraph 4 of Schedule 7; or
    (c) a variation or cancellation of such an exemption,
the requirement, condition, variation or cancellation shall not have effect while the appeal is pending.

(4) Where it allows an appeal against a requirement or prohibition, the court may, instead of cancelling the requirement or prohibition—
    (a) vary the requirement, or allow more time for compliance with it; or
    (b) if an absolute prohibition has been imposed, substitute for it a prohibition on using the premises after such time as the court may specify unless such specified requirements as the local authority had power to impose under paragraph 6 are complied with.

(5) Any requirement or prohibition specified or substituted by a court under this paragraph shall be deemed for the purposes of Part IX (other than this paragraph) to have been imposed by the local authority under paragraph 6 or (as the case may be) section 69.

(6) Where it allows an appeal against a refusal to make an exemption, a condition imposed in such an exemption or a variation or cancellation of such an exemption, the court may—
    (a) make an exemption;
    (b) impose a condition; or
    (c) vary the exemption.

(7) Any exemption made or varied under sub-paragraph (6), or any condition imposed under that sub-paragraph, shall be deemed for the purposes of Schedule 7 (but not for the purposes of this paragraph) to have been made, varied or imposed under that Schedule.

(8) Nothing in sub-paragraph (1)(e) to (g) confers any right of appeal on—
    (a) a person who is, or would be if exempted under Schedule 7, a local authority foster parent; or
    (b) a person who is, or would be if so exempted, a person with whom a child is placed by a voluntary organisation.

Extension of Part IX to certain school children during holidays

9—(1) Where a child under sixteen who is a pupil at a school which is not maintained by a local education authority lives at the school during school holidays for a period of more than two weeks, Part IX shall apply in relation to the child as if—
    (a) while living at the school, he were a privately fostered child; and
    (b) paragraphs 2(1)(d) and 6 were omitted.

(2) Sub-paragraph (3) applies to any person who proposes to care for and accommodate one or more children at a school in circumstances in which some or all of them will be treated as private foster children by virtue of this paragraph.

(3) That person shall, not less than two weeks before the first of those children

is treated as a private foster child by virtue of this paragraph during the holiday in question, give written notice of his proposal to the local authority within whose area the child is ordinarily resident ("the appropriate authority"), stating the estimated number of the children.

(4) A local authority may exempt any person from the duty of giving notice under sub-paragraph (3).

(5) Any such exemption may be granted for a special period or indefinitely and may be revoked at any time by notice in writing given to the person exempted.

(6) Where a child who is treated as a private foster child by virtue of this paragraph dies, the person caring for him at the school shall, not later than 48 hours after the death, give written notice of it—
  (a)   to the appropriate local authority; and
  (b)   where reasonably practicable, to each parent of the chid and to every person who is not a parent of his but who has parental responsibility for him.

(7) Where a child who is treated as a foster child by virtue of this paragraph ceases for any other reason to be such a child, the person caring for him at the school shall give written notice of the fact to the appropriate local authorioty.

Prohibition of advertisements relating to fostering

10   No advertisement indicating that a person will undertake, or will arrange for, a child to be privately fostered shall be published, unless it states that person's name and address.

Avoidance of insurances on lives of privately fostered children

11   A person who fosters a child privately and for reward shall be deemed for the purposes of the Life Assurance Act 1774 to have no interest in the life of the child.

SCHEDULE 9

Child Minding and Day Care for Young Children

Applications for registration

1—(1) An application for registration under section 71 shall be of no effect unless it contains—
  (a)   a statement with respect to the applicant which complies with the requirements of regulations made for the purposes of this paragraph by the Secretary of State; and
  (b)   a statement with respect to any person assisting or likely to be assisting in looking after children on the premises in question, or living or likely to be living there, which complies with the requirements of such regulations.

(2) Where a person provides, or proposes to provide, day care for children under the age of eight on different premises situated within the area of the same local authority, he shall make a separate application with respect to each of those premises.

(3) An application under section 71 shall be accompanied by such fee as may be prescribed.

(4) On receipt of an application for registration under section 71 from any person who is acting, or proposes to act, in any way which requires him to be registered under that section, a local authority shall register him if the application is properly made and they are not otherwise entitled to refuse to do so.

Disqualification from registration

2—(1) A person may not be registered under section 71 if he is disqualified by regulations made by the Secretary of State for the purposes of this paragraph.

(2) The regulations may, in particular, provide for a person to be disqualified where—
- (a) an order of a prescribed kind has been made at any time with respect to him;
- (b) an order of a prescribed kind has been made at any time with respect to any child who has been in his care;
- (c) a requirement of a prescribed kind has been imposed at any time with respect to such a child, under or by virtue of any enactment;
- (d) he has at any time been refused registration under Part X or any other prescribed enactment or had any such registration cancelled;
- (e) he has been convicted of any offence of a prescribed kind, or has been placed on probation or discharged absolutely or conditionally for any such offence;
- (f) he has at any time been disqualified from fostering a child privately;
- (g) a prohibition has been imposed on him at any time under section 61, section 10 of the Foster Children (Scotland) Act 1984 or any other prescribed enactment;
- (h) his rights and powers with respect to a child have at any time been vested in a prescribed authority under a prescribed enactment.

(3) A person who lives—
- (a) in the same household as a person who is himself disqualified by the regulations; or
- (b) in a household at which any such person is employed,

shall be disqualified unless he has disclosed the fact to the appropriate local authority and obtained their written consent.

(4) A person who is disqualified shall not provide day care, or be concerned in the management of, or have any financial interest in, any provision of day care unless he has—
- (a) disclosed the fact to the appropriate local authority; and
- (b) obtained their written consent.

(5) No person shall employ, in connection with the provision of day care, a person who is disqualified unless he has—
- (a) disclosed to the appropriate local authority the fact that that person is so disqualified; and
- (b) obtained their written consent.

(6) In this paragraph "enactment" means any enactment having effect, at any time, in any part of the United Kingdom.

Exemption of certain schools

3—(1) Section 71 does not apply in relation to any child looked after in any—
- (a)   school maintained or assisted by a local education authority;
- (b)   school under the management of an education authority;
- (c)   school in respect of which payments are made by the Secretary of State under section 100 of the Education Act 1944;
- (d)   independent school;
- (e)   grant-aided school;
- (f)   grant maintained school;
- (g)   self-governing school;
- (h)   play centre maintained or assisted by a local education authority under section 53 of the Act of 1944, or by an education authority under section 6 of the Education (Scotland) Act 1980.

(2) The exemption provided by sub-paragraph (1) only applies where the child concerned is being looked after in accordance with provision for day care made by—
- (a)   the person carrying on the establishment in question as part of the establishment's activities; or
- (b)   a person employed to work at that establishment and authorised to make that provision as part of the establishment's activities.

(3) In sub-paragraph (1)—
"assisted" and "maintained" have the same meanings as in the Education Act 1944;
"grant maintained" has the same meaning as in section 52(3) of the Education Reform Act 1988; and
"grant aided school", "self-governing school" and (in relation to Scotland) "independent school" have the same meaning as in the Education (Scotland) Act 1980.

Exemption for other establishments

4—(1) Section 71(1)(b) does not apply in relation to any child looked after in—
- (a)   a registered children's home;
- (b)   a voluntary home;
- (c)   a community home;
- (d)   a residential care home, nursing home or mental nursing home required to be registered under the Registered Homes Act 1984;
- (e)   a health service hospital;
- (f)   a home provided, equipped and maintained by the Secretary of State; or
- (g)   an establishment which is required to be registered under section 61 of the Social Work (Scotland) Act 1968.

(2) The exemption provided by sub-paragraph (1) only applies where the child concerned is being looked after in accordance with provision for day care made by—
- (a)   the department, authority or other person carrying on the establishment in question as part of the establishment's activities; or
- (b)   a person employed to work at that establishment and authorised to make that provision as part of the establishment's activities.

(3) In this paragraph "a health service hospital" includes a health service hospital within the meaning of the National Health Service (Scotland) Act 1978.

Exemption for occasional facilities

5—(1) Where day care for children under the age of eight is provided in particular premises on less than six days in any year, that provision shall be disregarded for the purposes of section 71 if the person making it has notified the appropriate local authority in writing before the first occasion on which the premises concerned are so used in that year.

(2) In sub-paragraph (1) "year" means the year beginning with the day on which the day care in question is (after the commencement of this paragraph) first provided in the premises concerned and any subsequent year.

Certificates of registration

6—(1) Where a local authority register a person under section 71 they shall issue him with a certificate of registration.

(2) The certificate shall specify—
    (a)   the registered person's name and address;
    (b)   in a case falling within section 71(1)(b), the address or situation of the premises concerned; and
    (c)   any requirements imposed under section 72 or 73.

(3) Where, due to a change of circumstances, any part of the certificate requires to be amended, the authority shall issue an amended certificate.

(4) Where the authority are satisfied that the certificate has been lost or destroyed, they shall issue a copy, on payment by the registered person of such fee as may be prescribed.

Fees for annual inspection of premises

7—(1) Where—
    (a)   a person is registered under section 71; and
    (b)   the local authority concerned make an annual inspection of the premises in question under section 76,
they shall serve on that person a notice informing him that the inspection is to be carried out and requiring him to pay to them such fee as may be prescribed.

(2) It shall be a condition of the continued registration of that person under section 71 that the fee is so paid before the expiry of the period of twenty-eight days beginning with the date on which the inspection is carried out.

Co-operation between authorities

8—(1) Where it appears to a local authority that any local education authority or, in Scotland, education authority could, by taking any specified action, help in the exercise of any of their functions under Part X, they may request the help of that local education authority, or education authority, specifying the action in question.

(2) An authority whose help is so requested shall comply with the request if it

is compatible with their own statutory or other duties and obligations and does not unduly prejudice the discharge of any of their functions.

SCHEDULE 10

Amendments of Adoption Legislation

Part I

Amendments of Adoption Act (1976 c. 36)

1   In section 2 (local authorities' social services) for the words from "relating to" to the end there shall be substituted—

"(a)   under the Children Act 1989, relating to family assistance orders, local authority support for children and families, care and supervision and emergency protection of children, community homes, voluntary homes and organisations, registered childrens' homes, private arrangements for fostering children, child minding and day care for young children and children accommodated by health authorities and local education authorities or in residential care, nursing or mental nursing homes or in independent schools; and

(b)   under the National Health Service Act 1977, relating to the provision of care for expectant and nursing mothers."

2   In section 11 (restrictions on arranging adoptions and placing of children) for subsection (2) there shall be substituted:

"(2)   An adoption society which is—

(a)   approved as respects Scotland under section 3 of the Adoption (Scotland) Act 1978; or

(b)   registered as respects Northern Ireland under Article 4 of the Adoption (Northern Ireland) Order 1987,

but which is not approved under section 3 of this Act, shall not act as an adoption society in England and Wales except to the extent that the society considers it necessary to do so in the interests of a person mentioned in section 1 of the Act of 1978 or Article 3 of the Order of 1987."

3—(1) In section 12 (adoption orders), in subsection (1) for the words "vesting the parental rights and duties relating to a child in" there shall be substituted "giving parental responsibility for a child to".

(2) In subsection (2) of that section for the words "the parental rights and duties so far as they relate" there shall be substituted "parental responsibility so far as it relates".

(3) In subsection (3) of that section for paragraph (a) there shall be substituted—

"(a)   the parental responsibility which any person has for the child immediately before the making of the order;

(aa)   any order under the Children Act 1989";

and in paragraph (b) for the words from "for any period" to the end there shall be substituted "or upbringing for any period after the making of the order."

4   For section 14(1) (adoption by married couple) there shall be substituted—

"(1)   An adoption order shall not be made on the application of more than one person except in the circumstances specified in subsections (1A) and (1B).

(1A) An adoption order may be made on the application of a married couple where both the husband and the wife have attained the age of 21 years.

(1B) An adoption order may be made on the application of a married couple where—

(*a*) the husband or the wife—

(i) is the father or mother of the child; and

(ii) has attained the age of 18 years;

and

(*b*) his or her spouse has attained the age of 21 years."

5—(1) In section 16 (parental agreement), in subsection (1) for the words from "in England" to "Scotland)" there shall be substituted—

"(i) in England and Wales, under section 18;

(ii) in Scotland, under section 18 of the Adoption (Scotland) Act 1978; or

(iii) in Northern Ireland, under Article 17(1) or 18(1) of the Adoption (Northern Ireland) Order 1987."

(2) In subsection (2)(*c*) of that section for the words "the parental duties in relation to" there shall be substituted "his parental responsibility for".

6—(1) In section 18 (freeing child for adoption), after subsection (2) there shall be inserted—

"(2A) For the purposes of subsection (2) a child is in the care of an adoption agency if the adoption agency is a local authority and he is in their care."

(2) In subsection (5) of that section, for the words from "the parental rights" to "vest in" there shall be substituted "parental responsibility for the child is given to", and for the words "and (3)" there shall be substituted "to (4)".

(3) For subsections (7) and (8) of that section there shall be substituted—

"(7) Before making an order under this section in the case of a child whose father does not have parental responsibility for him, the court shall satisfy itself in relation to any person claiming to be the father that—

(*a*) he has no intention of applying for—

(i) an order under section 4(1) of the Children Act 1989, or

(ii) a residence order under section 10 of that Act, or

(*b*) if he did make any such application, it would be likely to be refused.

(8) Subsections (5) and (7) of section 12 apply in relation to the making of an order under this section as they apply in relation to the making of an order under that section."

7 In section 19(2) (progress reports to former parents) for the words "in which the parental rights and duties were vested" there shall be substituted "to which parental responsibility was given".

8—(1) In section 20 (revocation of section 18 order), in subsections (1) and (2) for the words "the parental rights and duties", in both places where they occur, there shall be substituted "parental responsibility".

(2) For subsection (3) of that section there shall be substituted—

"(3) The revocation of an order under section 18 ("a section 18 order") operates—

(*a*) to extinguish the parental responsibility given to the adoption agency under the section 18 order;

(*b*) to give parental responsibility for the child to—
    (i) the child's mother; and
    (ii) where the child's father and mother were married to each other at the time of his birth, the father; and
(*c*) to revive—
    (i) any parental responsibility agreement,
    (ii) any order under section 4(1) of the Children Act 1989, and
    (iii) any appointment of a guardian in respect of the child (whether made by a court or otherwise),
extinguished by the making of the section 18 order.

(3A) Subject to subsection (3)(*c*), the revocation does not—
(*a*) operate to revive—
    (i) any order under the Children Act 1989, or
    (ii) any duty referred to in section 12(3)(*b*),
extinguished by the making of the section 18 order; or
(*b*) affect any person's parental responsibility so far as it relates to the period between the making of the section 18 order and the date of revocation of that order."

9   For section 21 (transfer of parental rights and duties between adoption agencies) there shall be substituted—

"21 Variation of section 18 order so as to substitute one adoption agency for another
(1) On an application to which this section applies, an authorised court may vary an order under section 18 so as to give parental responsibility for the child to another adoption agency ('the substitute agency') in place of the agency for the time being having parental responsibility for the child under the order ('the existing agency').
(2) This section applies to any application made jointly by—
(*a*) the existing agency; and
(*b*) the would-be substitute agency.
(3) Where an order under section 18 is varied under this section, section 19 shall apply as if the substitute agency had been given responsibility for the child on the making of the order."

10—(1) In section 22 (notification to local authority of adoption application), after subsection (1) there shall be inserted the following subsections—
"(1A) An application for such an adoption order shall not be made unless the person wishing to make the application has, within the period of two years preceding the making of the application, given notice as mentioned in subsection (1).
(1B) In subsections (1) and (1A) the references to the area in which the applicant or person has his home are references to the area in which he has his home at the time of giving the notice."

(2) In subsection (4) of that section for the word "receives" there shall be substituted "receive" and for the words "in the care of" there shall be substituted "looked after by".

11   In section 25(1) (interim orders) for the words "vesting the legal custody of the child in" there shall be substituted "giving parental responsibility for the child to".

12 In—
  (a) section 27(1) and (2) (restrictions on removal where adoption agreed or application made under section 18); and
  (b) section 28(1) and (2) (restrictions on removal where applicant has provided home for 5 years),
for the words "actual custody", in each place where they occur, they shall be substituted "home".

13 After section 27(2) there shall be inserted—
  "(2A) For the purposes of subsection (2) a child is in the care of an adoption agency if the adoption agency is a local authority and he is in their care."

14—(1) After section 28(2) there shall be inserted—
  "(2A) The reference in subsections (1) and (2) to any enactment does not include a reference to section 20(8) of the Children Act 1989."

(2) For subsection (3) of that section there shall be substituted—
  "(3) In any case where subsection (1) or (2) applies and—
  (a) the child was being looked after by a local authority before he began to have his home with the applicant or, as the case may be, the prospective adopter, and
  (b) the child is still being looked after by a local authority,
  the authority which are looking after the child shall not remove him from the home of the applicant or the prospective adopter except in accordance with section 30 or 31 or with the leave of a court."

(3) In subsection (5) of that section—
  (a) for the word "receives" there shall be substituted "receive"; and
  (b) for the words "in the care of another local authority or of a voluntary organisation" there shall be substituted "looked after by another local authority".

15 In section 29 (return of child taken away in breach of section 27 or 28) for subsections (1) and (2) there shall be substituted—
  "(1) An authorised court may, on the application of a person from whose home a child has been removed in breach of—
  (a) section 27 or 28,
  (b) section 27 or 28 of the Adoption (Scotland) Act 1978, or
  (c) Article 28 or 29 of the Adoption (Northern Ireland) Order 1987,
  order the person who has so removed the child to return the child to the applicant.

  (2) An authorised court may, on the application of a person who has reasonable grounds for believing that another person is intending to remove a child from his home in breach of—
  (a) section 27 or 28,
  (b) section 27 or 28 of the Adoption (Scotland) Act 1978, or
  (c) Article 28 or 29 of the Adoption (Northern Ireland) Order 1987,
  by order direct that other person not to remove the child from the applicant's home in breach of any of those provisions."

16—(1) In section 30 (return of children placed for adoption by adoption agencies), in subsection (1) there shall be substituted—
  (a) for the words "delivered into the actual custody of" the words "placed with";
  (b) in paragraph (a) for the words "retain the actual custody of the child" the words "give the child a home"; and
  (c) in paragraph (b) for the words "actual custody" the word "home".

(2) In subsection (3) of that section for the words "in his actual custody" there shall be substituted "with him".

17—(1) In section 31 (application of section 30 where child not placed for adoption), in subsection (1) for the words from "child", where it first occurs, to "except" there shall be substituted "child—
  (a) who is (when the notice is given) being looked after by a local authority; but
  (b) who was placed with that person otherwise than in pursuance of such arrangements as are mentioned in section 30(1),
that section shall apply as if the child had been placed in pursuance of such arrangements".

(2) In subsection (2) of that section for the words "for the time being in the care of" there shall be substituted "(when the notice is given) being looked after by".

(3) In subsection (3) of that section—
  (a) for the words "remains in the actual custody of" there shall be substituted "has his home with"; and
  (b) for the words "section 45 of the Child Care Act 1980" there shall be substituted "Part III of Schedule 2 to the Children Act 1989".

(4) At the end of that section there shall be added—
    "(4) Nothing in this section affects the right of any person who has parental responsibility for a child to remove him under section 20(8) of the Children Act 1989".

18—(1) In section 32 (meaning of "protected child"), in subsection (2) for the words "section 37 of the Adoption Act 1958" there shall be substituted—
    "(a) section 32 of the Adoption (Scotland) Act 1978; or
    (b) Article 33 of the Adoption (Northern Ireland) Order 1987."

(2) In subsection (3) of that section for paragraph (a) there shall be substituted—
    "(a) he is in the care of any person—
        (i) in any community home, voluntary home or registered children's home;
        (ii) in any school in which he is receiving full-time education;
        (iii) in any health service hospital";
and at the end of that subsection there shall be added—
    "(d) he is in the care of any person in any home or institution not specified in this subsection but provided, equipped and maintained by the Secretary of State."

(3) After that subsection there shall be inserted—
    "(3A) In subsection (3) 'community home', 'voluntary home', 'registered children's home', 'school' and 'health service hospital' have the same meaning as in the Children Act 1989."

(4) For subsection (4) of that section there shall be substituted—
    "(4) A protected child ceases to be a protected child—
    (a) on the grant or refusal of the application for an adoption order;
    (b) on the notification to the local authority for the area where the child has his home that the aplication for an adoption order has been withdrawn;

(c) in a case where no application is made for an adoption order, on the expiry of the period of two years from the giving of the notice;

(d) on the making of a residence order, a care order or a supervision order under the Children Act 1989 in respect of the child;

(e) on the appointment of a guardian for him under that Act;

(f) on his attaining the age of 18 years; or

(g) on his marriage,

whichever first occurs.

(5) In subsection (4)(d) the references to a care order and a supervision order do not include references to an interim care order or interim supervision order."

19—(1) In section 35 (notices and information to be given to local authorities), in subsection (1) for the words "who has a protected child in his actual custody" there shall be substituted "with whom a protected child has his home".

(2) In subsection (2) of that section for the words "in whose actual custody he was" there shall be substituted "with whom he had his home".

20—(1) In section 51 (disclosure of birth records of adopted children), in subsection (1) for the words "subsections (4) and (6)" there shall be substituted "what follows".

(2) For subsections (3) to (7) of that section there shall be substituted—

"(3) Before supplying any information to an applicant under subsection (1), the Registrar General shall inform the applicant that counselling services are available to him—

(a) if he is in England and Wales—
   (i) at the General Register Office;
   (ii) from the local authority in whose area he is living;
   (iii) where the adoption order relating to him was made in England and Wales, from the local authority in whose area the court which made the order sat; or
   (iv) from any other local authority;

(b) if he is in Scotland—
   (i) from the regional or islands council in whose area he is living;
   (ii) where the adoption order relating to him was made in Scotland, from the council in whose area the court which made the order sat; or
   (iii) from any other regional or islands council;

(c) if he is in Northern Ireland—
   (i) from the Board in whose area he is living;
   (ii) where the adoption order relating to him was made in Northern Ireland, from the Board in whose area the court which made the order sat; or
   (iii) from any other Board;

(d) if he is in the United Kingdom and his adoption was arranged by an adoption society—
   (i) approved under section 3,
   (ii) approved under section 3 of the Adoption (Scotland) Act 1978,
   (iii) registered under Article 4 of the Adoption (Northern Ireland) Order 1987,

from that society.

(4) Where an adopted person who is in England and Wales—

(*a*) applies for information under—

   (i) subsection (1), or

   (ii) Article 54 of the Adoption (Northern Ireland) Order 1987, or

(*b*) is supplied with information under section 45 of the Adoption (Scotland) Act 1978,

it shall be the duty of the persons and bodies mentioned in subsection (5) to provide counselling for him if asked by him to do so.

(5) The persons and bodies are—

(*a*) the Registrar General;

(*b*) any local authority falling within subsection (3)(*a*)(ii) to (iv);

(*c*) any adoption society falling within subsection (3)(*d*) in so far as it is acting as an adoption society in England and Wales.

(6) If the applicant chooses to receive counselling from a person or body falling within subsection (3), the Registrar General shall send to the person or body the information to which the applicant is entitled under subsection (1).

(7) Where a person—

(*a*) was adopted before 12th November 1975, and

(*b*) applies for information under subsection (1),

the Registrar General shall not supply the information to him unless he has attended an interview with a counsellor arranged by a person or body from whom counselling services are available as mentioned in subsection (3).

(8) Where the Registrar General is prevented by subsection (7) from supplying information to a person who is not living in the United Kingdom, he may supply the information to any body which—

(*a*) the Registrar General is satisfied is suitable to provide counselling to that person, and

(*b*) has notified the Registrar General that it is prepared to provide such counselling.

(9) In this section—

   "a Board" means a Health and Social Services Board established under Article 16 of the Health and Personal Social Services (Northern Ireland) Order 1972; and

   "prescribed" means prescribed by regulations made by the Registrar General."

21   After section 51 there shall be inserted—

"51A Adoption Contact Register

(1) The Registrar General shall maintain at the General Register Office a register to be called the Adoption Contact Register.

(2) The register shall be in two parts—

(*a*) Part I: Adopted Persons; and

(*b*) Part II: Relatives.

(3) The Registrar General shall, on payment of such fee as may be prescribed, enter in Part I of the register the name and address of any adopted person who fulfils the conditions in subsection (4) and who gives notice that he wishes to contact any relative of his.

(4) The conditions are that—

(*a*) a record of the adopted person's birth is kept by the Registrar General; and

(*b*) the adopted person has attained the age of 18 years and—

(i) has been supplied by the Registrar General with information under section 51; or

(ii) has satisfied the Registrar General that he has such information as is necessary to enable him to obtain a certified copy of the record of his birth.

(5) The Registrar General shall, on payment of such fee as may be prescribed, enter in Part II of the register the name and address of any person who fulfils the conditions in subsection (6) and who gives notice that he wishes to contact an adopted person.

(6) The conditions are that—

(*a*) a record of the adopted person's birth is kept by the Registrar General; and

(*b*) the person giving notice under subsection (5) has attained the age of 18 years and has satisfied the Registrar General that—

(i) he is a relative of the adopted person; and

(ii) he has such information as is necessary to enable him to obtain a certified copy of the record of the adopted person's birth.

(7) The Registrar General shall, on receiving notice from any person named in an entry in the register that he wishes the entry to be cancelled, cancel the entry.

(8) Any notice given under this section must be in such form as may be determined by the Registrar General.

(9) The Registrar General shall transmit to an adopted person whose name is entered in Part I of the register the name and address of any relative in respect of whom there is an entry in Part II of the register.

(10) Any entry cancelled under subsection (7) ceases from the time of cancellation to be an entry for the purposes of subsection (9).

(11) The register shall not be open to public inspection or search and the Registrar General shall not supply any person with information entered in the register (whether in an uncancelled or a cancelled entry) except in accordance with this section.

(12) The register may be kept by means of a computer.

(13) In this section—

(*a*) "relative" means any person (other than an adoptive relative) who is related to the adopted person by blood (including half-blood) or marriage;

(*b*) "address" includes any address at or through which the person concerned may be contacted; and

(*c*) "prescribed" means prescribed by the Secretary of State."

22—(1) In section 55 (adoption of children abroad), in subsection (1) after the word "Scotland" there shall be inserted "or Northern Ireland" and for the words "vesting in him the parental rights and duties relating to the child" there shall be substituted "giving him parental responsibility for the child".

(2) In subsection (3) of that section for the words "word '(Scotland)'" there shall be substituted "words '(Scotland)' or '(Northern Ireland)'."

23—(1) In section 56 (restriction on removal of children for adoption outside Great Britain),—

  (a)   in subsections (1) and (3) for the words "transferring the actual custody of a child to", in both places where they occur, there shall be substituted "placing a child with"; and

  (b)   in subsection (3)(a) for the words "in the actual custody of" there shall be substituted "with".

(2) In subsection (1) of that section—

  (a)   for the words from "or under" to "abroad)" there shall be substituted "section 49 of the Adoption (Scotland) Act 1978 or Article 57 of the Adoption (Northern Ireland) Order 1987"; and

  (b)   for the words "British Islands" there shall be substituted "United Kingdom, the Channel Islands and the Isle of Man".

24—(1) In section 57 (prohibition on certain payments) in subsection (1)(c), for the words "transfer by that person of the actual custody of a child" there shall be substituted "handing over of a child by that person".

(2) In subsection (3A)(b) of that section, for the words "in the actual custody of" there shall be substituted "with".

25   After section 57 there shall be inserted—

"57A Permitted allowances

(1) The Secretary of State may make regulations for the purpose of enabling adoption agencies to pay allowances to persons who have adopted, or intend to adopt, children in pursuance of arrangements made by the agencies.

(2) Section 57(1) shall not apply to any payment made by an adoption agency in accordance with the regulations.

(3) The regulations may, in particular, make provision as to—

  (a)   the procedure to be followed by any agency in determining whether a person should be paid an allowance;

  (b)   the circumstances in which an allowance may be paid;

  (c)   the factors to be taken into account in determining the amount of an allowance;

  (d)   the procedure for review, variation and termination of allowances; and

  (e)   the information about allowances to be supplied by any agency to any person who is intending to adopt a child.

(4) Any scheme approved under section 57(4) shall be revoked as from the coming into force of this section.

(5) Section 57(1) shall not apply in relation to any payment made—

  (a)   in accordance with a scheme revoked under subsection (4) or section 57(5)(b); and

  (b)   to a person to whom such payments were made before the revocation of the scheme.

(6) Subsection (5) shall not apply where any person to whom any payments may lawfully be made by virtue of subsection (5) agrees to receive (instead of such payments) payments complying with regulations made under this section."

26—(1) In section 59 (effect of determination and orders made in Scotland and overseas in adoption proceedings), in subsection (1) for the words "Great Britain" there shall be substituted "the United Kingdom".

(2) For subsection (2) of that section there shall be substituted—

"(2) Subsections (2) to (4) of section 12 shall apply in relation to an order freeing a child for adoption (other than an order under section 18) as if it were an adoption order; and, on the revocation in Scotland or Northern Ireland of an order freeing a child for adoption, subsections (3) and (3A) of section 20 shall apply as if the order had been revoked under that section."

27   In section 60 (evidence of adoption in Scotland and Northern Ireland), in paragraph (*a*) for the words "section 22(2) of the Adoption Act 1958" there shall be substituted "section 45(2) of the Adoption (Scotland) Act 1978" and in paragraph (*b*) for the words from "section 23(4)" to "in force" there shall be substituted "Article 63(1) of the Adoption (Northern Ireland) Order 1987".

28   In section 62(5)(*b*) (courts), for the words from "section 8" to "child)" there shall be substituted—

"(i) section 12 or 18 of the Adoption (Scotland) Act 1978; or
(ii) Article 12, 17 or 18 of the Adoption (Northern Ireland) Order 1987".

29   After section 65 (guardians ad litem and reporting officers) there shall be inserted—

"65A Panels for selection of guardians ad litem and reporting officers

(1) The Secretary of State may by regulations provide for the establishment of panels of persons from whom guardians ad litem and reporting officers appointed under rules made under section 65 must be selected.

(2) The regulations may, in particular, make provision—
(*a*) as to the constitution, administration and procedures of panels;
(*b*) requiring two or more specified local authorities to make arrangements for the joint management of a panel;
(*c*) for the defrayment by local authorities of expenses incurred by members of panels;
(*d*) for the payment by local authorities of fees and allowances for members of panels;
(*e*) as to the qualifications for membership of a panel;
(*f*) as to the training to be given to members of panels;
(*g*) as to the co-operation required of specified local authorities in the provision of panels in specified areas; and
(*h*) for monitoring the work of guardians ad litem and reporting officers.

(3) Rules of court may make provision as to the assistance which any guardian ad litem or reporting officer may be required by the court to give to it."

30—(1) Section 72(1) (interpretation) shall be amended as follows.

(2) In the definition of "adoption agency" for the words from "section 1" to the end there shall be substituted "—
(*a*)   section 1 of the Adoption (Scotland) Act 1978; and
(*b*)   Article 3 of the Adoption (Northern Ireland) Order 1987."

(3) For the definition of "adoption order" there shall be substituted—
"'adoption order'—
(*a*) means an order under section 12(1); and

(*b*) in sections 12(3) and (4), 18 to 20, 27, 28 and 30 to 32 and in the definition of 'British adoption order' in this subsection includes an order under section 12 of the Adoption (Scotland) Act 1978 and Article 12 of the Adoption (Northern Ireland) Order 1987 (adoption orders in Scotland and Northern Ireland respectively); and

(*c*) in sections 27, 28 and 30 to 32 includes an order under section 55, section 49 of the Adoption (Scotland) Act 1978 and Article 57 of the Adoption (Northern Ireland) Order 1987 (orders in relation to children being adopted abroad)."

(4) For the definition of "British adoption order" there shall be substituted—
"'British adoption order' means—
(*a*) an adoption order as defined in this subsection, and
(*b*) an order under any provision for the adoption of a child effected under the law of any British territory outside the United Kingdom."

(5) For the definition of "guardian" there shall be substituted—
"'guardian' has the same meaning as in the Children Act 1989."

(6) In the definition of "order freeing a child for adoption" for the words from "section 27(2)" to the end there shall be substituted "sections 27(2) and 59 includes an order under—
(*a*) section 18 of the Adoption (Scotland) Act 1978; and
(*b*) Article 17 or 18 of the Adoption (Northern Ireland) Order 1987"

(7) After the definition of "overseas adoption" there shall be inserted—
"'parent' means, in relation to a child, any parent who has parental responsibility for the child under the Children Act 1989;
'parental responsibility' and 'parental responsibility agreement' have the same meaning as in the Children Act 1989."

(8) After the definition of "United Kingdom national" there shall be inserted—
"'upbringing' has the same meaning as in the Children Act 1989."

(9) For section 72(1A) there shall be substituted the following subsections—
"(1A) In this Act, in determining with what person, or where, a child has his home, any absence of the child at a hospital or boarding school and any other temporary absence shall be disregarded.

(1B) In this Act, references to a child who is in the care of or looked after by a local authority have the same meaning as in the Children Act 1989."

31 For section 74(3) and (4) (extent) there shall be substituted—
"(3) This Act extends to England and Wales only."

PART II

AMENDMENTS OF ADOPTION (SCOTLAND) ACT 1978 (c. 28)

★ ★ ★ ★ ★ ★

SCHEDULE 11

JURISDICTION

PART I

GENERAL

Commencement of proceedings

1—(1) The Lord Chancellor may by order specify proceedings under this Act or the Adoption Act 1976 which may only be commenced in—
- (a)   a specified level of court;
- (b)   a court which falls within a specified class of court; or
- (c)   a particular court determined in accordance with, or specified in, the order.

(2) The Lord Chancellor may by order specify circumstances in which specified proceedings under this Act or the Adoption Act 1976 (which might otherwise be commenced elsewhere) may only be commenced in—
- (a)   a specified level of court;
- (b)   a court which falls within a specified class of court; or
- (c)   a particular court determined in accordance with, or specified in, the order.

(3) The Lord Chancellor may by order made provision by virtue of which, where specified proceedings with respect to a child under—
- (a)   this Act;
- (b)   the Adoption Act 1976; or
- (c)   the High Court's inherent jurisdiction with respect to children,

have been commenced in or transferred to any court (whether or not by virtue of an order under this Schedule), any other specified family proceedings which may affect, or are otherwise connected with, the child may, in special circumstances, only be commenced in that court.

(4) A class of court specified in an order under this Schedule may be described by reference to a description of proceedings and may include different levels of court.

Transfer of proceedings

2—(1) The Lord Chancellor may by order provide that in specified circumstances the whole, or any specified part of, specified proceedings to which this paragraph applies shall be transferred to—
- (a)   a specified level of court;
- (b)   a court which falls within a specified class of court; or
- (c)   a particular court determined in accordance with, or specified in, the order.

(2) Any order under this paragraph may provide for the transfer to be made at any stage, or specified stage, of the proceedings and whether or not the proceedings, or any part of them, have already been transferred.

(3) The proceedings to which this paragraph applies are—
- (a)   any proceedings under this Act;
- (b)   any proceedings under the Adoption Act 1976;
- (c)   any other proceedings which—
    - (i)   are family proceedings for the purposes of this Act, other than proceedings under the inherent jurisdiction of the High Court; and

(ii)   may affect, or are otherwise connected with, the child concerned.

(4) Proceedings to which this paragraph applies by virtue of sub-paragraph (3)(*c*) may only be transferred in accordance with the provisions of an order made under this paragraph for the purpose of consolidating them with proceedings under—
   (*a*)   this Act;
   (*b*)   the Adoption Act 1976; or
   (*c*)   the High Court's inherent jurisdiction with respect to children.

(5) An order under this paragraph may make such provision as the Lord Chancellor thinks appropriate for excluding proceedings to which this paragraph applies from the operation of any enactment which would otherwise govern the transfer of those proceedings, or any part of them.

Hearings by single justice

3—(1) In such circumstances as the Lord Chancellor may by order specify—
   (*a*)   the jurisdiction of a magistrates' court to make an emergency protection order;
   (*b*)   any specified question with respect to the transfer of specified proceedings to or from a magistrates' court in accordance with the provisions of an order under paragraph 2,
may be exercised by a single justice.

(2) Any provision made under this paragraph shall be without prejudice to any other enactment or rule of law relating to the functions which may be performed by a single justice of the peace.

General

4—(1) For the purposes of this Schedule—
   (*a*)   the commencement of proceedings under this Act includes the making of any application under this Act in the course of proceedings (whether or not those proceedings are proceedings under this Act); and
   (*b*)   there are three levels of court, that is to say the High Court, any county court and any magistrates' court.

(2) In this Schedule "specified" means specified by an order made under this Schedule.

(3) Any order under paragraph 1 may make provision as to the effect of commencing proceedings in contravention of any of the provisions of the order.

(4) An order under paragraph 2 may make provision as to the effect of a failure to comply with any of the provisions of the order.

(5) An order under this Schedule may—
   (*a*)   make such consequential, incidental or transitional provision as the Lord Chancellor considers expedient, including provision amending any other enactment so far as it concerns the jurisdiction of any court or justice of the peace;
   (*b*)   make provision for treating proceedings which are—
      (i)   in part proceedings of a kind mentioned in paragraph (*a*) or (*b*) of paragraph 2(3); and

(ii) in part proceedings of a kind mentioned in paragraph (c) of paragraph 2(3),

as consisting entirely of proceedings of one or other of those kinds, for the purposes of the application of any order made under paragraph 2.

PART II

CONSEQUENTIAL AMENDMENTS

The Administration of Justice Act 1964 (c. 42)

5 In section 38 of the Administration of Justice Act 1964 (interpretation), the definition of "domestic court", which is spent, shall be omitted.

The Domestic Proceedings and Magistrates' Courts Act 1978 (c. 22)

6 In the Domestic Proceedings and Magistrates' Courts Act 1978—
  (a) for the words "domestic proceedings", wherever they occur in sections 16(5)(c) and 88(1), there shall be substituted "family proceedings";
  (b) for the words "domestic court panel", wherever they occur in section 16(5)(b), there shall be substituted "family panel".

The Justices of the Peace Act 1979 (c. 55)

7 In the Justices of the Peace Act 1979—
  (a) for the words "domestic proceedings", wherever they occur in section 16(5), there shall be substituted "family proceedings";
  (b) for the words "domestic court", wherever they occur in section 17(3), there shall be substituted "family proceedings court";
  (c) for the words "domestic courts", wherever they occur in sections 38(2) and 58(1) and (5), there shall be substituted "family proceedings courts".

The Magistrates' Courts Act 1980 (c. 43)

8 In the Magistrates' Courts Act 1980—
  (a) in section 65(1) (meaning of family proceedings), the following paragraph shall be inserted after paragraph (m)—
    "(n) the Children Act 1989";
  (b) in section 65(2)(a) for the words "and (m)" there shall be substituted "(m) and (n)";
  (c) for the words "domestic proceedings", wherever they occur in sections 65(1), (2) and (3), 66(1) and (2), 67(1), (2) and (7), 69(1), (2), (3) and (4), 70(2) and (3), 71(1) and (2), 72(1), 73, 74(1), 121(8) and 150(1), there shall be substituted "family proceedings";
  (d) for the words "domestic court panel", wherever they occur in sections 66(2), 67(2), (4), (5), (7) and (8) and 68(1), (2) and (3), there shall be substituted "family panel";
  (e) for the words "domestic court panels", wherever they occur in section 67(3), (4), (5) and (6), there shall be substituted "family panels";
  (f) for the words "domestic courts", wherever they occur in sections 67(1) and (3) and 68(1), there shall be substituted "family proceedings courts";

(g)   for the words "domestic court", wherever they occur in section 67(2) and (5), there shall be substituted "family proceedings court".

The Supreme Court Act 1981 (c. 54)

9   In paragraph 3 of Schedule 1 to the Supreme Court Act 1981 (distribution of business to the Family Division of the High Court), the following sub-paragraph shall be added at the end—
"(e) proceedings under the Children Act 1989".

The Matrimonial and Family Proceedings Act 1984 (c. 42)

10   In section 44 of the Matrimonial and Family Proceedings Act 1984 (domestic proceedings in magistrates' courts to include applications to alter maintenance agreements) for the words "domestic proceedings", wherever they occur, there shall be substituted "family proceedings".

The Insolvency Act 1986 (c. 45)

11—(1)   In section 281(5)(b) of the Insolvency Act 1986 (discharge not to release bankrupt from bankruptcy debt arising under any order made in family proceedings or in domestic proceedings), the words "or in domestic proceedings" shall be omitted.

(2) In section 281(8) of that Act (interpretation), for the definitions of "domestic proceedings" and "family proceedings" there shall be substituted—
"family proceedings" means—
>   (a) family proceedings within the meaning of the Magistrates' Courts Act 1980 and any proceedings which would be such proceedings but for section 65(1)(ii) of that Act (proceedings for variation of order for periodical payments); and
>   (b) family proceedings within the meaning of Part V of the Matrimonial and Family Proceedings Act 1984."

SCHEDULE 12
MINOR AMENDMENTS

1 to 30   ...

The Matrimonial Causes Act 1973 (c. 18)

31   For section 41 of the Matrimonial Causes Act 1973 (restrictions on decrees for dissolution, annulment or separation affecting children) there shall be substituted—

"Restrictions on decrees for dissolution, annulment or separation affecting children
41.—(1)   In any proceedings for a decree of divorce or nullity of marriage, or a decree of judicial separation, the court shall consider—
>   (a) whether there are any children of the family to whom this section applies; and
>   (b) where there are any such children, whether (in the light of the arrangements which have been, or are proposed to be, made for their upbringing and welfare) it should exercise any of its powers under the Children Act 1989 with respect to any of them.

(2) Where, in any case to which this section applies, it appears to the court that—

(a) the circumstances of the case require it, or are likely to require it, to exercise any of its powers under the Act of 1989 with respect to any such child;

(b) it is not in a position to exercise that power or (as the case may be) those powers without giving further consideration to the case; and

(c) there are exceptional circumstances which make it desirable in the interests of the child that the court should give a direction under this section,

it may direct that the decree of divorce or nullity is not to be made absolute, or that the decree of judicial separation is not to be granted, until the court orders otherwise.

(3) This section applies to—

(a) any child of the family who has not reached the age of sixteen at the date when the court considers the case in accordance with the requirements of this section; and

(b) any child of the family who has reached that age at that date and in relation to whom the court directs that this section shall apply."

32 to 45 . . .

SCHEDULE 13

Consequential Amendments

* * * * *

SCHEDULE 14

Transitionals and Savings

Pending Proceedings, etc.

1—(1) Subject to sub-paragraph (4), nothing in any provision of this Act (other than the repeals mentioned in sub-paragraph (2)) shall affect any proceedings which are pending immediately before the commencement of that provision.

(2) The repeals are those of—

(a) section 42(3) of the Matrimonial Causes Act 1973 (declaration by court that party to marriage unfit to have custody of children of family); and

(b) section 38 of the Sexual Offences Act 1956 (power of court to divest person of authority over girl or boy in cases of incest).

(3) For the purposes of the following provisions of this Schedule, any reference to an order in force immediately before the commencement of a provision of this Act shall be construed as including a reference to an order made after that commencement in proceedings pending before that commencement.

(4) Sub-paragraph (3) is not to be read as making the order in question have effect from a date earlier than that on which it was made.

(5) An order under section 96(3) may make such provision with respect to the

application of the order in relation to proceedings which are pending when the order comes into force as the Lord Chancellor considers appropriate.

2 Where, immediately before the day on which Part IV comes into force, there was in force an order under section 3(1) of the Children and Young Persons Act 1963 (order directing a local authority to bring a child or young person before a juvenile court under section 1 of the Children and Young Persons Act 1969), the order shall cease to have effect on that day.

Custody Orders, etc.

Cessation of declarations of unfitness, etc.

3 Where, immediately before the day on which Parts I and II come into force, there was in force—
- (a) a declaration under section 42(3) of the Matrimonial Causes Act 1973 (declaration by court that party to marriage unfit to have custody of children of family); or
- (b) an order under section 38(1) of the Sexual Offences Act 1956 divesting a person of authority over a girl or boy in a case of incest;

the declaration or, as the case may be, the order shall cease to have effect on that day.

Family Law Reform Act 1987 (c. 42)

Conversion of orders under section 4

4 Where, immediately before the day on which Parts I and II come into force, there was in force an order under section 4(1) of the Family Law Reform Act 1987 (order giving father parental rights and duties in relation to a child), then, on and after that day, the order shall be deemed to be an order under section 4 of this Act giving the father parental responsibility for the child.

Orders to which paragraphs 6 to 11 apply

5—(1) In paragraphs 6 to 11 "an existing order" means any order which—
- (a) is in force immediately before the commencement of Parts I and II;
- (b) was made under any enactment mentioned in sub-paragraph (2);
- (c) determines all or any of the following—
  - (i)   who is to have custody of a child;
  - (ii) who is to have care and control of a child;
  - (iii) who is to have access to a child;
  - (iv) any matter with respect to a child's education or upbringing; and
- (d) is not an order of a kind mentioned in paragraph 15(1).

(2) The enactments are—
- (a) the Domestic Proceedings and Magistrates' Courts Act 1978;
- (b) the Children Act 1975;
- (c) the Matrimonial Causes Act 1973;
- (d) the Guardianship of Minors Acts 1971 and 1973;
- (e) the Matrimonial Causes Act 1965;
- (f) the Matrimonial Proceedings (Magistrates' Courts) Act 1960.

(3) For the purposes of this paragraph and paragraphs 6 to 11 "custody" includes legal custody and joint as well as sole custody but does not include access.

Parental responsibility of parents

6—(1) Where—
  (a) a child's father and mother were married to each other at the time of his birth; and
  (b) there is an existing order with respect to the child,
each parent shall have parental responsibility for the child in accordance with section 2 as modified by sub-paragraph (3).

(2) Where—
  (a) a child's father and mother were not married to each other at the time of his birth; and
  (b) there is an existing order with respect to the child,
section 2 shall apply as modified by sub-paragraphs (3) and (4).

(3) The modification is that for section 2(8) there shall be substituted—
      "(8) The fact that a person has parental responsibility for a child does not entitle him to act in a way which would be incompatible with any existing order or any order made under this Act with respect to the child".

(4) The modifications are that—
  (a) for the purposes of section 2(2), where the father has custody or care and control of the child by virtue of any existing order, the court shall be deemed to have made (at the commencement of that section) an order under section 4(1) giving him parental responsibility for the child; and
  (b) where by virtue of paragraph (a) a court is deemed to have made an order under section 4(1) in favour of a father who has care and control of a child by virtue of an existing order, the court shall not bring the order under section 4(1) to an end at any time while he has care and control of the child by virtue of the order.

Persons who are not parents but who have custody or care and control

7—(1) Where a person who is not the parent or guardian of a child has custody or care and control of him by virtue of an existing order, that person shall have parental responsibility for him so long as he continues to have that custody or care and control by virtue of the order.

(2) Where sub-paragraph (1) applies, Parts I and II shall have effect as modified by this paragraph.

(3) The modifications are that—
  (a) for section 2(8) there shall be substituted—
      "(8) The fact that a person has parental responsibility for a child does not entitle him to act in a way which would be incompatible with any existing order or with any order made under this Act with respect to the child";
  (b) at the end of section 9(4) there shall be inserted—
      "(c) any person who has custody or care and control of a child by virtue of any existing order"; and
  (c) at the end of section 34(1)(c) there shall be inserted—
      "(cc) where immediately before the care order was made there was an

existing order by virtue of which a person had custody or care and control of the child, that person."

Persons who have care and control

8—(1) Sub-paragraphs (2) to (6) apply where a person has care and control of a child by virtue of an existing order, but they shall cease to apply when that order ceases to have effect.

(2) Section 5 shall have effect as if—
- (*a*)   for any reference to a residence order in favour of a parent or guardian there were substituted a reference to any existing order by virtue of which the parent or guardian has care and control of the child; and
- (*b*)   for subsection (9) there were substituted—
       "(9) Subsections (1) and (7) do not apply if the existing order referred to in paragraph (*b*) of those subsections was one by virtue of which a surviving parent of the child also had care and control of him."

(3) Section 10 shall have effect as if for subsection (5)(*c*)(i) there were substituted—
       "(i) in any case where by virtue of an existing order any person or persons has or have care and control of the child, has the consent of that person or each of those persons".

(4) Section 20 shall have effect as if for subsection (9)(*a*) there were substituted "who has care and control of the child by virtue of an existing order."

(5) Section 23 shall have effect as if for subsection (4)(*c*) there were substituted—
       "(*c*) where the child is in care and immediately before the care order was made there was an existing order by virtue of which a person had care and control of the child, that person."

(6) In Schedule 1, paragraphs 1(1) and 14(1) shall have effect as if for the words "in whose favour a residence order is in force with respect to the child" there were substituted "who has been given care and control of the child by virtue of an existing order".

Persons who have access

9—(1) Sub-paragraphs (2) to (4) apply where a person has access by virtue of an existing order.

(2) Section 10 shall have effect as if after subsection (5) there were inserted—

       "(5A) Any person who has access to a child by virtue of an existing order is entitled to apply for a contact order."

(3) Section 16(2) shall have effect as if after paragraph (*b*) there were inserted—
       "(*bb*) any person who has access to the child by virtue of an existing order."

(4) Sections 43(11), 44(13) and 46(10), shall have effect as if in each case after paragraph (*d*) there were inserted—
       "(*dd*) any person who has been given access to him by virtue of an existing order."

Enforcement of certain existing orders

10—(1) Sub-paragraph (2) applies in relation to any existing order which, but for the repeal by this Act of—
  (*a*)   section 13(1) of the Guardianship of Minors Act 1971;
  (*b*)   section 43(1) of the Children Act 1975; or
  (*c*)   section 33 of the Domestic Proceedings and Magistrates' Courts Act 1978,
(provisions concerning the enforcement of custody orders) might have been enforced as if it were an order requiring a person to give up a child to another person.

(2) Where this sub-paragraph applies, the existing order may, after the repeal of the enactments mentioned in sub-paragraph (1)(*a*) to (*c*), be enforced under section 14 as if—
  (*a*)   any reference to a residence order were a reference to the existing order; and
  (*b*)   any reference to a person in whose favour the residence order is in force were a reference to a person to whom actual custody of the child is given by an existing order which is in force.

(3) In sub-paragraph (2) "actual custody", in relation to a child, means the actual possession of his person.

Discharge of existing orders

11—(1) The making of a residence order or a care order with respect to a child who is the subject of an existing order discharges the existing order.

(2) Where the court makes any section 8 order (other than a residence order) with respect to a child with respect to whom any existing order is in force, the existing order shall have effect subject to the section 8 order.

(3) The court may discharge an existing order which is in force with respect to a child—
  (*a*)   in any family proceedings relating to the child or in which any question arises with respect to the child's welfare; or
  (*b*)   on the application of—
       (i)   any parent or guardian of the child;
       (ii)   the child himself; or
       (iii) any person named in the order.

(4) A child may not apply for the discharge of an existing order except with the leave of the court.

(5) The power in sub-paragraph (3) to discharge an existing order includes the power to discharge any part of the order.

(6) In considering whether to discharge an order under the power conferred by sub-paragraph (3) the court shall, if the discharge of the order is opposed by any party to the proceedings, have regard in particular to the matters mentioned in section 1(3).

GUARDIANS

Existing guardians to be guardians under this Act

12—(1) Any appointment of a person as guardian of a child which—
  (*a*) was made—
         (i)   under sections 3 to 5 of the Guardianship of Minors Act 1971;
         (ii)   under section 38(3) of the Sexual Offences Act 1956; or
         (iii) under the High Court's inherent jurisdiction with respect to children;
                and
  (*b*) has taken effect before the commencement of section 5,
shall (subject to sub-paragraph (2)) be deemed, on and after the commencement
of section 5, to be an appointment made and having effect under that section.

(2) Where an appointment of a person as guardian of a child has effect under section
5 by virtue of sub-paragraph (1)(*a*)(ii), the appointment shall not have effect for
a period which is longer than any period specified in the order.

Appointment of guardian not yet in effect

13   Any appointment of a person to be a guardian of a child—
  (*a*) which was made as mentioned in paragraph 12(1)(*a*)(i); but
  (*b*) which, immediately before the commencement of section 5, had not taken
         effect,
shall take effect in accordance with section 5 (as modified, where it applies, by
paragraph 8(2)).

Persons deemed to be appointed as guardians under existing wills

14   For the purposes of the Wills Act 1837 and of this Act any disposition by
will and testament or devise of the custody and tuition of any child, made before
the commencement of section 5 and paragraph 1 of Schedule 13 shall be deemed
to be an appointment by will of a guardian of the child.

CHILDREN IN CARE

Children in compulsory care

15—(1) Sub-paragraph (2) applies where, immediately before the day on which Part
IV comes into force, a person was—
  (*a*) in care by virtue of—
         (i)   a care order under section 1 of the Children and Young Persons Act
                1969;
         (ii)   a care order under section 15 of that Act, on discharging a supervision
                order made under section 1 of that Act; or
         (iii) an order or authorisation under section 25 or 26 of that Act;
  (*b*) deemed, by virtue of—
         (i)   paragraph 7(3) of Schedule 5A to the Army Act 1955;
         (ii)   paragraph 7(3) of Schedule 5A to the Air Force Act 1955; or
         (iii) paragraph 7(3) of Schedule 4A to the Naval Discipline Act 1957,
         to be the subject of a care order under the Children and Young Persons
         Act 1969;

(c) in care—
    (i) under section 2 of the Child Care Act 1980; or
    (ii) by virtue of paragraph 1 of Schedule 4 to that Act (which extends the meaning of a child in care under section 2 to include children in care under section 1 of the Children Act 1948),
    and a child in respect of whom a resolution under section 3 of the Act of 1980 or section 2 of the Act of 1948 was in force;
(d) a child in respect of whom a resolution had been passed under section 65 of the Child Care Act 1980;
(e) in care by virtue of an order under—
    (i) section 2(1)(e) of the Matrimonial Proceedings (Magistrates' Courts) Act 1960;
    (ii) section 7(2) of the Family Law Reform Act 1969;
    (iii) section 43(1) of the Matrimonial Causes Act 1973; or
    (iv) section 2(2)(b) of the Guardianship Act 1973;
    (v) section 10 of the Domestic Proceedings and Magistrates' Courts Act 1978,
    (orders having effect for certain purposes as if the child had been received into care under section 2 of the Child Care Act 1980);
(f) in care by virtue of an order made, on the revocation of a custodianship order, under section 36 of the Children Act 1975; or
(g) in care by virtue of an order made, on the refusal of an adoption order, under section 26 of the Adoption Act 1976 or any order having effect (by virtue of paragraph 1 of Schedule 2 to that Act) as if made under that section.

(2) Where this sub-paragraph applies, then, on and after the day on which Part IV commences—
    (a) the order or resolution in question shall be deemed to be a care order;
    (b) the authority in whose care the person was immediately before that commencement shall be deemed to be the authority designated in that deemed care order; and
    (c) any reference to a child in the care of a local authority shall include a reference to a person who is the subject of such a deemed care order,
and the provisions of this Act shall apply accordingly, subject to paragraph 16.

Modifications

16—(1) Sub-paragraph (2) only applies where a person who is the subject of a care order by virtue of paragraph 15(2) is a person falling within sub-paragraph (1)(a) or (b) of that paragraph.

(2) Where the person would otherwise have remained in care until reaching the age of nineteen, by virtue of—
    (a) section 20(3)(a) or 21(1) of the Children and Young Persons Act 1969; or
    (b) paragraph 7(5)(c)(i) of—
        (i) Schedule 5A to the Army Act 1955;
        (ii) Schedule 5A to the Air Force Act 1955; or
        (iii) Schedule 4A to the Naval Discipline Act 1957,
this Act applies as if in section 91(12) for the word "eighteen" there were substituted "nineteen".

(3) Where a person who is the subject of a care order by virtue of paragraph 15(2) is a person falling within sub-paragraph (1)(b) of that paragraph, this Act applies as if section 101 were omitted.

(4) Sub-paragraph (5) only applies where a child who is the subject of a care order by virtue of paragraph 15(2) is a person falling within sub-paragraph (1)(*e*) to (*g*) of that paragraph.

(5) Where a court, on making the order, or at any time thereafter, gave directions under—
(*a*)   section 4(4)(*a*) of the Guardianship Act 1973; or
(*b*)   section 43(5)(*a*) of the Matrimonial Causes Act 1973,
as to the exercise by the authority of any powers, those directions shall continue to have effect (regardless of any conflicting provision in this Act) until varied or discharged by a court under this sub-paragraph.

Children placed with parent etc. while in compulsory care

17—(1) This paragraph applies where a child is deemed by paragraph 15 to be in the care of a local authority under an order or resolution which is deemed by that paragraph to be a care order.

(2) If, immediately before the day on which Part III comes into force, the child was allowed to be under the charge and control of—
(*a*)   a parent or guardian under section 21(2) of the Child Care Act 1980; or
(*b*)   a person who, before the child was in the authority's care, had care and control of the child by virtue of an order falling within paragraph 5,
on and after that day the provision made by and under section 23(5) shall apply as if the child had been placed with the person in question in accordance with that provision.

Orders for access to children in compulsory care

18—(1) This paragraph applies to any access order—
(*a*)   made under section 12C of the Child Care Act 1980 (access orders with respect to children in care of local authorities); and
(*b*)   in force immediately before the commencement of Part IV

(2) On and after the commencement of Part IV, the access order shall have effect as an order made under section 34 in favour of the person named in the order.

19—(1) This paragraph applies where, immediately before the commencement of Part IV, an access order made under section 12C of the Act of 1980 was suspended by virtue of an order made under section 12E of that Act (suspension of access orders in emergencies).

(2) The suspending order shall continue to have effect as if this Act had not been passed.

(3) If—
(*a*)   before the commencement of Part IV; and
(*b*)   during the period for which the operation of the access order is suspended,
the local authority concerned made an application for its variation or discharge to an appropriate juvenile court, its operation shall be suspended until the date on which the application to vary or discharge it is determined or abandoned.

Children in voluntary care

20—(1) This paragraph applies where, immediately before the day on which Part III comes into force—
  (a) a child was in the care of a local authority—
        (i)   under section 2(1) of the Child Care Act 1980; or
        (ii) by virtue of paragraph 1 of Schedule 4 to that Act (which extends the meaning of references to children in care under section 2 to include references to children in care under section 1 of the Children Act 1948); and
  (b) he was not a person in respect of whom a resolution under section 3 of the Act of 1980 or section 2 of the Act of 1948 was in force.

(2) Where this paragraph applies, the child shall, on and after the day mentioned in sub-paragraph (1), be treated for the purposes of this Act as a child who is provided with accommodation by the local authority under Part III, but he shall cease to be so treated once he ceases to be so accommodated in accordance with the provisions of Part III.

(3) Where—
  (a) this paragraph applies; and
  (b) the child, immediately before the day mentioned in sub-paragraph (1), was (by virtue of section 21(2) of the Act of 1980) under the charge and control of a person falling within paragraph 17(2)(a) or (b),
the child shall not be treated for the purposes of this Act as if he were being looked after by the authority concerned.

Boarded out children

21—(1) Where, immediately before the day on which Part III comes into force, a child in the care of a local authority—
  (a) was—
        (i)   boarded out with a person under section 21(1)(a) of the Child Care Act 1980; or
        (ii) placed under the charge and control of a person, under section 21(2) of that Act; and
  (b) the person with whom he was boarded out, or (as the case may be) placed, was not a person falling within paragraph 17(2)(a) or (b),
on and after that day, he shall be treated (subject to sub-paragraph (2)) as having been placed with a local authority foster parent and shall cease to be so treated when he ceases to be placed with that person in accordance with the provisions of this Act.

(2) Regulations made under section 23(2)(a) shall not apply in relation to a person who is a local authority foster parent by virtue of sub-paragraph (1) before the end of the period of twelve months beginning with the day on which Part III comes into force and accordingly that person shall for that period be subject—
  (a) in a case falling within sub-paragraph (1)(a)(i), to terms and regulations mentioned in section 21(1)(a) of the Act of 1980; and
  (b) in a case falling within sub-paragraph (1)(a)(ii), to terms fixed under section 21(2) of that Act and regulations made under section 22A of that Act,
as if that Act had not been repealed by this Act.

Children in care to qualify for advice and assistance

22   Any reference in Part III to a person qualifying for advice and assistance shall be construed as including a reference to a person within the area of the local authority in question who is under twenty-one and who was, at any time after reaching the age of sixteen but while still a child—

    (*a*)   a person falling within—
           (i)   any of paragraphs (*a*) to (*g*) of paragraph 15(1); or
          (ii)   paragraph 20(1); or
    (*b*)   the subject of a criminal care order (within the meaning of paragraph 34).

Emigration of children in care

23   Where—
    (*a*)   the Secretary of State has received a request in writing from a local authority that he give his consent under section 24 of the Child Care Act 1980 to the emigration of a child in their care; but
    (*b*)   immediately before the repeal of the Act of 1980 by this Act, he has not determined whether or not to give his consent,

section 24 of the Act of 1980 shall continue to apply (regardless of that repeal) until the Secretary of State has determined whether or not to give his consent to the request.

Contributions for maintenance of children in care

24—(1)   Where, immediately before the day on which Part III of Schedule 2 comes into force, there was in force an order made (or having effect as if made) under any of the enactments mentioned in sub-paragraph (2), then, on and after that day—
    (*a*)   the order shall have effect as if made under paragraph 23(2) of Schedule 2 against a person liable to contribute; and
    (*b*)   Part III of Schedule 2 shall apply to the order, subject to the modifications in sub-paragraph (3).

(2)   The enactments are—
    (*a*)   section 11(4) of the Domestic Proceedings and Magistrates' Courts Act 1978;
    (*b*)   section 26(2) of the Adoption Act 1976;
    (*c*)   section 36(5) of the Children Act 1975;
    (*d*)   section 2(3) of the Guardianship Act 1973;
    (*e*)   section 2(1)(*h*) of the Matrimonial Proceedings (Magistrates' Courts) Act 1960,
(provisions empowering the court to make an order requiring a person to make periodical payments to a local authority in respect of a child in care).

(3)   The modifications are that, in paragraph 23 of Schedule 2—
    (*a*)   in sub-paragraph (4), paragraph (*a*) shall be omitted;
    (*b*)   for sub-paragraph (6) there shall be substituted—
          "(6) Where—
         (*a*) a contribution order is in force;
         (*b*) the authority serve a contribution notice under paragraph 22; and
         (*c*) the contributor and the authority reach an agreement under paragraph 22(7) in respect of the contribution notice,
the effect of the agreement shall be to discharge the order from the date on which it is agreed that the agreement shall take effect"; and
    (*c*)   at the end of sub-paragraph (10) there shall be inserted—
          "and

(c) where the order is against a person who is not a parent of the child, shall be made with due regard to—
  (i) whether that person had assumed responsibility for the maintenance of the child, and, if so, the extent to which and basis on which he assumed that responsibility and the length of the period during which he met that responsibility;
  (ii) whether he did so knowing that the child was not his child;
  (iii) the liability of any other person to maintain the child."

SUPERVISION ORDERS

Orders under section 1(3)(b) or 21(2) of the 1969 Act

25—(1) This paragraph applies to any supervision order—
  (a) made—
    (i) under section 1(3)(b) of the Children and Young Persons Act 1969; or
    (ii) under section 21(2) of that Act on the discharge of a care order made under section 1(3)(c) of that Act; and
  (b) in force immediately before the commencement of Part IV.

(2) On and after the commencement of Part IV, the order shall be deemed to be a supervision order made under section 31 and—
  (a) any requirement of the order that the child reside with a named individual shall continue to have effect while the order remains in force, unless the court otherwise directs
  (b) any other requirement imposed by the court, or directions given by the supervisor, shall be deemed to have been imposed or given under the appropriate provisions of Schedule 3.

(3) Where, immediately before the commencement of Part IV, the order had been in force for a period of more than six months, it shall cease to have effect at the end of the period of six months beginning with the day on which Part IV comes into force unless—
  (a) the court directs that it shall cease to have effect at the end of a different period (which shall not exceed three years);
  (b) it ceased to have effect earlier in accordance with section 91; or
  (c) it would have ceased to have had effect earlier had this Act not been passed.

(4) Where sub-paragraph (3) applies, paragraph 6 of Schedule 3 shall not apply.

(5) Where, immediately before the commencement of Part IV, the order had been in force for less than six months it shall cease to have effect in accordance with section 91 and paragraph 6 of Schedule 3 unless—
  (a) the court directs that it shall cease to have effect at the end of a different period (which shall not exceed three years); or
  (b) it would have ceased to have had effect earlier had this Act not been passed.

Other supervision orders

26—(1) This paragraph applies to any order for the supervision of a child which was in force immediately before the commencement of Part IV and was made under—
  (a) section 2(1)(f) of the Matrimonial Proceedings (Magistrates Courts) Act 1960;
  (b) section 7(4) of the Family Law Reform Act 1969;
  (c) section 44 of the Matrimonial Causes Act 1973;
  (d) section 2(2)(a) of the Guardianship Act 1973;

(e)   section 34(5) or 36(3)(*b*) of the Children Act 1975;
(*f*)   section 26(1)(*a*) of the Adoption Act 1976; or
(*g*)   section 9 of the Domestic Proceedings and Magistrates Courts Act 1978.

(2) The order shall not be deemed to be a supervision order made under any provision of this Act but shall nevertheless continue in force for a period of one year beginning with the day on which Part IV comes into force unless—

(*a*)   the court directs that it shall cease to have effect at the end of a lesser period; or

(*b*)   it would have ceased to have had effect earlier had this Act not been passed.

PLACE OF SAFETY ORDERS

27—(1) This paragraph applies to—
(*a*)   any order or warrant authorising the removal of a child to a place of safety which—
  (i)   was made, or issued, under any of the enactments mentioned in sub-paragraph (2); and
  (ii)   was in force immediately before the commencement of Part IV; and
(*b*)   any interim order made under section 23(5) of the Children and Young Persons Act 1963 or section 28(6) of the Children and Young Persons Act 1969.

(2) The enactments are—
(*a*)   section 40 of the Children and Young Persons Act 1933 (warrant to search for or remove child);
(*b*)   section 28(1) of the Children and Young Persons Act 1969 (detention of child in place of safety);
(*c*)   section 34(1) of the Adoption Act 1976 (removal of protected children from unsuitable surroundings);
(*d*)   section 12(1) of the Foster Children Act 1980 (removal of foster children kept in unsuitable surroundings).

(3) The order or warrant shall continue to have effect as if this Act had not been passed.

(4) Any enactment repealed by this Act shall continue to have effect in relation to the order or warrant so far as is necessary for the purposes of securing that the effect of the order is what it would have been had this Act not been passed.

(5) Sub-paragraph (4) does not apply to the power to make an interim order or further interim order given by section 23(5) of the Children and Young Persons Act 1963 or section 28(6) of the Children and Young Persons Act 1969.

(6) Where, immediately before section 28 of the Children and Young Persons Act 1969 is repealed by this Act, a child is being detained under the powers granted by that section, he may continue to be detained in accordance with that section but subsection (6) shall not apply.

RECOVERY OF CHILDREN

28   The repeal by this Act of subsection (1) of section 16 of the Child Care Act 1980 (arrest of child absent from compulsory care) shall not affect the operation of that section in relation to any child arrested before the coming into force of the repeal.

29—(1) This paragraph applies where—
(*a*)   a summons has been issued under section 15 or 16 of the Child Care Act 1980 (recovery of children in voluntary or compulsory care); and

(b)   the child concerned is not produced in accordance with the summons before the repeal of that section by this Act comes into force.

(2) The summons, any warrant issued in connection with it and section 15 or (as the case may be) section 16, shall continue to have effect as if this Act had not been passed.

30   The amendment by paragraph 27 of Schedule 12 of section 32 of the Children and Young Persons Act 1969 (detention of absentees) shall not affect the operation of that section in relation to—
(a)   any child arrested; or
(b)   any summons or warrant issued,
under that section before the coming into force of that paragraph.

Voluntary Organisations: Parental Rights Resolutions

31—(1) This paragraph applies to a resolution—
(a)   made under section 64 of the Child Care Act 1980 (transfer of parental rights and duties to voluntary organisations); and
(b)   in force immediately before the commencement of Part IV.

(2) The resolution shall continue to have effect until the end of the period of six months beginning with the day on which Part IV comes into force unless it is brought to an end earlier in accordance with the provisions of the Act of 1980 preserved by this paragraph.

(3) While the resolution remains in force, any relevant provisions of, or made under, the Act of 1980 shall continue to have effect with respect to it.

(4) Sub-paragraph (3) does not apply to—
(a)   section 62 of the Act of 1980 and any regulations made under that section (arrangements by voluntary organisations for emigration of children); or
(b)   section 65 of the Act of 1980 (duty of local authority to assume parental rights and duties).

(5) Section 5(2) of the Act of 1980 (which is applied to resolutions under Part VI of that Act by section 64(7) of that Act) shall have effect with respect to the resolution as if the reference in paragraph (c) to an appointment of a guardian under section 5 of the Guardianship of Minors Act 1971 were a reference to an appointment of a guardian under section 5 of this Act.

Foster Children

32—(1) This paragraph applies where—
(a)   immediately before the commencement of Part VIII, a child was a foster child within the meaning of the Foster Children Act 1980; and
(b)   the circumstances of the case are such that, had Parts VIII and IX then been in force, he would have been treated for the purposes of this Act as a child who was being provided with accommodation in a children's home and not as a child who was being privately fostered.

(2) If the child continues to be cared for and provided with accommodation as before, section 63(1) and (10) shall not apply in relation to him if—
(a)   an application for registration of the home in question is made under section 63 before the end of the period of three months beginning with the day on which Part VIII comes into force; and
(b)   the application has not been refused or, if it has been refused—
    (i)   the period for an appeal against the decision has not expired; or

(ii)   an appeal against the refusal has been made but has not been determined or abandoned.

(3) While section 63(1) and (10) does not apply, the child shall be treated as a privately fostered child for the purposes of Part IX.

Nurseries and Child Minding

33—(1) Sub-paragraph (2) applies where, immediately before the commencement of Part X, any premises are registered under section 1(1)(a) of the Nurseries and Child-Minders Regulation Act 1948 (registration of premises, other than premises wholly or mainly used as private dwellings, where children are received to be looked after).

(2) During the transitional period, the provisions of the Act of 1948 shall continue to have effect with respect to those premises to the exclusion of Part X.

(3) Nothing in sub-paragraph (2) shall prevent the local authority concerned from registering any person under section 71(1)(b) with respect to the premises.

(4) In this paragraph "the transitional period" means the period ending with—
  (a)   the first anniversary of the commencement of Part X; or
  (b)   if earlier, the date on which the local authority concerned registers any person under section 71(1)(b) with respect to the premises.

34—(1) Sub-paragraph (2) applies where, immediately before the commencement of Part X—
  (a)   a person is registered under section 1(1)(b) of the Act of 1948 (registration of persons who for reward receive into their homes children under the age of five to be looked after); and
  (b)   all the children looked after by him as mentioned in section 1(1)(b) of that Act are under the age of five.

(2) During the transitional period, the provisions of the Act of 1948 shall continue to have effect with respect to that person to the exclusion of Part X.

(3) Nothing in sub-paragraph (2) shall prevent the local authority concerned from registering that person under section 71(1)(a).

(4) In this paragraph "the transitional period" means the period ending with—
  (a)   the first anniversary of the commencement of Part X; or
  (b)   if earlier, the date on which the local authority concerned registers that person under section 71(1)(a).

Children Accommodated in Certain Establishments

35   In calculating, for the purposes of section 85(1)(a) or 86(1)(a), the period of time for which a child has been accommodated any part of that period which fell before the day on which that section came into force shall be disregarded.

Criminal Care Orders

36—(1) This paragraph applies where, immediately before the commencement of section 90(2) there was in force an order ("a criminal care order") made—
  (a)   under section 7(7)(a) of the Children and Young Persons Act 1969 (alteration in treatment of young offenders etc.); or
  (b)   under section 15(1) of that Act, on discharging a supervision order made under section 7(7)(b) of that Act.

(2) The criminal care order shall continue to have effect until the end of the period of six months beginning with the day on which section 90(2) comes into force unless it is brought to an end earlier in accordance with—
  (a) the provisions of the Act of 1969 preserved by sub-paragraph (3)(a); or
  (b) this paragraph.

(3) While the criminal care order remains in force, any relevant provisions—
  (a) of the Act of 1969; and
  (b) of the Child Care Act 1980,
shall continue to have effect with respect to it.

(4) While the criminal care order remains in force, a court may, on the application of the appropriate person, make—
  (a) a residence order;
  (b) a care order or a supervision order under section 31;
  (c) an education supervision order under section 36 (regardless of subsection (6) of that section); or
  (d) an order falling within sub-paragraph (5),
and shall, on making any of those orders, discharge the criminal care order.

(5) The order mentioned in sub-paragraph (4)(d) is an order having effect as if it were a supervision order of a kind mentioned in section 12AA of the Act of 1969 (as inserted by paragraph 23 of Schedule 12), that is to say, a supervision order—
  (a) imposing a requirement that the child shall live for a specified period in local authority accommodation; but
  (b) in relation to which the conditions mentioned in subsection (4) of section 12AA are not required to be satisfied.

(6) The maximum period which may be specified in an order made under sub-paragraph (4)(d) is six months and such an order may stipulate that the child shall not live with a named person.

(7) Where this paragraph applies, section 5 of the Rehabilitation of Offenders Act 1974 (rehabilitation periods for particular sentences) shall have effect regardless of the repeals in it made by this Act.

(8) In sub-paragraph (4) "appropriate person" means—
  (a) in the case of an application for a residence order, any person (other than a local authority) who has the leave of the court;
  (b) in the case of an application for an education supervision order, a local education authority; and
  (c) in any other case, the local authority tro whose care the child was committed by the order.

MISCELLANEOUS

Consents under the Marriage Act 1949 (c.76)

37—(1) In the circumstances mentioned in sub-paragraph (2), section 3 of and Schedule 2 to the Marriage Act 1949 (consents to marry) shall continue to have effect regardless of the amendment of that Act by paragraph 5 of Schedule 12.

(2) The circumstances are that—
  (a) immediately before the day on which paragraph 5 of Schedule 12 comes into force, there is in force—
    (i)   an existing order, as defined in paragraph 5(1); or
    (ii) an order of a kind mentioned in paragraph 16(1); and

(*b*)   section 3 of and Schedule 2 to the Act of 1949 would, but for this Act, have applied to the marriage of the child who is the subject of the order.

The Children Act 1975 (c. 72)

38   The amendments of other enactments made by the following provisions of the Children Act 1975 shall continue to have effect regardless of the repeal of the Act of 1975 by this Act—

(*a*)   section 68(4), (5) and (7) (amendments of section 32 of the Children and Young Persons Act 1969); and

(*b*)   in Schedule 3—

(i)   paragraph 13 (amendments of Births and Deaths Registration Act 1953);

(ii)   paragraph 43 (amendment of Perpetuities and Accumulations Act 1964);

(iii) paragraphs 46 and 47 (amendments of Health Services and Public Health Act 1968); and

(iv)   paragraph 77 (amendment of Parliamentary and Other Pensions Act 1972).

The Child Care Act 1980 (c. 5)

39   The amendment made to section 106(2)(*a*) of the Children and Young Persons Act 1963) by paragraph 26 of Schedule 5 to the Child Care Act 1980 shall continue to have effect regardless of the repeal of the Act of 1980 by this Act.

Legal aid

40   The Lord Chancellor may by order make such transitional and saving provisions as appear to him to be necessary or expedient, in consequence of any provision made by or under this Act, in connection with the operation of any provisions of the Legal Aid Act 1988 (including any provision that Act which is amended or repealed by this Act).

SCHEDULE 15
REPEALS

*   *   *   *   *

Index